DENYS ARCAND

A LIFE IN FILM

RÉAL LA ROCHELLE

Translated by
ALISON STRAYER

McArthur & Company
Toronto

First published in English in Canada in 2005 by
McArthur & Company
322 King St., West, Suite 402
Toronto, Ontario M5V 1J2
www.mcarthur-co.com

Library and Archives Canada Cataloguing in Publication

La Rochelle, Réal, 1937-
Denys Arcand, a life in film : a biography / Réal La Rochelle.

Translation of: Denys Arcand, l'ange exterminateur.
ISBN 1-55278-537-8

1. Arcand, Denys, 1941- 2. Motion pictures—Québec (Province).
3. Motion picture producers and directors—Québec (Province)—
Biography. I. Title.

PN1998.3.A72L3713 2005   791.4302'33'092   C2005-903714-8

The publisher would like to acknowledge the financial support of the
Government of Canada through the Book Publishing Industry Development
Program, the Canada Council for the Arts, and the Ontario Arts Council
for our publishing activities. We also acknowledge the Government of
Ontario through the Ontario Media Development Corporation Ontario
Book Initiative.

Design and Composition by *Mad Dog Design*
Printed in Canada by *Friesens*

10 9 8 7 6 5 4 3 2 1

Basically I'm a writer.

Allure, August 1986

Denys Arcand, why do you make films?

For no reason. Because it's my job. Because I don't know how to do anything else. Because there are people crazy enough to pay me for filming. Because it's a pleasant way to wait for death.

Unpublished manuscript, 1995

TABLE OF CONTENTS

PROLOGUE

MONTREAL, "EVENING IN THE WOODS"

Sunday, November 3, 2002. Day 41 of shooting on *The Barbarian Invasions*. The set has been prepared in an amphitheatre in the Desmarais Building at the Université de Montréal. Denys Arcand is about to shoot the sequence in which Rémy says goodbye to teaching and his students. A scene of great cruelty, terrifyingly apt, chilling in its realism.

Whereas other directors would be content with shooting the classroom scene alone, Arcand says, laughing, that he's adding some melancholy shots, in the spirit of German writer W.G. Sebald. Rémy stands hidden behind a window, hunched with grief and helplessness, taking one last look at his indifferent students. Then, like a weary ghost, he leaves the university forever. His courses carry on as if nothing had happened, conducted by a fashionable-looking, career-minded young replacement. A minute before, Rémy was questioned by a contemptuous young student as to whether the due dates for term papers and exams would remain the same.

The same student will visit Rémy in hospital, hired by Sébastien, the millionaire son. Sébastien Huberdeau, the actor who plays this minor role of the arrogant student, plays the lead in Rodrigue Jean's *Yellowknife*. In *The Barbarian Invasions*, he is on screen for only a few minutes. He quips: "For Denys Arcand, I'd play a door-knob!" During a break, while I am smoking outside with Rémy Girard, he affirms that shooting the scenes in the order in which they appear in the script, rather than out of sequence, has greatly helped him play the role of a dying man.

After shooting has ended for the day, outside the Desmarais Building beneath a stunning autumn sky, Arcand recalls that in 1960 there was a forest in the place where we are standing. We are several metres from the Ernest Cormier Building, the only one that existed at the time, where we took our literature and history courses. "It's also where I shot my first film, *Seul et avec d'autres*. Just yesterday, in 1961."

This brief flashback takes us both back to the middle of the 1960–1961 school year and the Faculty of Literature at the Université de Montréal.

Once upon a time.

On the evening of December 7, 1960, Denys Arcand was busy marvelling over the most beautiful voice to sing Mozart in the twentieth century, that of tenor Léopold Simoneau. This discovery took place in Plateau Hall, in Lafontaine Park, where the Montreal Symphony Orchestra was playing. In the program for this "Evening in Salzburg," the group was conducted by Josef Krips, featuring the opera singers Pierrette Alarie and Léopold Simoneau. During the intermission I ran into Denys, whom I had known since the beginning of the school year at the Université de Montréal. He shared his great enthusiasm with me. It was the first time either of us had attended the symphony and we were both on the verge of lyrical frenzy.

A few days later, in the university corridors, Denys declared for all to hear that on that same December 7, 1960, a major event had also occurred at La Scala in Milan, where the opera season always opens on the feast day of Saint Ambroise, December 7. That year, Maria Callas was making a much awaited return after a two-year absence.

"La divina has come back to the Scala!" announced Arcand. "In Donizetti's *Poliuto*."

"In what?"

"P-O-L-I-U-T-O, a rarely performed opera that la Callas has brought to life again! Yet another triumph!"

Music was not all—there was also theatre, creative writing, history, film, an entire cyclorama of cultural activity in which Denys Arcand immersed himself at the beginning of a decade that would also see the beginning of the Quiet Revolution in Quebec. At that time, the end of 1960, were we aware for a single moment that this revolution was right at our door? Certainly not in any clear way, but our consuming passion for cultural events surely served as a catalyst for our awareness.

For me, Denys Arcand was unquestionably the kind of person who sets off a cultural revolution. In his deep bass voice that echoed through the hallways of the Ernest Cormier Building he proclaimed his insatiable thirst for communication; with uncontainable joy he told us about Vittorio de Sica's *Umberto D*, Gogol's *Revizor*, Sartre, Gide and Camus, whose works he already knew, about Mozart and Léopold Simoneau, and the phantasmagorical opening chords of *Don Giovanni*, as conducted by Krips, at the "Evening in Salzburg" concert.

That this initiatory concert took place in Lafontaine Park enhanced the aura of the brilliant intellectual that was Denys. Since 1951 he had lived near the park, at 3818 rue Parc-Lafontaine. His family had left the village of Deschambault, near Quebec City, to live in Montreal close to the excellent classical college run by the Jesuit priests of Sainte-Marie. The college was located on rue de Bleury between rue Sainte-Catherine and Dorchester Boulevard, since renamed boulevard René-Lévesque. Thus, Arcand's youth was spent between two inner-city forests, in Lafontaine Park and on Mount Royal, reminding him perhaps of the "evening in the woods" evoked by the composer A. Flégier in "Le cor," a song that had marked the filmmaker's childhood, based on a poem by Alfred de Vigny. Across from Lafontaine Park was the main branch of the Montreal public library; close by, on rue Amherst, were bookstores and movie theatres. Denys was the oldest of four children (along with Bernard, Suzanne and Gabriel), and was a teenager during the Duplessis years of the 1950s; though the neighbourhood did not cover a large area, it was criss-crossed with streetcar and trolley-bus lines and had much to offer in the way of books, films and plays.

During the intermission at the Mozart concert, cigarette in hand, Denys exulted: "It's extraordinary, live music and singing! So different from recordings! Even more beautiful than theatre, films and literature!" He added, "We should make a pact: forget all the rest and stick with music, only go to concerts."

So it was settled. A few days later, meeting at the university, we were a little abashed by this display of youthful chivalry, understanding that it would have been a little stupid never to go to the cinema again or to our theatre workshop on Gogol's *Révizor*, never again to read those beautiful, provocative books that were covertly passed from hand to hand. Let us try and imagine it for a moment. The following summer, at the Montreal World Film Festival, we would have missed Fellini's *La dolce vita*, a culture shock more essential, more luminous and formative than even the Mozart evening. And then let's try to write the script of Denys Arcand's life without film. He would have become a history scholar, an undistinguished little professor (so he thought), assiduously attending symphony concerts and the opera. Luckily, our "agreement" was buried without further discussion. Nonetheless, I noticed a kind of mocking stubbornness in Denys ("We should keep our pact," he repeated) that would later appear to be more a kind of perseverance.

Earlier, in October, another kind of lyric art had taken Montreal and the university by storm. The Peking Opera arrived at the Théâtre Saint-Denis, making its first appearance in North America since the Chinese Revolution of 1949, the rise to power of the Communist Party and of Mao-Tse Tung to the head of the People's Republic of China.

On rue Saint-Denis, the opera *In the Forest of the Wild Boars* had become a religious and political *cause-célèbre* that generated a number of tracts and demonstrations on the part of the Jesuits and the Chinese Catholic Mission of Montreal. The protesters attempted to dissuade spectators from entering the theatre; according to their reasoning, the fabulous secular art of the Peking Opera could not camouflage "the face of Christ, swollen and crowned with thorns," or the photos of sisters of the Immaculate Conception of Montreal, chained up by Chinese communists. *Le quartier latin*, the student newspaper of the Université de Montréal, covered the dispute in its edition of September 29, 1960. The musician Stéphane Venne denounced the propagandist slogan "A penny for the Peking Opera—A penny for Mao" and declared that the show was "not to be missed." A number of students rushed to see it, crossing the lines of the protesters, whom they judged as right wing. Besides, they told themselves, the Peking Opera was born with the people, belonging neither to Mao nor the Chinese Communist state.

On October 4, *Le Devoir* published a letter of opinion, a somewhat jumbled diatribe defending free access to art, the rejection of all censorship, as well as the freedom to criticize all political regimes, of whatever kind. The students were touchy about the interventions of righteous Catholics. That same autumn, the Quebec board of censors cut the first fourteen minutes of Alain Resnais's lyrical classic *Hiroshima mon amour*, turning the film into what Stéphane Venne termed "a clumsy short."

At the Université de Montréal, that year of 1960–1961, Denys Arcand was the embodiment of artistic passion, holding forth *fortissimo*, like an operatic bass, at once self-assured and anxious, always on the alert. "I've always doubted myself," he has said for decades. No one believes him. In the art deco Ernest Cormier Building, whose tower was referred to as the phallus of Mount Royal, and of Montreal in general, he loved to recount all sorts of facts and anecdotes, new discoveries and strange explorations that often (if not always) revolved around opera: the triumphs of Callas in Milan, Schwarzkopf's recording of Mozart, "especially *Exultate jubilate*, inCREDible!"

One of his own feats from that period makes for an unforgettable story. While still a teenager attending the Collège Sainte-Marie, the theatre-mad Denys volunteered as an extra for the touring company of the Metropolitan Opera, which was performing *Aïda* at the Montreal Forum. Arcand played a scantily clad Ephebian, bearing an enormous and bedraggled peacock-feather fan. What struck him most was not the music, which could not be heard backstage, but the loud buzz of activity in this "hive" as it prepared for the great Triumphal Scene. At the top of their lungs the singers ran through their vocal exercises, which echoed among the milling crowd of chorus singers and extras being ordered about by the American stage managers: *Stand by! In line, extras! Go on now, go on, GO ON STAGE! C'mon, move your ass, MOVE!* Serious in his role of a fake Egyptian slave among the Pharaohs of the Met, as disciplined as one could be amidst the commotion of this New York show, intoxicated by the activity both on and off stage, Denys Arcand saw his wildest acting dreams come true to the rhythm of Verdi's trumpets.

That is about all I knew, up until that point, about Arcand's college days, of course, other than the wonderful books, banned and condemned to Library Hell, that only the "brains" of Collège Sainte-Marie were allowed to read in the 1950s. Indeed, the Jesuits were possessed of the following contradiction: in Quebec and the Catholic world in general they enforced their infamous code of censorship (the "alphabetical index of 10,000 authors with 40,000 of their works classified as to their moral value" by G. Sagehomme, Society of Jesus). Yet, at the same time, for the elite of Collège Sainte-Marie, all was permitted by the men in black robes: Gide, Sartre, Malraux, Camus. Arcand, moreover, prided himself on having discovered works by the Marquis de Sade with the discreet help of the bookseller Henri Tranquille. In the eyes of provincial schoolboys and seminary students, the uneducated and awkward children of Marie and *Athalie*, the lucky and glorious of Collège Sainte-Marie seemed to glide through life with their heads held high, offspring of sultry and poetic Phaedra, daughter of Minos and Pasiphaé, condemned, wonderful, altogether bewitching. "Phaedra," in their greedy hands, took the form of *The Outsider* and *The Caves of the Vatican*, *The Human Condition*, *Nausea* and *The Memoirs of Hadrian*. André Brochu walked around carrying *Being and Nothingness* (or was it Pierre Maheu?); Arcand provided a résumé of *Philosophy in the boudoir* (or did I dream it?). We were virgin intellectuals, strong of will and true disciples of our magisterium. The students of Sainte-Marie made the best teachers; they could teach anything, despite the fact that they were themselves still learning.

For some members of this cohort, Denys Arcand had become the *maestro*. First of all, because he had panache, *maestria*, like Corneille's Matamore, Rostand's Cyrano de Bergerac, or Theophile Gautier's actors, as revisited by Ettore Scola in *Captain Fracasse*. And finally, because he was already a "master."

PART ONE

HAVE GUN, WILL TRAVEL

*I feel more and more marginal.
I'm developing a criminal, negative
mind. I feel more and more sympathetic to bandits, petty criminals, and
all marginal characters. I have no
more ideas about anything, just
nightmare images. Soon I'd like to
make a film about the incredible corruption, the stupidity and deprava-
tion of the people in power. I'm a
filmmaker by trade:* "Have Gun, Will
Travel . . ."

Conseil québécois pour la diffusion
du cinéma, 1971

1
ARIA AND VARIATIONS ON THE THEME OF LOVE AND HATE

Over four decades have passed since Denys Arcand's apprenticeship years at the Université de Montréal, forming a buried stratum that awaits archaeological excavation. For example, we will have to refer to the film *Seul ou avec d'autres* (*Alone or with Others*), made in the autumn of 1961, to see the institution as it was at a time when students kicked over the traces to assert their youthful will for change. Since the beginning of the sixties, the campus has considerably expanded, so *Seul ou avec d'autres* remains a rare document, revealing one of the important backdrops for the biography of Denys Arcand. The singular trajectory of a Québécois artist who has expressed himself primarily through film, and secondarily through writing, in a Quebec rocked by more jolts, metamorphoses and shock waves than at any other time in its history. As the filmmaker has often said, until 1960, the climate in Quebec was quiet and gloomy, following the conquest of New France by the British Empire in the eighteenth century.

The path of this little-known director, or one who is primarily famous for the more spectacular and showy moments of his career, is worth examining at length and down to its most essential details on account of its originality and singularity. So that we may fully appreciate its density and complexity, Arcand's filmic and literary œuvre must be brought to light, its haziest and most shadowy recesses illuminated, those "grey zones" so dear to the filmmaker. Both his completed works and those unpublished or unproduced will be examined, his projects and even his most wild and spectral dreams. What is needed is a kind of "Arcand by Arcand." For, could this really be Denys Arcand, the high-profile filmmaker on whom fame and fortune have smiled on more than one occasion? Can we believe that in 1986, at the time of *Le Déclin*'s domestic and international triumph, the public that hailed Arcand was almost completely unaware that he had been making films for twenty-five years?

Now, after almost half a century of Quebec cinema and Quiet Revolution, Denys Arcand, the most famous enfant terrible of the Québécois postwar generation of filmmakers, is also the most underappreciated or least venerated, the object of love and hate. He has garnered not only rave reviews and numerous awards, but also a closetful of harsh and trenchant invective. Throughout his very up-and-down career, he has been called defiant, arrogant, dangerous, iconoclastic, mocking, contemptuous, cynical, pessimistic. He has often been considered a troublemaker by funding agencies. The invective has come from all sides, from Marxist-Leninist groups or Parti Québécois members, major newspapers and trade magazines, feminists, and even a backbencher MP in Ottawa's House of Commons. On receiving his award at Cannes for *Jesus of Montreal*, Arcand quipped: "Better a grand jury prize from Cannes than first prize at the festival of Rouyn-Noranda." Gabriel Desjardins, at that time Conservative MP for the Témiscamingue riding, complained about this remark in federal Parliament, demanding that the filmmaker apologize to the people of Abitibi! In an anti-Arcand "auto-da-fé" in the summer of 2002, the film magazine *24 images* pronounced Arcand anathema; it pilloried the filmmaker and his "disappointed and bitter baby-boomer cinema," for "blasé fanaticism that has today become the fashionable pose for idiots [. . .] a vision which, given the way things are going, can longer be considered acceptable."

In the spring of 2002, when shooting for *The Barbarian Invasions* was announced, rumours started to fly. After his failures of the 1990s, was Arcand so short on inspiration that he had to make do with a well-timed remake of his best-known feature, a sort of *Decline II*? Could he have fallen as low as Pierre Falardeau, who was making an *Elvis Gratton III*? Poor Denys Arcand! He'd already missed out on two Oscars, for *The Decline of the American Empire* in 1987 and then for *Jesus of Montreal* in 1989; in the spring of 2000, when *Stardom* came out, how many media commentators expressed their chagrin that the film had obtained *nothing more* than the (prestigious) closing screening at Cannes! Was he a washed-up "boomer," no longer capable of "re-enchanting us," as Marie-Claude Loiselle concluded in her editorial in *24 images?*

Was Denys Arcand a new Savonarola, fit for the bonfire of the vanities? Or, to use the words of the Jesuit Marc Gervais in *Cinema Canada* when *The Decline of the American Empire* came out in 1986, ". . . a kind of impish Savonarola castigating the sexual mores of his own world." *Vanitas vanitatum, et omnia vanitas*—"vanity of vanities, all is vanity." The fathers of the Roman Catholic Church have repeated it for centuries; Denys Arcand's mother repeated it to her oldest son throughout his childhood. How can we help but think of Savonarola, who lived in Florence in the second half of the fifteenth century, at the time of the Medicis? Girolamo Savonarola, Dominican prior of the San Marco convent who preached the renunciation of material possessions, convincing rich citizens to cast their most precious belongings into a huge public bonfire—jewellery, paintings, books and silks. Great was the success of this "bonfire of the vanities," an expression later borrowed by American novelist Tom Wolfe for the title of a book that Arcand dreamed of filming one day. But Savonarola also aroused the suspicions of the papacy, whose luxuries and corruption he had denounced. Excommunicated by an order of Rome, the famous preacher was thrown into the bonfire he had started. A true story of love and hate.

Now in his sixties, Arcand offers a view of himself that is rich with contradictions as well as zones of illumination. He speaks of his deep attachment to Quebec and sense of belonging in Deschambault; his happy childhood; his parents' far-sightedness with regard to higher education for their children; the important contributions of certain Jesuits at Collège Sainte-Marie; his dazzling first encounter, at the National Film Board, with the principal founders of Quebec filmmaking, during the making of *Seul ou avec d'autres* in the autumn of 1961; the sense of wonder inspired by his history professors at the Université de Montréal, and of Maurice Séguin in particular; the capital influence, on his filmmaking, of the three women who have shared his life. Despite caustic remarks he has made about the conservative aspects of Quebec society, he names the above factors as those that have helped make him what he is: a personality that has forged its own freedom, often in the heat of confrontation, while remaining firmly rooted in the various dynamics that have helped to shape it.

Both famous and little known, sometimes adulated but often the object of suspicion or contempt, Denys Arcand remains the most enigmatic figure in the intellectual and cultural life of Quebec today. A kind of evil genius, angel of melancholy, or "court jester," as he calls himself, a dandy with the soul of a bandit, like Fantomas. His trajectory in modern-day Quebec is in every way atypical. A detached free-thinker and at the same time ultrasensitive, a bundle of contradictions that he owns and assimilates, Arcand has produced with great perseverance a filmic and literary œuvre that reflects a sort of "controlled madness," to borrow the term used by Stendhal in reference to Rossini's *The Barber of Seville*, an operatic masterpiece greatly cherished by Arcand.

Armed with a degree in History, which would play an instrumental role in his career, mad about theatre (clearly, he could have been a stage actor or director), an insatiable reader, a film and music lover who for a time remained torn between the careers of professor and artist, the future director of *Réjeanne Padovani* made his entry into filmmaking "by accident," or so it seemed. Filmmaking *chose him*, as a priest is said to be summoned to by the voice of God. However, it was also a trade he chose in a most wholehearted, definitive and conscious manner, quickly becoming an expert. "I'm a filmmaker by profession," he would declare at the height of the Quiet Revolution years. A filmmaker he has remained, without wavering or straying from his course, in spite of setbacks, defeats, failures and uncertainties, while keeping a cool head in the face of success; also in spite of the fact that his father never understood his choice of profession, feeling that it condemned his eldest son to perdition, marking him as a failure.

Since the beginning of the 1990s, for certain people Arcand's films have become *unacceptable* and are to be avoided. Once again we can almost hear the Jesuit priests of Collège Sainte-Marie lamenting the fate of their brilliant student, or the caustic reprimands of the Marxists-Leninists from the *Cahiers du Conseil québécois pour la diffusion du cinéma*, who in 1971 subjected their "comrade and friend Denys" to the question torture with inquiries such as: *"In approaching drama, do you plan to introduce political issues?"*

At the time of this first in-depth interview, though Duplessis had been dead for twelve years, it seemed to Arcand as if he were still alive and well. To all appearances, the ghost of the former obscurantist premier of Quebec roamed freely outside his whitened tomb, moralizing and denouncing with the same kind of sermon that had bored Arcand to tears since his first days at the NFB. True, there were one or two periods of respite, first, with the release of *Réjeanne Padovani*, then at the time of *Jesus of Montreal*; for the latter film, Arcand even received the award of the ecumenical jury—a postmodern, face-lifted version of the former Vatican award—but we no doubt must understand this truce as related to the laicization of Quebec, which is generally recognized. Hostilities resumed with *Love and Human Remains* and *Stardom*, both filmed "in English, with Toronto money"; *Lettres d'une religieuse portuguaise* (*The Portuguese Nun's Letters*) and *Joyeux calvaire* were received with little enthusiasm, being "just television." Quebec film magazines practically ceased to do in-depth interviews with Arcand, whereas in the days of *The Decline* and *Jesus*, they abounded.

If there is one factor that has remained unchanged throughout Denys Arcand's filmmaking career, and it is significant, it is these repeated attacks, bearing witness to a vigorous anti-intellectualism in Quebec, particularly evident when a free-thinker of Arcand's calibre who doubles as a writer of formidable style and a matchless humorist-satirist expresses himself through film.

Internationally, Arcand has the stature of Pasolini, whom he resembles in some ways, Godard, Woody Allen or Scorsese. Among domestic filmmakers, he names Claude Jutra and Gilles Groulx as his masters. Moreover, he is almost of the same generation as these two filmmakers, though the media would have us think that he did not step up to the baptismal font until the mid 1980s, with the success of *The Decline*. Arcand is also one of the rare filmmakers of this generation who is still active, in top form both physically and intellectually. Thus, thanks to his experience and perseverance, the stubborn and exacting coherence of his productions, as a creative mind and thinker he is a rare witness to the development of *modern Quebec cinema as a whole*.

In the wake of Jutra and Groulx, Denys Arcand is incontestably one of the great Quebec filmmakers; if not the "top of this class," he surpasses in terms of his thought and themes filmmakers such as Pierre Perrault and Gilles Carle, whose "glorious" reputations, viewed in retrospect, have been overrated—that, at least, is my conviction—in the case of Perrault, apparently due to pronounced cultural nationalism and in the case of Carle, on account of his populist philosophy.

No one has managed better than Arcand to think and live with this difficult cohabitation of opposites, which is rare in Quebec. In Quebec film, Arcand is perpetually and constantly loved and hated. He's the filmmaker who can be neither "lived with or lived without"— national and international, French and English, flying back and forth to Montreal, Cannes and Hollywood, penniless jet-setter, rich bohemian, Jesuit ladies' man, smiling introvert, gentle and arrogant, in short, a dyed-in-the-wool Québécois wearing the mask of a foreigner, of a "barbarian," bearing the mark of the survivor.

In *The Barbarian Invasions*, the filmmaker explores in greater depth his melancholic, saturnine vision of the decline of Western society after nearly half a century of Quebec history, filmmaking and cultural sovereignty. Now is an interesting time, at the start of this new millennium, to explore the trajectory of Denys Arcand and to attempt to shed light on its essential and most distinctive characteristics. His is an exceptional and atypical artistic itinerary. Enigmatic, symptomatic, exemplary and metaphorical—in a word, emblematical.

If I have chosen to write this biography, it is because I have the fortune and the pleasure to be living at the same time as the person whom I consider to be Quebec's greatest filmmaker, and practising a profession that has brought me into contact with him since the early sixties. He has also treated me to the "friendship" of his films, a form of companionship like any other. Film is the street we've both been walking down for over forty years, a sort of multicoloured "Main" or flashing Broadway. We walk down this "Sunset Boulevard" at the same time, but on opposite sidewalks: he as a creator, I as a teacher, analyst and critic. We have ambled over this immense set on parallel paths, crossing the street from time to time to say hello, arrange to meet, stop for a chat or a smoke under a tree or in a pub. Four, five times, this kind of ritual, at the office of the Conseil québécois pour la diffusion du cinéma, at the Cinémathèque québécoise, in my book *Cinéma en rouge and noir,* at the Festival de Namur, in the

office of MaxFilms while putting together the book later published by
Flicks Books in London, *Auteur/provocateur: The Films of Denys Arcand*.
This time, we met on the production site for *The Barbarian Invasions*, at
the crossroads of Cinémaginaire and "Denys Arcand Films."

My vision of the filmmaker may seem contradictory: empathetic
and passionate on one hand, removed and analytical on the other. I am
not one of those idealistic critics who say, "Stick close to the films and
stay away from the filmmakers." On the contrary, though I do believe
that one must keep a cool head about the finished works, which objectively exist, independent of the conditions in which they were produced,
I've always thought that one should try as much as possible to explore
the groundswells and the accidents that go into making creative people,
as well as the tools they use—money, techniques, collaborators—in
order to hone their works. A distance must be maintained in order for
the works to be examined, but that does not mean one has to overlook
small gestures or exchanges that in the long run can contribute to a more
refined filmic analysis. If that aspect is neglected, there is a tendency to
get wrapped up in a kind of metaphysical viewpoint, in analytical
abstractions or aesthetic formalism, which more often than not lead one
to make lofty and removed judgments, to establish a tribunal that is
greedy for diktats, a mighty congregation of beautiful and hideous, or
even a Jesuitical Bible of good taste and moralistic labels, such as "rec-
ommended," "to be avoided," "masterpiece," "bomb," et cetera.

Having taken account of the available means, I decided to limit my
exploration of Arcand's career by staying as close as possible to the subject and his friends and associates. In this sense my approach is consistent with Arcand's concept of cinema, which is to make films to please
himself and his friends, and in doing so cultivate a few new friendships.
It was Arcand himself who told me about his sister Suzanne, a criminologist and an invaluable consultant on his films of the seventies. He
named the three women in his life who have influenced his career, Édith
de Villers, Johanne Prégent, Denise Robert, and suggested that I talk
with some of his friends and fellow sportsmen, Jacques Poulin, François
Ricard, Yvon Rivard. I also wished to meet with two important witnesses from Arcand's college days, André Brochu and Jacques Brault, as well
as several other individuals whom I asked to enlighten me on certain key
aspects of Arcand's work. These include the writer Jacques Benoit, film

editors Monique Fortier and Isabelle Dedieu, filmmakers Jacques Leduc, Marcel Carrière and Catherine Martin, Jacques W. Benoit, first AD (assistant director) on four of Arcand's films, as well as Marc Laurendeau, journalist and former member of the Cyniques comedy troupe. I am aware that many other colleagues, technicians, filmmakers, actors, co-scriptwriters, producers, could have shed light on further aspects of Arcand's work, but research was limited for financial reasons and not because these inquiries lacked interest.

Denys Arcand provided the essential part of the documents in this book, at least in terms of the unpublished writings. Moreover, he agreed to participate in over twenty hours of new interviews, conducted for a period of more than a year (from the end of 2002 to January 2004), and whose transcriptions he revised. Thus, in a sense, he has authored the play based on the story of his filmmaking and the fragments of his personal life that are associated with it. My role was to edit or direct this unique script, in some ways as seething and busy as a Shakespearean drama. Arcand, first violin, myself, viola.

Several important leitmotifs recur throughout the career of Denys Arcand. First, that of saturnine melancholy, which has pervaded Western civilization and left its mark on culture and philosophy, from the works of ancient Greece up to contemporary works such as *Saturn and Melancholy* by the philosopher Klibansky or the essays of W.G. Sebald. The exhaustive works of Klibansky, in particular, clearly demonstrate the role played by melancholy in our cultural history, studied by doctors and philosophers, and permeating all the arts; Dürer's engraving *The Angel of Melancholy* is a fascinating, emblematical illustration of this phenomenon.

Another leitmotif is the filmmaker's love of Western history, which is ever-present, informing his analysis of the events and people of Quebec. A distinguishing characteristic of Arcand's artistic and intellectual production is that it is very rooted in the micro-realities of Quebec of yesterday and today, though these grains of sand are never isolated from the larger history to which they belong. For example, in his first film, *Champlain,* which came out in 1964, the filmmaker drew a parallel between modern Quebec and the colonial adventure of the founder of New France, reminding us that this seventeenth-century life with its vast expanses of forest and snow was contemporaneous with

Shakespeare's *Hamlet* and Monteverdi's sojourn in Venice.

As a third leitmotif, we might be tempted to name Machiavelli. But instead it is Buñuel who should be named, with his cinema that is at once ethnographical and surreal. Of course, Buñuel was no stranger to Machiavellianism, but unlike the famous Florentine he did not disdain poetry and music. One last leitmotif, the filmmaker's passion for books, libraries and bookstores. Which brings us directly to the subject of Arcand's writing.

To some it may come as come as a surprise to hear of the *literary* works of Denys Arcand, given that he chose filmmaking in such a clear and exclusive way. Of course, he never made writing a profession, not even a secondary one, and categorically denies that he is a writer. He explains that writing does not come naturally to him, is a laborious task; he can only produce a page a day, and it always seems like torture! And yet the range, variety and quality of his writings deserve to be fully recognized. His bibliography in this domain is impressive: numerous newspaper and magazine articles for the *Sainte-Marie* newspaper, *Le quartier latin, Parti pris, Format cinéma* and *Lumières*, prefaces, incisive essays on history and sports, commentaries on documentary films, and of course, numerous scripts (*Réjeanne Padovani, Gina*, the *Duplessis* series for Radio-Canada television, *The Decline of the American Empire, Jesus of Montreal, Stardom* and *The Barbarian Invasions*), several unproduced scripts such as *Nesbitt's Trip, Maria Chapdelaine, 1960: En mai nos amours, Dernier amour* and *C'est la vie*, not to mention a number of plays, an opera idea, research reports, synopses and various rough sketches.

Though this list is impressive, there's more to it than that. These texts, practically all of which relate to film and the art of representation, performance and simulacrum, also reflect a very thorough spirit of inquiry, research and documentation; and finally, above all, they are undeniably well written. This corpus possesses literary merit in its own right, and is especially well suited to the task of illuminating the filmic œuvre, a product and extension of a substratum of writing, of thought and structured discourse: the Word, lyrical and passionate. Denys Arcand the writer is one of the keys to the strength and coherence of his film work; his writing no doubt constitutes the essential characteristic of his œuvre, which is that of an artist-intellectual, a thinker who expresses himself through an audiovisual medium.

The second part of this book illustrates this aspect with a selection of some of the "best pages" of Arcand, who in 1958 was nicknamed "the little Voltaire" by Jacques Brault, then a professor of literature in Rhetoric at Collège Sainte-Marie. Arcand's qualities as a writer also extend to his way of speaking. The many interviews with Arcand, a brilliant talker, reflect the same quality of thought, the same gift for flights of oratory, satire and lapidary turns of phrase. Some of these interviews have been revised by Arcand himself, which gives them the unquestionable status of belonging among his writings. All these reasons go to justify the inclusion, in the present essay, of this literature that is the hidden face of the planet Arcand, whose luminous and visible side appears in his cinema.

The filmmaking face, generally speaking, is better known. However, we must take a closer look, if only to describe the totality and coherence of an œuvre whose most prominent aspects are often all we see, such as *The Decline of the American Empire, Jesus of Montreal*, and now *The Barbarian Invasions*. An attempt must also be made at creating a synthesis of a very long career which has received a great deal of attention from the media but has nonetheless been "up and down," provoking both admiration and annoyance, passionate love and hatred.

And finally, several visuals from this biography reveal one last, little-known facet of the filmmaker, his photographic work. During the sixties and seventies, armed with his Leica, Arcand applied himself to photography. "A good hobby for a filmmaker, it helps you get a better fix on the subject and learn how to frame it properly. One day, someone stole my Leica M3, and I stopped doing it."

Forty-two years after our first Mozart concert at Plateau Hall, while hearing the music of the same composer, I would once again be with Arcand, in the beautiful autumn of 2002 on the shoot of *The Barbarian Invasions*. This time Mozart was there with the andante from the *Sonata in D major for four hands* (K 381, 1772). This moving passage, at once serene, melancholy and lyrical, accompanies the death at the end of the film of the baby-boomer Rémy, one of the young people whose vigour and anxiety was featured in *Seul ou avec d'autres*. Yet another indication of Denys Arcand's great sense of continuity, intellectually, methodologically and musically as well.

2
THE BARBARIAN INVASIONS: ON MELANCHOLY

It is often our mightiest projects that most obviously
betray the degree of our uncertainty.
W.G.Sebald, *Austerlitz*

In February 1982, *Le Devoir* asked Denys Arcand, "Do you believe it is still possible to have dreams in Quebec?" This was at the time when his film *Le confort et l'indifférence* was being launched, a political essay and one of Arcand's most controversial films, about the failure of the 1980 referendum on Quebec sovereignty. "No," the filmmaker replied. "That's just my problem at the moment. I don't have dreams and I don't know many people who do. I don't see a dream for Quebec anymore. I'm not aware of an identifiable pattern of dreams that we could all share. My impression is that the Parti Québécois was the last dream. Their practice of power, so disappointing, killed the dream of an entire generation. Will other dreams be possible? I really don't know. Let's talk again in twenty years."

Twenty years passed. What was Arcand dreaming about in 2002? Unperturbed, he continued to examine the concrete issues of political administration in which Quebec and Canada were mired, crises in health care, education, justice; the theme of death, which had haunted him for twenty-five years; generational solitude, strained relations between parents and children. Arcand was busy scripting and directing his new dramatic feature, *The Barbarian Invasions*. A title that refers as much to the defeat of the sovereignist government in Quebec and the events of September 11, 2001, as to the waves of warriors in antiquity who dealt the coup de grâce to the Roman Empire. "With *The Barbarian Invasions*," the filmmaker told *La Presse* on May 11, 2002, "I just want to make a good film."

A good film first of all depends on a solid screenplay, and this one would be developed over three drafts, those of April, June and August of 2002. It could be read in one sitting, and was lively, incisive, resonant and well-thought-out, with a lot of drive, rhythm and luminosity. The text opened with a dedication in the form of an *in memoriam*: "In fond memory of Réo Grégoire, Pierre Maheu, Claude Jutra, Hubert Aquin, Yves Navarre, Jay Moloney." Six tragic deaths, six friends of Denys Arcand: a director of photography, two filmmakers, two writers, and one Hollywood agent.

For more than two decades, the filmmaker had been haunted by the shadow of death, particularly "controlled death," euthanasia or suicide—the Roman emperor in Marguerite Yourcenar's *The Memoirs of Hadrian* called it the desire to "step towards death with the eyes wide open." This leitmotif appeared as early as 1976 in a screenplay entitled *Nesbitt's Trip*, which was commissioned and then turned down by CBC Toronto shortly after the failure of Arcand's *Gina*. Later, in the early nineties, after the huge success of *The Decline of the American Empire* and *Jesus of Montreal*, Arcand proposed a script to MaxFilms whose three different versions were titled *La femme idéale, La vie éternelle* and finally, *Dernier amour*. Roger Frappier rejected the project. Shortly after that, in 1993, Arcand wrote some eighty pages of an autobiographical script on the death of his father, a first draft entitled *C'est la vie*, which remained unfinished.

Death is the structuring theme of *The Barbarian Invasions*. The film returns to a work that Arcand conceived as an image of his own death. But to avoid morbidity and add a certain levity to his subject, he reintroduced some of his former characters/actors: five from *Jesus of Montreal*—Father Leclerc, Sister Constance, a security guard, a police inspector and an ambulance driver, as well as seven from *The Decline of the American Empire*—Rémy, Louise, Dominique, Diane, Claude, Pierre and Alain. The main subject of *The Barbarian Invasions* is Rémy's death. In *The Decline*, of course, though there were no literal deaths there was a kind of fracture at the end, a metaphorical death lurking in the twilight over Lake Memphremagog and evoked in the deathly light of the paintings of Caravaggio. *Jesus of Montreal* depicted the death of a young actor. Death is such a recurrent theme in the filmmaker's work of the past twenty-five years that it is pointless to view *The Barbarian Invasions* as merely a *Decline* revisited, or as its "sequel and end."

In a Montreal hospital that is in a state of great upheaval, Rémy will learn that he has an incurable illness. Joking and sarcastic as ever, he says to his son Sébastien, "You know the proverb: 'Christmas in the scanner, Easter in the cemetery.'" It is October, an autumn full of colour that Rémy will never see decline into winter. But his own end he will see very clearly, being fortunate enough to be able to enter into death with eyes wide open, fully lucid.

The origin of this "providence" is his son, who has arrived from London with his fiancée Gaëlle at the insistence of his mother, Rémy's ex-wife. Sébastien has to be prodded at first, having violently severed ties with his father several years earlier before going on to become a very rich young trader in the City. In the beginning he grumbles quite a lot about his father's illness, but little by little, faced with the breakdown of the Quebec health system, and thanks to his mother and the sensible advice of the humane and progressive Sister Constance, he sets about orchestrating a dignified, euphoric death for his father, a voluntary departure in a serene environment. First, he manages to come up with a private room for the dying man, and then he procures heroin to ease his pain. But most of all, he tracks down his father's old friends, who gather, as in the old days, to drink and smoke, savour fine food and make sarcastic, world-weary reflections. This unusual "class reunion" will follow Rémy to a beautiful house on the shores of Lake Memphremagog and accompany him in his last moments. Once again, friendship (that unspoken value of *The Decline*, as Arcand says) triumphs over all the vicissitudes of sexual life and the difficulties of being parents. Just before the last "page" of Rémy's life, Sébastien clumsily embraces his father, his new friend.

As ever with Arcand, no matter what story is being told, History upholds and illuminates the filmic edifice. This time it is the *Memoirs* of Saint-Simon, which Rémy quotes to Constance, that sheds light that is both sharp and iridescent on the edifice as a whole: "To write the history of one's country and one's times is to show oneself the futility of the world, of its fears, its desires, its disgraces, its fortunes. It is to convince oneself of nothing and everything by the short and rapid duration of all these things and the life of man; it is to remind oneself that neither bliss nor even tranquillity is to be found here on earth."

In the company of this lucid and implacable historian, one feels almost as if one were at the heart of Sebald's *The Rings of Saturn* or meandering dizzily through history in *Saturn and Melancholy* by Klibansky, Panofsky and Saxl. Sebald was an author whom Arcand had only started to read at the time our meetings began in the spring of 2002 (speaking of necessary archives for this biography). *The Rings of Saturn, Vertigo, The Emigrants, Austerlitz* and *On the Natural History of Destruction* were books that accompanied him like brothers in melancholy throughout the entire production of *The Barbarian Invasions*.

In Scene 36 of the script, after Rémy reads her the passage from Saint-Simon, Sister Constance makes the following remark:
– Saint-Simon was a pessimist.
– RÉMY. He was a historian.
– SISTER CONSTANCE. Like you.
– RÉMY. Oh, not me, I was just a history professor. It's not at all the same thing.

At this moment, Rémy makes us think of Arcand himself, who in interviews constantly repeats that he is "just a filmmaker" or says, "I was never a professor. I just did a degree in History, I'm not a historian either" (*24 images*, autumn 1986).

Arcand is at his best in these first days of the twenty-first century, in the wake of the catastrophe at Ground Zero in New York: lucid, shaken, a jester at the courts of today's "kings" of democracy, deeply moved, wounded, cut to the heart. Only "trendy" columnists and superficial critics could see this new film as an opportunistic sequel to *The Decline of the American Empire*. Indeed, *The Barbarian Invasions* is not a remake, or another chapter in a "serial," but a new trajectory, a profound new "reading" not only of *The Decline* and *Jesus of Montreal*, but also of all the films Arcand has made in the past forty years.

The film functions in the same way as most of Arcand's filmic works, which form diptychs or triptychs; this time he has merged all his films into one, like the synthesis of a long chain. *The Barbarian*

Invasions contains *La route de l'Ouest* (*The Westward Road*) as well as *Réjeanne Padovani, Les Montréalistes* (*Ville Marie*) and *Québec: Duplessis et après . . .* (*Quebec: Duplessis and After . . .*), contains the young people from *Jesus of Montreal* and *Love and Human Remains* as well as the teachers and students in *The Decline*; deepest Quebec, stagnating, as well as the globalization jet set and international beauty economy, as in *Stardom*; insignificant Canada and the petty life of an intellectual dying of cancer, one hand held by a nun and the other by a heroin addict who offers him an artificial paradise in the here and now instead of an unlikely Beyond on the other side of nothingness.

Like Fellini and so many other creative minds, Arcand incessantly repeats himself. We all make the same film over and over again, write the same novel and compose the same music. Each individual, while singular and irreplaceable, relives the lives of a million other people. Civilizations succeed and jostle each other, are more often than not struck down by natural disasters, trampled or beheaded in barbarian invasions. This perpetual turmoil is part of the great disintegration of the universe described in astrophysics, evoked in *Jesus of Montreal* in the scene featuring a film about the universe, an idea also demonstrated by Nicholas Ray in the planetarium scene in *Rebel Without a Cause*.

What doesn't fall apart? One day, the professor has to give his last course, the Quebec Roman Catholic Church must auction off its religious artefacts that can no longer be used. Even books, ideas and intelligence dissolve, but so do film and its erotic and imaginary power. Pasolini said that films disappear more quickly than books. In the screenplay we come upon a fleeting reference to the great warehouses of goods in *Citizen Kane* or the radiant image of the legs of d'Inès Orsini, who plays Saint Maria Goretti in *Cielo sulla palude* (*Heaven over the Marshes*), not to speak of the evocative repetition of the music of Handel from the opening scene of *The Decline*. Even cinema is mortal—especially cinema, the most fragile cultural product of all: so many films have disappeared, can no longer be found or viewed, a phenomenon that is harder to imagine in the case of literary classics or sound recordings, to say nothing of visual art works, which now can be so finely reproduced. The cinema—an artistic device of the twentieth century, even of the nineteenth century according to Godard—is handicapped by its own technique, like a rich soldier in too-heavy armour that impairs his agility and flexibility. At his dying moment, all that remains of Rémy's entire life is this cinematic image of the legs of Inès Orsini, fleeting, sensual and erotic, charged with meaning. A flash of light before the great black hole.

Moreover, this sequence becomes a metaphor for Arcand's view of cinema, his choice of cinema: a device for conveying, in a whisper, the ephemeral essence of life, its fleeting tragedy, the little etching that so touches us by its very existence and its inability to bear witness, to leave behind a kind of graffiti to mark its passage. But they are better than nothing, these pencil strokes between two voids, or between two states of material reality, between the Big Bang when it all expands and the Big Crunch, when it contracts, followed by yet another explosion; and so it continues, back and forth. Rémy is inconsolable for having made a bad job of his time on earth: "If only I'd been able to write . . . I'd have left something behind. It's important to succeed at something in life, even in a small way. To be able to say that you did what you could, that you did your best. I'm sure that makes death more peaceful. But I failed at everything."

What else was in the screenplay for the *The Barbarian Invasions?* The political poverty ensuing from Quebec's explosive laicization in 1966, the gloomy insignificance of Canadian history, the stupidity of Americans, who keep building more prisons, and police who act as "guardians of the peace" rather than hunting down criminals. These distressing facts are contrasted with the memory of the great collective intelligence of classical Athens, the Italian Renaissance, the *Declaration of Independence* of the United States. In parallel, or written between the lines, are the barbarian invasions of today, the attack on the World Trade Center, the down-at-the-heel clan of university professors, stock markets, international art and beauty markets.

Described at the end of the screenplay are several floating images from Rémy's imagination (just as the books of Proust, Wittgenstein and Tocqueville "wander" through his uninhabited apartment): Françoise Hardy singing "L'Amitié," Mao Tse-Tung on a tribunal, Chris Evert winning at Roland-Garros, Julie Christie, Neil Armstrong on the moon, Katarina Witt, the bombs of the *Front de libération du Québec* (FLQ), Thelonious Monk at the piano. These fragments of Arcand's intellectual cosmogony, sounds and images of sports and culture, writing and audiovisual media, art and social history, are some that have managed to escape the barbarians for an instant; they make their quiet music, spiralling from one nation to another, transiting towards a future in which no music will exist but the music of the spheres, which no animal or human ear will hear and no civilization will be there to conserve.

I was lucky enough to witness the development of this screenplay (from which certain scenes and images would be eliminated at the shooting and editing stages), to see its progress step-by-step and from every angle, over a period of ten months: preproduction, shooting, image and sound editing, sound mixing, even some of the marketing efforts undertaken in the summer of 2002. Not to mention numerous private conversations with the filmmaker and crew members.

For the first time, I was front-row centre for the making of a film, observing the work done in the main stages of the production process. It was a film analyst's dream, reminiscent of the diagram made by Bertolt Brecht in the early 1930s during the filming of *The Threepenny Opera*, demonstrating the necessity of understanding all the steps involved in this creative process, material, industrial and commercial. The objective: to achieve an overview of the complex "conditions in which a work of art is produced in an era of mechanical reproduction," to borrow the title of an essay by Walter Benjamin.

It was also the first time I'd seen Denys Arcand at work, though we'd talked on numerous occasions outside the studio. For reasons that escape me entirely, until then I had never asked him for permission to observe. On *The Barbarian Invasions*, I at once became a member of the crew, wonderfully accepted, as well as an outsider, the "barbarian," in the Greco-Roman meaning of the word, the one whom everyone likes to tease: "Here comes the biographer, watch what you say!" I kept a little journal in order to understand the complex tapestry that was the film's long production process, running from the summer of 2002 until spring of the following year, when sound mixing was concluded just as arms were taken up in Iraq.

The calendars and preproduction schedules indicate that the fifty-day shoot for *The Barbarian Invasions* will extend over ten weeks, from September 8, 2002, until mid-November. A large part of this work is done in a Montreal hospital.

Thursday, August 29. First, AD Jacques Wilbrod Benoit leads a delegation of the heads-of-teams for image, sound, set design and props, lighting and production management: Guy Dufaux, Patrick Rousseau, François Séguin, Caroline Alder, Claude Fortier, Hélène Grimard. Locations are visited in anticipation of shooting. Site chosen and rented: the Lachine General Hospital, built in 1951, closed for seven years. Denise Robert, the film's producer, explains that the location is the choice and request of the director. As the hospital has never been used for a film shoot, several complicated procedures had to be undertaken with a union to obtain permission to rent the building from the ministry of health. In the script, there are several scenes that take place on an empty floor in a fully functioning hospital. In the Lachine Hospital, every floor is deserted, though the building is in excellent shape and could be reopened with a day's notice. It is a wonderful place to shoot and it comfortably accommodates the various production teams. Producer Daniel Louis, from Cinémaginaire, like the director, is very satisfied with the location: "It's the equivalent of a big studio, and we have it all to ourselves." The outdoor parking lot and the facade of the front entrance, the foyer, corridors, rooms, the floor for administrative offices, a little chapel, all are to be used in shooting. On the ground floor, several rooms will be set up as an infrastructure for costumes and makeup, the cafeteria, and the rest. Jacques Benoit explains to the troupe that the plan for shooting will more or less respect the dramatic progression of the film script, an interesting vector, conceived to help the actors play the gradual death of Rémy. The sound engineer Patrick Rousseau indicates to the first AD that he prefers natural sound, a room with reverberation rather than a soundproofed effect, which would not convey a hospital atmosphere.

Wandering through this empty hospital, one is struck by the fact that not only is it a good solid construction that is no longer used to provide health care, but that it seems to have been abandoned and emptied in great haste. All the washrooms are functional, the "Reserved" plaques are still visible in the parking lot as well as the "Coffee Club" sign in the lobby; the name of one "Dr. Sicotte" is still pinned to the door of an office in the Emergency; another room is decorated with paper ornaments from a recent farewell party and on the blackboard, written in chalk, are the words: *Bye, bye Lachine, Montreal Here We*

Come!!, a sarcastic allusion to the "Montréal, une île, une ville" campaign, aimed at the fusion of numerous local municipalities.

This ghostly hospital exudes a surreal and chilly atmosphere, identical to that of *The Barbarian Invasions*. It is as if this place, described by the filmmaker as "Dante-esque," had arrived at its irreversible denouement. Let us imagine a follow-up: once Rémy has left the hospital to die in the country, in the Eastern Townships, the institution closes its doors forever, the Quebec health system itself terminally ill, bound for destruction due to silence and neglect. Quebec is full of these abandoned, empty buildings, churches, old town halls, schools, and now hospitals, waiting for unlikely budgets to transform them and put them to new uses. These are the cemeteries, warehouses, and archaeological sites of the Duplessis regime and the Quiet Revolution.

September 8, daybreak, first day of shooting. It's autumn and back to work for Arcand, the curtain rises on what we hope will be a pivotal work in the filmmaker's career and the history of Quebec cinema. From 6:30 to 9:00 a.m., I look around in the various departments. I wish Denys luck upon his arrival at the studio, and on the set for Rémy's Room #1, observe the final plotting details for the first scene. The filmmaker works with the actors. First, he blocks out the scene, watching the actors' movements around the set, and then he decides with the director of photography how the scene will be divided into shots. This method was initiated during shooting for *The Decline*: in the first stages of work, flexibility and open-mindedness with a bit of improvisation, followed by fine-tuning and rigour once the final shooting script has been determined. As Arcand explained in *Philosopher* in 1987, "just enough of an element of imponderability, as in jazz improvisation." Similarly, Arcand listens to the actors' suggestions and ideas and talks them over, but once he has a clear idea, he sticks with it. Generally speaking, he always asks the actors to use the mute pedal in their acting, to "underplay," avoiding overtly theatrical gestures and a declamatory style. Interiority, always and above all.

I have to leave during the break between the scene blocking and the start of shooting. In the parking lot, I meet Denys, who has come out to get a cigarette from his car. I comment upon how cool and collected he seems on this big shoot. "Not as much as I may seem," he says.

Wednesday, September 11. Fourth day of production. I can't stay for the scene in which Rémy reads the passage from Saint-Simon to Sister Constance. (I will find out later that there is another disappointment in store for me in relation to this astonishing, emblematic scene.) Still, I manage to catch the blocking and shooting of the moment when the nun scolds Rémy for not noticing the efforts made by his son Sébastien. During the break, Denys talks to me about opera and launches into a description of Coline Serreau's splendid staging of *The Barber of Seville*, which I was lucky enough to see at the Opéra-Bastille in Paris the previous June. He still dreams of staging a musical production, an ambition and fantasy he has nurtured since the 1980s.

Sunday, September 29. Day 16 of shooting. In the morning, two flocks of Canada geese pass overhead, heading west over Lac Saint-Louis. In the afternoon, Arcand's daughter Ming Xia comes to visit with her mother, Denise Robert, president of Cinémaginaire and producer for *The Barbarian Invasions*. The little girl has a miniature walkie-talkie and a Polaroid camera. She takes photos of her director father, all of which are low-angle shots due to her height. Denise Robert tells me that arranging financing for the film was no rest cure. She had to fight tooth and nail to oppose negative readers' reports and a fairly widespread sentiment that Arcand's last two films, *Love and Human Remains* and *Stardom*, had not brought in the expected returns. In such conditions, financial support for a new film could not be taken for granted.

On the set for Rémy's new room, on the third floor of the hospital, the "patient" grimaces with pain just after expounding upon his youthful fascination with the legs of Inès Orsini in the melodramatic film about Maria Goretti, "the one who said no." He knew he was getting old, he says, the day he dreamed "about the Caribbean. . . . Women had deserted my dreams." At another moment, during some test shots, close-ups on Rémy's face that could be viewed on the video monitor, I am surprised to see that all of a sudden, by concentrating on his character, Girard has death in his face. Only a moment before he was laughing heartily with the other actors. And how can we not be touched by Dominique Michel's melancholy reply: "If you knew how long it's been since I've dreamed of a man . . .," after joking in her inimitable fashion about Portugal, the shepherdess who saw the Virgin Mary, and the secret of Fatima?

Monday, September 30. Day 17. Three students emerge from Rémy's room, looking for Sébastien, who pays them for visiting their former professor! What cruelty, yet what a realistic way of conveying the absence of ties or memory. The girl student ends up refusing Sébastien's money. In the first drafts of the screenplay, all three accepted money for their visit.

I think of yesterday. The props department outdid themselves, preparing plates of spaghetti for the scene of the friends' meal in Rémy's new room. To provide for the three or four scenes to be shot the same day and maintain continuity, several kilos of pasta were required; the plates of spaghetti had to be shown steaming—or not— with or without sauce, freshly served or half-eaten, et cetera. The books scattered here and there in Professor Rémy's antechamber, bought or rented by art director Patrice Bengle, further reveal this maniacal concern for concrete detail. This little library was put together to correspond to the character, but reflects the tastes of Arcand and the logic of his screenplay. One would almost think these books came from his own library. Marvelling, I go through the row of books: A. Haury, *Humour and Irony in Cicero*; Hans Licht, *Sexual Life in Ancient Greece*; Jean Delumeau and Yves Lequin (dir.), *The Misfortunes of Time: History of Plagues and Calamities in France*; the *Journal of Jean Héroard: Doctor to Louis XIII*, two large volumes in a case; Verena Zinserling, *Women in Greece and Rome*; Ivan Cloulas, *The Borgias*; Otto Kiefer, *Sexual Life in Ancient Rome*; Robert Rumilly, *Brother Marie-Victorin and His Times*; Bernard Sergent, *Initiatory Homosexuality in Ancient Europe*; Max Pohlenz, *Greek Liberty: The Nature and Evolution of a Life Ideal*; Verlaine, *Erotic Works*; K.J. Dover, *Greek Homosexuality*; Raymond Bloch, *The Etruscans*; Pierre Grimal, *Roman Cities*. We never see these books on screen, but with an art director like Bengle in charge of the set, Arcand can direct his shoot in a relatively relaxed manner.

After lunch, rushes from Thursday, September 26, are screened: exterior shots of the hospital, with patients smoking outside; the arrival of the Quebec Minister of Culture, played by Suzanne Lévesque (a scene that will be discarded at the editing stage); in the corridor, outside the room that this lady has entered, a press attaché and a bodyguard listen in embarrassment to the dying man's ex-mistress, who showers him with recriminations.

Sunday and Monday morning, October 6 and 7. Days 21 and 22 of shooting. The village of Austin near Magog in the Eastern Townships of Quebec, in an elegant old house on Lake Memphremagog. Sunday, in particular, is a superb autumn day full of colours that are radiantly reflected in the lake. Shooting is going smoothly on the scenes of Rémy's last meal with his friends, as well as the memorable sequence of "isms"—separatism, Maoism, sovereignism, et cetera—ending with a melancholy shot of the friends on the veranda, sitting motionless, side by side and facing the lake, like a row of sad statues. Scenes like this are now referred to as "Sebald scenes," in honour of the German writer W.G. Sebald and his works of melancholy. The atmosphere grows more relaxed with the arrival of Denise Robert and little Ming Xia. The producer tells us how the little girl asked Denys the other day: "When Mr. Ford invented the car, was it because it made him happy or was it for money?" A real little Arcand!

And then, in the middle of the day, comes the surprise visit of humorist Clémence DesRochers. A neighbourly visit that quickly turns into an improvised monologue. "I'm staying at a friend's place, close by. When I heard you were shooting, I thought I'd come say hello. Hello, Dodo, Denys, hello, Rémy and Louise and Dorothee. My, my, don't you all look young! Incredible. Why make a sequel fifteen years later if you all still look the same! Make another film. If at least you were all withered like me, it'd be different, but look at you . . . though I mean, it's obvious all that's been lifted . . ." And everyone laughs at her number. "Excuse me, I really just wanted to drop by unnoticed and not disturb anything. Bye-bye, bye-bye . . ."

October 13. Day 27. Screening of the rushes from Magog, Rémy's farewell and death scenes. Very moving, tear-rending. I discover an important element that I did not grasp while reading the screenplay: the identity of the "Prince of the Barbarians." It is perhaps the most unexpected of all scenes and, suddenly, by its brevity and concision, the most forceful and disturbing. Even more moving than the farewell scene of Rémy and his friends, a kind of funeral rite from antiquity, in itself very poignant. Sébastien is the central character of this key scene. Rémy is in a state of delirium. In his hallucination, he speaks of the barbarian invasions, evokes an apocalyptic vision of their chief: "Tomorrow . . . the

Middle Ages . . . barbarians everywhere. . . . Here comes their Prince." His son arrives. Sébastien is the "Prince of the Barbarians," the same person with whom, only a little while before, Rémy was joined in a great emotional reconciliation.

In other words, even in his dying moments, having recovered the love of his son, Rémy has not lost his wits. He is alone, and still lucid enough to recognize that his own child is the lord of the modern barbarians, a child of the new generation of technocrats, of cold and uncultivated millionaires who believe only in the virtues of money, the political power of money, electronic gadgets, and goal-managed skill-driven programs for success. Rémy recovers his son's affection, yes, but the progenitor realizes that he has engendered a monster. The words uttered by Rémy, slurred but lucid, about "the prince who is coming," are the equivalent of Caesar's roar as the conspirators' daggers strike him down: *Tu quoque fili, tu quoque Brute!*—"You too, Brutus, my son!"—you too plunge a blade into my heart, Sébastien, my son, you are killing me!

Children play the central role in these "barbarian invasions," which is something new in the works of Arcand. They resemble the young people we met in *Love and Human Remains*, endearing but suicidal, or murderous. Affectionate, devoted, smiling, angelic barbarians. In the February 14, 1987, issue of *Le Figaro*, during a promotional tour for *Le Déclin* in France, Arcand affirmed that he had no idea what the future held, either for himself or his characters. "They're alone, and they will probably grow old alone. How can you raise children when you don't have a model to transmit to them?" By 2002, he had clearly changed his point of view on this question, for his film is primarily centred on the new generations.

On October 21 and 22, at the hospital, shooting in the "Dante corridor," as first AD Jacques Wilbrod Benoit calls it in his work jargon: long dolly shots that will form the background for the film's title sequence. I am only present for one take, but it is a gripping one, with its 150 extras, François Séguin's surrealistic set, and the glaucous lighting effects of director of photography Guy Dufaux. Sister Constance makes her way down the corridor interminably, followed by the heavy steady cam, valiantly borne by François Daignault.

Thursday, October 24. Day 35. Last day of shooting at the Lachine Hospital. An atmosphere of feverish joy and near-exaltation. Shooting in the little mirrored police office, with the Prince of the Barbarians, Sébastien, the inspector (Roy Dupuis) and his colleague (Sofia De Medeiros). Two things have become clear: that everyone has gotten used to this place that has housed the production for over a month, and that the building has enveloped the entire shoot in its aura of emptiness and neglect, of recent disaster, to the point where certain members of the team, more sensitive to spirits than others, never wanted to set foot in the four rooms of the ground-floor operating unit, not to speak of the morgue and autopsy room in the basement. One security guard sighs: time will weigh heavy on his hands from now on; he will miss the colourful hustle and bustle of *The Barbarian Invasions* troupe.

Viewing yesterday's rushes, what a hilarious surprise to see Denys Arcand in the self-cast role of sidekick to the union boss, a sort of hulking Hells Angel with a bodyguard at his side. Impossible to miss the irony of this character as played by the director, once seen as a staunch supporter of the struggles of workers and the people, now transformed through simulacrum into a rogue in expensive black leather, working for a new-style trade union straight out of the narcotics Mafia. "Yes," confirms Denys, laughing, "there *is* a 'subtext'!" Politicians, administrators for health care centres and trade unions, all are part of the new millennium of the barbarians.

Shooting ended quietly on November 14, 2002. As ever, and as he told *La Presse* en 1992, Arcand wanted to maintain "a very comfortable atmosphere" on set. The director, he maintains, "doesn't need to try and be the best of his team." Jacques W. Benoit, Arcand's right-hand man, alludes to his "postpartum" blues. It's never easy to break with the euphoria of a set, especially this one, magnificent and relaxed. Jacques had the fortune of working as first AD on *The Crime of Ovide Plouffe* and *The Decline*, as well as *Joyeux calvaire*. "It's been a while since I've been on such a pleasant shoot; it went so smoothly. It's rare for a shoot to go so well, without a hitch, without arguments, without fatigue."

Wednesday, November 20. A day of observing the editing at Splice in Old Montreal. If a shoot can sometimes resemble a solemn high mass at

Christmas in a huge, packed cathedral, coloured with a thousand little lights and filled with the murmurs of a thousand chants, editing takes place in an enclosed little chapel, dark and quiet. The computer is the tabernacle, where a lamp burns night and day; Arcand presides, the all-powerful officiate with co-celebrant Isabelle Dedieu, who also worked as editor on *Jesus of Montreal* and *Stardom*; Denise Robert, the film's producer and first Egeria. For example, in the very beginning of the process she suggested shooting the scenes with Rémy's daughter Sylvaine on the sailboat. These prefilmed sequences were very helpful to the actors, who saw them for the first time when doing their scenes.

The day is spent tightening the first twenty-five minutes of the film: pretitles, the title sequence with the "Dante corridor," the arrival of Sébastien and Gaëlle in Montreal, the scenes of Rémy's first room, etc. The editing is rapid-paced, almost breathless. It calms down a little in the scene in which Rémy's ex-wife and Gaëlle visit his apartment and when we see close-up shots of the anxious hospital patients at night, unable to sleep with death lurking around them. Quite cheerfully Arcand cuts down certain pieces of dialogue and alternative shots. The idea is to tighten and tighten again, find the greatest possible interiority in the acting, which doesn't prevent parts of certain sequences from being zany and tumultuous, almost kitsch. The idea is to cut down and tighten in order to guarantee the musical rhythm and pacing, the alternation between calm and "breathless." The hallucinatory walk down the "Dante corridor" is judiciously slowed so that Sister Constance can give communion to a patient, and then the frenetic walk picks up again *da capo*. Arcand has a very keen sense of music.

During a break, he explains that he was more nervous than usual on this shoot. In the past, he says, he wrote, filmed and edited quickly and in a relaxed manner. But not anymore. Due to the burden of responsibility? Because of who or what may be around the corner? Age? Whatever the reason, we can have no doubt that nervousness weighs more heavily on him this time.

Wednesday, December 4, 2002, Astral Media. Screening of the first assembly of *The Barbarian Invasions*. A long version of 135 minutes. The film works very well from start to finish. A steady rhythm, either too quickly paced or heavy, with just a few sustained shots and notes, none of which are held for too long. The pacing flows throughout, lively without being breathless, exactly as it needs to be to describe a world in constant movement: complex, composite, and in which various threads, described by cars, planes, television, cell-phones, computers and satellites, combine to produce a huge spider web. A great sobriety and restraint in the emotional scenes, which give the film a colouring all its own. Nothing excessive, the descent into death occurring in a stoical manner, *alla romana*. No melodrama either, the dramatic structure being inspired by tragedy, that is, the notion of death is present right from the beginning, conveying us as if in a train; we go along with the voyage it has planned, all the way to its destination, our main question being, "How will we get there?" We are aboard a streetcar named desire, the desire to "enter into death with eyes wide open."

What creates this very particular tone is, of course, the lucidity and ongoing introspection of all the characters—the recalling of historical facts concerning Quebec, America or the entire planet; also there's the fact that everyone has their "two cents" to add, from the enraged nurse to the police inspector, the police inspector to the drug pusher. None of which takes away from the mystery that envelops the whole in an aura of tragedy, with death in the foreground, and all these people who are ignorant of what is happening to them, or who are resigned like the hospital patients in hostage to the health system. In short, the mystery is more difficult to understand than death itself, but it leads us back to the fold, to the lake, to nature which endures far longer than human beings and their history, moving at its own, slower rhythm, serene and stoical, also coming to an end, but which instead of sinking into nothingness can transform.

The good roles: that of Rémy, of course, but also the cohort of Fates: Sister Constance, Nathalie the heroin addict, the compassionate nurse; and Sébastien, in his smiling robotic coldness, Prince of the barbarians, enigmatic and indispensable, an exterminating angel. This last character brings us back to that other mystery: how are monsters and patricides produced, such as Oedipus, both king and murderer. Sébastien is death incarnated, the boatman who conveys Rémy across a modern-day River Acheron between Montreal and Magog, from the cosmopolitan whirlpool to the autumnal lake. The image of Rémy, sitting in his wheelchair at the end of the dock, turning back towards his son and smiling like a sad child, makes for a heart-rending shot. Rémy finally smiles at his death, which will take him in his arms, envelop him in a chilly and comforting blanket, and hold his hand at the moment of his final journey.

The "postmortem" segment of the story is also very interesting. Nathalie, in Rémy's apartment, gazes at some of the professor's books, filmed in close-up: *The Gulag Archipelago* by Solzhenitsyn; *If This Is a Man* by Primo Levi; *History and Utopia* by Cioran; the *Diary of Samuel Pepys*, books from Arcand's personal library this time. And then there is the magnificent short scene of the piano lesson that Louise is giving to young girls of different races and cultures, the new world, the voice of tomorrow singing along with Diabelli.

To live one's life well is perhaps, above all, a matter of knowing how to die well, at peace with oneself, reconciled with friends, music, nature, matter. This film, which makes effective use of the classical code of dramatic art as well as that of popular television, is doubtless one of the most contradictory or subversive works that Arcand has ever made, for every moment is punctuated by flashes of inquiry and unnameable anxieties, an explosive mixture of ancient and contemporary cultures, all of it treated with deceptive lightness, touched with a passing glance, a near-banal reflection, a trembling landscape: like flowing water, ever changing but always itself. Fluidity and musicality.

The touching placidity of this master shot at the end of the film, when Louise is teaching two young girls the slow movement of Diabelli's *Sonata no. 1, opus 32*. A shot that is all the more moving because it contains, as a silent and attentive extra, Ming Xia, Denys Arcand's daughter, sitting quietly beside the teacher. This little Chinese girl and the two young Vietnamese women comprise a metaphor of the third generation in *The Barbarian Invasions*. While the first generation is dead or petrified in its emptiness and melancholic despair, and the second generation, that of Sébastien and Nathalie, represents the "barbarians," the third, in gestation, marks the beginning of the future.

A racially mixed future, a little society of nations weaving the Quebec of tomorrow, French-speaking, multi-ethnic, artistic. The antithesis of the barbarians and the deceased. A new life born in and through music, the alchemy of transmission, of teaching, thanks to a survivor of the hecatomb. A moment earlier we saw Nathalie, in recovery, looking through Rémy's books, a treasure that has been entrusted to her care. Similarly, Louise acts as a ferrywoman for her three young students; music is the cool water with which she moistens these new shoots and which she transmits to these young women of a new Quebec, radically different from that of the Quiet Revolution.

Two more work screenings after the holidays, in the beginning of the New Year 2003. The Québécois and Canadian film milieu is already pinning its hopes, both economic and cultural, on *The Barbarian Invasions*. From now on, pressure will weigh on the film like a yoke of lead. Editor Isabelle Dedieu, directed by Arcand, continues to tighten the film, pruning, cutting, reducing to the essential and indispensable, working towards a smooth rhythm. A second version of the film has been reduced to about one hour and fifty minutes, just under two hours. Entire scenes are eliminated: the one in which Rémy reads and comments upon the passage from Saint-Simon; the entire scene with Rémy's third ex-mistress, who has become the Quebec Minister of Culture; overly emphatic flashbacks to *The Decline*; numerous images at the end of the screenplay; shots where the camera work is too obvious, lacking simplicity and precision; shots that are overtly melodramatic. For Arcand this work of cutting back is a matter of course, rigorous, classical, devoid of forced effects.

The later work on the sound track at Covibec is carried out in the same spirit, with Marie-Claude Gagné and Yves Laferrière composing, and Michel Descombes and Gavin Fernandès on sound-mixing. To be eliminated: sound atmospheres that are too enveloping or loaded, and seem superfluous; to be retained: only "realistic" or metaphorical sounds, only those that correspond to a minimalist style. The placing of music must obey the same logic: a few phrases from Arvo Pärt and the title track by Pierre Aviat (Handel and scratch) complement short sonatas by Mozart and Diabelli, played "live" in the last part of the film. Finally, Arcand chooses and places his dedication: "To my daughter Ming Xia," definitively rejecting the dedication from the screenplay addressed to five friends who died tragically.

In the first days of spring 2003, the film is finished, the final mix wrapped, Arcand has turned the final page on two years of work on *The*

Barbarian Invasions. Now all that remains is for an invitation to Cannes in mid-May to be confirmed. In the meantime, the film's distributor, Alliance Atlantis, sets the date of May 9 for the Quebec premiere. On April 15 at the Ex-Centris, a screening and press conference is planned and then a preview screening for the crew. And finally, the great Montreal premiere is planned for early May at the Theâtre Maisonneuve. A gigantic promotional blitz is already underway. The entire crew touches wood, with Arcand in the lead.

In playing one last musical chord with the children in the end of the film, Arcand comes full circle, linking these young faces to those of his own childhood in the 1940s, returning to his roots in Deschambault. *The Barbarian Invasions* is a film that emerges from this matrix. Its first working title was *Père et fils*, "father and son." In the preface to the published version of his script, the filmmaker writes: "I accompanied, to our hospitals, my grandfather, father and mother, who all died of cancer. I never told my grandfather nor my mother, and especially not my father how much I loved them. I should have." W.G. Sebald, in his book *Austerlitz*, observes that the work of photography "is the moment when one sees the shadows of reality, so to speak, emerge out of nothing on the exposed paper." Perhaps, in the end, the work of cinematography in *The Barbarian Invasions* was Denys Arcand's way of conjuring the shadow of his father, of telling him at last how much he loved him.

3
THE OPERA HOUSE OF DESCHAMBAULT-DE-PORTNEUF

"**M**y father, an opera enthusiast, was friends with Raoul Jobin. They knew each other from school. The famous Quebec tenor came to visit sometimes. As a child, I remember how I would creep up to the bathroom door while he was shaving. I would listen to him sing to himself."

As far back as Denys Arcand can remember there has been opera in his life. His mother often played Chopin polonaises, veritable lyric tragedies in miniature. With his father, he listened religiously to the direct broadcasts from the New York Metropolitan Opera on Radio-Canada on Saturday afternoons. He liked them very much. Once in a while, Raoul Jobin would whistle a phrase, from *Romeo and Juliet* perhaps, or the song "Je t'ai donné mon cœur."

That is one good reason that the Arcand home, at 276 chemin du Roy in Deschambault, could have been called an "opera house." In the United States, this rather surprising name was given to tiny theatres in small towns, villages or urban neighbourhoods that hosted all sorts of events and performances: films, lectures, musicals, meetings of local associations, et cetera. There was one such magnificent building in Stanstead in the Eastern Townships, straddling the Quebec-Vermont border, called the Haskell Free Library and Opera House.

A second reason: the Arcand household was always filled with music. "My mother had studied piano in the village with the Sisters of Charity, called the 'grey nuns'; she played very well." A guitar, a saxophone, a drum-set, and a harpsichord would later join the piano. All the children would study music. Suzanne attended the conservatory before choosing criminology. Bernard, Gabriel and Suzanne formed a trio for the fun of it; the group Beau Dommage, friends of Gabriel's, started out by rehearsing in the Arcand's new house in Montreal, on rue du Parc Lafontaine.

A third reason for referring to the Arcand as an "opera house" was that the family itself was like a sort of operatic sextet, constantly discussing or laughing about something, living in its cocoon and at the same time open to the world and to culture. It was a family in which everyone was allowed to have his or her say and defend even the most disputable ideas, strictly Catholic and moralistic in its outlook but with a sidelong glance at the libertarian idea. "In our house," says Suzanne Arcand, "the big private joke was that our parents dreamed of seeing their children become doctors, lawyers, parish priests. They ended up with a filmmaker, an anthropologist, a criminologist, and an actor. They were out of luck!" In 1987, while a dossier on Arcand was being prepared for *Copie zéro* at the Cinémathèque québécoise, when asked to comment upon the unusual fact of three famous brothers in one family, Denys, Bernard and Gabriel, the filmmaker replied, "You don't know our sister Suzanne, the most intelligent of all. She's a criminologist, a scientist."

To describe in epic-film style the arrival and the place of Denys Arcand on this planet, one might say he arrived in the early 1940s, at the portals of the American Empire. The Second World War is raging in the "old countries," just prior to the decline and fall of this modern imperialism. The future filmmaker makes his first appearance in the village of Deschambault during the Duplessis era, in that strange province of Quebec, or Lower Canada in the former French colonial American empire, where nothing has happened since the British conquest in 1763. "Indeed," says Arcand, "nothing has happened here since 1642 when they established the Chavigny *seigneurie*, the ancestor of Deschambault." Soon, however, Quebec will wake up to the modern age. The 1948 *Refus global* manifesto is the first important catalyst for what will become the Quiet Revolution in the fifties and sixties. Arcand will become one of the leading figures in this revolution that plays itself out in both euphoria and pain, though later Arcand will say it was only a secondary phenomenon. However, this does not prevent him, at Collège Sainte-Marie, the Université de Montréal, and in filmmaking, from espousing a line of thought that will soon be expressed in the journal *Parti pris*'s platform of revolution. In any case, he explains, in Canada and Quebec, we sit on our glaciers watching the American Empire burn, and the barbarians have barrelled across our territory, heading straight for that giant and have set about destroying him.

After the failure of the 1980 referendum on Quebec sovereignty, Arcand will completely lose interest in politics. He turns instead to the examination of souls, his own, first of all, and those of the people close to him, treating these zones of shadow and mystery as territory for scientific research, exposing them to the light of an ever-broadening historical awareness. Start off with the detail and work towards the universal. He proceeded in the same way in making documentaries, but now his work will take the exclusive form of documented fiction.

In the candid eye cinema mode, Arcand's story goes more or less as follows. Georges Henri Denis Arcand is born in Quebec City at the Saint-Sacrement hospital on June 25, 1941, second offspring of marine pilot Horace Arcand and Colette Bouillé, residents of Deschambault, in the county of Portneuf. A first son, stillborn on July 17, 1939, as indicated by an inscription on the family monument reading F.G. Arcand, precedes Denis. Thus, the newborn becomes the oldest child in the family. The baby is baptised on the day of his birth by Father Jos. Émile Létourneau, at the Saints Martyrs Canadiens parish church in Quebec City. His godfather is his maternal grandfather, Henry Bouillé, also a Saint Lawrence river pilot, his godmother is Olévine Gauthier, his godfather's wife; he is held by Priscilla Paquette, Madame Georges Arcand, his paternal grandmother. The birth register cites the child's main given name as "Denis." Changing the spelling to "Denys" is not a literary affectation or a teenage whim, but his mother's idea. When the boy is five, realising that there is another Denis his class at primary school, she changes the spelling to distinguish him. A sister and two brothers, in the following order, will follow Denys: Bernard (April 18, 1945), Suzanne (April 23, 1948) and Gabriel (June 4, 1949).

In Deschambault, there is opera but also death. Two close companions. One day, Denys receives an unusual gift from his grandmother

Olévine. She has an inscription made on a tombstone in her cemetery plot, reading *D. ARCAND*. She bequeaths the plot to him. In the family it is believed that in doing so, the good woman hoped that young Denys would reflect more often upon death. It is a surprising anecdote, well worth hearing in full from the filmmaker himself: "When she sold me her house, in the end of the sixties, my grandmother was well aware that I didn't go to church and that my wife didn't either. For my grandmother, anyone who did not practise religion or think of their end was a frivolous person. For her, to be agnostic was unthinkable. There is a God in heaven who created us, and that's how it was. Only someone completely stupid could deny it. Since she did not feel I was stupid, she believed I must be frivolous, that I was just having fun, that I did not think about my end, that one day I'd be confronted with illness and death, that I was in danger of going to hell. She bought this plot in the graveyard, had a tombstone made with my name on it. I've often joked with my friends: "You don't know where you're going in life. I do. It's a very specific place." Women in my childhood said that you had to think of your death every day. My mother thought so, even more than my grandmother, who didn't have my mother's completely exalted temperament. She was a fine old lady, very Catholic, very much a believer, but without my mother's ultrareligious, tense side. The fact that I had a tombstone in the Deschambault cemetery didn't affect me in the least. Since childhood, I've thought about death every day. My parents passed this bit of data from their genetic baggage onto me. Believer or nonbeliever, it makes no difference. I think constantly of death, I make films on the subject, like *Réjeanne Padovani*, *Love and Human Remains* and *The Barbarian Invasions*. I am completely saturated with it."

So Grandma Olévine Gauthier bought her own plot at the Deschambault cemetery. In doing so, she made a place for her grandson Denys, but also fulfilled another last wish: *not* to be buried in the *Tancrède Bouillé* family plot where her husband lay below the monument inscribed: "Henry Bouillé, pilot, deceased December 1, 1967 at the age of 83." Suzanne Arcand explains that by doing this, Olévine Gauthier meant to find peace in the cemetery! She only reserved a place beside her for the filmmaker's future coffin. But this did not prevent the good woman from having her epitaph inscribed with the not very feminist name of "Madame Henry Bouillé, 1890–1980."

Deschambault, not far from Sainte-Anne-de-la-Pérade and Quebec City, is a unique rural village in deepest French Canada, a remnant of New France—among other things, it possesses a very rare old presbytery left over from the French regime—slumbering since the middle of the seventeenth century in its humdrum rural environment, enveloped in its monotonous seasons and ongoing succession of days, each one the same as the one before. This village with its picturesque, monasterial torpor is unique in that its Catholic heart is not housed, as in other villages, on the chemin du Roy, the "king's road" (the name usually given to a village main street), but at the end of the little rue de l'Église, on Cap Lauzon, a pretty promontory with a view of the river. On this hillock, arranged in a circle as if around a kitchen table, are the usual buildings: the church of Saint-Joseph, the presbytery, the convent, the former "*habitants*' hall," the people's bank. The general store is nearby; the cemetery stretches out in front of the church like an old cat. The presbytery, not unexpectedly, is as vast as a seigniorial manor. Next to the church, it is the proudest, most handsome and elaborate building in the village.

Beneath this balcony of Roman Catholic faith and the French Canadian "race" flows the powerful river, dotted with ships like the ones piloted by Denys's father. Horace Arcand was a specialist of the Saint Lawrence, as one had to be in order to navigate this changeable and difficult waterway, one of Canada's biggest marine cemeteries, a burial ground for countless three-masted battleships from the English and French empires, as well as the *Empress of Ireland.*

Denys Arcand, in 1989, told the Quebec City daily *Le Soleil:* "You never get away from where you come from." Indeed, though one might get the impression that the filmmaker is an urbanite, a resolute Montrealer, when reading his biography we become aware of the importance of Deschambault in his life. He spent his childhood there, until the age of ten; during his years at Collège Sainte-Marie, from 1951 to 1960, the family returned every summer and at Christmas; after 1966 and his marriage to Édith de Villers, he moved into the house of his grandmother Bouillé and the couple lived there until the early 1980s, almost fifteen years. "My roots are in Deschambault. First, the attachment comes from birth, an involuntary factor. Four days after my birth in Quebec City, I was back in Deschambault, I lived there for my entire early childhood, a crucial period."

In the filmmaker's view, Deschambault, a very small village of about eight hundred inhabitants, must have been very pretty at the turn of the twentieth century. Arcand has seen a few magnificent old photos: Normandy-style architecture, gabled roofs, skylights, stone houses. After 1900, the place started to deteriorate, at first a little and then a lot. But certain spots have been preserved and restored by local inhabitants, young people attached to their patrimony. These villages between Quebec City and Trois-Rivières are the loveliest in Quebec, located on both the south and north shores: Cap-Santé, Neuville, Deschambault, Les Grondines. On the other side of the river: Lotbinière, Deschaillons. "I don't know if this environment influenced my love of history. My paternal grandparents' house, for example, goes back to about 1690. We're talking the seventeenth century. These are certainly some of the oldest spots, the most permanent fixtures in North America. If you go to the village cemetery, you see all your grandparents, your great-grand-parents, and your great-great-grandparents. It gives you a kind of great stability. Probably too much, because it's also extremely stifling."

In his home parish of Saint Joseph, the future filmmaker is an altar boy, often participating in the ringing of the bells, shown in a beautiful scene in his unproduced screenplay *C'est la vie*, written in 1993. This incomplete manuscript describes the death of an old *pater familias*, struck down with cancer, a Saint Lawrence River pilot by the name of Adrien Gauthier. It is the story of a family's life in a small Quebec village, told in the present tense or in flashbacks to the childhood of the oldest son, Éric, an architect. The other characters include the mother, a sister and two brothers. Despite a number of imaginary plot twists, it is obviously a near-exact depiction of Denys Arcand's family and his father Horace's death. The ballet of bell ringing occurs at the end of the film. The film-maker comments upon it with a smile, à la Buñuel: "I was an altar boy, all little boys were, give or take a few. Five cents per mass. The church marked your life with nonstop ceremony: mass and vespers, feast-days every two weeks, the Immaculate Conception, Assumption, the Annunciation, Rogations, Advent, Lent, All Saints' Day. . . . Life would stop, everybody went to church. Tocqueville noticed that about the Québécois when he visited in the nineteenth century. Like in *Mon oncle Antoine*, people went to church with horses. As I say this, I feel as if I were talking about a Tolstoy novel. The choir was very important. Madame Blandine Paré played the organ; the choir sang the masses of Charles Gounod or Theodore de La Hache. Being an altar boy gave you a kind of social status, especially if you were an assistant or an incense bearer. The latter of the two had the responsibility of spreading incense through the crowd. He'd walk along with the censer, and the whole crowd had to stand up. I loved it—it's my theatrical side—going along with the censer and the crowd standing up on cue. Very pleasant, the way it would be for an actor who's just performed a monologue. I have other images: in autumn, taking off on my bicycle. The first mass was at five-thirty in the morning. I left at five-fifteen. It was still dark. No cars, nothing. Nineteenth-century images. I was a believer myself. I prayed. I was quite happy."

During the summer, thanks to the Bouillé grandparents, the Arcand children have the use of a nearby cottage by the river, to the west of the village in the direction of the La Chevrotière mill and Les Grondines. This summer cottage is an unexpected haven of peace, even more cosy than their nest in Deschambault. There is a beach; the children can swim in the river. Not far, there is a group of rocky islets. Each Arcand child chooses one and gives it his or her name. The first one, closest to the shore is, of course, "Denys's Island." The rest of the time is taken up with various forms of entertainments and parties.

It is also during childhood that Denys learns to read the New Testament, as he wrote in 1989. "*Jesus of Montreal* was born from juxtaposing with the themes of the Passion according to Saint Mark my memories of life as an altar boy in a remote village that had been Catholic for centuries, and my daily experience as a filmmaker in a big cosmopolitan city. I will always be nostalgic about that time of my life, when religion provided a soothing answer to the most insolvable problems, while remaining quite aware of the how much obscurantism and demagogy these false solutions contained. Even today, I can't help but be moved when I hear: 'Where your treasure is, there will your heart be also,' and 'If you love those who love you, what merit is there in that?' Through the thick fog of the past, I hear the echo of a profoundly disturbing voice." Today Arcand adds: "All my films exude this loss of faith. It's always with me."

Within this Catholic cocoon, Denys's mother dreamed of her

eldest son becoming a priest. "Not a priest," quips Denys, "she wanted me to be a cardinal, even the pope!" Colette Bouillé had her own version of the story: "It was Denys who wanted to become pope!" This well-behaved schoolboy who first learned to write beneath the rod of the nuns, and who would continue to write with a round, well-formed hand, even started to think he could become a saint, as he told the *Globe and Mail* in 1989. At the age of fourteen, while studying with the Jesuits of Collège Sainte-Marie, he made the wish of becoming a saint, through missionary work in Africa or preaching the theology of freedom in Latin America. "Until I was a teenager, like my mother, I was a mystic," he declared on the television show *Viens voir les comédiens*.

As a marine pilot, Horace Arcand (December 24, 1906–November 13, 1986) was a leading citizen of Deschambault, of about the same social rank as the doctor, notary or parish priest. The son of Georges Arcand, he lived with his mother, who was widowed in 1933, and eight brothers and sisters at 200, chemin du Roy, a house built about 1715, in the French regime period. His mother, Priscilla Paquette, died on May 11, 1964, at the age of eighty-nine. After doing his secondary studies and serving as a seaman, Horace Arcand trained as a marine sailor. After becoming a captain of ocean-going vessels, he trained as a Saint Lawrence River pilot, sailing to several countries and continents, and around Cape Horn. His itinerant status lasted quite a long time. Future pilots left Quebec at around the age of sixteen and spent fifteen years at sea. They returned at the age of thirty, married young women just out of the convent, never wanted to talk about their long voyages, their life at sea and its various ports, a sacred subject, almost taboo. Very late in life, Horace Arcand let a few details slip, discreetly confiding to Denys, "Spanish women are often very pretty" or "In Singapore, Chinese merchants sold us opium on the docks. We put it in our pipes at night. We slept well. It was wonderful, that stuff, better than what you take these days." Colette Bouillé, his wife, also came from a family of Saint Lawrence pilots. She received her grade-twelve education from the sisters of La Charité in Deschambault, and studied piano and painting.

There was an unspoken but very obvious social structure, Denys Arcand explains. His father socialized with other pilots, the doctor, the notary, the Liberal MP (Dr. Pierre Gauthier), the parish priest. But he would never have gone to visit a farmer or country people. He was friendly and polite with them, but there were pronounced social strata and distances that had always existed. People like his father were part of a long line of river pilots, and it had been that way for as long as any-one could remember. It was a kind of freemasonry: fathers passed down the secrets of Saint Lawrence navigation, a mysterious and very compli-cated science. It was almost a social structure from the *Ancien Régime*. "That's the milieu I was brought up in; it had a great influence on me, though I can't say in exactly what way."

Close to the village of Deschambault, near a part of the river called the Devil's Hole, is the La Chevrotière mill, now transformed into an art gallery and small museum. In the basement is a room devoted to sea pilots, with an exhibition entitled *Magicians of the Water*. Here, in par-ticular, we find several newspaper articles celebrating Horace Arcand, who one day became "the Queen's Pilot." He had the honour of pilot-ing the royal yacht *Britannia*, a distinction that came to him as president of the Saint Lawrence pilots' association, on June 26, 1959, for the Canadian inauguration of the Saint Lawrence Seaway. Pinned on a bul-letin board is a photocopy of his secret notes on seamarks or landmarks, navigational guidelines for ships. One example almost makes one think of Joseph Conrad: "Going downriver, the Boulard sand bar begins when you reach the road to Bouillé, and ends when the statue of Saint Louis shows its back between the two clock towers in Lotbinière." Denys Arcand notes that his father was proud of showing people the compli-mentary letters he received from captains of ships that he had led down the Saint Lawrence. "One day, I'd like to make a film about my father."

In the seventies and eighties, Denys Arcand would say, for exam-ple, in *TV-Hebdo* in 1982, that he came from a "working-class back-ground." Today, he amends this. The term "working-class background" was not well chosen. His father earned a good living, the equivalent of what an airline pilot would earn today. Their situation was therefore comfortable enough that the parents could pay for a good education for their children, but not enough for them to board at school. This is why the family had to move to Montreal, so the children could attend school as day students. "Not a tight budget, but one with clear limits." The filmmaker specifies that he does not come from an upper-middle-class background like Pierre Perrault, Michel Brault or Claude Jutra, who lived in the Town of Mount Royal or Westmount, that he could not count on his father, later in life, to help him out or ask him to finance his research and filmmaking. "We didn't come from the upper-middle class, but from a small village of eight hundred people where there were these two rather strange, special people, my father and mother, difficult to pigeonhole, who dreamed of culture, of having children who would lead the lives they could not have themselves."

However, the filmmaker confirms that he was raised on Black Sea caviar, absolutely delicious, as well as scotch! These were gifts given to his father by the captains of British or Russian ships. His father brought home caviar as if it were peanut butter. Denys loved the taste, not knowing that it was a very expensive item. He ate it in the morning on his toast made with Weston bread, drinking Nescafé. His father often repeated that the most beautiful places in the world were Monte-Carlo and Los Angeles. He thought the Quebec climate was awful. Though he was still very attached to his village, his family and the people around him, he basically looked down on the Quebec people. Arcand remembered his father saying that they were sawers of wood and water-carriers. They had no education. They made good fisherman, miners, and lumberjacks, that was all. It was lamentable, they didn't know how to express themselves, had no culture, nothing. For Horace Arcand, culture was the Paris Opera, La Scala in Milan, travelling. "I learned at my father's knee that the most beautiful place in the world was the orange groves of Los Angeles." To live in Quebec was to be stuck there, trying to do your best. His mother would have liked to be more cultivated, stay in school longer, live in Europe or go back there to visit. His father never liked Montreal, where he lived for twenty years. The filmmaker's parents sacrificed their lives by deciding to do all they could to help their children succeed and be the most educated of all. Their energy was completely devoted to this.

In 1987, in the Cinémathèque's magazine *Copie zéro*, Denys Arcand confided: "My relations with my parents were not conflictual, they were mute." Today he specifies that he lied and kept things from them. His father never talked about his life on the boats. Moreover, as a teenager, Denys, who worked as a sailor for two summers, had it clearly explained to him that what happens or is said on boats remains an absolute secret. Nor did Arcand ever talk to his father about his life as a student or filmmaker, because it didn't interest him. Horace Arcand knew nothing about film; he looked down on it. For him, it was entertainment for the lower classes and the jobless, as he had so often seen during the crisis of the 1930s, in Quebec City, Trois-Rivières, Montreal. "When I first started at the NFB at the age of twenty-one, it was a catastrophe for my father and the entire family. My grandfather Bouillé said to my father: 'It's really a shame to have made so many sacrifices, all for this. He'll be a federal civil servant making films.'"

Like the character of Éric, in the unproduced screenplay *C'est la vie*, or like Tina in *Stardom*, Denys Arcand was wounded by the fact that he always disappointed his father, who thought his oldest son was a bad hockey player, and because he preferred tennis, learned from his mother. In front of the Bouillé home, Colette's father built a games area, and it was on this private court, rare in a Quebec village, that Denys took up this sport that his father thought effeminate. It is no surprise, given the context, that the future filmmaker locked horns with the father he loved so much. It happened twice, Arcand says, as he evoked in *C'est la vie*. The first time, he must have been seventeen. He fell in love with an English-Canadian girl, sent by her parents to Deschambault for the summer to study French with the nuns. He saw her everywhere, they ran on the beach together. Suzanne Arcand explains that their grandfather Bouillé had a very big orchard, which started at the chemin du Roy and extended almost all the way down to the river: "A very good place to hide one's youthful loves." Horace Arcand found Denys's conduct unacceptable, feeling that his oldest son was dishonouring him in the eyes of the village. "I wouldn't stand for it: 'I'm going to do what I want, and you're not going to stop me.' We were yelling at each other in the kitchen. At that time, I was already tall and strong. We yelled at each other at the top of our lungs for two hours. I doubt either of us slept that night. And after that, we never talked about it again." Another time, it was an argument about his sister. She had gone off to live with a young man, they weren't married, and so she was "living in sin." They had rented a house in a neighbouring village. Horace Arcand said: "She's not my daughter anymore, I disown her." So Denys, who had gotten married in a church, was thus beyond reproach and had a solid basis for attack, called his father a "crazy old reactionary, and not a pretty sight."

Colette Bouillé (February 22, 1913–February 11, 1990) entered the Montreal Carmelite monastery in 1932, having decided to become a nun. It was an austere, cloistered community. Why did she leave to marry Horace Arcand?

There are two quite different accounts of this event, like two drafts of the same screenplay. First, there was her own story: a knee wound from playing tennis, followed by surgery, rendered her unfit for religious life. The Carmelites had to refuse to admit her to the novitiate and proceed to her final vows. The second version, which the prioress Sister Lucille told filmmaker Catherine Martin in 1989, goes as follows: Colette's sweetheart and suitor Horace Arcand came to see her at the convent and begged her to leave it to marry him, intent on supplanting his rival, Christ the husband.

Today, Suzanne Arcand tells this lovely story that she heard from her mother and resembles a scene from a film: "Colette Bouillé returned to Deschambault to convalesce. She walked with a cane. Her father Henry was delighted, as he had been very distressed when she had entered the convent. One evening in May, the month of the Virgin Mary, she went to pray in the darkness of the church. After finishing her prayers, who did she see standing at the end of the centre aisle? Horace. He had not seen her since her return; he had been waiting for her. He had sworn that he would marry her—she was the love of his life. She said: "OK, if I can't be a nun, I'll make myself useful, we'll get married, have children, and that'll be that!"

Even in 2003, one of the sisters still remembers Colette's much-noticed stay at the convent. She confirms that the young woman remained only six months as a postulant, and had not worn the novice's habit because of having to return to her parents' home due to illness. However, the sister specifies in the same breath, it is true that Horace Arcand came to meet the prioress and plead with her: "Give me back my Colette." On her departure, Colette apparently said: "I will give him my hand, but my heart remains with the Carmelites." And indeed, Colette Bouillé continued to write the prioress on a regular basis, telling her at great length about her marriage, her honeymoon in Europe, the arrival of the children, et cetera. For Denys Arcand's mother, it seemed the Carmelites would always remain her first family. It was not surprising that, several years before she died, she saw and very much liked *Jesus of*

Montreal, whereas she had hated *The Decline of the American Empire*. In summary, Arcand says: "My mother was a Carmelite in training and a mystic in training. She took her secret from the convent to the grave."

"The fundamental thing is that my parents were deeply Catholic, and not for social reasons. They went to mass every day, said the rosary when the family was together each evening, and religious order defined their entire life. What's more, it was their great tragedy: they never realized that their ambitions were contradictory, that in pushing their children to do higher education they were opening a Pandora's Box, that their children would lose their faith. My mother was too intelligent to be only rigid. It's very complicated. She was the sort of person who, if I asked her, for example: "Can I go on a picnic with the neighbours on Saturday?" would say: "Saturday, we may all be dead, we don't know when Jesus will come to take us away. So if you are still alive on Saturday, we'll see." She was obsessed by the idea of death, by the idea of God's presence in our lives, and repeated that we were not on earth to be happy. It went much deeper than simply being rigid, scrupulous, Puritanical . . ."

In *C'est la vie*, several scenes revolve around beauty. The character Éric asks his mother if he is handsome. She does not want to answer him, because, she says, it is vain to talk about such things. The young man concludes that he must be horribly ugly, that she had said this to hide the truth, so as not to hurt his feelings. It takes him a long time to understand that his mother finds her children and husband repellent. Today, the author explains this scene: "The term 'repellent' is perhaps a little exaggerated. My mother was someone with a sense of duty, of family, of religion. In her eyes, romantic love, physical love, were things that degraded human beings and made them like animals. Her Puritanism was abominable. In this scene, I make reference to a moment from my childhood, when I was four or five. She answered me: "Beauty has no importance. What counts is the soul. We must have a beautiful soul." I concluded that she told me that because I was extremely ugly. And I lived my entire adolescence, until I was twenty, with the idea that I wasn't handsome and so I had to be very nice and very intelligent to try and get by in life, because no girl was ever going to be interested in me. Paradoxically, the male physique my mother liked best was the Tino Rossi type, which she would go contemplate in secret on film screens during the 1940s between two bits of shopping."

Horace Arcand and Colette Bouillé were married on December 11, 1937. A social columnist reported in a Quebec City newspaper: "The bride wore a wool suit, French cut, ruby trimmed with black fox, with a matching hat and black antelope accessories. [. . .] During the mass, a magnificent selection of music was presented. Madame B. Paré played the organ." The honeymoon was rather unusual, for the young couple benefited from certain advantages, thanks to Horace's status as pilot and his friendship with Raoul Jobin. The Arcands spent four months travelling around Europe, from December to April. As Colette Bouillé wrote in her diary, on December 28, at the comic opera they heard Jobin sing in *The Tales of Hoffman*. Around the New Year, it was Maurice Chevalier at the Petit Paris, then Fernandel in *Regain*, on boulevard de la Madeleine. After Paris, they went to Switzerland and Italy, then to the French Midi. Returning to Paris on March 11, they saw Madame Jobin, who was worried about rumours of world war, with her husband singing in Barcelona and then in Belgium. Finally, on March 30, Raoul Jobin was back in Paris, performing in Verdi's *Rigoletto*. In the southwest of France, the newlyweds heard the distant thunder of the Spanish Civil War, echoed in this dialogue from the screenplay for *C'est la vie*: "We stopped in Biarritz during our honeymoon. Your mother wanted to travel across Spain. We couldn't, because there was a civil war at that time. At night, we heard gunshots." They had to cut the trip short and get back home before World War II began. On the return voyage, on April 5, 1938, they passed another ship for the first time since they had left on April 1st from Cherbourg. Colette Bouillé wrote: "It was a German cargo ship. We shouted, and a flag with a swastika was raised." Denys Arcand concludes: "For them, their honeymoon was a magical event; they never did anything like it again. They talked about it all the time. They had an album of photos they often looked at, as if they were the most beautiful memories of their lives."

Their financial situation was more difficult during the war, because merchant ships were almost out of circulation. But after 1945 work picked up again. Thanks to their sense of economy, the Arcands were able to raise a family of four children, hoping to find them the best teaching institutions in Quebec. After making inquiries, Horace Arcand set his sights on Collège Sainte-Marie, "less snobbish than Brébeuf," but also run by Jesuits. The three boys would do their pre-university studies there; Suzanne would attend Collège Jésus-Marie in Outremont. The father decided to move to Montreal in 1950, and bought the house at 3818 rue Parc-Lafontaine.

The Arcand parents were cultivated people, lovers of the "great" arts (music, opera, painting), and at the same time very devout, practising Catholics, to the point of rigorism and austere moralism. They were fond of giving charity to the poor. It was a duality that Denys would later discover among the Jesuits, whose contradictions would profoundly mark his youth. In this peculiar clerical context, and even in the bosom of the family, where debate and discussion were encouraged, the exercise of individual freedom remained an ongoing struggle. Denys will always retain a rather dark memory of this, crushed as he was by narrow-minded moralism and his parents' dismay at seeing their eldest child become an artist and filmmaker. He will always feel that his father believed he failed in his career, and that his mother was convinced that he'd gone astray by making films. In a rare interview, Colette Bouillé commented that her Denys, "idealistic, very shy, very tactful, generous, attentive, prudish, very closed," basically "is not very happy; but one can't have everything in life."

"I agree pretty much with what she says," remarks Arcand with a smile. "Our mothers know us well, in the end. What can I say? It's quite correct, completely right, quite right." He concludes, laughing: "Bravo, Maman."

Two things marked Denys Arcand early in life: film and literature. The story of his "first kiss" with cinema resembles the beginning of Ettore Scola's *Splendour*. "The first film I saw, at the convent of Deschambault, was about the Incas. The Grey Nuns showed it to us one day in 16 mm. A missionary film. I can still see the image of an Inca prince wearing a long tunic, accompanied by a queen who had to give up her kingdom. It was very sad and I was very touched. I also had an uncle, Antoine Roy, an agronomist for the Quebec ministry of agriculture, who had a 16 mm projector and showed farmers films on seeding and other practical things. Sometimes on summer nights he hung a sheet over grandfather Bouillé's garage door, under the stars, and showed us films on corn growing, but also NFB animation films, like *C'est l'aviron*. And strange films too, like a concert by the opera singer Ezio Pinza singing, "I love the sound of the horn, when the day has died, deep in the woods." It left a strong impression on me; there was a very low note at the end of the aria. We also saw features like *Petit Papa Noël* with Tino Rossi."

Another time, in 2000, in a short speech he gave as president of the Images du Nouveau Monde festival in Quebec City, Arcand recalled: "When I was a child, my aunts, my grandmother, sometimes my mother, came to Quebec City by train or bus to do their shopping at Compagnie Paquette, the Syndicat or J.B. Laliberté's, and they often took advantage of the opportunity to see a French film starring Raimu, Fernandel, Tino Rossi or Jean-Pierre Aumont, a film that changed every week thanks to the France-Film company, which also screened Italian or Spanish films once in a while."

Early in life, Denys Arcand developed an immoderate appetite for reading, as well as a taste for freedom and free-thinking, all of which would be fostered at Collège Sainte-Marie. Deschambault was more like a prison or cloister. "No books in the house." The only books in the house during his early childhood were those his mother had won as prizes and left at his grandmother's, "beautiful" books, "good" books, bound in red leather and very big, with illustrations by Gustave Doré, *Sacred History*, a kind of watered-down Bible, or *The Epic of Napoleon* or indeed *The Epic of the Vendée*. "Unreadable books, ugly, poorly written, boring, but that created a flamboyant visual effect on a bookshelf." His parents never read anything but the newspaper. There were two schools in the village, one for the farmers' children, the public school financed by the department of public instruction where one teacher taught grades one to twelve. For the children of eminent citizens, there was a private convent school run by the Sisters of Charity, where boys could go up until grade seven. Denys attended this school, where the teachers were very good, devoted and fond of children. He went to school with his girl neighbours and girl cousins. Whereas boys had to leave after grade seven, girls could continue up until grade twelve. In this school, there were four or five books. Students had to put their name on a list to borrow them and wait their turn. The most popular book was called *On the Double Steel Ribbon* and was the story of a railroad. Alas! The young Arcand never had the chance to read the book. He put his name on the list, but then the end of the year came, and he missed his turn. "I'd never read a book before arriving in Montreal at the age of ten."

A small school is always good, you don't have to force yourself too hard and you still get 98 per cent. Denys went to school, listened in class; he was a good student, well mannered but already headstrong. He did his homework, passed his exams, and then waited until school ended so he could go play outdoors. "The country was a paradise for children: we made ourselves rafts on the ponds, we skated when they froze over, we went fishing in spring or autumn. We lived outdoors like little savages. I had no kind of intellectual or artistic life for my first five years at school. It was a very happy time, in a very peaceful village, not a poor village where there were hotels and drunks. Nothing had happened for three centuries, ever. Life from day to day, quiet, the days counted out an hour at a time. That's it. A very happy childhood. My parents were good parents, gentle, generous. The sisters at the convent were very kind. We were surrounded by nature, we had a rowboat, in the winter we caught little fish in the channels. A great sweetness."

The young Denys Arcand did not yet know what his life lacked. "Later I would learn what I was missing. There'd be the Jesuits, but that's another chapter."

4
"LITTLE VOLTAIRE" OF SAINTE-MARIE

The 1950s are a prelude to a long struggle, the Quiet Revolution, which will take almost two decades to run its course, and be marked by a great deal of turmoil. Denys Arcand will take a very active part in this struggle, but for the time being, the *padre padrone* Horace Arcand has chosen Collège Sainte-Marie for his son and must be obeyed. Denys is ten years old. The famous Jesuit college has existed for over one hundred years, and hence seems almost immortal. But it will not survive the collapse of the Church in Quebec in the mid-1960s. As Father Leclerc remarks in *The Barbarian Invasions*: "At a very specific moment—it was in 1966—the churches suddenly emptied in a matter of months. A very strange phenomenon that no one has ever been able to explain."

Rather than being transformed into a university, as the Jesuits hoped, the Collège Sainte-Marie Building at the corner of rue de Bleury and Dorchester Boulevard was closed after the 1968–1969 school year, sold to real estate developers and torn down in 1975. The site where it once stood has since remained a vacant lot, emblazoned with the name of its owner, SNC-Lavallin. Several ruins of the college walls remain, with two bricked-up doors, one of them decorated with sculpted stones. Next to the surviving Church of Gesù, at the site of the phantom college, the Historic Sites and Monuments Board of Canada erected a bilingual commemorative plaque: "The Company of Jesus. From the beginning of the seventeenth century, the Jesuits occupied a place of choice in the history of Canada, as missionaries, explorers, seigneurs and educators. In 1635, they founded the country's first college, in Quebec City. After the Conquest, British authorities prevented all recruitment in the community and seized its goods. Invited back into Canada in 1842, the Jesuits devoted themselves to education. They established institutions of learning in several large cities, including the Collège Sainte-Marie, which formerly stood here."

Can we guess for which academic subject Denys Arcand received his very first First Prize at Collège Sainte-Marie at the end of 1951–1952? *Religion!* This is no invention. The prize must have brought an enigmatic smile to the face of this future atheist or agnostic. In any case, the event is reported in the yearbook for the college's 104th academic year, published by the prefecture of studies under the heading "A.M.D.G." (*Ad Majorem Dei Gloriam—For the greater glory of God*). Receiving this prize for his thorough knowledge of Roman Catholic religion, young Denys recalled the music of the church bells in his native parish, Saint-Joseph de Deschambault, or the sacred songs of Charles Gounod being sung by the village choir, the same music that we would hear twenty years later, in *Quebec: Duplessis and After* . . . .

And that's not all. We must add, in his defence, that in "Éléments français," year one at Sainte-Marie, he received first prizes in parsing and Canadian History, both of which foreshadowed his future profession of filmmaker, as well as four honourable mentions in Geography, Precepts, Excellence and Diligence. This last quality is defined in the *Webster's Dictionary* as "interested and persevering application." As for "precepts," those have to do with the commandments of God, the Church, the Gospel; the filmmaker would remember them for *Jesus of Montreal.*

"Éléments français" was a transitional year, a seventh "special" year given at private colleges, a kind of qualifying year between elementary school and classical studies. *Collège classique*, a system that no longer exists, lasted eight years in all and included high school and college level education. Those eight academic years, in which Denys Arcand was enrolled as of the 1952–1953 school year, each had names that have today become outmoded. It is important here to provide a list of these: (1) Éléments latins, (2) Syntax, (3) Method, (4) Versification, (5) Belles-Lettres, (6) Rhetoric, (7) Philosophy I, (8) Philosophy II. The accomplished and tenacious student emerged from this long cycle with a baccalaureate (*baccalauréat ès arts*), required at that time to enter university. Denys graduated from Sainte-Marie in 1960, to enrol in the faculty of literature at the Université de Montréal. During his *collège classique* years, he received several second prizes (in elocution, French composition, French discourse, Greek translation, dissertation), a few firsts (elocution, Latin translation, French narration), quite a number of honourable mentions in the same subjects and in history and geography, natural science, and the analysis of drama. It may be noted that Arcand's parents were in the habit of making donations to Collège Sainte-Marie for student prizes.

In his Rhetoric year, Denys received his ultimate first prize, for brilliant elocution. However, he says, "Though I like the art of oratory, I've always hated speeches. Even today, I'm unable to listen to anything in this genre, which to me is the most repulsive in the world. When I was young, my uncle Antoine Roy often took me, with his daughter, my cousin Francine, on his agronomical tours of agricultural exhibitions in Saint-Hyacinthe or Chicoutimi. Every evening there was a prize ceremony for the breeders of Ayrshire cattle. It always began with speeches, by the parish priest, the agronomist, the federal MP, the provincial MP, the bishop of Saint-Hyacinthe, the bishop of Chicoutimi. . . . We literally lay under the table, my cousin and I, sleeping until the speeches ended. They lasted for hours. The introduction alone took three minutes: "Your Grace the prelate, dear friends, my Lord Bishop, your Excellency, your Honourable," et cetera. Since that time, I've never been able to stand speeches. Even today, when someone wants to speak, I generally get up and leave the room. I pretend that I feel faint, and withdraw."

While pursuing his studies, the oldest Arcand son takes part in all kinds of activities: sports, theatre, choir, lectures, "extracurricular evenings," the student newspaper, television and radio quizzes. In 1960, during a variety evening referred to as "a philosophical festival," his first amateur film was presented, *À l'est d'Eaton* (*East of Eatons*), co-directed by Stéphane Venne. "Collège Sainte-Marie," explains Arcand, "had a very diversified and heterogeneous population composed of children from working-class and wealthy families. I was a day student, very shy. The young Montrealers of my age seemed very strange to me. I'd arrived from the country, I was badly dressed, the height of ridicule, my mother still dressed me in short pants and knee socks at the age of eleven. All the boys wore long pants. My mother thought I was very cute in short pants, but I was the butt of all sorts of teasing." During recess, Denys remained alone, talked to no one, did not play, waited for the moment when he could go back to class. That is, until the day in his second year, Syntax, when the titular professor, Father Gérard Deslisle, who was also in charge of recreation and sports activities, called him into his room. A priest's room also served as his office, containing a bed, a prayer stool, a missal and a little office space where students usually arrived in a state of terror, "because when one of the priests summoned you to his room, it was usually for a very serious reason. That time, Father Deslisle said to me: 'Listen, my young friend, people who don't do sports have trouble passing their exams with me.' It was terrifying. I knew about all the sacrifices my father had made to move the family and pay for my studies. I told myself that I was going to be failed if I didn't do sports."

From then on, Arcand signed up for all the sports—baseball, basketball, football, swimming—trying to be in the good graces of Father Deslisle. This decision would have a double effect. First, the teenager would earn the good graces of the priest. Next, he would prove to be physically gifted enough to *make* the teams. This provided him with an extraordinary advantage, for he immediately made friends and became "socialized." In a college, the athletic hierarchy is very important. The class bullies, the brutes who shove people or trip them in the stairways, don't try it with people who are on the hockey team, because they'll have the whole club on their back. They prefer to harass people who are more isolated and vulnerable. "It gave me a kind of assurance. Sports became a part of my life, and to this day provides me with a rich and enjoyable social life."

"Intellectual or cultural activities were a second step, beginning around sixteen. I received a note ordering me to go see the study prefect. This one had me in his office and gave me the opposite speech, as terrifying as the one before: "Listen, my young friend, you're on all the sports teams, that's very good, brilliant, but we've looked at your psychological aptitude tests. You have definite intellectual ability but at the moment you're wasting it by playing hockey and football. . . . I'm warning you, we're going to have to be very severe with you. You're going to have to do something else." Once again, Denys panicked. He ran to sign up with the choir, the theatre workshop, the college newspaper . . . an about-face just as abrupt as the one that made him throw himself into sports four or five years before. He happened to possess the required aptitude to do well in these new intellectual extracurricular activities. From that time on, he neglected sports somewhat, except for lacrosse, "the activity I did the least badly." At this time, he often listened to classical music on Radio-Canada, on the program called *Chefs-d'œuvre de musique* and participated in the recording of a pilot for a television quiz hosted by Gérard Pelletier. "Oddly enough," he emphasizes, "this pilot was preserved, though Radio-Canada threw out tons of archives."

In November 1958, Arcand's first interview appeared in the school newspaper, *Le Sainte-Marie*, an independent publication, though supervised from the "watch tower" of a Jesuit. Fifteen days earlier, he had participated in a radio broadcast, *Nos collèges au micro*, a kind of literary debate between the young women students of Collège Marguerite-Bourgeoys and four students from Sainte-Marie. Raymond Lafontaine questioned Denys Arcand as he emerged from the old boys' lounge, where the program had taken place. A false interview, a student prank. Arcand replies that the students prepared themselves for the debate in "the rare leisure time that our many philosophical occupations allow us," that the experience had not enriched them "because [we] did not earn a cent," that they had gained only the satisfaction of "having perhaps given a few minds thirsting for truth some new elements of a solution for an ongoing problem," and finally, that they are not carried away with enthusiasm for Saint-Exupéry but find him interesting. "There's a difference," concludes Arcand. André Brochu sees this performance in another light: "My fellow team-members were so talkative, erudite, brilliant and uncivilized, letting no one from the opposite team speak, that the prize went to the young ladies." Brochu, a poet, essayist and novelist, was at Sainte-Marie at the same time as Arcand. They got to know each other better at the Université de Montréal, where they were in some of the same literature courses, then as flat-mates in an apartment "where Denys concealed his first loves."

In Montreal, Arcand discovered books. Across from Lafontaine Park, at the big main library, Youth Section. Particularly the Biggles novels, about the R.A.F. colonel who defended Great Britain against the

Germans during the Battle of Britain, books written by Captain W.E. Johns, also read by the young Michel Tremblay, who refers to them in *A Horned Angel with Tin Wings*. They enchanted Arcand: "The entire Captain Johns collection, forty volumes I think, I read them all. I devoured them. I read morning, noon and night, on the bus or streetcar. It was sheer bliss. After that, I read the entire Youth section in the library. A great discovery." Later, at the Tranquille bookshop on Rue Sainte-Catherine, near Collège Sainte-Marie, Arcand consumed books of a more provocative variety, the kind described, during the 1950s, in Gérard Bessette's novel *Le Libraire* (*Not for Every Eye*), in which a teenager is thrown out of college for having bought and read a book written by the satanical Voltaire. These intensive readings would prepare the student Arcand for writing.

His very first article was published in the school newspaper *Le Sainte-Marie* on March 21, 1957. Its author was, at that time, in his fifth year, Belles-Lettres. The subject? "Boy-scouting in the College." It begins with the mocking lead, which could have come straight out of *Le confort et l'indifférence/Comfort and Indifference*: "If the college were a republic, most assuredly we would say that the scout troop is a 'State organization.'" What follows is a short but detailed inquiry into the "very learned vivisectionist," the Jesuit Taché, in order to trace the history of scouting at Sainte-Marie and decide whether it was a thousand-year-old organization whose origins "have been lost in the dust of time" or "one of those young modern revolutionary organizations with monopolist tendencies." After examining the question, Arcand concludes that scouting is "one of today's powerful and lofty organizations," made up of "men of the cloth, professionals of conscience, valued technicians, actors of repute, television directors . . ." Whence comes "the absolute necessity of scouting in the college"! Here, Arcand's sarcasm is plain to see, though he is ostensibly praising scouting for fostering the development of talents required for practical accomplishment, such as "learning to finish" a piece of work, blocking the wind in order to build a successful campfire, and organizing voyages of discovery to "the mysterious forest." In the same dossier, scouting is presented as potential matrix for "perfect camaraderie, a life where every breath is shared, so that we may together achieve our fine and noble goal of serving." Several short years later, the motto of "serving" would feed the entire Quiet Revolution in Quebec, in which the students of "Sainte-Marie-de-la-Culture" would be among the avant-garde.

Denys Arcand publishes several other pieces in the *Le Sainte-Marie*, sometimes under the name of Georges-Denys, in a team of free-lancers including Marcel Saint-Germain and Stéphane Venne. These texts are about music, hockey, sadness and death (*De tristitia*), as well as a surprising essay on Ancient Greece, on May 2, 1958, *Païdeia Politeia* (the education of youth and politics), which concludes with the portrait of a young Athenian, Antistenes. Half real, half dream, it is a near-autobiographical text from which emerges an odd combination of politics and beauty. This is the piece that opens the section of selected writings by Arcand the writer at the end of this book.

Arcand's most unexpected and unusual article from those years is on the composer Arthur Honegger, and the presentation on Radio-Canada television, on November 20, 1958, of the dramatic oratorio *Joan of Arc at the Stake*. In this review, Arcand takes issue with Dominique Michel, who said on the radio: "*Joan of Arc at the Stake*, I didn't buy it. Joan of Arc complained for two hours and the fire didn't even burn her!" This rankled with Arcand, who felt that "poor Honegger has good reason to be bitter." To counter this example of rampant anti-intellectualism, Arcand takes pains to praise Honegger, the "bold fellow," the "independent" composer whose works, unfortunately, "do not reach the public, though he has every right to claim that he is a man of his time." As for the little jab at Dominique Michel, how ironic it is that twenty-five years later, Arcand would choose her for one of the best roles in *The Decline of the American Empire*, which would give this stand-up comic the status, in France, of an "intellectual comedian," as she herself asserts.

One of the last files on which Arcand collaborates, in *Le Sainte-Marie*'s edition of January 28, 1959, deals with the new college library, a "canteen of the mind" administered by Georges Cartier, who at the end of the sixties will become founder and head of the Quebec national library. Arcand delights in describing some of the buried pearls in the treasury of 50,000 books in the Jesuit Fathers' library, "millions of yellowed pages compressed between thick pigskin bindings." He lets his mind glide into this cultural labyrinth, "among these walls of shelves black with print": Saint Augustine, Bossuet, Bourdaloue, catechisms in twenty-eight volumes, "casuistry manuals of 922 pages in which all possible sins are explained and commented upon, from premeditated murder to the fencing of stolen safety pins."

What other titles? Plato's *Republic,* several editions of the Bible, the *Summa Theologica* of the saintly doctor Thomas Aquinas, the diabolical Karl Marx, Montaigne, Buffon, Kant and Sartre; but also La Fontaine, Voltaire, Chateaubriand, Hugo, Louis Veuillot, Camus, Malraux, Steinbeck, Caldwell, Hemingway and so many other classics, Shakespeare, Corneille, Racine, Molière, Schiller, Gogol, as well as other rich books of history: *The Memoirs of Trévaux*; *Report made to the King on the history of the East Indies* by the Jesuit priest Duierric; the Jesuit *Relations*; Ferland's *History of Canada.* And then, all the works of "sad French Canadian literature." And finally, our whirlwind tour ends with a few books for frivolous minds such as *The Gallant Women* or *The Woman with Two Smiles.*

The professional establishment of this new library was seemingly part of a Jesuit plan to create a new French-language university in Montreal on the foundations of Sainte-Marie. With this end in mind, the founders wanted to lay down a solid biblioeconomic foundation. However, in the following decade, the Quiet Revolution was quick to bury this dream. The greater part of Sainte-Marie library would be merged with that of the École normale Jacques-Cartier to stock the library of the new Université du Québec à Montréal (UQAM); the old, rare and precious books would be conserved by the Jesuits at their Maison Bellarmin in Montreal, or their central archives in Saint-Jérôme. But despite the Jesuit's initiative to create a modern library in the late fifties, it must not be forgotten that students had been deprived of the "Fathers' Library" for quite some time, and that the Jesuits had done their part to abort a project for the creation of a big public library in Montreal in the early twentieth century. Indeed, the American philanthropist Andrew Carnegie wanted to provide the Quebec metropolis with the necessary funds to establish such a library. The politicians refused Carnegie's gift on the advice of the Catholic hierarchy (in which the Jesuits played the role of "prompters"). It was feared the library would have a bad influence on people's reading. We may also recall that the infamous Hayes Code of film censorship that was inflicted upon Hollywood was the work of Jesuit, Father Daniel A. Lord. Denys

Arcand's passion for literature and film would never let him forget that at Sainte-Marie, he was one of many "idiots savants," a term that he used in *Copie zéro*.

What was it that provoked this kind of conflagration among the youth of Sainte-Marie? During the fifties, the horizon seemed blocked by the conservative government of Duplessis, by an ineradicable and triumphant Church that had recently endowed Montreal with a Scarlet Prince, Cardinal Paul-Émile Léger; the Jesuits were an immovable fortress and the Company of Jesus was preparing its megalomaniac project of creating two new universities in Montreal, one French speaking, the other English speaking.

The young wolves howled at the top of their lungs for freedom without limit, freedom of thought, radiant intelligence, and a hypersensitive hedonism coupled with sincere humanism. Being teenagers, they did not mince words; their vanity and sarcasm intimidated more than a few people and excluded others from their circle. But they were killingly funny; the humour of the Cyniques would emerge from this mould, as would Arcand's satires and the sarcastic novels of André Brochu, which depict the era so well. Their humour, to paraphrase filmmaker Chris Marker, was the politeness of their despair.

The poet Jacques Brault, a secular teacher among the Jesuits, clearly understood this explosive mixture of libertarian outcry and melancholy. He taught Canadian history in Versification (fourth year), and was titular professor of Arcand's Rhetoric "B" class. He still speaks of these young people with emotion: "Like those who came before them, they dig and search our melancholy earth, our history of sadness, and turn our gloomiest fears into words of consent to rage mingled with love of life, and at last death passes through the sieve of our bodies that vibrate with covetousness, passes from the future to the conditional." Here, Brault is mainly referring to young poets such as Pierre Maheu, André Brochu, Paul Chamberland, but at the same time he is describing the entire intelligentsia of new officiates of French Canadian *antiprêtrisme*. "*Prêtrisme*" ("priestism"), was a word invented by Stendhal to designate all forms of ultraconservatism, whether secular or clerical, and which obviously did not apply to progressive priests. In Montreal, one of these was the Jesuit Ernest Gagnon, a collector of African art and an extraordinary professor of literature, an influential and greatly loved master.

Denys Arcand moved in the orbit described by Jacques Brault. However, he passed for a big-talking dilettante, a jack-of-all-trades spreading himself thin between theatre, essay- and review-writing, debating, music, and shooting his first film. The melancholy and tragic filmmaker-writer could not yet be divined beneath this rowdy and sarcastic facade. At Sainte-Marie, Denys was like a jay in peacock feathers. Our grandparents used to say that you shouldn't judge a toad by watching it jump. Jacques Brault, who was won over by Arcand's literary work, today expresses surprise that his student chose film, but notes that the filmmaker takes a classical approach to his art, favouring no innovation or form for the sake of itself. "He takes great care in directing the actors, always maintaining a kind of distance, a detachment that is not coldness and does not exclude sensitivity. His cinema is never heavy, but manifests a certain lightness and gravity at the same time. His satires are tasteful and measured. A very modest cinema. His dramas are always founded on meticulous research, enriched with concrete fact, they are dense and there is nothing superficial about them. Arcand's cinema is truly a kind of history project on modern Quebec, on the Quiet Revolution, the dream of sovereignty. Arcand has not let himself be submerged by the drama caused by this upheaval, he has created, has allowed himself to criticize, sifted through these transformations, a form of cure and regeneration."

In André Brochu's novel *Le maître rêveur*, the character of Jean-Robert is inspired by Arcand. This character is not an exact copy of the filmmaker, but borrows a few of his character traits, enlarged for the purpose of caricature. Different behaviours that the novelist has given him are quite believable, but fictional. Jean-Robert is the hard-working student who asks the teachers the most killing questions, can cleverly hold forth in front of the cafeteria supervisor about the disgusting quality of the food without being accused of rebelliousness and insubordination. Jean-Robert holds court in the schoolyard, assembling a group "with unpleasant rituals." He makes fun of the character of Sylvain, a projection of Brochu himself, "cynically declaring that I had no sense of wonder, and that a good story is worth a hundred times more than dull, flat reality. He is upheld by the others' laughter, and someone even sings the praises of lying, whose explanatory value, he says, from a strictly logical point of view, surpasses that of truth." Jean-Robert says later in the book: "Truth is the opposite of communication. [. . .] Read Machiavelli [. . .]," concluding in his grand and sardonic way: "The destiny of intelligent people is a very difficult one!"

Today Brochu admits: "The main image I have of him at that time is of a slightly intimidating presence, not because he attacked others but because he embodied a system of values that could indirectly exclude more delicate and idealistic beings such as myself. His laugh, his infinite power of mockery gave him a kind of superiority, reinforced by his physical size, his deep voice and his self-assurance. His level of culture, his dilettantism, his detachment from everything that was sacred made him as admirable and distant as some kind of Don Juan or Voltaire. His passion for film, which at that time did not exist or that no one knew about, provided an axis for his many gifts, which were in danger of going unused."

André Brochu, author of such passionate apprenticeship novels as *La Croix du nord*, *La vie aux trousses* and *Le maître rêveur*, explains the free-thinking attitudes of the Sainte-Marie avant-garde in terms of their great attachment to postwar French existentialism. In music and literature, Juliette Gréco lends her aura to this movement, as do Sartre, Camus and Malraux. This saturnine form of thought, emerging from the smouldering ruins of ravaged Europe and France, seems so vital that in 1957, in the Rhetoric "A" class, Brochu took on the direction of a little newspaper called *Libre-Pensée*, printed with old-style Gestetner stencils. A very modest publication that runs the risk of "being condemned by a gallery of Jesuits looking for something to criticize." The poetry of nothingness slips in, too: "We got along well, you, Death, with your great ashen antlers, and I, the skull, cracked open, smiling, eyes pierced . . . ."

Thus, Arcand spends nine long initiatory years at Sainte-Marie, his entire adolescence, with all its burning impatience. Sports and culture, learning, mind and body, all in an unbridled effort to attain the ideal of *Mens sana in corpore sano*, "a healthy mind in a healthy body," a slogan dear to Catholic institutions of learning, intent upon combating with Spartan physical exercise the temptations of the young flesh and spirit, in other words, sex, but also poetry and morbid philosophies.

Denys participates in a number of sports, but at the same time is passionate about theatre, film, literature and music. Though not a film-club fanatic, he follows the advice of one of his Belles-Lettres teachers to go out and lose his innocence by seeing, imperatively, Fellini's *La strada* at the Snowdon Palace, an illumination and a shock. "I had very good Jesuit teachers, exceptional people with a great deal of culture. I tried to model the character played by Gilles Pelletier, in *Jesus of Montreal* and *The Barbarian Invasions*, on these teachers. Extremely cultivated people, unfortunately Québécois, thus who came from farms and working-class families, for whom entering the Company of Jesus was a door to salvation; they were artists, aesthetes, philosophers, writers who never fulfilled their potential. Rather sad people, in the end. The religious order gave them a way out of Québécois mediocrity to study in Paris or at the Jesuit college in Rome. They had seen Renaissance paintings in Italy. Actually, they were often brusque, harsh; they had sexual impulses and desires that they couldn't assuage. Later, during the sixties, they all became defrocked."

In an unfilmed dialogue in *Jesus of Montreal*, Father Leclerc explains: "My father was a textile worker. He was a trade union member. He lost his jobs; he was coshed, put in prison. From time to time, he managed to make a dollar more per month, a day of paid vacation or what have you. He struggled all his life. Today the same factories belong to the Japanese; the looms are controlled by computer. Fifteen technicians produce more and better goods than two thousand workers in the old days. What good were the sacrifices my father made?" Arcand continues: "Father André Paquet was my Belles-Lettres professor: 'You think you know film, the films you see are worthless. You're just a lot of young fools. If you want to get away from the mediocrity that surrounds you, there's a film playing right now in the western part of the city—*La Strada*, it must be seen.' It was an absolute masterpiece, a revelation. The Jesuits were often like that, they pushed us. Wonderful pedagogues. They had Catholic tastes, quite particular, but I take my hat off to them. I owe what I am to them."

As Marc Laurendeau recalls, theatre was valued and encouraged at Sainte-Marie by Father Paquet, Julien Laferrière and André Bédard. Arcand sparkles on stage, in 1958, in Hochwalder's *On Earth as in Heaven* in which he magnificently plays an obsequious and spiteful bishop.

Moreover, he never misses any of the "extracurricular evenings," big music-hall-type revues organized by the classical colleges. All over Quebec, these evenings will give birth to artists such as Raoul Duguay, the comedy troupe Les Cyniques, the comedy team Ding et Dong. During one of these revue evenings, the short film *À l'est d'Eaton (East of Eatons)* is shown, reminiscent of early films shown at fairs, circuses or variety theatres. "The title was a joke, a reference to the magnificent film by Elia Kazan *East of Eden*. Our film has been lost. It was about the ideal or mythical day of a student. Tired of walking up the stairs, floor after floor, he falls down; then he goes to class and falls asleep. Then he makes fun of the teacher. A comedy, a silent film, poorly synchronized with a sound track played on a tape recorder. We showed it once at Sainte-Marie, then at the Élysée, the art cinéma programmed by Patrick Straram, who had invited submissions of amateur or experimental films shot in Montreal. It was an honour for Stéphane Venne and I."

Filmed in 1959 with a camera belonging to Venne's father, *À l'est d'Eaton* had its premiere the following year during the Sainte-Marie winter carnival, an arts evening held by the students in Philosophy in which caricatures and parodies of courses were presented alongside poems by André Brochu and songs by Venne. In *Le Sainte-Marie*, March 22 edition, the film receives rave reviews for its "originality, its surprise effects and suspense."

A brilliant and sarcastic jack-of-all-trades, Denys is also enthusiastic about music and has the rare opportunity of attending a concert by Glenn Gould. He later writes about this in his preface to the published version of François Girard's script for *Thirty-Two Short Films About Glenn Gould*. It's not that he is averse to writing. Leaving Sainte-Marie with his baccalaureate in hand, Denys Arcand appears to be a singular "budding evil-genius," multitalented, a bundle of potential. André Brochu remembers: "Denys did not play up to the Jesuits at all, which was quite remarkable. Never to my knowledge did he manifest sympathy for any of them. And his teachers treated him in kind. Of course they admired him (the Jesuits never concealed their admiration for their talented students, future pillars of society in whom they ogled their own reflections unreservedly), but they didn't like him. They saw in him a will, a resistance to be curbed, and someone very clever who would never give them a chance to bring him to rein. His intellectual gifts were considerable. He wilfully let them go uncultivated, and as he showed so little interest in science or even literature—at least, in creative writing—he could pass for a dilettante unconcerned with planning a future career. Given his attitude, all joker and all negative, offhand, without passion or commitment to anything in particular, one couldn't have guessed at the great talent that he would later manifest."

Sainte-Marie's 1960 graduating class in Philosophy took as their motto, "*Solitaire. Solidaire.*" André Brochu: "We borrowed the formula from a Camus story called *Exile and the Kingdom*. Camus was greatly appreciated by "advanced" Jesuits and left-leaning Catholics in the class, *beaux esprits*, humanists and full of themselves, like some of the students. Denys must have liked Camus, but not exclusively. I don't think he ever spoke in a humanistic vein." After graduating, Arcand chooses a career in literature. The newspaper covering the graduation describes him as follows: "A face hidden beneath frizzy, curly hair like an African's, in his eyes and his rosy complexion we can see all the charm of his personality. A smile that never leaves his lips reveals the likeable loquacity of the guy from Sainte-Marie. His eyes emanate the delicacy of a polite young man who is serious when he has to be, and is always distinguished. Whether you talk to him about Homer, Sophocles, Socrates, Pascal, Boileau, Rousseau or even Brigitte Bardot, he is difficult to impress. You can aim at him all the satires you can invent and he will send them back to you with greater finesse and ease than if they were simple hellos. Even on his death bed, he would find some way of saying something witty."

So as to appear serious and not disappoint his parents too much, he opts for history at university, a discipline associated with the department of literature. Thus, he climbs Mount Royal, which will play a major role in *Jesus of Montreal*, and contemplate the university's art deco phallus, designed by architect Ernest Cormier, with forest all around it, like the "dense woods" in a Rameau opera, and the Côte-des-Neiges cemetery.

Sex, knowledge, opera, death.

5
THE PHALLUS OF THE UNIVERSITÉ DE MONTRÉAL

On April 6, 1995, the year of the one-hundredth anniversary of the cinematograph, Denys Arcand receives an unusual gift from the Université de Montréal, an honorary doctorate in film. As of that day, the filmmaker could be legitimately addressed as "Doctor Arcand."

According to the usual ceremonial, he and his sponsor, as well as a cohort made up of the rector, the dean, the Secretary-General and department head, not to mention four students in charge of music, take their places on stage in an amphitheatre in the Cormier Building. In his pompous costume of gown and mortarboard, Arcand is playing the most preposterous role of his entire acting career. With mock seriousness, he delivers his speech, cue cards in hand, recalling "the memory of the first Quebec filmmaker, Ernest Ouimet, who in 1921 burned all his films in a vacant lot in the east end of the city and ended up as a branch manager for the Quebec liquor commission [SAQ]." He also recalls the first film he ever participated in, "shot on this campus," and "the student film club, which held their screenings in this room, the same room where I received my diploma in literature thirty-three years ago. All this is to say that if it is relatively easy to call oneself a musician in Vienna, a dancer in Saint Petersburg, a writer in Paris, a singer in Milan or a cameraman in Los Angeles, to say you wanted to become a filmmaker in Montreal in 1962 was to fatally condemn yourself to a marginal and somewhat shady existence."

This archaic ceremony, laughable with its faded costumes and rituals, makes a peculiar stage for this provocative former student, known for his resonant voice and ideological pranks, a student for whom this university may never have been anything but a theatre: dramatic arts, the student newpaper *Le quartier latin*, the arts society of the general students' association (the AGEUM), but especially filmmaking, starting with *Seul ou avec d'autres* (*Alone or with Others*).

This enigmatic title, as film professor Yves Lever has commented, refers to the question asked by a priest in the confessional when a sin of the flesh is confessed: "My child, did you do it alone or with others?" This film produces effects similar to those of photography, making the shadows of reality emerge out of nothing. *Seul ou avec d'autres* illuminates the ghost of the Université de Montréal as it was in the beginning of the sixties. Despite the meanderings of the script through a story of first love on campus, this dramatic feature made in the autumn of 1961 allows us to see the exact layout of a group of structures, smaller than today's, around the central Cormier Building. The campus is surrounded by gardens and forest. An asphalt path leads east towards the social centre and the student residences: one for young men and on the opposite side, one for young women nicknamed "the virgins' tower." Off campus, in the background, city streets lined with big triumphal American convertibles.

This so-called cinéma-vérité setting documents sites of forty years past: a classroom, the great hall, an amphitheatre in the central building for the debutants' ball; the entrance to the social centre, a big stairway leading down to rue Maplewood, since renamed Edouard-Montpetit. In and among the threads of romance and derision that make up the plot, certain truths are bluntly asserted. Pierre Letourneau explains to Nicole Braün—using the words of scriptwriters Arcand and Stéphane Venne—that the faculty of arts is an "accident" at the university; we witness a hilarious course in Thomist philosophy on the theme of sexuality, preceded by an insistent close-up of the phallic tower of the Cormier Building; the sociologist Guy Rocher maintains that the Université de Montréal is not equipped to develop individual, autonomous thought. Next in line in this back-to-school scene are two budding members of the Cyniques comedy troupe. Marcel Saint-Germain, standing in the doorway of the social centre, does a sketch next to the distributor for *Le Devoir* newspaper, which you pay for or not, depending on your mood.

Then comes Marc Laurendeau, in a first performance at the Grand Salon, doing his monologue called *La soirée de culte* (meaning "evening worship," a parody of *La soirée de lutte*), rolling his "r's" and making fun of Cardinal Paul-Emile Leger, who was at that time the supreme authority of the (Catholic) Université de Montréal.

At this time, Marc Laurendeau is a second-year law student. He knows Denys Arcand and Stéphane Venne well, having been one year ahead of them at Sainte-Marie. Passionate about theatre, he is already performing comic monologues, and is soon to become founder and director of Les Cyniques, who in their own way, and with their own set of hilarious and cruel weapons, will play a role in the surge of cultural development that feeds the Quiet Revolution. Today a journalist, Laurendeau provides the following explanation of the sketch and its context. *La soirée de lutte*, Wednesday wrestling night on Radio-Canada television, was narrated by sports commentator Michel Normandin, a peculiar nonstop talker who used astonishing metaphors for the wrestlers' manœuvres, such as the "airplane hold," or "the rictus spread." As for Cardinal Paul-Emile Leger, he said the rosary each day on the program entitled *Le chapelet en famille*, on CKAC radio. The program included the intoning of prayers such as "I believe in God," "Our Father," "Hail Mary," "Glory to the Father." The reciting of three chaplets was called a rosary, and the sequences of rosaries were grouped under the name of "mysteries," characterized as sorrowful, joyous or glorious. Laurendeau also made a pun based on Red Cap beer (a brand that no longer exists) and the cardinal's scarlet cap. This beer was produced by Dow breweries, which gives rise to another play on words, "Dow-minus vobiscum," a spoof on the liturgical phrase *Dominus vobiscum* ("The Lord is with you"). One last liturgical phrase in Latin used in the sketch—"*Et verbum caro factum est*"—means "and the Word became flesh." The author has checked the following transcription of the monologue, taken from *Seul ou avec d'autres*, and given his permission to publish it here for the first time.

(Psalmody) Star of the morning, Queen of the Holy Rosary.

Good evening, good evening, rosary fans! Direct from Montreal, you're listening to *Soirée de culte*, brought to you by Dow Breweries and Casgrain Rosaries Limited.

Good evening, prayer buffs! We have a real crowd here this evening at the cardinal's palace. There's a great clergical turnout. The place is packed!

Our feature this evening: *Sorrowful Mysteries*, in a return rosary match, three chaplets to finish.

(Imitating the voice of Michel Normandin) But do you believe our rugged rosarists are in good shape this evening? I'll pass it over to you Paul-Emile. What's your belief?

(Imitating the voice of Cardinal Paul-Emile Leger) "I believe in God, the almighty Father."

"Yes, yes, my dear Card, no doubt you do. I meant, what's the state of our gladiators?"

"Very much a state of grace."

"Yes, yes, my dear Card. Obviously I won't ask you what you favourite kind of beer is. I know it's Red Cap. It's the family beer. A family that gets sloshed together stays together."

[. . .]

. . . What a fine procession! Ding! Ding! Oh! The official has given the signal. The mystics are attacking the classical creed. There's the hold of conscience, the scissors of the mystic body and the Franciscan foot box. Here comes the blow! Pow! And it's a magnificent Glory-be-to-God, dealt by Sister Emilie of the Force, the Masked Marvel, an expert on the veil hold. The official calls time. Pow! A gladiator is sent crashing to the floor. *Et verbum caro factum est.*

We'll be back tomorrow, all you prayer fans, when Dow Breweries presents *Soirée de culte.*

And until then . . . *Dow . . . minus vobiscum.*

According to one story about *Seul ou avec d'autres*, Johanne Harelle sang "Ti-z-oiseaux" during the variety evening but in the end, the scene was was given to Claude Jutra for his feature *À tout prendre* (*Take It All*).

Seul ou avec d'autres, one of the first dramatic feature films to be made in this new style of Québécois filmmaking, was a kind of subversive cultural enterprise. The arts society of the AGEUM (the Université de Montreál student association), headed by Arcand, let itself be convinced by Denis Heroux to replace the annual "Bleu et Or" variety-revue evening with a film production, which would cost less money and reach a wider audience. Arcand often remembers that *Seul ou avec d'autres* was his first film. But the first script he wrote with Stéphane Venne, all dialogue, was thrown into the wastebasket by its authors; the second draft was just a rough sketch for directing the actors' improvisations. What could have seemed to Arcand like a one-time event among his studies and theatre pursuits, planted the seed of what would become his first career choice, filmmaking.

Since childhood, Arcand has been passionate about film. During his university years, he risks anything to catch all the films from all the new waves that hit Montreal and New York. He haunts the film clubs, the Montreal World Film Festival, as well as the Élysée, the first art cinema in Quebec, an historic monument that was demolished in 1995 by Daniel Langlois, the SoftImage millionaire and philanthropist, founder of Montreal's Ex-Centris.

Earlier, in the fifties, with the Arcands' move to Montreal, Denys goes from watching films in 16 mm on makeshift screens to 35 mm and movie theatres. Not far from rue du Parc-Lafontaine, are two neighbourhood cinemas, the Amherst and the Electra; to the west, on rue Sainte-Catherine, in the vicinity of Collège Sainte-Marie, movie palaces such as the Comédie-Canadienne, the Orpheum, the Loew's, the Capitol. . . . The prince from Deschambault has found another kingdom. The first movies the young teenager sees are Catholic films, the only ones his mother allows: Joan of Arc by Victor Fleming with Ingrid Bergman, and of course, *Cielo sulla palude* (*Heaven over the Marshes*), the story of Maria Goretti, starring the immortal Inès Orsini, as well as a film on the children of Fatima. "It's a very strange thing, and I talk about it in *The Barbarian Invasions*, for me these pious Christian films were erotically charged." Instead of being edified by the religious content of the films, the teenager is attracted to the beautiful actresses. These feminine images will haunt him for a long time and then be forgotten, until the day he reads Michel Tremblay's *Les vues animées*. While reading the author's account of *Cielo sulla palude*, Arcand suddenly remembers that he too was obsessed by Inès Orsini as a child. The student also experiences a huge shock upon seeing *The Robe* at the Loew's cinema, a magnificent palace with a giant screen, later the site of the first Montreal World Film Festival. Watching *The Robe*, Arcand is, of course, enthralled by the Cinemascope, the first of its kind, and most of all, by another erotic discovery. "It was the first time I saw a kiss on screen. I was thunderstruck by the close-ups of mouths pressed together, and I asked myself: 'Do people really do that? It's absolutely incredible!' At home, we didn't have a television. My parents didn't kiss, or anyway, when they did, it was very chastely, on the cheek. Seeing it the screen gave me an absolutely terrible shock, which I have barely gotten over, to this day. There were also scenes of Jesus on the cross, things I would use later in my own films." Finally, at fifteen or sixteen, Arcand arrives at his own "road to Damascus" at the Comédie-Canadienne, with his first great cinematographic experience: *Hamlet* with Laurence Olivier, dubbed in French. A double discovery: an extremely well-done film—academic yet noble in its intentions—and Shakespeare, yet unknown to him, due to a gaping hole in Quebec culture.

The fifties in Quebec saw the birth of a cinephile underground and film club networks. There was even one for professionals at the NFB, equipped accordingly, set up by Guy-L. Côté and run by Claude Jutra. Everywhere, from colleges to convents, film clubs sprang up by the dozen, all in the hands of the Catholic Church, as was the case with education and social services. Montreal was exceptionally lucky: at the end of the decade, thanks to Doctor Jean-Paul Ostiguy and Patrick Straram, an art cinema moved into the Élysée; the Montreal World Film Festival was born; several commercial cinemas occasionally showed *films d'auteur*. In 1960–1961, aficionados rushed to see Chaplin (*The Gold Rush*, *Modern Times*) at the System, a little cinema on rue Sainte-Catherine, or to the Regent on avenue du Parc near Laurier, to see *Stella* with Melina Mercouri, or *Orfeu negro*.

Despite his passion for film, Arcand is the antithesis of a film-clubber. He has always had a difficult rapport with film clubs, and that is why he has sometimes said that he is not a cinephile. To have to discuss a film after it ends has always repelled him. After the projection, the lights come back on and you can't run away, you have to talk. "I've always had a very personal rapport with film, sitting there in the dark in the afternoon, almost on the sly. The first times I went to the Amherst cinema, which was on my way home from school, it was in secret; I could never have admitted it to my parents."

Arcand the student picks all the forbidden fruit he can before forming his own pantheon of seventh art geniuses. "Among the giants of film, Buñuel has always seemed like the one closest to me. First of all, because of his humour. I love humour, I like to put it my own films when I can. I'm not comparing myself to Buñuel, but I hope my films have a smile to them. Buñuel, like Fellini, is a nonbeliever, and both of them know how to deal with serious subjects with a smile. What's more, Buñuel is a very simple filmmaker who makes his films with modest means. Of all forms of artistic expression, I prefer simple things, an apparently banal story. I don't like films that put style first. I like téléro- man-type stories combined with situations that grow nightmarish, insane. In that sense, Buñuel was always a kind of idol for me. He made films that are like exterminating angels, they attack without warning. I prefer a between-the-lines kind of cinematographic style; I like styles that don't draw attention to themselves." Perhaps Arcand has so thoroughly absorbed the films of Buñuel that he unconsciously borrowed a scene from *The Phantom of Liberty*, in which one of the characters says: "We are all someone's barbarian."

Between 1960 and 1967, at the time of the first Montreal World Film Festival (some said it was the only real one, with a Critics' Week to follow), Arcand saw all the films from the golden age of cinema, which he roughly situates between 1955 and 1970. It was a time when all the great filmmakers except Eisenstein and Chaplin attained the height of their art. Antonioni, Fellini, Visconti, Rossellini, Jean Renoir, Hitchcock, Bergman, Howard Hawks, John Ford, Kurosawa, Kobayashi. He didn't miss a single one. "Now I tell young people, grumbling the way all old-sters do: 'You don't know what you missed.' Because in those days, at the film festival, every second day there was a masterpiece. Films that will last for centuries to come, as long as we can preserve the celluloid, *La dolce vita, The Seven Samurais, Rashomon*. It was absolute bliss, it was brilliant." In 2002, *Sight and Sound* asked hundreds of filmmakers to name their ten favourite films. Arcand chose *The Bicycle Thief* (Vittorio de Sica), *Citizen Kane* (Welles), Buñuel's *The Discreet Charm of the Bourgeoisie*, Fellini's *8 1/2*, *General della Rovere* (Rossellini), *The Man Who Shot Liberty Valance* (John Ford), Jean Renoir's *Une partie de campagne*, Kurosawa's *The Seven Samurais*, Bergman's *The Silence* and finally, *The Triumph of the Will* by Leni Riefenstahl. Today if we ask him the name of the best Quebec film, he names *Pour la suite du monde* (*The Moontrap*) by Brault and Perrault. This does not mean he does not consider Perrault "right wing," as he declared on the occasion of the fortieth anniversary of the Cinemathèque québécoise. "Perrault who, at the NFB, only believed in individual action and never participated in collective actions."

Another thing: because so many films were banned by Quebec censors, Arcand and his friends crowded into a Volkswagen and drove down to New York to see films. They saw twelve in two days, a total immersion. They left on Friday evening, drove all night, entered the film theatre at eleven o'clock or noon, saw five films in a row. The next day they began again, then drove through the night to be back at the university for their courses on Monday morning.

Of all the literature and history courses in which Arcand was enrolled, there was only one that he really followed. Called "Normes historiques," it was given by Maurice Séguin, whose instruction would indelibly influence him. He wrote a magnificent text on the subject that was praised by the novelist Jacques Poulin: "I'm touched that he was attached to this professor. One can sense his affection and admiration. There is a little sentence at the end that intrigues me, when he says: "I remember a polite, ironic tormented and extremely secretive man. In winter, he wore a beret. My father did too." Why does he say, 'My father did too'? Perhaps Maurice Seguin was his spiritual father? This little phrase gives a human quality to the whole text, it's quite touching." It is an exceptional piece of writing, included in the "Selected Readings" in this book. Arcand also has positive memories of courses given by another historian, Michel Brunet. Through him, the student learns about his family's famous cousin, the fascist Adrien Arcand, founder in the thirties of the *Christian National Socialist Party* and the newspapers *Le patriote* and *Le fasciste canadien*. The children never heard him mentioned by their parents because the family was ashamed of him. Horace Arcand, like all sailors, described himself as "apolitical." When the children tell him about their discovery of Adrien Arcand, their father confirms that he is a cousin he never sees because he finds him "a bit of an extremist."

Between 1960 and 1962, after the death of Duplessis in 1959, the

Université de Montréal is a veritable steam engine, shooting ahead at breakneck speed and in a state of near anarchy, in search of new spaces. In 1963, a new phase begins with the founding of the journal *Parti pris*, which fights for an independent, secular and socialist Quebec. This revolutionary journal is born at the Catholic university of Mont-Royal, under the authority of Cardinal Paul-Emile Leger, the Cyniques' scapegoat, whose base anti-worker and anti-union manoeuvres would later be described by Madeleine Parent in *On est au coton* (*Cotton Mill, Treadmill*).

At the heart of the avant-garde of this revolution, which controls the student newspaper *Le quartier latin* and the arts society of the Université de Montréal student association, are people such as Jacques Guay, Denis Heroux, André Brochu, Denys Arcand, Stéphane Venne, Marc Laurendeau, Marcel Saint-Germain, Serge Grenier, and others. In the background, a battle is raging: the Jesuits want to create two universities, one French speaking (Sainte-Marie), the other English speaking (Loyola); the student newspaper expresses opposition to the idea, as does the publication of the AGEUM, calling for a commission of public inquiry into the Quebec system of education. Thundering noon-hour debates are held in the social centre, between the founders of the Mouvement laïque de langue française (French-language secular movement) on the left, including Jacques Godbout, and on the right, the "Cathos" headed by the formidable Dr. Gilles Poupart, who crusades for "the inseparable unity of the Mystical Body of Christ," proclaiming: "At the call of the Living God they will move forward, and they will vanquish!" Moreover, Quebec's direct cinema has just been born at the NFB. Commandos of artists from Radio-Canada insist on being served in French, in stores and English restaurants in West End Montreal. The historian Michel Brunet asks, in *Le quartier latin*: "Can three-and-a-half centuries of history be remade? Will Quebec sovereignty be driven by naive optimism or terrorist agitation?" The Quiet Revolution has begun, though it does not yet have a name and no one is sure if it will mark an epoch or not.

Denys Arcand is interested in history on Saturday mornings, but most of his time is devoted to theatre. He fights tooth and nail to save the theatre arts workshop, which goes from bad to worse and finally closes its doors in early 1962. I regularly met Denys in Ernest Gagnon's creative writing workshop, but we had also worked together, for several weeks, at the theatre workshop directed by Gilles Marsolais, who had us do Gogol's *Revizor*. Alas! The project came to an abrupt end.

The Jesuit Ernest Gagnon had enormous success with his creative writing course, which was part of a university program that otherwise, at the time, says André Brochu, "had more or less ceased to evolve." This course, once attended by Monique Bosco, numbered among its students Antonine Maillet ("Tonine," as we called her), Jean-Guy Sabourin, Jean Pierre Lefebvre, Claude Grenier, Jacques Benoit, not to speak of Arcand, Brochu and dozens of others. The classroom was always full to bursting. The former students from Sainte-Marie, the "Sartrians," were already very familiar with the movements that interested Gagnon, so they experienced less of an impact from his teaching. Still, they recognized his importance, as well as his limitations, he whom the "most enlightened made their prophet."

André Brochu draws this portrait of him: "Ernest Gagnon introduced the study of the symbolic to Quebec. At the same time, though a Jesuit, he introduced the works of Freud at a time when Freud was very poorly regarded in the Jesuit community and by the Church in general. Gagnon was primarily a Jungian, but Jung implies Freud. Moreover, with his book *L'homme d'ici,* Gagnon was the great theorist of interiority for an entire generation that had explored and put this concept to use both culturally and existentially. It was the generation of Saint-Denys Garneau, Jean LeMoyne, and Robert Elie. Gagnon outlined the philosophical bases of the concept, espoused by left-leaning Christians for whom no doubt the unconscious existed but contained more mystery and instinct than drives."

Arcand, meanwhile, has not yet been "chosen" by film. Theatre is his centre of gravity; he works hard at dramatic arts and participates in the production, at the Gesù, of *Twelve Angry Men*. Marc Laurendeau chose and directed this American play written by Reginald Rose. It is one of the annual activities organized by the Faculty of Law under the name of "Law on Trial," an event designed to present legal issues in relation to theatre. Laurendeau saw Arcand act at Sainte-Marie, then at the university's theatre workshop. He gives him the main role of Juror Number Eight, played by Henry Fonda in the Sydney Lumet film. *Twelve Angry Men* is presented with success in February and March of

1961, several months before the filming of *Seul ou avec d'autres*. In presenting the play on February 21 in the student newspaper, *Le quartier latin*, the "Cynique" Laurendeau starts out by saying that the twelve men in question are not "the twelve apostles" of the gospels: "we'll save that for next time." The Cyniques are created at the end of that year and at first Arcand plays an active role in the group. Denys, whom the student newspaper calls the "cine-goth," plays in several numbers, takes care of stage management and lighting, accompanies the little troupe on its first shows in Montreal and Quebec City. He even becomes their propagandist in *Le quartier latin*, presenting the new group, on October 26, 1961, as "a permanent cabaret group; they are wickedly funny, ferociously funny, sadistically funny. For them, nothing is sacred. Their victims will number in the thousands by the end of the year, they are Attilas of the joke. For shooting people down, they are real sharp-shooters. They are commanded by Marc Laurendeau, artist of the jugular, clinician of ridicule, master of the scalpel-joke, of sepulchre humour, who runs the show with an open tomb." Arcand's collaboration comes to an end several months later, in the summer of 1962, when he starts working at the NFB. It is due to his predilection for the stage that Denis Heroux asks him to write the dialogue for *Seul ou avec d'autres* with Stéphane Venne and supervise the actors' improvisations. The essential elements of the film are created by NFB professionals, and that is why this feature is in fact a co-production. Hence, Arcand's two first nonprofessional film experiences, between 1959 and 1961, fall halfway between theatre and film.

As for his writing skills, Arcand puts them abundantly to use in *Le quartier latin*, composing over twenty-five articles in two years, though without thinking of making a career of literature or journalism. He writes primarily about the performing arts, theatre or song, and very little on film. Still, his first article, on the French new wave, begins with this typically melancholy sentence: "For there is nothing less solid, less substantial, less absolute, than the rising and falling movement of a wave." On September 20, 1962, while reviewing a production of Shakespeare's *Richard II* at the Theâtre du Nouveau Monde in Montreal, in a flight of saturnine oratory, Arcand notes "the great lyrical passages in which Richard laments the fragility of the human condition," or the fact that "the fall and the death of the king transpire in a climate of historical inevitability," borne by a kind of contemplative Shakespearean poetry. One of his last articles, published on October 9 of the same year, when he had already started working at the NFB, is a political paper on "the necessity of Machiavellianism," asserting the need for intelligent manœuvering in the provincial elections by supporting the Liberal Party rather than the NDP, because "the current state of evolution of the Quebec people forces us to vote for the Liberal Party, which can fully commit itself to educational reform," even though we know that this party "has hit the jackpot in terms of crooked bosses and century-old idiots."

One last memory of university courses. Albert Legrand, a young secular instructor, freshly graduated from literary studies in Paris, taught the course in French Canadian literature with another course that was sensitive and explosive at the time, contemporary French literature: Sartre, Gide, Camus. When introducing the course, Legrand gives students the choice of writing an end-of-term exam or delivering an in-class paper on one of the authors on the curriculum. Most of the students know nothing of this corpus, and only the former students of Sainte-Marie-de-la-Culture volunteer to do seminars. Legrand is in a difficult position: the Sainte-Marie students are far more impressive than himself. Through them, the class finally learns something about these great modern authors, more than they would from the poorly prepared and slightly haughty titular professor. What did Arcand choose as his subject? Albert Camus's *Letters to a German Friend*. Perhaps the future filmmaker retained, from this work, the following reflection: "I love my country too much to be a nationalist."

In Quebec, the Quiet Revolution would alter the way the wind blew. Arcand, too, would change direction, move away from theatre. The feature film *Seul ou avec d'autres* would open the doors of the NFB to him, though he did not yet know it. However, film had taken hold of the young man to such a degree that he would confide to his girlfriend Édith de Villiers in a letter of May 22, 1962: "Barely six months ago I didn't know what I was going to do with my life. I even thought about signing up for the Faculty of Law. What's more, I'd started work on a risky feature film on which my whole future might have depended. I still haven't found work, and in that regard, the future doesn't look too bright. Now

I know that ideally, I'd like to spend my life making films, but I also know that I'm a long way from making this desire come true. In other words, I'm in a state of total insecurity about life."

After completing his diploma in history and literature, which at that time took two years, Arcand thinks of entering the Ministry of External Affairs to pursue a diplomatic career, or go to Berkeley for a PhD in history. It was the era of the free speech movement and Berkeley seemed a veritable hive of ideas and protest. He looks for work, if only for the summer, and sends off three job applications at once: one to Radio-Canada for the job of announcer, one to the newspaper *La Presse* for the position of journalist, and one to the NFB. In the latter case, his application was preceded by a kind of recommendation to producer Fernand Dansereau from the filmmakers who met Arcand on the shoot for *Seul ou avec d'autres*. Dansereau needed a historian to analyze the production of a film series on the French Regime. Arcand is offered a contract that he immediately shows up to sign, travelling all the way across the city to the head office on rue Côte-de-Liesse, in Ville Saint-Laurent. The next day, he also receives offers from Radio-Canada and *La Presse*, which he has to turn down. Farewell, theatre and journalism, film chose him first. In France, during the seventies, people would say that Arcand started out at the NFB as an "educational consultant."

Thus, in the spring of 1962, the NFB asks Arcand to "study the future orientation of a series of historical film reconstructions on the French Regime, currently in production at the NFB." For three hundred dollars, Arcand produces his analysis, which he submits in May, a text of thirty-four pages typed on official PhD thesis paper from the Université de Montréal. A resonant report, as we might expect, that starts with a crack of the whip: "It's got to be one or the other: either the NFB makes historical films or it doesn't. In the case of the second hypothesis, there is no reason for writing this report. But if, on the other hand, the NFB decides to make a film series on the French Regime in the history of Canada, to my mind, it should submit itself to a strict scientific discipline, and all the films should be made under the direction of a producer who will make sure they contain unity of thought in their interpretation of the history of French Canadian history."

Here, the history student delivers a rigorous, implacable analysis of already existing films, such as Pierre Patry's *Lafontaine* whose "workmanship and dramatic atmosphere" he appreciates, but "without having the slightest idea of the context in which the described actions occurred, what imperatives they were meant to fulfil, and what their consequences were." Or he comments on works at the writing stage, such as Charles Dumas's *Cartier*, "a pure fiction that is in no way proven by the original historical documents"; *Champlain*, "chaotic script; we have to realize that in history, the losers are ALWAYS wrong. Champlain is to blame"; one by Gilles Carle, *Jacques Cartier*, "done with an alert intelligence [. . .] but without great value, I'm afraid, for a rational comprehension of the history of Canada"; a script by Alec Pelletier, *Les missionaries*—which would become *Le festin des morts*—whose analysis ends on this extraordinary note: "The majority of Jesuit missionaries, faced with the impossibility of creating the French country they had dreamed of, were surely aware of the futility of their enterprise; but perhaps they pursued it all the more, in order to punish and sanctify themselves rather than from true love of the native population?"; and finally, a project by Bernard Devlin, *Ceux de Ville-Marie*, which "unfortunately does not describe the religious fanatic members of the Société de Notre-Dame."

Besides these analyses, Arcand proposes thirteen interesting films that could be done on the French Regime, and in doing so, implicitly or unconsciously draws a blueprint for his future début as NFB director with *Champlain*, *La route de l'Ouest* (*The Westward Road*), and *Les Montréalistes* (*Ville Marie*). Other projects will never see the light of day, on the Amerindians, Jean Talon, d'Iberville, Madeleine de Verchères, the Conquest. . . . His report, until now unpublished, is at once a thorough analysis, a notebook of specifications, script ideas and directing methods. Reason enough to include a few excerpts among the "Selected Readings."

Rediscovering this text after forty years, Arcand comments: "I find it pretty accurate. I haven't changed my mind about those films or the ones I was going to propose. But I'm irritated by my offhand tone, which I still have at times and am trying to get rid of, the fact of brushing aside the work of twenty-five other filmmakers, saying it's crap and that I can do much better. Youthful bravado, understandable, but it still irritates me a little. I worked like crazy. After only three weeks I'd seen all the films made by the NFB, a week later I'd already written my report. I wrote day and night; I didn't eat."

Events start to accelerate for Arcand, who recounts how Fernand Dansereau said to him: "If you're so smart, what's your idea of a good script on the history of Canada? Write me one." Arcand is free. By the end of the summer, the twenty-five page script is ready: *Samuel de Champlain: Une ré-evaluation*. The text is at such an advanced stage that it has already been divided into seventy-five shots. The scriptwriter has read the entire works of Champlain and written his text over a three-week writing marathon, having returned to Deschambault and shut himself up in his grandparents' house. "I can't understand how I managed to work so quickly that time."

One last anecdote from this intense chapter on Arcand's beginnings in film: "Thirty years later, I was sitting with Dansereau on the board of directors of the Société des auteurs. I said to him: 'After all, Fernand, it was you who gave me my first contract, it's thanks to you that I got my start in film. You were the first to recognize my talent.' He answered: 'No, I never recognized any talent. The thing I liked about you was your energy, the amount of energy you had.'"

In September, after writing the report and the *Champlain* script, Arcand starts PhD courses in history, and writes several articles for *Parti pris*. Two weeks later, the NFB asks him to direct his own script. When Dansereau makes this request, he is addressing someone who has been ready to do the job for two years. Perhaps this gives credence to the filmmaker's paradoxal statement that his film career has been "a series of accidents and premeditated flukes." In other words, Arcand's encounter with film directing corresponds to the following mysterious aphorism from the Bible, "You would not seek me had you not already found me." Having made his choice to become a filmmaker, Arcand leaves the university for good, returning only thirty years later to pick up his honorary PhD, earned with great care and effort through his films. Though he will never completely abandon dramatic arts and writing, from now on, film will be his main occupation, his tool of choice and his weapon of exterminating expression, soon allowing him to proclaim that he has become a filmmaker by trade.

6
THE CINEMA OF HISTORY

While working on *Seul ou avec d'autres*, Denys Arcand was dazzled by the NFB filmmakers. Less, at first, by their control of the audiovisual elements of film writing and editing than by their lifestyle. "They were always ready to party. They smoked, drank, stayed up all night. They were completely free spirits." The student was equally enthused by their way of dressing, their constant travel (to France, Nigeria, the United States and all over Quebec and Canada), their bohemian flair, their money and their culture. Whereas Arcand had a classical education in music, Gilles Groulx was a walking encyclopedia of jazz, of which the aspiring filmmaker knew nothing—Groulx had known Paul-Emile Borduas and the Automatistes. Michel Brault held forth about photography, Cartier-Bresson and Steichen. Claude Jutra knew the works of Cocteau, Truffaut and Bertolucci and talked about these filmmakers as if they were friends. In no time, Arcand would catch up with them. *Seul ou avec d'autres* was his calling card, the research and report on the French Regime his entrance exam.

Arcand's report of May 1962 soon shows results. He becomes the writer-director of a first professional film that he shoots and edits in the fall of 1962 and in 1963. Two veteran historians, Maurice Careless and Gustave Lanctôt, are asked to examine Arcand's written commentary for *Champlain*. They give their seal of approval. This short film, entitled *Champlain: Une réévaluation* is meant to be anything but a hagiographical, mythomaniac work. It depicts the founder of Quebec with the greatest possible historical accuracy, with particular attention to the Amerindians and a sarcastic view of the ultracommercial way in which the explorer's name is used in contemporary society.

When the film was released in 1964, there was an outbreak of "priestism." Father Henri-Paul Sénécal, from *Séquences*, denounced it as "a film written in a haughty, offhand style" with an "ambitious, chatty, eloquent and ridiculous" commentary, attacking its "unhealthy obsession with truth" and its "virulent zeal for historical objectivity," which has the effect of "singularly diminishing the historic stature of Champlain." Next, the film is ostracized at its opening night in Quebec City in 1965, at the annual meeting of the ACEF (the Canadian association for French-language educators), where it is judged incompatible with the school curriculum. Negative commentaries are relayed in *Le Devoir* and *La Presse*. The first of the two dailies report the opinion of a teacher who wondered "if it was necessary to portray a man so much in terms of his sadism," another who says, "the documentary, being too intellectual and because of its form, is not a film for distribution in the schools." *La Presse* writes: "The director's scalpel slices into a cherished legend, exposing open wounds and emphasising the resistance of flesh that is greedy for life, in the end leaving us speechless with the skeleton of a being who for us has always been 'a god of French Canada,' the artisan of a glorious past . . . ."

In the wake of this outcry, *Champlain* is subtly but radically condemned at the NFB, foreshadowing the prohibition of *On est au coton* in 1970. Arcand's first short film falls prey to a full-scale revisionist undertaking, and not just once but twice. The NFB first approaches screenwriter Alec Pelletier, asking her to construct a dramatic feature on the same subject. Madame Pelletier is the wife of Gerard Pelletier, one of the three doves of the Liberal party, along with Pierre Elliott Trudeau and Jean Marchand, who will accede to power in Ottawa in 1968. The work of Alec Pelletier comes to nothing, but the NFB persists. It has the film re-edited by Réjane Charpentier in a new so-called educational version called *Quebec 1603*, "based on the film by Denys Arcand," as the title reads, for circulation in the schools. This version expurgates all the contemporary scenes from Arcand's film, keeping only the drawings of Frederic Back and tacking on a more "suitable" commentary. Oddly enough, the NFB has never removed Arcand's film from their catalogue, perhaps fearing bad publicity for censorship; however, by keeping both versions, the organization only highlights the triviality of the bland remake, whitewashed for the schools.

"Right from my first film, the tone of my relations with the NFB was established. The NFB didn't know how to react to controversy and outcry. This official reaction never really touched me. I was acknowledged right away by filmmakers and cinephiles, *Champlain* won the prize for best short film of the year. But I was in trouble with the authorities. My boss Fernand Dansereau asked me to remove certain scenes, including one drawn by Frederic Back in which there was question of pedophilia on the part of Champlain. His marriage at the age of forty-five to a girl of twelve, Helène Boulle ("a dowry of six thousand *livres* was among the bride's wedding presents"), was unusual at the time, except in the case of royal unions for the perpetuation of the dynasty. And that is not to mention a strange gift from the Amerindians of three very young girls called Faith, Hope and Charity. These facts give historians reason to suspect pedophilia. The NFB administration categorically objected. You couldn't say that about the founder of Quebec, it was intolerable! Just imagine our canons going up their crimson walls! I always had trouble with NFB management. Why? Because of my training in history, the desire to think for myself? I don't know. I've always been headstrong, right from primary school. Top of the class, they couldn't kick me out, but at the same time I was the one who sat in the back row, always with a sort of mocking smile. Never absent, never a trouble-maker, I was very good, but I still had my own ideas. This iconoclastic attitude carried over to my filmmaking. Always thinking in a different way or in the opposite way from the majority, that's the way I've always been."

Arcand, of course, has every reason to be proud of his first professional film. His written commentary is unique in that it links Champlain's movements in Canada to contemporaneous events in other colonies or in Europe. For example, in 1603, as the geographer travels down the Saint Lawrence, sighting Île aux Coudres and Montmorency Falls, "Shakespeare is doing Hamlet." During the difficult winter of 1608 in Quebec City, "The Jesuits were in Paraguay. In Paris, people were reading *Introduction to the Devout Life* and in Madrid, *Don Quixote*. Kepler was studying the elliptic trajectory of the planets.

Scurvy killed sixteen of Champlain's twenty-eight men." In 1613, as Champlain makes his expedition down the Ottawa River, "Monteverdi becomes chapel master at San Marco in Venice." In 1616, "Galileo is put in prison by the tribunal of the Inquisition" while the founder of Quebec recovers from a wound received in battle with the Iroquois. Around the time of Champlain's death on Christmas Day in 1635, "the Académie française is founded, Corneille writes *Le Cid* and Descartes *Discourse on Method*. In Quebec City, the college of Jesuits is founded, in Boston, Harvard University. There are one hundred and fifty inhabitants in Quebec, and twenty-nine thousand in the United States." Another interesting trait of this "historical" film is that it writes a page of contemporary Quebec history through the mythic and ever-present image of the founder of New France. One face in particular that serves as a kind of leitmotif is that of a young Mohawk woman. During a seminar at Concordia University on April 4, 1995, Arcand explains that this young Native woman was his girlfriend at the time of shooting and that he had learned from her how much, and how viscerally, the Mohawks hate the Québécois!

Arcand considered this first period of 1962 to 1966 at the NFB as "film school" and his first three short films as a refresher course, as he often explains during the seventies and eighties in *24 images*, *Cinema Canada* and *This Magazine*. In 1961, he learned from observing the NFB filmmakers at work on *Seul ou avec d'autres*. As a greenhorn writer-director, he interned as first-camera assistant for Michel Brault and Bernard Gosselin, and on sound for Marcel Carrière. He also interned with Claude Jutra, who came around from time to time, and most of all with Gilles Groulx in the editing room. He spent hours and entire nights with Groulx, working until dawn in a sinister second-floor editing room on rue Wellington in Verdun. Arcand was also attending courses at the time, sleeping only a few hours at around daybreak. "Only a twenty-year-old can get away with that without dropping dead. I wouldn't be able to do one-hundredth of it today." These were all-important lessons: in documentary, editing is essential, even more so than directing with good technical teams, as Arcand explains to *This Magazine* in 1974. Also with Groulx he learned the importance of the sound track and collage, as he indicated in our interviews for the monograph *Auteur/provo-*

cateur, published in London. "My first films had nothing to do with *cinéma direct*, maybe none of my films did; they were totally different, the short films especially. At that time I was mad about the the NFB sound library. I spent hours listening to loops of every kind of noise, all very well inventoried. I was especially fond of the different kinds of winds; I used a lot of them. If you ask me from whom I might have learned this way of doing free-sound collage with music, voice-overs and images, I guess I'd have to call myself a disciple of Gilles Groulx. I often talked to him about cinema and music. That must have influenced me."

The historical film series comes to an abrupt end after *La route de l'Ouest* (*The Westward Road*) and *Les Montréalistes* (*Ville-Marie*), both shot in 1963 and released in 1965. Pierre Juneau terminates the program and Arcand must abandon two projects at the planning stage, *La société sous le Régime français* and *La Conquête* (fortunately, the story summaries for both can be found in his 1962 Report). In *The Westward Road* and *Ville- Marie* he was nonetheless able to apply a concept of history based on the teachings of Maurice Séguin about the economy/politics/culture triad, the interaction between the three and their influence on the material and intellectual works of human beings. He applies the triad to historical cinema, as we can see in his essay for UNESCO, *The Cinema of History*, in which he calls for films built on fact, conceived and structured by a certain view of history (for the conclusion of this study, see the "Selected Readings" in this book).

These films are not so much didactic or propagandistic works but personal films based on historical and ethnographical fact. This explains Arcand's enthusiasm for a film like Rossellini's *The Rise to Power of Louis XIV*: "In my profession I have often grappled with historical problems, in my history films at the NFB, my documentaries on politics and the *Duplessis* series on Radio-Canada." Arcand believes that costume dramas always miss the essential. Knowledge of historical phenomena is extremely difficult to illustrate on film without resorting to didacticism, putting oneself on screen with a blackboard and chalk. In his view, Rossellini's *The Rise to Power of Louis XIV* is one of the only examples, the most brilliant example, of a film that manages to explain some fundamental part of history: in this case, Louis XIV's centralization of power in France at the Château de Versailles. At the time, France had just been unified, but there was still a danger that provincial nobles would revolt against the king. Not only was the Château de Versailles sumptuous, it also fulfilled a very astute political goal. The nobility was brought to live there so they could more easily be controlled. "How does Louis XIV manage it? By creating fashion and cultural phenomena: costumes, theatre, celebrations and music that keep the Court in the net. Versailles becomes a gilded cage for the nobility so the king can maintain his power over it. To film Versailles and the Hall of Mirrors is all very well, it's grandiose, but it's all just insane ostentation, like in Sacha Guitry and some of the wig-and-powder films. Whereas in the Rossellini film, you understand a very precise phenomenon that generally requires pages and pages of commentary in a history book to explain. In an hour and a half, it's all explained, and at the same time it's spectacular. I've always had great admiration for that film."

Shortly after entering the NFB, Arcand has the fortune of meeting Rossellini, who is invited to Montreal by the World Film Festival. Claude Jutra organizes a get-together at his home with the great Italian maestro. Arcand says that he was too shy even to ask a question of this god of Italian neorealism, who inspired new waves in cinema all over the world. Content just to listen, he retains Rossellini's response to the Quebec filmmakers' complaint of having no money to make films. "There's never money for film. You always have to beg. After the war, I started by going to see my tailor and having two suits made on credit. Then, appropriately dressed, I went to a bank and asked for a loan that would allow me to shoot *Rome Open City*. The secret is to have a good tailor to make an impression on the bankers." Arcand has a vivid memory of this anecdote on the relation between money and the art of cinema.

In 1963, during his first full year at the NFB, Arcand also becomes involved in political writing for the journal *Parti pris*, whose founders include Pierre Maheu and some of Arcand's other friends, such as André Brochu and Jean-Marc Piotte. Arcand collaborates with them until 1964, producing several essays for the journal, most of them on cinema. It is the third time Arcand will have participated in this kind of activity, after writing for *Le Sainte-Marie* and *Le quartier latin*. It will also be the last, not counting occasional contributions to filmmaker-run journals *Format cinema* and *Lumières*. Other than that, after his *Parti pris* days, he will write only prefaces, testimonies, acknowledgments, a few letters and replies to questionnaires on the filmmaking profession.

In *Parti pris*, his system of criticism is again based on the history teaching of Maurice Séguin, "criticism in the philosophical sense," as Arcand explains in his 1963 article "Les divertissements": "[criticism] in the sense of the examination and global meaning of such and such a cultural gesture. Nothing to do with normative criticism. Indeed, the problem is not that of knowing whether a work of art is well or badly made, technically speaking, or whether it reflects certain influences in its conception or uncovers an original aspect of its author's personality. That's just chit-chat. It's a question of knowing whether the appearance of that work has profound cultural meaning, and seeing the relationship between this meaning and its cultural, political and economic environment."

It was Pierre Maheu who convinced Arcand to become involved in the launching of *Parti pris*, a real intellectual journal founded in opposition to *Cité libre*, at that time the medium of Pierre Elliott Trudeau and his generation. *Parti pris* aimed to revolutionize the intellectual history of Quebec. Occupied with his films at the NFB, Arcand could not be a full-time member. During his involvement with the journal he "did something a little strange." He wrote reviews of Quebec films, including the first features of Claude Jutra and Gilles Groulx. "By chance, I heard an interview with François Truffaut on Radio-Canada: 'There is a barricade that cannot be crossed. Some people make films, others judge them. I'm on one side of the barricade, I'm not going to cross it.' I realized that he was right, I reread my reviews and asked myself who was I, a filmmaker, to judge the films of other filmmakers? Since that day, I've completely refused to write film reviews or sit on film festival juries, because there's a very clear dividing line between creating and reviewing. Both are valid, but they can't be done at the same time. I'm ashamed of my reviews in *Parti pris*, I'm uncomfortable with them, and it doesn't make me happy to reread them." In the 1987 edition of *Copie zero*, Gerald Godin notes that Arcand disowns his "arrogant texts" in *Parti pris*.

For Arcand, the *Parti pris* adventure comes to an end in 1964, shortly after the journal publishes a file on the NFB and Quebec cinema, put together by filmmakers Jacques Godbout, Gilles Carle, Clément

Perron, Denys Arcand and Gilles Groulx. "*Intra muros* we were rounded up like unruly pupils by the commissioner Guy Roberge, whom we usually never saw: a former diplomat, a gentleman with a big reputation. He said: 'This cannot happen again. You are employees of the NFB, which does not accept being criticized outside its walls in a subversive journal. It's all right this time, but don't do it again.' Gilles Groulx, indomitable, asked: 'Could you write down this opinion for us?' 'It's an oral communication and it's going to stay that way,' the commissioner answered sharply."

What is to be retained from Arcand's brief but productive collaboration with *Parti pris*? In the winter of 1972, the journal *La barre du jour* published a file called "Écrire sur *Parti pris*" ("Writing about *Parti pris*"). Arcand's contribution to the issue sees the journal's short trajectory as mainly positive, including its act of self-sabotage." There were accusations about giving up the cause, but those mostly came from confirmed leftists, who generally speaking were socially and emotionally maladjusted individuals." Arcand writes this commentary shortly after his participation in the *Cahiers* of the "Marxist" *Conseil quebecois pour la diffusion du cinema*, a monograph in which he is reproached for giving up revolutionary struggle in his filmmaking. André Brochu, in his contribution to "Ecrire sur *Parti pris*," expresses a more melancholy point of view: "I know that certain members of the *Parti pris* had problems with fashion (and modernity). We were humanists, a little in spite of ourselves. In any case, we were idealists, with all the fervour that went with our age. It's difficult, when one isn't yet thirty, to be late for a revolution." He adds this commentary, revealing the flirtation between *Parti pris* and materialist, even Marxist ideas: "*Parti pris* was essentially a political journal; the cultural dimension was subordinated to the demands of the revolution." In his article Brochu also alludes to a certain "survival of the metaphysical": "We had faith. Our religion was Quebec. We awaited its resurrection, its epiphany. We even believed that we could play an active role in this birth—our own, that of our people. Every political event threw us into abysses of hope or despair."

After leaving *Parti pris*, Arcand's "last stand" is an article for *Liberté*. The journal is preparing a special issue on the history of the *Patriotes'* insurrection against the British colonial government in 1837-

1838. The introduction to the issue presents the Lower Canada Rebellion as "a national failure singularly repressed." Arcand's contribution, an essay entitled "1837 at school," describes how events are depicted in history textbooks for the schools. His analysis covers works written between 1873 and 1960.

The first constant that he remarks upon: "No evolution in historical thinking, no re-evaluation of the insurrection." His examination reveals that according to the textbooks, the cause of the insurrection was administrative; the insurgents were a small minority, were mad and had no chance of succeeding, though they were extremely courageous. Colborne and the English behaved abjectly, the conduct of the clergy was wise and far-seeing, and "in spite of everything, the insurrection was profitable for the French Canadians." Concluding his analysis of the French and English textbooks, Arcand notes the moralistic character of the vocabulary used: "Words like obligation, respect, established authority, social order, disobedience and punishment envelop what was a strictly political event with the atmosphere of a confessional." In fact, the textbooks reflect an "official" line of thinking, the party line of Church or State, and the essayist concludes: "What's worrying is that this line of thought has not budged since 1873. One might ask how a 'thought' could remain inert for such a long time."

In the autumn of 1963, Arcand makes *Ville-Marie* and *The Westward Road*. His first trilogy of short historical films is made in rapid-fire succession. The first film describes the mystical founding of Ville-Marie/Montreal by the "God-crazy" French of the Société Notre-Dame. The second film deals with the great and mysterious westward expeditions of Europeans at the time when Canada and America were discovered. While shooting his films, Arcand sees Bergman's *The Silence* in Sweden and writes about it with passion in *Parti pris*. He works closely with Monique Fortier on the editing of *Ville-Marie* but says he is dissatisfied with the editing of *The Westward Road*, which he is not able to supervise. It seems that everything this director does is subject to controversy.

For the first film, NFB commissioner Pierre Juneau obliges the filmmaker to cut a scene in which a sister of the Notre-Dame Congregation flagellates herself, a reconstitution done with an actress. In the place where the scene is cut, the filmmaker suggests inserting a black title card on which the following excerpt from a historical text appears: "As our Lord has marked us with his love all the more through the trials that He was willing to suffer for us during his mortal life, so will his faithful servants, animated with his spirit of penitence, work incessantly to mortify their flesh, which they regard as the enemy of Jesus Christ . . . but finding they were not yet satisfied with this, added the worst of all disciplines: chains of iron and other lacerations that were its daily bread. Sister Marie Morin, Ville-Marie, 1659."

Upon its release in 1965, *Ville-Marie* is subjected to Catholic outrage from *Séquences* magazine. Father Sénécal, the permanent spiritual delegate in such matters, disparages the "tendentious interpretation of French Canadian history" and the "masochistic besmirching" of the past. *The Westward Road*, which seems to go unnoticed, is the only one that is not labelled anathema by priests and nationalists. In 1971, however, the film cannot escape the Marxist-Leninist indictment, for which I happened to be the loudspeaker, maintaining that its discourse was idealistic, "favouring sumptuous, all-enveloping images and music, a 'charm,' through which the past is depicted with romanticism and nostalgia." In fact, *The Westward Road* contains enchanting historical music interpreted by Kenneth Gilbert, Olav Harstad, Sorcha ni Ghuairim and the *Société de musique d'autrefois*. Its saturnine commentary is one of the most beautiful historical texts the filmmaker has ever produced. This account of journeys and darkness has also been included in the "Selected Readings."

Also in 1963, Arcand agrees to write the screenplay for Denis Héroux's second film *Jusqu'au cou*, produced by the AGEUM: "I wrote a screenplay that was all dialogue because I wasn't satisfied with the improvisation techniques used in *Seul ou avec d'autres*. In this script—and I'm more than a little proud of it—I anticipated the existence of the Front de libération du Québec (FLQ), of terrorists who commit a murder. It's fiction, entirely written in the traditional mode. Héroux showed it to our old co-conspirators at the NFB, who burst out laughing and found the script completely ridiculous. They made fun of me, calling me 'Denys de La Patellière,' because of the spelling of my first name. My other contribution consisted of lending them my girlfriend, Édith de Villers, to play the main role. End of my involvement in *Jusqu'au cou*." Unfortunately or not, this script cannot be found, which does not prevent its author from saying he would be curious to take a look at it.

The next year he begins work on a project that will have a considerable impact on his later career. He writes the script for a dramatic feature, *Entre la mer et l'eau douce* (*Drifting Upstream*). Of course, he already has some experience writing drama, with Stéphane Venne for *Seul ou avec d'autres* and solo for *Jusqu'au cou*, but it is his first time writing a professional work from beginning to end. The project belongs to Michel Brault. He thinks he can direct it at the NFB and he asks Arcand to write the screenplay. The first version is completed on December 30, 1964.

When Brault described the project a few months earlier, on September 4, 1964, he put the emphasis on the Saint Lawrence River, the young protagonist's attachment to the North Shore and his attraction to the city of Montreal: "This film is intended to be the portrait of a river, in the sense that one gets to know a country by living among its inhabitants. It will be the portrait of a young man who is born and grows up on the shores of the river and who ultimately makes his living from the river. He doesn't question this ferocious element, for the river is part of his life; he doesn't respect it, often insults it, neither disdains nor venerates it. We want to do the story of a voyage, almost a round-trip voyage."

Arcand proposes a different outlook and angle of attack: "The proposed film is above all an itinerary. An itinerary that begins with a schooner in Sept-Îles and ends one evening at a concert at the Comédie-Canadienne. On the one hand, it's a journey from country to city, at once physical and spiritual. But it is also a rise to success, with all the patience and determination that involves, in a domain that has become well known to French Canadians: song. Through the story of a singer, this film reflects upon two objectives that obsess French Canadians (and many other people): urbanization and success. From Alexis Tremblay, the old captain at Île aux Coudres, to Steve, the journalist from the *Monde des vedettes* showbiz magazine, the hero frequents a motley crowd whose sole common denominator is that of living in the same country and not knowing how to live there." From this point of view, Arcand's script reflects his own world of sailors and navigators, village roots and the departure to Montreal, higher education and a career in the arts. The "itinerary" of the young Claude Tremblay is a kind of professional trajectory, a self-portrait.

Pierre Juneau does not approve the project for production by the NFB, so Michel Brault makes his film in the private sector with Coopératio, founded in 1963 by Pierre Patry. It is shot intermittently over the autumn of 1965 and then in November and December of 1966. In the film's titles, under the heading "screenwriter," the director inserts Arcand's name but also those of Marcel Dubé, Gérald Godin, Claude Jutra and himself. However, judging from the documents produced by the NFB in 1964, and in spite of changes made to the original screenplay for *Drifting Upstream*, it would seem that Arcand is quite justified in claiming to be its progenitor.

To compare Arcand's scripts with his finished films is very revealing. The differences between the two are well worth examining as relics from his vast workshop. The Michel Brault feature is a complex case. The director makes two major changes to Arcand's original script. He develops and goes into detail about the political dimension of the story, making direct references to the colonized situation of Quebec and its need for independence. He keeps almost none of the original dialogue, replacing it with exchanges that are less developed and more commonplace, which mean the same thing as the original dialogue but are less explicit. Moreover, the director adds numerous proto-documentary shots, short improvisations with ambient sound but no dialogue—for example, shots of people at work or a midnight supper on Christmas Eve. He also adds voice-overs, for Reggie ("I'd rather die standing up than live kneeling"), for Aude, Claude's sister, and for Claude himself throughout the film, a kind of spoken logbook describing his work as a sailor. Finally, Brault chooses original songs by Claude Gauthier rather than the music mentioned in the screenplay: Félix Leclerc and Gilles Vigneault, Pierre Lalonde and Monique Leyrac, *Le Canadien errant* and *Notre chanson d'amour*. Nor does the director keep the detail of Aude reading Machiavelli's *The Prince*, an authentic Arcand signature-piece.

In 1965, now officially a filmmaker, Arcand participates in the creation of an independent production company, Cinéastes associés, with Jean Dansereau, Gilles Groulx, Bernard Gosselin and Michel Brault. Cinéastes associés appears at the same period as Coopératio and Onyx Film. The latter, founded by André and Pierre Lamy in 1962, will become the fiefdom of Gilles Carle. According to Jean Dansereau and André Bertrand, Cinéastes associés was founded on February 18, 1965.

The group was dissolved in 1967, though the firm lingered on until 1971, when Dansereau created a new entity, les Ateliers du cinéma québécois. Thanks to Cinéastes associés, for a time Arcand could believe that the private sector would be profitable for his filmmaker colleagues and himself.

In 1965, Montreal is already busily preparing for Expo 67. In 1965, Arcand directs *Montréal un jour d'été* (*Montreal on a Summer Day*), with Bernard Gosselin on camera and music by Stéphane Venne, a promotion of Montreal, Expo and the Quebec Pavilion. He also does the editing. "The director of the pavilion asked if it was possible for a Quebec filmmaker to film properly in 35 mm Eastmancolor. I went away with Gosselin for five days and we shot anything and everything in Eastmancolor: the façade of Le Roi du Smoked Meat, Saint-Hubert shopping plaza, Cap Saint-Jacques, Parc Lafontaine. The director of the Quebec Pavilion thought it was very good and said: 'You just have to edit it and it's a film.' You can see the front of the Roi du Smoked Meat, et cetera." But there is a postmortem story, which Arcand tells in the *Cahiers du Conseil québécois pour la diffusion du cinéma*. To illustrate how poorly the Cinéastes associés adventure turned out, he explains: "The director of the pavilion was very satisfied and took the opportunity of giving the biggest film contract to an English-speaking company. As for me, the Quebec Pavilion later asked me to make little 16 mm black- and-white clips about the fur trade. That was it."

The same year, Arcand also makes a short documentary called *Volleyball*, one of the most underestimated works of his career. It describes a game between the American and Soviet Olympic teams at Montreal's Maurice-Richard Arena in October 1965. The film is unusual in two respects. First, its form is a tribute to Gilles Groulx, whose editing work left such an impression on Arcand during postproduction for *Seul ou avec d'autres*. Second, it is the only film Arcand has ever made on sports, one of his favourite fields. He says of the film: "The Physical Fitness Department of the Ministry of Health asked the NFB for a film to promote volleyball. The film was given to me by Jacques Bobet. I thought that showing the world's best volleyball players would be an interesting form of 'promotion.' Four cameramen and eight assistant cameramen shot the film in a single evening at the Maurice Richard

Arena in Montreal. It took four months to edit. At the end, we had the idea of adding two little animation sequences to the original to satisfy the sponsor's educational requirements. Kaj Pindall drew the scenes and I wrote the commentary. The film was turned down by the Ministry of Health, who found it vulgar and boring." The voice-over commentary is a little satiric gem, a send-up of educational films illustrated by Pindall's grinning and delirious caricatures.

Even before the film's rejection by its sponsor, Arcand had to perform the thankless and stupid task of writing a complete script for his documentary. As he emphasizes when the film is shown for the fortieth anniversary of the Cinémathèque québécoise, on November 1, 2003: "To do this kind of script is an aberration, you just don't do that! How are you to supposed know in advance what's going to be in a film, if shooting is how you find that out?" Yet in 1965, a script is still current practice at the NFB and the Ministry of Health insists on having one. On October 4, Arcand sends the script to producer Jacques Bobet, introducing it as "a detailed script of the film." In fact, it is a bogus script, made up of an exaggerated number of quotes from the Canadian Volleyball Association's *Annual and Rule Book 1965*, accompanied by ad hoc images. This script, entitled *How to Play Volleyball*, is a cynical farce, a clever satire in which the filmmaker presents the twelve players as follows: "Twelve people. Twelve young men, twelve young women, twelve elderly people, twelve professional athletes, twelve retired colonels. Anyone."

On a more serious note, in 1966 when the film is completed and then refused, the NFB undertakes to make another one that is more to the taste of the Ministry of Health's fitness and amateur sports division. As with *Champlain*, the NFB orders a second "revisionist" film on the same subject. This time, the educational documentary is entrusted to director Hector J. Lemieux, a kind of piece-worker whose filmography includes dozens of films in the same mould. His film, called *The Name of the Game Is Volley-Ball*, is produced with the Canadian Volleyball Association, and comes out in 1967. This time, it is perfectly educational, that is, perfectly flat and insipid. There is no doubt that this script by Lemieux and Jacques Bensimon could have been written in full before shooting! The NFB still has this film in its catalogue, along with Arcand's. The latter is the original minus Pindall's cartoons and his own biting commentary.

"Alas!" Arcand says, again at the Cinémathèque, *Volleyball* is the only film I've ever done on sports." There are traces of a similar regret in some of the filmmaker's other works and projects. *Le confort et l'indifférence* (*Comfort and Indifference*), made at the end of the seventies, was supposed to take place in a hockey stick factory in Drummondville; in the *15 Moments* version of the film *Stardom*, young Tina is discovered while playing on a girl's hockey team and her father is a professional player who bears a resemblance to Steve Bourque of the New York Rangers. For Arcand, sports, like film or the gospels, go back to his childhood in Deschambault. Hockey and tennis, guidance from father and mother. At Collège Sainte-Marie, the child learns from the Jesuit Delisle that practising a sport is the only way to earn respect and avoid being bullied for liking literature and the arts, considered "girly." Lacrosse and hockey act as his carapace and armour. In the student paper *Le Sainte-Marie,* on November 14, 1959, Arcand publishes a text about hockey, "La glace brûlante" ("burning ice"). "Since ancient times, crowds have been fascinated by athletic competition. Does the phenomenon of catharsis lie at the root of this deep need of man? Could physical exertion play, at an intellectual level, a role similar to that of theatre? Yes."

Jacques Poulin has known the filmmaker-sportsman for a long time. He recalls that in 1972, Édith de Villers was studying at the École des Beaux-Arts in Quebec City along with his wife. The two women met there. "That year, we went to Denys's place in Deschambault for the first time. What struck me was their force of personality, especially Denys's, but Édith's too. They were obviously lively, dynamic people. This impression was later confirmed, in all circumstances, whether related to tennis or work." Jacques Poulin was Arcand's tennis partner for about ten years. The sport brought them together more often than film or literature. "I played tennis with the flaws of someone who hadn't taken lessons." The novelist explains that he learned tennis on his own, at around the age of six, on a court behind his house in Saint-Gédéon-de-Beauce. "Denys was interested in the theory of tennis and he gave me books to read." Poulin read everything in Arcand's library on the subject of tennis, bought other books, took lessons with Richard Legendre in Quebec City and with Jack Hérisset, but found it more interesting to play with Denys because they were at about the same level.

They played in tournaments together, such as the Rondeau in Quebec City, and did fairly well. Denys's strong points, he says, are the overhead strokes, that is, the serve and the smash, characteristic of people who are very assertive and extroverted. Poulin's own game depends more on regularity and ground strokes, typical of more reserved and introverted people. He remarks: "I'm sure that Denys is a very sensitive person. Just one little example, again to do with tennis: in the old days, we played with wooden racquets. The two most popular racquets were the Maxply and the Wilson. The Maxply was a flexible racquet, the one used by McEnroe; the other was more rigid. Denys played with that one; I used a softer racquet. Once I pointed out this difference, he said: 'Between that and saying I'm a great brute isn't much of a stretch.' It was just a joke, but it showed his sensitivity."

A year before *Volleyball*, Arcand worked with Jean Lemoyne on the commentary for Jean Dansereau's *Parallèles et grand soleil*. In an otherwise conventional and descriptive narration of the gymnastics trials at the fourth Pan American Games, Arcand's ideas and style stand out all of a sudden, in ringing flights of lyricism:

> What have these proud athletes from the two Americas come looking for, if not glory? If they consented to austere preparations for these trials, was in not in the hope of contemplating the metallic brilliance and clamour of glory, the same hope that makes filmmakers dream of Lions d'Or, journalists of Pulitzers and even peace-makers of Nobels?

> The gymnast never flies off the handle. He has no gestures of self-protection. He does not throw or hit anything, or anyone. Rage sometimes saves the boxer, but if the gymnast even slightly loses control, he's out. With training and the final exercises, a perfect event is constructed, one that entirely is entirely lodged in the body. The gymnast has a preoccupied, anxious expression; people's encouragements have no more meaning than a vague liturgy of camaraderie. The trial is too close. The gymnast is reduced to his own inexpressible expectation of performing an immaculate gesticulation.

The objective existence of the gymnast depends on one thing, success. Failure for him can only be a disaster. Short of recognition of his perfection he is nothing. What a combat it is to emerge from the drama. The pugilist's failure arouses compassion. Or disappointment. The gymnast's failure interests no one. The gymnast is never triumphant. He triumphs over himself, by himself, and if something is remembered, it is a fact rather than an event.

These are the same traits we find in one of Arcand's rare texts on sport, "The Rigour of Sport" (see "Selected Readings" later in this book), an incisive reflection on the contradictions and syncretism between physical activity and creativity. "At Sainte-Marie, the Jesuits' guiding principle and Utopia was the famous *Mens sana in corpore sano*. It was their ambition to achieve the perfect sum of a human being, flesh and spirit. That's what they dreamed of. Did they succeed? I don't know. I was just happy to do sports, theatre, sing in the choir—that's what was important."

At the NFB, Arcand would have very much liked to do a documentary on hockey. But the project went to Gilles Groulx, in 1964, becoming the film *Un jeu si simple*. As for *Maurice Richard*, producer Pierre Maheu's project on four mythical Quebec figures, it was taken over by Gilles Gascon in 1971, whereas Arcand agreed to do *Duplessis est encore en vie*. To this day, the filmmaker dreams of making a film on sport, and on hockey in particular.

Arcand recounts that in the spring of 1966, he neglected to renew his contract as an NFB staff member. He recalls in a 1990 speech, at the retirement of Jacques Leduc from the NFB: "I wanted him to understand that I left the NFB staff in 1966. He understood 1990. He took twenty-four years to understand that the ideal rapport between a filmmaker and the NFB was based on freelancing. It's easy enough to understand: each time imbeciles are appointed to important positions at the NFB, and unfortunately, as we know, it happens quite often, the freelancer can immediately say: 'Bye!' and go work elsewhere; the staff member is condemned to come here to the cafeteria, drink the worst coffee in the world, and waste three or four years of his life repeating to his friends, who don't need convincing, that Sidney Newman or someone else is an idiot."

The end of 1966 and the beginning of 1967 are difficult for Arcand financially but also a time of great change. He moves to Deschambault, where he will remain until the mid-eighties. To be able to live with his companion Édith de Villers, he gets married. The ceremony takes place in Montreal on November 10, 1966, at the Église Saint-François d'Assise in Longue-Pointe, a new building that replaced the older temple, demolished to make way for the Louis-Hippolyte Lafontaine tunnel. During their long stay in Arcand's native village, Édith de Villers, a university graduate, works as a high school teacher in history, visual arts and music. At a more personal level, she lends Denys Arcand her support, scrupulously respecting his work and periods of isolation, while offering hospitality to their numerous friends, filmmakers and otherwise.

Arcand explains that he settled in the village for a very simple reason—money. He was quite poor until the age of forty-five and *The Decline of the American Empire*. At the end of the sixties, people were moving to the country, "going back to the earth." It was the time of Flower Power, the Beatles and growing marijuana in your fields. He and Édith de Villers wanted this lifestyle too. Horace Arcand still had his house in Deschambault, where the family spent summers and holidays. It was available, and the couple moved in without necessarily intending to stay for long. It was a winter of doing nothing, of sleeping and taking walks . . . : "During our stay, my grandfather Henry Bouillé died, on December 1, 1967. I was with him when he died at the hospital in Quebec City. My grandmother ended up alone. She found the house at 277, chemin du Roy too big for her, and offered to sell it to me for almost nothing. I liked country life. I often embark on long intellectual projects, like reading all of Shakespeare, all the plays and sonnets. In Deschambault, having this kind of project to do all winter long, as well as cross-country skiing and playing hockey, was very pleasant. I did it for over fifteen years. Once in a while I'd come back to Montreal to make films, to work, but the country had a particular attraction for me. It allowed me to withdraw from the world."

The detail about reading Shakespeare in Deschambault over the winter of 1966–1967 is an interesting one. We already know that Arcand's films are always preceded or accompanied by intense reading. Readings in history feed his first three short films. He reads Suetonius in preparation for *Réjeanne Padovani*. During the making of *Le confort et l'indifférence* (*Comfort and Indifference*), the filmmaker goes through the works of Aristotle, Clausewitz and Tite-Live. And Machiavelli, of course. For *The Barbarian Invasions* it is Saint-Simon. Who would have imagined that *On est au coton*, which triggered one of Quebec's biggest political scandals of the early seventies, would gestate in the wake of the complete works of Shakespeare?

7
THE GUN TRILOGY

In 2001, while working on the complete edition of the films of Gilles Groulx, author of *Chat dans le sac*, Arcand remarks upon the filmmaker's love-hate relationship with the NFB, a kind of "can't live with you, can't live without you" relation. Though not identical, Arcand's rapport with the NFB is similar. Instead of mouldering away on the permanent Board staff, Arcand leaves for the private sector in 1966. However, he soon returns as a freelancer and works there until 1971 on three full-length documentary projects about Quebec and an idea for a script called *La Chine des poètes*. In 1972, he first submits his project for the dramatic feature *Gina*, but the NFB refuses it. After three dramatic features in the private sector, Arcand returns to the NFB to propose a film on Quebec tourism in Mexico and, at the end of the seventies, to make *Le confort et l'indifférence*. Moreover, it is within this organization that *The Decline of the American Empire* is first conceived in the early eighties. Arcand maintains his ties with the NFB from 1962 until the 1980s. Over twenty years. In film, that's a lifetime.

The years of 1966 and 1967 mark a turning point in Arcand's brand new career in film, years that remain a little obscure to this day. The young Arcand couple have barely settled into the deceptive torpor of Deschambault when the "the years of the furnaces" are upon them. In May of 1967 there is Expo, the world exhibition held on the islands of Montreal. In July, there is General de Gaulle's journey down the chemin du Roy, a sumptuous piece of classical theatre with its three unities of time, place and action; the General's deft crescendo and dénouement, an exultant *deus ex machina,* his "Vive le Québec . . . libre!" uttered from the "set" of the balcony of Montreal City Hall. Not long after that come the upheavals of May 1968.

"I missed that whole wonderful period of youth in rebellion, Expo 67 and May '68. I was working all the time. De Gaulle passed my house on the chemin du Roy at around ten in the morning. My wife's family, who lived in Lotbinière on the other side of the river, crossed the river to come see the general in Deschambault. That crossing is difficult because of the sandbanks. It's totally foreign to my nature to be a groupie. I asked myself: how is it that people cross the river to see the president of the French Republic go by? I wouldn't even cross the street to see him." In *Stardom* Arcand reflects on groupies of all kinds, in politics, sports and film. He thinks of going back to the subject one day. When de Gaulle cried, "Vive le Québec . . . libre," he thought it was funny, likeable, iconoclastic. The politicians in Ottawa almost swallowed their gum; Gérard Pelletier choked. For Arcand it was amusing but nothing more. As for the student movements, he liked them too. He thought the students were right to make their demands but was not convinced that the movement would change the course of history. "What changes history are social classes, and youth isn't one of them. So I let all that pass me by. I was married, I lived quietly, I was working."

People used to joke about the comings and goings of NFB filmmakers: out the main entrance, back in the side door. Arcand will soon follow suit. In 1966, as a freelancer, he finishes editing *Volleyball,* shot the previous year at the Maurice Richard Arena, and directs the short film *Parcs atlantiques/Atlantic Parks* (1967), a documentary promoting resorts in the Atlantic Provinces of Canada. For this project he creates a fairly elaborate script containing "dream images" and "ideal settings," as in sophisticated commercials. The spectator, he feels, must not be bored with "a documentary on the need to protect beavers in the ponds of Fundy." For his exploration of the Cabot Trail in Cape Breton, the beaches of Prince Edward Island and Fundy National Park, Arcand decides to use actors: a young model, a very handsome couple and a baby to achieve a "family feel," all of it cast in fantasy and far removed from "the heaviness of an ordinary travelogue." He retains a bitter memory of the film, "my shortest film, which cost the most money. A real Film Board film, meant to get everyone to go and swim around Ingonish, Nova Scotia, and places where I wouldn't send my worst enemy." In this production, it may be noted that for the first time since *Champlain* and *Ville-Marie*, the filmmaker uses a mixture of documentary and drama.

Before returning to eat his fill at the NFB as a freelancer, Arcand is obliged to earn his bread elsewhere. In December 1966, for the private company Adaptel, which produces for Radio-Canada television, he agrees on the spur of the moment to replace André Rufiange, Marc Beaudet and Marcel Dubé and write the scripts for the better part of nineteen thirty-minute episodes of the téléroman *Minute, papillon!* He works flat out until April 1967, sustained by bottles of scotch from his father's cellar, gifts from British sea captains. The official description of the téléroman is as follows: "In spite of themselves, Conrad and Léon become permanent hosts for their cousin Gérald. Rather cynical by nature, Gérald is always ready to make others work in his stead. As soon as he moves in, he starts throwing his weight around, appointing himself Conrad's adviser to the detriment of Léon. For reasons of greed or fantasy, he gets Conrad to abandon his job as a vacuum cleaner salesman to build outlandish accessories that transform the characters into meat-grinders or turntables. A series of misadventures ensue for the three cronies and their friends, Sophie and Mme Saindon." Scripts and videotapes for the series have been lost, everything but a three-page document dated January 16, 1967, entitled "Writer's Notes for the Development of the Program," in which Arcand enumerates the "numerous difficulties" he faces when he begins work on the series. However, in this document he is more optimistic about the ten or so texts he has left to write, which he says will make fun of clairvoyants, hypnotism, "fear of hospitals," politics and showbiz. There will even be a babysitting scene in which a twelve-year-old girl reviews her lessons, an opportunity, as Arcand puts it, "to demystify historical reality and teach the child the real facts of history." It is all held together by the concept of "a naive and inexperienced character who is advised by a cynical and disillusioned character." In short, Arcand hopes to enrich the series "at the level of fantasy and freedom of thought."

Minute, papillon! may be one of the worst bread-and-butter jobs Arcand has ever done, but he manages to slip in a few details that are meaningful for him and that he will use one day in other scripts. Though as he remarks to Michel Coulombe, he considers the result "catastrophic" and finds the program "dreadful," Arcand shows great consistency in his work.

In July 1967, Arcand plays the lead in Jacques Leduc's film, *Nominingue . . . depuis qu'il existe.* A cross between documentary and drama, the film tells the story of two young Montrealers—Paul, an academic, and his girlfriend Isabelle—who are visiting a holiday resort. Their summer love evolves over scenes in which local elders tell stories and village legends. "I agreed to act," explains Arcand, "because I desperately needed money."

Far from playing a small role as he does in other films, in *Nominingue* he is the main protagonist. Moreover, he literally invents his character through controlled improvisation, a sort of "live" screenwriting, reminiscent of *Seul ou avec d'autres*, from which several revealing Arcand themes emerge. First of all, solitude and village roots: the city and the telephone are presented as sources of stupid and futile distraction. The young man attempts to conserve the family patrimony by protecting the general store. The idea is echoed in the words of a song: "The past lives in you, oh, my dear house." Next, Arcand develops the theme of forgetting with a letter from a man in Tunisia, and the theme of suicide with the story of a rich exile in the States who kills himself. History is introduced through the anecdote about the bell of Saint-Eustache, broken by a British cannonball during the *Patriotes'* rebellion in 1838 and then given to the parishioners of Nominingue. Finally, love is presented as an ephemeral entity, seen through the prism of a holiday affair. The young man writes the word "love" in the sand and then erases it in the presence of the girlfriend he is about to leave, who is played by Françoise Sullivan. "Between takes," recalls Arcand, "I talked to her with great interest. In 1948, she had been one of the people to sign the *Refus global* manifesto of Borduas."

Arcand could not stay for the whole screening of *Nominingue.* As usual, he says, he found it difficult to see himself on screen. Today, having agreed to watch the whole film attentively, he states that its themes express the personality of the director and not that of the lead actor. Arcand and Leduc had certain points in common, for example, the fact of living in a village rather than a city. The two filmmakers lived in little hamlets in the days when "the hippie movement was going back to the earth to watch the sunflowers grow and cultivate cannabis." Otherwise, all the themes of *Nominingue* are Leduc's and cannot be considered as belonging to Arcand himself, who moreover says he hardly recognizes himself in the role he played. "Unlike Leduc, I've never been much of a bell-of-Saint-Eustache type."

Jacques Leduc spent all the summers of his adolescence in Nominingue. He envisaged a film both cruel and tender about the holiday community of the place and his own emotions at that time. His script is largely inspired by personal memories of those formative years, which he spent in a paradoxical zone between the transitory reality of summer and the old village with its long-time inhabitants. The name Nominingue comes from an Indian word for red earth, or iron earth, "in the place where the Laurentians are almost no longer the Laurentians." Leduc concludes, "Choosing Denys Arcand for this film gave me the chance to work with a very articulate being with great analytical ability. I asked Denys and Françoise Sullivan to improvise their scenes and dialogue. Sometimes we had magnificent conversations after shooting, about astronomy, for example, beneath a beautiful northern night sky."

Years later, Arcand will ask Jacques Leduc, as director of photography, to shoot the nature scenes for *The Decline of the American Empire* and the great nocturnal urban landscapes for *Jesus of Montreal*.

In 1967, the federal government founds the Canadian Film Development Corporation (CFDC), a step ahead of Quebec whose *Cinema Act* will not appear until 1975. Henceforth, funding for "private sector" Quebec cinema will primarily come from the federal government, on top of the contribution from the NFB, which for several years has fostered the development of a Quebec *cinéma d'auteur*. At the end of 1967 Arcand submits two rather contradictory works: in November, a project for a full-length documentary called *Les informateurs*, and a research project entitled *Film Program for the National Arts Centre of Canada*. Commissioned by producer Clément Perron, the study gives Arcand the chance to research new technologies developed in the wake of Expo 67, by the Scopitone firm in particular. He will also visit the Library and Museum of the Performing Arts at New York's Lincoln Center and examine the plans for the future National Arts Centre in Ottawa—yet another job he does for money, far removed from *Les informateurs*, the future *On est au coton*, which will have such an important impact on his filmmaking career.

A striking contrast. On the one hand, "steak jobs," television comedy, pretty films to promote tourism and a serious report on audio-visual infrastructure. On the other hand, a cavalry charge of punch-out films with machine-gun camera work. The May '68 effect. In Quebec, there is a strong wind that is "blowing wherever it wants to." The FLQ has been around for years, the first bombs exploded in Montreal in 1963, the year in which *Parti pris* was created and writer Jacques Ferron founded the *Parti rhinocéros*, an Ubu-esque caricature of a Canadian political party. Ferron states on this occasion: "Between masquerade and violence there is only one step. We are completely in line with the FLQ. Only the weapons differ."

At about the same time, works considered fundamental to the Quiet Revolution are published: *La vie agonique (The Agonised Life: Poems and Prose)* by Gaston Miron and *La fatigue culturelle du Canada français (The Cultural Fatigue of French Canada)* by Hubert Aquin. The year 1968 sees the publication of *Nègres blancs d'Amérique (White Niggers of America)* by Pierre Vallières, who goes to New York with Charles Gagnon to picket for Quebec's liberation in front of the UN. Both men are arrested as FLQ members and put in Parthenais prison in Montreal. There is the *L'osstidcho* concert on May 28, 1968 (with Robert Charlebois, Louise Forestier, Mouffe and Yvon Deschamps), and a week of political film at the Verdi, where Godard and many others showed up. And it does not stop in 1968. In 1969, there are Montreal police strikes, described by criminologist Suzanne Arcand in her article "De la bureaucratisation policière" as "wildcat strikes" marked by "police illegality." There is a violent strike by the typesetters of *La Presse*, illustrated in the film *24 heures ou plus* by Gilles Groulx. It is "the hour of the furnaces," to borrow the title of the long revolutionary film by the Argentinean Solanas *(La hora de los hornos)*, which is widely circulated in Quebec at this time. On October 8, 1970, the famous FLQ *Manifesto* is read on Radio-Canada television. Several days later, on October 16, 1970, after the FLQ kidnappings of British diplomat James Richard Cross and the Liberal minister Pierre Laporte, the federal government declares the *War Measures Act.*

Pierre Perrault, in his essay "L'art and l'état," praises the October manifesto in a nationalist-populist incantation reminiscent of the storming of the Bastille: "Every people needs heroes. Men who act, who refuse to be confined. We must remember the great joy of *October.* [. . .] The *felquistes* [FLQ members] stole the word as in other times fire was stolen [. . .] having the word, they had the power. [. . .] My people feared the consequences and feared death. [. . .] They are not politicized. [. . .] So the creative minds of Quebec are taking over. A people cannot stand on its feet without these examples of bloody courage." *La nuit de la poésie* in March 1970 at the Gesù had reflected the same spirit; Gérald Godin performed his provocative poem "Énumération," Michèle Lalonde her poem "Speak White." In January 1971 comes a second edition of *Chants et poèmes de la résistance.* The same year, Pierre Falardeau makes his first film, *Continuons le* combat, with Vidéographe. It marks the beginning of a nationalist and populist œuvre whose political ideology, described by politicologist Jean-Guy Prévost as "chauvinistic *sans-culottisme,*" follows in the lineage of *Le père Duchesne* (a radical newspaper that came out of the French Revolution), as do the FLQ *Manifesto* and the speeches of trade-unionist Michel Chartrand, in Prévost's view.

It is the time of the great Arcand scandals at the NFB. Gérald Godin is behind the scenes, along with Pauline Julien and Édith de Villers. Arcand is constructing his documentary trilogy, *A Portrait of Quebec Today.* Pierre Maheu becomes a producer at the NFB. The first two films he produces, Jacques Leduc's *Cap d'espoir* and Arcand's *On est au coton* (co-produced by Guy-L. Côté and Marc Beaudet), will be guillotined by political censorship, the first incident of its kind in the history of the NFB since its founding in 1939. Shortly after, the NFB will also come down on *24 heures ou plus* by Gilles Groulx and *L'Acadie, l'Acadie* by Michel Brault and Pierre Perrault. As for Arcand, his dreamed-of trilogy will be reduced to a shadow of itself: *Coton* is censored, *Duplessis est encore en vie* amputated, *Les terroristes* refused. This triptych and the polemics that surround it are complex; considerable time and effort would be required to untangle all the threads.

To begin with, let us talk about *On est au coton* (the title is a popular expression meaning "we're fed up!" that also refers to textiles with its use of the word "*coton*"). The film evolves out of *Les informateurs*. When starting it in 1967, Denys Arcand has no idea that it will make him a name by provoking the greatest politico-cultural scandal of the Quiet Revolution. The first film to be censored in the history of the NFB, it becomes a *cause célèbre*, a kind of *Macbeth* in the filmmaker's budding career. It is also his longest production, including three projects and two different cuts over the period of 1967–1971. Once censored, the film goes to hell for five years. The NFB does not lift its ban until 1976, after Arcand has gotten even with the federal organization in *Gina*. Almost ten years of love's labours lost. The story of this five-act tragedy deserves to be told in detail.

Act I

Arcand submits his project in November 1967. His first report comes out the following March, a real MA thesis as Arcand describes it, about state technocracy in Quebec and "the technocrats who are the informers of power." The report is the product of several months' research conducted during the winter of 1967–1968. It is a twenty-five-page document that includes a bibliography of about fifteen works, such as publications by Jacques Billy *(Les techniciens et le pouvoir)*, J.K. Galbraith and James Burham, particularly his essays "The Managerial Revolution" and "The Machiavellians." Moreover, Arcand conducts nearly twenty-five in-depth interviews with personalities from Radio-Canada (including Gérald Godin) and International Business Machines (IBM), the societies of applied mathematics from the Université Laval and the Université de Montréal, and technocrats from eight Quebec government ministries, for example, Jacques Girard, an "old boy" from Collège Sainte-Marie, and Bernard Landry.

The study primarily describes how these new technocrats propose to conduct their government careers. "They have a notion of professionalism that is new in Quebec" and they have "freely agreed to make their careers in Quebec." The characteristics of the group: all have advanced university degrees and decent salaries, are in favour of the depoliticization of the public service, are interested in their work, possess the dynamism of a small organization, and are increasingly willing to work for the interests of Quebec and the greater awareness of its society. This group is intended to preside over the emergence of "professional 'government men,' men with inside experience of high-level governmental activity and who are automatically destined for a ministry."

Based on his initial research, Arcand became convinced that "a film about technocratic reality had to be made," that it was necessary to return to the main premises of "inhumanity in the world and its outcomes." This approach requires "considerable intellectual work," more than what is required to describe "emotional explosions" about the Vietnam War or underdevelopment; it means forgetting about films on the Pentagon, the World Bank or the International Monetary Fund. The planned film is to be made with limited equipment and a small crew, in 16 mm and in black and white. Arcand concludes with a smile à la Buñuel: "Like all great films, this one will be made on an absurdly low budget."

Act II

A second report, in June 1968, states that the basic hypothesis was false and "grossly incomplete." Technocracy is not an independent and isolated phenomenon: "It now seems that we cannot avoid adding to the reflection on technocracy a reflection upon our entire political system." Thus, "the reality of the people" must be observed, and the documentary focused "on the total dichotomy between the traditional political world of the worker and the power of economic trends, a dichotomy which directly leads to alienation, which recently formed citizens' committees are combatting." The result is a new structure for the film: "An industry closes its doors. Trade unions, municipalities, citizens' committees vigorously protest. To the point where the Minister of Industry has to act. He asks his deputy minister to conduct a study of the situation. [. . .] A confidential report is drawn up; it naturally questions the entire politics of industry in Quebec, goes on at length about the policies of manpower and education. [. . .] Tensions arise between technocrats and the government, begin to infiltrate the public via the media. The government compels the technocrats to keep quiet. Then it is the media's turn to fall silent. The problem of the closing of the industry in question remains." In concluding his report, Arcand asks the NFB to assign him Gérald Godin as co-writer.

Act III

After a new stage of research that goes from August to October 1968, Arcand indicates in a project of October 18, 1968, that his new focal point is the Quebec textile industry, "which has been failing since about 1950, and whose decline will accelerate in the next five years to the point where it is possible the entire industry will disappear within ten years." He wants to film the closing of a factory in this sector, which is the second biggest employer in Quebec, as well as the commission of inquiry that is studying the phenomenon. He also wants the roles of minister and deputy minister to be played by actors. Shooting for "this film that is documentary in basis and experimental in form," could be completed in April or May of 1969. The documentary project evolved over one year, becoming *On est au coton*, an essay on the decay of an industry and the resignation of the rejected workers. A very Quebec tragedy. The film is shot between September 1968 and February 1970.

The project had undergone radical changes. In his interview for the *Cahiers du Conseil québécois pour la diffusion du cinema*, Arcand emphasized that with the new subject of *Coton* "we're a long way from technocracy." "A long way" because meanwhile he has shot *Québec: Duplessis et après . . .* and *La maudite galette*, and also because he has completely changed his first project on technocrats to focus instead on textile workers. Why this about-face? The explosive circumstances, of course, both at the international level and that of Canada and Quebec. For example, on June 24, 1968, the new Liberal prime minister, Pierre Elliott Trudeau, has to leave the traditional Saint-Jean-Baptiste parade in Montreal because of a riot; consequently, the yearly parade of the little French-Canadian sheep will be cancelled for years to come. There is also the influence of Gérald Godin, invited by Arcand to help research and write the film after the former journalist loses his job at Radio-Canada for expressing opposition to Trudeau's ideas on language. "Very early," writes Godin, "the film started to become the portrait of a social class: the workers." And that is not to mention the combativeness of the entire NFB French Team. In 1969, Fernand Dansereau, president of the NFB's Social Research Group, which included Michel Régnier, Maurice Bulbulian and Robert Forget, notes that the collective intends to enlist part-time collaborators, including Denys Arcand. His film on the textile industry is a production-in-progress "which looks as if it will be easily integrated in the program." The collective shares his preoccupation with mass communications and the necessity of "giving a voice, through cinema, to all those who live on the fringes of society," of "contesting authority in all its forms."

And then there is Édith de Villers. Arcand specifies: "She shared twenty-two years of my life. I talked to her about all my films, I told her the stories of all my scripts, she saw all my shoots, the different cuts of my films, she gave her opinion." Édith de Villers was born in Montreal, and comes from a large family. Her parents were from Lotbinière, a South Shore village across from Deschambault. Édith is left-wing and an active union member in the teaching milieu, her middle-class family comprising teachers, technicians and specialized workers. Arcand liked this family environment, he who came from a family of village notables. It allowed him more intimate contact with workers.

Act IV

Still in 1970, Arcand agrees to make a first essential change in his film: to re-do his first cut, removing all the footage of Edward F. King, director of Dominion Textile, who no longer wanted to appear in a film praising class struggle. Despite this guillotine, the first *On est au coton* still exists, in a double-band copy (image on one side of the film, sound on the other), a work copy removed from a Steenbeck editing table. A certain mystery surrounds the existence of this copy, which apparently was carried off one night and hidden somewhere away from the NFB. The four reels have wandered from basement to storage vault and legend has it that Gérald Godin or producer Marc Beaudet was responsible for this historical legacy.

The copy was first screened for the public in 1994, during an evening organized by the André-Guérin foundation, a nonprofit organization opposing censorship. The original version is very enlightening. We see the dynamic Arcand created with his cross-cuts between King and the textile workers, a dialectical form that is lost in the second version. This dynamic is clearly illustrated in a document by researcher François Gagnon entitled "Scene Breakdown of the Original *On est au coton.*" In the original, Edward F. King is presented in two types of scenes, interviews and documentary sequences. During the interviews, King is sitting at his desk and filmed face on as he answers Gérald

Godin's questions. There are a total of seventeen interview scenes. In the documentary scenes, King is at work, filmed from a certain distance and from the side. Except in one instance, King is in his office. There are a total of seven scenes of this kind. In the film's official version, Denys Arcand replaced these twenty-four sequences of King with two black title cards, the first one thirty-six minutes from the beginning of the projection, the second one at fifty-two minutes. The cards may lead one to believe that the cuts were only made at these two places, but examination of the initial structure reveals a whole other story.

The scenes with Edward F. King appear in parallel montage with shots of the workers' confusion at the closing of the factory and the explanations they are given. The workers' tasks are shown in parallel with those of the president, King, the president's biography with those of workers Bertrand Saint-Onge and Carmen Bertrand. For example, an opening scene shows a round table of Penman's employees. A worker says: "We asked him a question. Why's it doing that, closing? We got no answer." King appears in the next shot and gives his explanation: *It's closing principally because the volume of business was getting in the lower end of the underwear business and is not sufficient to keep that plant, Saint-Hyacinthe and the Paris, Ontario, plant going. We had to make a contraction somewhere. That's one reason. The other reason is that if we did have enough business—which we haven't got—we will have to spend a lot of money on that plant B and the power plant is finished. We have spent, I think, something like 90 thousand dollars. Well, you know, the whole building is not worth that kind of money.*

In the final shot in the sequence, a forty-six-year-old worker and mother of five says: "A few times we heard it was going to close, but I don't know, we took it for a routine . . ." In an interview, the same worker says: "It's okay for a woman who has nothing but herself to think about. Forty bucks a week for life. But the other one who's got six around the table, they can't get by." Cut back to King: *"We've discussed it very, very frankly with the union people and they see it. There is no argument with the thing. We've got to go, we've got to go, so . . . so that's the Coaticook . . . thing."* Last shot: an employees' roundtable. A woman worker says: "Even if we pressured them, there'd be rumours that it wouldn't close, but it's closing, it's been decided."

Arcand agrees that the dynamic of the first version is lost in the second. "My secret hope, now that Mr. King is dead, is to take the original copy from its secret vault, for which no one but ourselves have the key, and have a friend reconstitute *On est au coton* to the way I conceived it in the beginning. It would be far better than the copy that's now in circulation."

For the entire year of 1970, the NFB is under considerable pressure about the film, as Luc Perreault writes in *La Presse* on July 17, 1971. The members of the Canadian Textiles Institute are invited to a screening so they can make a report to their board. Certain company administrators decide to take *"every possible legal means"* to prevent the film's release. King demands the removal of the scenes in which he appears; later, after the second cuts, W.M. Berry, president of the Textiles Institute "even sends the NFB document in which he accuses Godin of being a card-carrying Marxist. Then the new Liberal government in Quebec starts to worry about Robert Bourassa's role in the film." Finally there comes a series of resignations at the NFB. Jacques Godbout, Hugo McPherson and Gérard Bertrand leave their jobs as head of French production, commissioner and assistant commissioner respectively. And that is nothing compared to what happens next in the scandal.

Act V

Coup de théâtre in 1971. In the wake of the October Crisis of 1970, when Quebec minister Pierre Laporte is assassinated, NFB commissioner Sydney Newman prohibits the distribution of *On est au coton*. This unprecedented event makes the front page of *Québec-Presse*: "The NFB," says Newman, "is an organization dedicated to the defence of capitalism and Canadian unity." Now it is Arcand's second version of the film that is censored. *On est au coton* has become forbidden fruit that many are eager to taste. The new cut is circulated in secret, largely thanks to light video technology, new at the time. The pirated copies in VHS are passed around under increasingly esoteric and vague titles: *Vidéo Drummondville, The John A. Macdonald Story, Les fleurs de mai.* Finally on January 8, 1972, the NFB publishes a warning in the newspapers: "All persons or organizations who reproduce without authorization cinematographic documents that are property of the National Film Board of Canada may be prosecuted. The same applies to whomsoever may collaborate with these persons or organizations in order to program the said documents. These persons or organizations are hereby requested to return to the National Film Board of Canada all copies of films that have been illegally obtained and held in this manner."

The warning is issued to no avail. Citizens' committees, leftist or Marxist-Leninist cells, trade unions, film students and teachers, everyone watches, analyses and discusses *Coton*. It is the first great paradox in the director's career; *Coton* becomes very well known for a film that officially does not exist. Even in Paris, in *Écran 72*, Guy Hennebelle writes that Arcand's first feature has been "locked away by the National Film Board of Canada for reasons of Marxism and treason against employers. [. . .] In my opinion, *On est au coton* is the equivalent of *La hora de los hornos (The Hour of the Furnaces)* for Argentina. [. . .] Denys Arcand is to be praised for depicting Quebec's political problems in terms of class struggle. In this sense, he differs from the likes of Perrault, who at times gets lost in the muddle of an insufficiently controlled direct cinema and the discreet charms of a quasi-metaphysical nostalgia."

The NFB will not return the film to official circulation until 1976. In late 2004, the NFB launched Arcand's documentaries in a boxed set of DVDs that include the original version of *On est au cotton*.

End of the five-act tragedy of *On est au coton*.

In 1969, while this saga is going on, Arcand agrees to sign a petition opposing the presentation of Claude Fournier's documentary *Le dossier Nelligan*. He does so at the urging of Gérald Godin and signs it, eyes closed. When the petition is published in *La Presse* and *Le Devoir*, Arcand is horrified by the tone of the letter, which borders on personal attack. He takes the time to write to the newspapers to retract his name from the petition. Indeed, the document describes Claude Fournier as "a gossip, a filmmaker without morals and without ethics [. . .] a depraved person who cannot be excused"; as for the film, it is called "a sinister and superficial enterprise, bearing the mark of the filmmaker's contempt for his subject." Two professional associations, the directors and producers of Quebec, take a stand against the petition-signers and observe that the five filmmaker signatories constitute a minority.

Arcand has not seen the end of his troubles. We might say he knows it ahead of time, being headstrong, with an innate intellectual tendency for anarchy and iconoclastic thinking. In the beginning of the new decade at the NFB Arcand's plans are overturned: the project for *Terroristes*, the last part of his documentary trilogy, presented in June 1970 is refused; *Coton* is re-edited and censored; there are difficulties with *Duplessis est encore en vie*, shot between April 6 and October 15 . Of these three projects, only *Duplessis* will be released, on the eve of Quebec's national holiday in 1972 just after *La maudite galette* is invited to Critics' Week in Cannes.

The idea for *Duplessis* comes from Pierre Maheu, who had conceived a series of four films on "great French-Canadian men." He described his project as follows: "French Canada, now defunct, was a very picturesque country. I believe we are all mature enough to acknowledge it and undertake a folko-analytical cure, take a look at what we once were in light of a quest that is at once lucid and heavily emotional. There is a special way of doing this that helps us relive the past, focuses our attention and liberates emotion all at the same time. That way is film." This end can be achieved by "choosing exemplary cases and illustrating them in a nondidactic way." Duplessis the politician, Brother André the founder of Saint-Joseph's Oratory, Maurice "the Rocket" Richard, country-western singer Willie Lamothe. Politics, religion, hockey, country music and to finish, a surprise: "These four Greats are like the three Musketeers: there are five of them. The fifth is to poetry what Duplessis is to autonomy. He is, in unhappiness, what the Rocket is in speed and brilliance. He is, in doubt, what Brother André is in faith. He is the Willie Lamothe of intellectuals. He is Saint-Denys Garneau. With this last subject, we can be sure the leftist intellectuals will no longer want to laugh. Caught with their pants down, Gitane or no Gitane, the little dears. It will be a very good film." This fifth "Great" does not exist at the NFB whereas the other ones do.

On March 15, 1970, Arcand submits his project on Duplessis, "a logical follow-up to *On est au coton*, which indeed, ends with the bitter affirmation of Quebec's political vacuum. That is the starting point for *Duplessis* [. . .], which is, above all, a documentary on Quebec political consciousness." The film will describe the next Quebec Provincial election in three counties: "It looks as if it might really be an election *à la Duplessis*. Election day is a Wednesday, as in the great Duplessis tradition, in honour of St. Joseph and also for superstitious reasons." A basic structure over which "the shadow of Duplessis-the-myth will hover, then a reflection upon the myth. The only Canadian politician capable of understanding Duplessis is Pierre Elliott Trudeau, who is part of our political star-system, Duplessis's twin brother." Arcand once again ends his text with a Buñuelian smile: "Because I'm a serious filmmaker, I talk seriously about the structure of my film. I'm keeping a few ideas in reserve, a few goodies, for example, the idea of having schoolchildren recite *The Voters' Catechism*, published by Duplessis in 1936."

In 1971, he clarifies his concept of history for this film. "My working hypothesis was that what we called the 'Quiet Revolution' of the sixties was in fact a creation of the mind and a relatively secondary phenomenon in our society. I never noticed any particular historical discontinuity between 1935, 1955 and 1970." But Arcand's *Duplessis* will not be approved without complications. Management even threatens not to distribute the film unless its director agrees to make cuts and changes. Arcand decides to comply rather than lose his film. Several days before the première, Arcand provides his own description of his documentary essay, a text published in *Québec-Presse* on June 18, 1972 (included in the "Selected Readings" in this book). Some find its conclusion disconcerting, especially Quebec nationalists who at this time have the wind in their sails. "The film suggests that without a profound modification of economic and cultural structures, the appearance and disappearance of various political parties, as well as the rise or fall of charismatic political 'personalities' (Kennedy, de Gaulle) are merely superficial phenomena that can play only a secondary role in the historical evolution of a people, be it the Quebec people or another."

On the day of the launch, Arcand tells Luc Perreault of *La Presse* about the "variations" he was obliged to accept: "Three cases of censorship. I learned from my producer that we couldn't keep the title. He came to me with *Québec: Duplessis et après. . . .* Then a little allusion to Pierre Laporte was taken out. . . . At that time, the memory of Laporte was still fresh. But the biggest cut was the film's opening with Rémi Paul. From a cinematographic more than a political point of view, I find the current first half-hour lamentable. We don't know where we're going, whereas the film originally began with the speech of Rémi Paul. Next we saw him on stage, putting his hand in his pocket and taking out an enormous wad of bills that he separated into three piles and gave to three of his organizers sitting next to him. The orator finished his speech, and Rémi Paul went up to the mike and discovered the little mike we'd attached to theirs. For five hours we'd been looking for ways to avoid being noticed. We were hiding in the corridor and could see the room through a little window. When he noticed the little mike, we saw Rémi Paul remove it and show it to the audience, asking who it belonged to. After a moment's confusion, he threw it on the ground and started jumping on it with both feet. We could hear the crackling of the mike as it died. Then some kind of farmer in suspenders started demolishing the little mike with the pedestal of the big microphone. After that, we didn't hear anything. The man threw what was left of the little mike backstage. Then the cameraman moved his camera to film the electric clapperboard used for synchronization, and we finished with the sound engineer hiding at the end of the corridor. The film began in darkness, where we saw the title appear: *Duplessis est encore en vie (Duplessis still lives)*. It was wonderful!"

As promised, this *Duplessis* contained a few cinematographic "goodies," a few embellishments, including schoolchildren with their beautiful teacher, Gisèle Trépanier, reciting excerpts from the *Voters' Catechism*. We also hear fragments of the Durham Report, written in 1839, read in voice-over by filmmaker Robin Spry. And finally, as a personal touch, the filmmaker has us listen to the religious songs of his childhood, sung by the Deschambault choir.

Les terroristes, the last film in the full-length documentary trilogy, is stillborn. It is presented as a "cinematographic study of Quebec terrorism, explaining why terrorism is rejected as compared with more social forms of protest—animation, militant trade unions, organization." The project summary concludes: "Because terrorism is the expression of a minority group that considers itself as such, it appears to be a dead end street. However, our hypothesis is that terrorism will exist in North America for many years to come. The reason is that here, there is no blueprint for anyone who wishes to work towards transforming an advanced industrial society."

Arcand saw the interest of making a film on *felquisme*, an important factor in Quebec society at this time. The filmmaker knew some of the FLQ militants at the Université de Montréal or through *Parti pris*. He had filmed a few of them on their release from prison in *On est au coton.* He had also exchanged letters with Pierre-Paul Geoffroy, who planted the bomb at the Stock Exchange ("interesting, from a symbolic point of view") and was handed 124 life sentences, the heaviest sentence in the entire history of the British Empire. "Geoffroy was very intelligent and very articulate. There was a film to be made on all that, but I never made it." The project has remained unknown until now, and needs to be taken out of limbo in the NFB archives and presented. The text in its entirety is included in the "Selected Readings."

At the time that Denys Arcand proposes his project for *Terroristes,* the programming committee of the NFB is being bombarded with other projects on the same subject. In July 1970 Hubert Aquin, as researcher, presents his *Histoire de l'anarchie,* to be directed by Jacques Godbout. The project features two young Montrealers who "establish a dialogue with students who are deeply involved in the protest movement or who are simply clear-sighted. Hence the film would be anchored in contemporary society, on one hand, and on the other offer a broad and searching perspective on the past: the days of February 1848, the Commune of 1870, the blossoming of Marxism all over Europe, wars in Russia and Spain, as well as the wave of student protests in 1968." On July 13, 1970, the filmmaker Louis Portugais presented his project *Sur la violence* to the NFB's Challenge for Change program. In this project he views violence as "one of the most basic elements of social change." Violence is a phenomenon that is becoming more and more widespread, with the Black Panthers, May of '68, the FLQ, student demonstrations, exemplary suicides and random murders. According to Portugais, the romanticism of action is such that protesters "have ceased to be reformers and become revolutionaries," seeking less to change the system than to replace it. The film will refer to the theories of Jean-Paul Sartre and Marcuse, examine the parameters of the French Revolution and others that can be perceived in neocapitalist societies or the experience of Cuba.

This project, like Arcand's, and that of Aquin and Godbout, does not get beyond the Programming Committee of the NFB or commissioner Sydney Newman. To close the file of stillborn projects dealing with the anarcho-terrorism of the 1970s, it may be of interest to quote the following note, written by Jacques Godbout. Replying to suggestions that *Descendre dans la rue* would "overlap with a project by Louis

Portugais and another by Denys Arcand," Godbout writes: "there is no relation." One might ask: was Godbout really sure of that?

The year of 1971 also yields two other projects by Arcand, which are now completely forgotten. The first one has to do with a collective work on utopias created by Jacques Leduc, Marcel Carrière and himself. "*Utopia*," Arcand recalls, "was a short-lived project. In cinema, the most charming, the most extraordinary utopia is the spectacle of destruction, as in Laurel and Hardy: the demolition of cars or Christmas trees, battles, cream-pie cataclysms. I would have liked to make a film in a spirit of innocence-in-destruction, silent-film style. Cinema creates a space for this kind of dreaming. I'd like to do it one day, if I live long enough." Meanwhile, the NFB is making a colossal effort to develop projects for films on China. Arcand submits an idea called *La Chine des poètes*. He starts with the statement that Canadians, and especially Quebecers, know nothing about China. Whence comes the idea of "trying to present the people of China. [. . .] In order to do this, the Chinese people must be shown from a point of view and group of references that are familiar to people here. It seems to me that popular Chinese poetry is particularly accessible; its simplicity, sincerity and almost naive charm cannot fail to touch my compatriots. [. . .] The greater part of our own poetry is attached to winter, the forest and the need to overcome the climate, snow, winds and tides. [. . .] In China, it seems that nature itself is perceived as a revolutionary force: the East wind, the spring of four seasons, the seas of wheat, the moon on the lake of the West, the importance of the Chinese rivers." This project will come to nothing, like the one on Utopias.

When Arcand participates in his first monograph in the Quebec filmmakers' series (*Cinéastes du Québec*), he goes into detail about the setbacks he experienced at the NFB while working on his great documentary trilogy, though he adds that it has not dampened his interest in doing fiction. During this interview Arcand, "fed up," expresses himself with great and almost frightening clarity: "I feel more and more sympathetic to bandits, petty criminals and all marginal characters. . . . A far cry from technocracy! I have no more ideas about anything, just nightmare images. [. . .] I'm not yet spiritual enough to become Zen and go weave baskets in Majorca, but that day will come. Already I'm growing a garden. I have an orchard. The objective conditions of film production oblige me to make *Calibre 45* or nothing, other than commercial films or sponsored films. [. . .] I've been studying the decadence and fall of the Roman Empire. It's a historical period which reminds me of our own. Have you ever thought of the fate of the people under Caligula? I see a striking resemblance with our current situation. [. . .] Soon I'd like to make a film in the style of Suetonius about the unspeakable corruption, the stupidity and depravity of the people in power [. . .] I'm a filmmaker by trade: 'Have Gun, Will Travel . . . .'"

Arcand's full-length documentaries were described as militant and propagandistic, especially *On est au coton.* This has led to great misunderstandings about his early career. For in fact, the filmmaker has always insisted on calling these works films of observation, personal films. "The documentary is not a combat weapon," he says in 1972. The following year he tells Robert Lévesque: "My films are not mobilizing. They are despairing." And then in 1974, in *This Magazine:* "What we were doing was not a film [*On est au coton*] about revolt, but a film about resignation."

While finishing *Duplessis est encore en vie,* Arcand puts his cards on the table. In interviews for the *Cahiers du Conseil québécois pour la diffusion du cinéma,* naturally he is talking "from inside Marxism" but wishes to assert, loudly and clearly, that his films are observations of the Quebec people's resignation with regard to industrial capitalism and national politics. Again in *This Magazine,* he describes himself as "a politically conscious person," "vaguely leftist" but not militant. His "filmic portraits of Quebec today" express his personal views, influenced by the historian Maurice Séguin, for example, the idea that it is impossible for Quebec to emerge from its age-old torpor. Seen from this point of view, *On est au coton* is a tragedy, not a revolutionary film; *Québec: Duplessis et après . . .* shows the persistent and all-pervasive influence of Duplessism up until the Quiet Revolution. To his mind, the Quiet Revolution is "overestimated," the only deep transformation in Quebec society being the disappearance of religion in the mid-sixties, a phenomenon that remains unexplained to this day.

In this context, the only radical and violent reaction that could arise in Quebec is not a revolution, but a chain of terrorist actions, extremist and isolated, initiated by exasperated subgroups. These include *felquisme* and the criminal activities of small-town gangs, illustrated in *La maudite galette* and the first version of *Gina*, but also the metaphorical and cultural *felquisme* of poets, chansonniers and filmmakers. Since his early days in film, Arcand has kept his distance from political militancy. What's most important, he tells *The Gazette* in 1972, is not political action in itself, "but the fact that people will look more at what they're doing themselves." He will be relentlessly reproached for political "de-commitment" after *Réjeanne Padovani*. In spite of his acute political awareness, he has never signed up for any cause, party or movement. In 2000 he will explain to Richard Martineau on the program *Les francs-tireurs* that there are no contradictions in his filmmaking and that he has always wanted to do films on unsolvable problems, not on solutions. Years before, in *Cinéma 73* he had asserted: "Film is a craft, not an individual mission."

8
GINA OR THE DEATH OF QUEBEC CINEMA

A rcand's trilogy of full-length documentaries will be a partial failure at the NFB. His first triptych of dramas will succeed, though not without obstacles and contradictions, despite the success of *La maudite galette* and *Réjeanne Padovani*. *Gina*, which closes the cycle in the mid-seventies, also appears to be a failure. Arcand will have a hard time getting on his feet again. Using the devices of fiction, *Gina* tells the story of the filmmaker's "red years" at the NFB but more than that, marks the point at which he moves from enlightened documentary to commercial drama.

Arcand's first three features were said to be produced in private industry *after* the documentaries. This has been taken for gospel truth for over thirty years, but it is not accurate. From 1969, while doing *On est au coton*, Arcand is working on a dramatic project based on the chasse-galerie legend. Later, while he is presenting his idea for *Les terroristes* to the NFB and shooting *Québec: Duplessis et après . . .* , Arcand is also supervising the script for *La maudite galette* (*The Damned Dough*), written by Jacques Benoit and produced by Cinak. In 1971, when *Coton* is banned, the filmmaker is already working on an idea that will become *Réjeanne Padovani*. In 1972, when *Galette* and *Duplessis* are released by the NFB, Arcand presents his idea for *Gina*. In other words, the filmmaker works on his full-length documentaries and his first dramas *at the same time*; they overlap in a sort of intensive, sustained blitz.

Like his arrival at the NFB, Arcand's entry into dramatic film is to some degree the result of accident. Even before he finishes *On est au coton* and starts working on *Duplessis* at the NFB, Jean Dansereau from Cinéastes associés and Jean Pierre Lefebvre from Cinak invite him to do a dramatic feature. Another "premeditated fluke." Arcand already had experience with fiction, having worked as a screenwriter on *Seul ou avec d'autres* in 1961 with Stéphane Venne, on *Jusqu'au cou* for Denis Héroux in 1963, and even more significantly, on *Entre la mer et l'eau douce* (*Drifting Upstream*) for Michel Brault the year after. And this is not to mention the dramatic segments he wrote for his short documentaries, his improvisational acting in Jacques Leduc's *Nominingue*, and his own use of actors in documentaries. As his work with Cinéastes associés suggests, Arcand was attracted by the relative independence of private film production, which would be instrumental in developing the feature-length drama. As of 1966, he chooses to work with the NFB on a freelance basis.

Even before he starts working with Jean Pierre Lefebvre and Cinak, Arcand approaches the novelist Jacques Benoit, whom he knows from Ernest Gagnon's creative writing course at the Université de Montréal. Benoit has already published a novel, *Jos Carbone*, which has done well, and he is interested in writing for film. In *Séquences*, and then in *La Presse*, Benoit describes how Arcand first asked him to write something based on the chasse-galerie legend for Cinéastes associés. Moreover, in February 1969 it is announced in *Photo Journal* that Arcand will be doing a film on the subject. But Benoit specifies that Arcand was dissatisfied with the script and rejected it. The novelist says, "I wrote a modern adaptation of the chasse-galerie. A crazy story that would have made a good surrealist film. But it was quite poorly constructed. Denys Arcand wasn't at all satisfied and I don't blame him. So then I talked to him about the idea for *La maudite galette*, and he was interested." It would appear that nothing remains of either the research or the script for *La chasse-galerie*.

Early in his career, Arcand developed an intellectual and theoretical framework for his dramas. The instant success of *La maudite galette* and *Réjeanne Padovani* led to invitations to Cannes and a warm reception in France, Quebec, English Canada and New York, bringing

Arcand numerous opportunities to air his views on drama and the connection between drama and documentary.

In general, Arcand describes film drama as a way of "organizing a coherent discourse that takes account of all the data of reality." For his fictional subjects, he takes his inspiration from the *auteur* policy, that is, he writes his ideas himself before shooting them, as he explains in a 1980 interview for the publication of the eighth edition of the *Semaine du cinema québécois*. However, in this regard as in others, Arcand sometimes contradicts himself; at times, he strays from the *auteur* principle. This is what happens with *La maudite galette*, which he does not write himself but entrusts to Jacques Benoit, who will also be involved in the writing of *Réjeanne Padovani*. Three times in the 1990s, Arcand makes this exception, directing but not writing *Vue d'ailleurs*, one of the sketches in *Montréal vu par . . . (Montreal Seen by . . . a.k.a. Montreal Sextet)*, *Love and Human Remains* and *Joyeux calvaire*. Today he states that these experiences were not entirely satisfying but left him with a "feeling of incompletion" as a writer-filmmaker.

According to Arcand's theoretical framework for drama, it is impossible to marry documentary and fiction. As he explains in *Écran 73*, he is against the mixing of film genres. In his first three dramas, he applies this principle, but with a few exceptions: there are short documentary sequences in *Réjeanne Padovani*, such as bulldozers destroying a working-class neighbourhood in Montreal's East End to make way for a highway; in *Gina*, Arcand does a kind of docu-fictional (or dramatized documentary) rendition of the censoring of *On est au coton*. Dramatized sequences were planned for some of the films in the French Regime series. Arcand also experimented with genre-mixing in *Ville-Marie* and *Atlantic Parks*. He thought of using actors in *On est au coton* and does use them in *Québec: Duplessis et après . . .*Gisèle Trépanier and Robin Spry. In *Le confort et l'indifférence* he once again circumvents the principle of not mixing genres. The documentary's powerful structure is built around appearances of the character of Machiavelli, played by Jean-Pierre Ronfard. And finally, in *The Barbarian Invasions*, images of the World Trade Center are woven into the fiction, as well as clips from archival film stock, images from *Cielo sulla palude (Heaven over the Marshes)*, of Françoise Hardy, Julie Christie, Chris Evert and Karen Kain. With Arcand, just as accident is never entirely random, principles are never dogmatic.

There is a third aspect of Arcand's system that may seem contradictory. He repeats that in the development of Quebec cinema, the emphasis on documentary worked against drama. But this does not prevent him from recognizing that certain skills used in the documentary can actually nourish drama. Reading, research, facts, interviews and personal memories all stoke the imagination. In *Image et son*, in 1973, he explains, "*cinéma direct* can be extraordinarily fertile." It helps writers develop something other than "films of films," subjects enriched by the "wonderful" habit of the direct and the use of real characters. "The direct approach inspires a total wonder at the millions of possibilities of human behaviour." This explains why all of Arcand's "fictions" are fuelled with facts, attitudes and manners of speaking, ultimately resembling an ethnographer's cinema.

Even more importantly, when Arcand starts making dramas, he claims the status of artist, as he explains in 1974 to *This Magazine* and *Cinema Canada*. He develops to a greater degree the stylistics of the self and the personal viewpoint. He makes films for his own pleasure, seeking to reach an audience of friends and co-conspirators. At a crucial moment when the FLQ, Marxist-Leninists and Parti Québécois enter the political scene, Arcand tells *The Gazette* that he believes introspection is what is most important. Later, in *Copie zéro*, he specifies that being an artist does not mean cultivating vague yearnings or woolly thinking. The artist is first and foremost the person "who possesses the techniques to make cultural objects and develops his ability to do so." For Arcand the two pillars of drama are know-how and self-expression via real and objective data. A drama is the structure of "a coherent discourse." To organize this discourse, Arcand always favoured the "Greek tragedy mould" or the mould of neoclassical French tragedy, with three unities of time, place and action. This is patently obvious in *Réjeanne Padovani*, which Arcand considers as the last in a trilogy after *Coton* and *Duplessis*, both of which emerged from the matrix of tragedy. This structure provides Arcand with a very simple foundation on which to build his stories and characters, and apply the Buñuelian principle of subversion from within.

Arcand makes his first dramas at a time of effervescence and contradictory self-assertion in the world of Quebec film. From all sides its artisans protest the absence of a cinema law in Quebec, especially considering that Trudeau's federal Liberal government has created the Canadian Film Development Corporation (CFDC/SDICC). Thus Canada has been endowed with a law of assistance to private film, primarily thanks to Gérard Pelletier, the secretary of state (the true minister of Canadian culture, who is not called by that name because according to the constitution, the cultural domain falls under provincial authority). This broke the NFB/Radio-Canada duopoly and meant that Quebec feature-film development fell under the provision of the federal government. From that moment on, the dramatic feature in Quebec would benefit from this manna.

The situation lent wings to the *Canadian Film Awards* organization, whose annual Etrog trophies were the Oscars of the brand-new commercial feature industry. In 1973, the organization decides to hold its gala evening in Montreal. A cultural bomb explodes: fourteen filmmakers sign a petition, refusing to attend the ceremony or even accept whatever awards their films might win. For them, the Etrogs represent a willingness to dissolve Quebec cinematography in the grand whole of Canadian culture. Arcand, whose *Réjeanne Padovani* has been nominated, adds his signature to those of Gilles Carle, Claude Jutra, André Melançon, Jacques Gagné, Denis Héroux, Marcel Carrière, Gilles Therien, René Avon, Clément Perron, André Bélanger, Jean Saulnier, Roger Frappier and Aimée Danis. Ironically, Arcand's film is awarded an Etrog for screenplay, whereas everyone expected it to be named best film of the year, especially after its great success at the Directors' Fortnight in Cannes.

Other demonstrations are organized among Quebec filmmakers. In Montreal, in 1974, they occupy the Bureau de surveillance du Québec, threatening to prevent films from getting their exhibition permits, and thus leave the screens blank. The diehards demand that a Quebec film act be filed immediately. Arcand firmly supports the gesture though does not directly participate in the occupation of the bureau. "I lived in Deschambault, I couldn't come to Montreal." At that time, he was also working intensively on his film *Gina*.

When Arcand takes the plunge into drama, thanks to Cinak and Jean Pierre Lefebvre, he is still in the middle of his documentary trilogy. The working title of his first dramatic feature, which changes from *Une maudite galette* to *Calibre 45*, clearly indicates that his subject is violence in Quebec and its culmination in terror. The film develops, in an imaginary vein, Arcand's idea for the would-be documentary *Les terroristes*. It is the story, at once banal and extraordinary, of a modest urban family who decide to rob a rich old uncle who lives in the country. The robbery turns out badly. The uncle resists and is beaten to death, and the family's lodger, the mentally deficient but crafty Ernest, short-circuits the robbers, kills part of the band and leaves with the uncle's hoard, though not before throwing his body in the river. The lodger can now live in high style. He rents a prostitute and succeeds in outsmarting a sleazy Mafioso who is hot on his trail. The whole mad escapade ends at the home of the lodger's parents, where in a final scene of carnage, Ernest is killed. In the end the parents, who have hidden everything from the police and are above suspicion, gaily depart for Florida with the hoard that they have "miraculously" inherited.

La maudite galette employs a kind of Brechtian distance and understatement, but it is also an "American anti-gangster film," made with great attention to detail and sociocultural exactitude. Arcand wanted it to be "a repugnant film," a political film, for "politics cannot be personalized." The preface he writes sheds light on his dramatic objectives and methods. Though on the whole Arcand is quite faithful to Jacques Benoit's script, he makes two changes: he considerably shortens the scene of the uncle's arrival at the apartment of Roland and Berthe, and completely cuts an episode in which Ernest goes to a grocery store, paying for his cookies and fruit with money from the suitcase. A mad car chase ensues. Moreover, Arcand's staging is more hieratic than what was planned in the script. For example, after torturing Uncle Arthur, Ernest is described in the script as having "crazy eyes, a wild expression like a rabid dog's," but this is not at all true of how the scene goes in the film. The same goes for a scene in which the killers are described as ferocious beasts shaken by maniacal laughter. Finally, in a nighttime scene on a country highway, the director replaces a love song on the radio, sung by Tino Rossi, with a beautiful country-folk song in music-over, by Michel Hinton, Gabriel Arcand and Lionel Theriault.

Shooting runs from May 25 to June 25, 1971. The same year, Arcand finishes new cuts of *On est au coton* and *Duplessis est encore en vie*. Foot to the gas pedal, the filmmaker is doing both documentary and drama, at the NFB and elsewhere. Suddenly, in 1972, Arcand begins to shine beneath the halo of thorns with which political censorship has crowned him. Two films are released in a matter of weeks, *Québec: Duplessis et après . . .* on the eve of Saint-Jean-Baptiste day, and *La maudite galette* in the autumn. Moreover, Denys Arcand is celebrated in France as well as in Quebec, *La maudite galette* having been invited to Cannes for Critics' Week in May. In autumn of the same year, he shoots *Réjeanne Padovani*. He says today: "At that time, I made one film after another with a speed and ease of which I was no longer capable when it came to *The Barbarian Invasions*."

Everyone seems to have forgotten it, but *Gina*, first called *Les jarrets noirs*, starts out as a drama project presented to the NFB in April 1972. "News item occurring on Saturday, July 31, 1971, at the Les Pins motel in Valley-Jonction, in Beauce. A gogo dancer is raped by twenty-odd bikers from the Jarrets Noirs gang. The next night, the dancer's 'bosses' arrive, track down the bikers in their den and set it on fire. Later everyone is arrested by the police except the dancer, who has fled to Mexico."

The subject fascinates the filmmaker, for whom the story contains "such a concentration of violence that it almost seems exemplary. Especially because this was premeditated, willed violence and not someone losing his head for a moment. [. . .] I would like to apply to this situation the research methods of Truman Capote when he wrote *In Cold Blood*." Arcand primarily wishes to focus on the structure and function of deviant subgroups in small and isolated Quebec towns—the role of unemployment, of economic underdevelopment, urbanization and social fragmentation in the birth of deviant groups; the mutual exploitation of subgroups, the underworld and workers; the underworld as an outgrowth of legal leisure structures, the bookie as a natural extension of a legal bet made at a horse race; rape as a classical expression of sexuality within certain subgroups; the collective aspect of this sexuality; the use of violence as a normal form of recourse in cases of conflict among deviants; the ineluctable logic of this violence; the subgroup as a homogenous society, completely closed, having no economic ties with the dominant society.

On May 30, NFB commissioner André Lamy gives his verdict. The project is refused: "As the number of features we do is limited, as much due to costs as to distribution networks, it has been decided for the moment that production will be reserved to NFB filmmakers. Consequently, we cannot allow Denys Arcand to work on the project for *Gina*." In 1973, in a document entitled *Contre la censure*, distributed during Quebec film week at Collège Saint-Laurent, Arcand declares: "I am not going back to the NFB. Management refused the last project I submitted. It was a research project on a news item that happened in Beauce." In the early stages, *Gina* does not contain the plot thread of the documentary film crew whose shoot on the textile industry has been canned by the "National Cinema Board." This important element will be added later, when the independent firm of Carle-Lamy produces the film. However, an enigmatic sentence is to be noted in the first project Arcand submitted to the NFB. He writes: "We must not neglect the hypothesis that further research leads us towards characters and facts that do not appear in the above-mentioned events." This "hypothesis" implies that Arcand might already have had something else in mind (maybe a story about filmmakers who have their film banned?). When presenting the *Gina* project to the NFB in the spring of 1972, the film-maker could not, of course, explicitly mention the idea. But no doubt he was thinking of it all the same . . . .

As he cannot begin research and writing for *Jarrets noirs*, Arcand throws himself into shooting *Réjeanne Padovani*. The shoot runs from October 26 to November 28, 1972. The idea goes back to the year before, when Arcand said he was working on a film called *La mort de Lucie Patriarca*. He wrote a twelve-page synopsis and asked Jacques Benoit to write the screenplay. Benoit explains: "Denys's synopsis already contained the entire structure of the film. I suggested that he write the screenplay himself, but he insisted I do it. I worked on the screenplay, composing all the dialogue, from the end of 1971 until August 1972, when I left to study in Aix-en-Provence. For the heroine's name we looked at a map of Sicily, then found 'Padovani' (which comes from Padova), to which we added a first name that sounded like Quebec working class. When I saw the final dialogue and all the changes Denys had made, at first I was offended. Today, I wouldn't be." Arcand confirms that he was responsible for over 80 percent of the *Réjeanne*

Padovani screenplay, whereas the major part of the *Maudite galette* screenplay is Benoit's.

Réjeanne Padovani is the story of a party at the luxurious residence of Montreal millionaire contractor Vincent Padovani. His guests of honour are the mayor of Montreal and a Quebec government minister. The party is spoiled by the arrival of militant leftist journalists, then by the unexpected return of the Mafioso's ex-wife, Réjeanne, who has come back to see her children. Réjeanne left her husband for another "businessman" and then fled to the United States to escape Padovani's reprisals. She tries to make an appointment with him, but he refuses and has her killed by one of his men. The following day, Réjeanne's body is dumped into one of the enormous pillars used for pouring concrete. Padovani, who has directed the construction of Montreal's Ville-Marie expressway, inaugurates before the authorities while an aria plays from Gluck's *Orpheus and Eurydice*. It is "I lost my Eurydice," the same aria performed live at the previous night's dinner as a gift from Padovani to the mayor, who is wild about opera and female vocalists.

Between the screenplay and the finished film, few content changes are to be noted. Arcand shortened the film slightly by not shooting the scene in which the musicians arrive at the Padovani residence, a scene that was to serve as a backdrop for the opening titles. He entirely cuts the end of the dinner, when the guests are discussing the lateness of the government minister Bouchard. In other places, the director is content to simply tighten scenes, for example, by removing bits of dialogue and an extra aria sung by the vocalist Stella. However, an important change is made during the shoot: the servants who in the screenplay are grouped in the Padovani kitchen gather instead in a more symbolic setting, the basement, allowing Arcand to highlight the contrast between "upstairs and downstairs." The greatest variation is in the editing, the major example being the grouping of the images in which Réjeanne Padovani herself appears. In the screenplay, these scenes are alternated with those of the Mafioso's dinner party; in the film, the shots are presented in two blocks. In the first block, Réjeanne is being followed by Di Muro in the streets of Montreal, in the second she takes refuge in her ex-husband's big greenhouse.

The film brings Arcand his first great moment of recognition and glory. In 1973, it astounds audiences in both Quebec and France, where it is first presented at the Directors' Fortnight at Cannes. The filmmaker makes the rounds of all the French film journals and magazines, *Image et son*, *Jeune cinema*, *Téléciné*. *Les cahiers du cinema*, which in 1967 had praised *Ville-Marie*, raves about Arcand's acute sense of staging and publishes an exemplary analysis written by Pascal Bonitzer, called "L'espace politique." Later, Arcand's work will be panned by both *Les cahiers du cinema* and *Liberation*. But for the moment, *Liberation* celebrates "one of the best filmmakers in Québécois cinema today" and the film it calls "Hands over Montreal." In *Cinema* magazine, Arcand gives one of the best interviews of his career, in which he calls himself a "despairing ethnographer," and says he feels "that he has reached an ideological dead-end." Finally, he makes this highly significant declaration: "My sole criterion is Denys Arcand: his coherence and sincerity."

To his eyes, *Réjeanne Padovani* deals with the theme of decadence, of disintegration. As we have seen, his script was inspired by his readings of Suetonius and the murder of Empress Messalina. In the despairing climate of what he considers to be a "little art film," against all expectations, the portrait of a woman emerges, one of the most beautiful (though brief) portraits in Quebec cinema. Réjeanne is at once memory and conscience. The sole objective of this woman, who has returned in secret from the United States, is to see and kiss her children again, risking death to accomplish this furtive gesture. Tragedy prevents her from doing so. In Montreal and with an aura of decadence reminiscent of Rome, Arcand has already reached the gates of the decline of the American empire. Because English Canada, or at least Toronto, is now interested in him, he declares loud and clear to the *Globe and Mail* that we live in a society in which everything is rotten, that political corruption is everywhere. It's always the bad guys who win, he says; we are governed by madmen! Organized crime, political corruption and power all go hand in hand in a chain of scandal and catastrophe, he repeats in *Cinema Québec*. In short, as he states in *Québec-Presse*, his film is more or less Francesco Rosi's *Hands over the City*, along the same lines as *Québec: Duplessis et après . . . .*

Réjeanne Padovani is also discovered and remarked upon in New York, where it is invited to the autumn film festival of 1973. The film is praised by the *Village Voice* (which will later drag Arcand over the coals for *The Barbarian Invasions*) for its matchless demonstration of "the seductive, almost sexual charge of power's inner lining." Molly Haskell's review notes that the rivalry between the Tannenbaum clan of New York Jewish Mafia and that of the Montreal Padovanis represents a conflict "similar to that of The Guelfs vs. The Ghibellines in Dante's Florence." Finally, the article praises how Arcand's "suave mise-en-scene so perfectly imitates the velvety duplicity of his milieu." *Variety* writes: "The characters are blocked out with a cold, visual precision that gives them the air of decadent Romans." *The Independent Film Journal* is more reserved in its judgments, though it recognizes the value of the film's attentive observation of corruption, conceding, ". . . the fat cats ring true as men, if not as political barons."

Arcand's action films have been extensively researched. "My brother Bernard, an ethnographer, and my sister Suzanne, a criminologist, are real scientists. They have taught me a lot," he declares in *Cinema 73*. Arcand's first dramatic trilogy deals with crime in many forms, police forces and their ties to political corruption. All these dramas are fed by research, reading and fact-checking, the filmmaker having found excellent script consultants within his family. He makes a point of underlining the pertinent remarks of his brother Bernard, an anthropologist. Later, in *Le Confort et l'indifférence*, he acknowledges Gabriel for having lent him the complete works of Machiavelli and suggested the idea of introducing this character as commentator of current events in Quebec and Canada at the time of the 1980 referendum.

Such acknowledgments are not new for Arcand. Like himself, his brothers attended the Collège Sainte-Marie and André Brochu notes: "He has great admiration for his younger brothers, both as tall as himself, as airy and extraordinary. I find this attitude unusual for an eldest child. Denys also has a sister, whom he must admire a lot too." We may recall that Arcand refers to his sister Suzanne as "a real scientist." During the seventies she is given a consulting credit as a specialist in criminology, the study of police forces. She collaborates on *La maudite galette*, *Réjeanne Padovani* and *Gina*. In the acts of a 1980 conference of the Canadian association for French-language sociologists and anthropologists, we find a paper presented by Suzanne Arcand on the "bureaucratization of the police" and police power. She analyzes the strange phenomenon of the police-industrial complex, a form of "social and professional alienation of police officers," even a "political alien-ation," to which the 1969 wildcat police strike testifies. This kind of "police illegality" allows these "inflexible guardians of orthodoxy" to exercise a power that is sometimes acquired by force over "the politics of their work." The criminologist concludes: "If there was a time when it might have seemed more pertinent to consider the police phenomenon primarily from the general angle of the State's power over police, it now seems more urgent to examine the power of the police over the State and citizens." This takes us back to Socrates' eternal question, Who shall guard our Guardians? "at a time when these 'public servants' that police are supposed to be are gradually becoming, or have become, their own servants above all."

Suzanne Arcand's task as script consultant was to give expert advice about the police and its organization, and on the structure and dealings of organized crime. For *Réjeanne Padovani*, she checked facts and information, for example, in Scene 9, when Officer Bertrand refers to his bonus of "about 150 to 175 dollars per month." She checked for truth and realism in Scene 73, in which police enter the meeting place of a citizens' committee: "Five guys enter. They have iron bars. They knock out four young men and one young woman. They ransack the place, taking the bodies outside. Once the room has been emptied, Lieutenant Gosselin enters. He dumps out the filing cabinet and looks for address books, putting everything in his leather briefcase."

The roots of *Réjeanne Padovani* go all the way back to the decline of the Roman Empire. The film makes a kind of jump-cut between Suetonius and the Montreal Mafia, between the twilight of the great empire of Antiquity and the contemporary empire of North America. Again we can see how, in the works of Arcand, Quebec current events and the unique destinies of real and fictional characters are informed by a keen knowledge of history. Points of view are fed by an overview of the past or by archaic sediments from the long, slow movements of societies and civilizations. This film is one of the most powerful moments in Arcand's quest to evoke, in the style of tragic opera or as an endless melancholy elegy, the singular destiny of Quebec, of Montreal in particular.

The same year, as a result of the success and renown of *Réjeanne Padovani*, Pierre Lamy offers Arcand a golden opportunity, a solid budget for the writing and shooting of *Gina*. This producer, to whom the filmmaker pays tribute at the Cinemathèque québécoise in the early eighties, is one of the very good producers with whom he has worked. The budget for *Gina* is $350,000, as compared to $150,000 for *Padovani*. The script is no longer the same as the one he proposed to the NFB in 1972. A documentary film team has been added, whose story is told in parallel with that of the raped dancer. In January 1975, Arcand tells *Le Devoir*: "I can't make a film that's totally faithful to banal reality. I have to add fiction. I've done research on news items; I've built a character, Gina. Maybe this isn't really consistent with my method or is contradictory. But I am contradictory; I like different things. I like Jean-Luc Godard and *The French Connection*. I like it when the good guy punishes the bad guy in the end, even if that's no longer realistic at all. Let's just say that *Gina* is a film that's as divided as I am."

The first draft of the scenario is dated November 1973, the second, February 1974. The film is shot between March 11 and May 10, 1974. The story's violence is now localized in two heterogeneous, though parallel, zones: on one hand, there is deviant subgroup of pimps and snowmobile hoodlums, on the other, the politicocultural powers-that-be who censure the group of filmmakers and confiscate their film. What is told here is a transparent depiction of what happened to Arcand's own film *On est au coton*. When *Gina* is released, Arcand's comments on the film are contradictory. In *Le Jour*, he declares that *Gina* "is not my way of getting even with the NFB"; in *La Presse*, however, he acknowledges the film as "getting even without bitterness." Today he openly asserts that it was his vengeance against the NFB.

There is very little difference between the script and the film version of *Gina*. However, there are two scenes that present interesting variations. In one scene, which was discarded, the textile factory's director of personnel Léonard Chabot explains that he has been interviewed for a program on Radio-Canada. He boasts about the quality of this program, its "objectivity." Here, Arcand is making reference to a Radio-Canada documentary, produced after the censoring of *On est au coton*, whose goal it was to propagate the federal position vis-à-vis the textile industry. At the time, Arcand made cutting comments on this documentary. Another scene, very much an object of discussion, was a monologue by the worker Dolorès on "the satisfactions of being poor." In the script, this soliloquy comes at the end of the film; in the film, it is cut into Gina's striptease. Both screenplay and film have other surprises to offer. The most astonishing of these, spoken by the pimp Ricky, is a reflection on the fact that public statues are almost always of despots, an idea that comes from Emil Cioran's *History and Utopia*, a work we will see in close-up at the end of *The Barbarian Invasions*.

With *Gina*, Arcand's luck takes yet another turn. The feature is not invited to Cannes and reviews in Quebec are lukewarm, when not overtly hostile. Arcand is starting to be reproached for no longer making politically committed films. However, as he has explained on numerous occasions since 1971, from the time he started out at the NFB, he makes films of personal observation, informed with intellectual, political and historical awareness. We may recall the motto of his graduating class at Sainte-Marie in 1960, "*Solitaire. Solidaire.*" For Arcand, the personal point of view and the presence of the "I" take nothing away from social consciousness. He has never been a militant or propagandist filmmaker. The debate on the role of the "I" in intellectual life goes back to Montaigne by way of Rousseau, and is continued by Stendhal. Filmmaker Johanne Prégent confirms that Arcand has read all the essays of Montaigne. That says it all. Since the sixties, Arcand's cinema foreshadowed this mode of thinking, in which Stendhalian egotism is neither selfishness nor social blindness.

Gina's poor reception puts a damper on Arcand's career. Gilles Marsolais, in *Vie des arts*, sets the tone: "It would seem that Denys Arcand has reached a limit that he does not know how to overcome without falling into the most questionable kind of complacency and self-satisfaction." In France, the film is considered even more disappointing. Despite an adulatory article by Henry Chapier in *Le Monde*, *L'Aurore* and *Positif* assert that "the film suffers from an obvious lack of unity"; *France Soir* writes that "Canadian cinema is a little short on imagination." Unlike his first two dramas, *Gina* appears to be a failure.

A sort of bad spell seems to have been cast on the film. When producing the trailer, the distributor Cinépix manages to erase all reference to the documentary shoot and filmmaking team, except for a brief and incomprehensible shot of Gabriel Arcand telling the workers that the film is over. Otherwise, the trailer shows only the striptease, the fights, the drag race between cars and snowmobiles. To draw the public, *Gina* is presented as nothing more than a thriller full of sex and gore. Arcand tells the following anecdote.

One day, a young Cinépix employee calls him in Deschambault, wanting to apologize: "My bosses are forcing me to mutilate your film." The filmmaker has only one concern. "Don't touch the negative at the Cinemathèque québécoise." The other assures him that he is not working with the negative. There are no further developments and Arcand forgets the incident. Several years later, he is invited to a retrospective of his films in Syracuse, New York. He arrives at the end of the projection of *Gina* to talk to the public. The filmgoers are astounded: "What have you done, Mr. Arcand? There are no documentary scenes on the textile industry. We've just seen a forty-minute film with nothing but stripteases, car chases and murders." Only then did Arcand understand to what extent the film had been mutilated by Cinépix. *Gina* was re-edited as a short film for drive-in screenings in the United States. In America, the director is not recognized as an *auteur* as he is in France and cannot protect the original version of his film.

At the heart of the *Gina* misunderstanding is the situation of Quebec film in general, whose death the film describes. What does Arcand want to talk about? In the days of *Parti pris*, ten years earlier, he had believed in the emergence of a cinema "whose destiny is inseparable from the fate of French Canada. If our cinema has made progress in the last while, this progress runs parallel to Quebec's self-awareness. Our cinema of the present time, to paraphrase André Brochu, provides us with a glimpse of what Quebec cinema could be—no longer a cinema of failure but of conquest, in which culture and everyday life would finally intersect." However, a decade later, the trend is reversed. Arcand explains in *Écran 73*, when *Padovani* is released: "I make the films they let me make. It is out of the question for the NFB, which in my opinion is being slowly but surely dismantled, to produce another *On est au coton*. And since the system is pushing me towards commercial filmmaking, I try as much as possible to use it in a progressive way."

In March 1973, in *Image et son*, Arcand paints an implacable portrait of the state of the film industry in Canada and Quebec, maintained on one hand by the NFB, and on the other, by the very young private sector, also supported by Ottawa. "Basically, Canada is almost an unliveable country, one that lives off theoretically antagonistic contradictions." Quebec cinema is fed by a vast nationalist movement, so it produces a great many films made by "separatists," financed by organizations that cannot be "propagandists for Quebec independence"; however, "federalist films" do not exist. Where federal organizations become intransigent is not so much when Quebecers assert their integrity and their language but when films "show that French Canadians are an oppressed social class."

On its release in 1975, *Gina* is not understood as the story of the death of Quebec cinema. Its value as metaphor will not be appreciated until the eighties, when the film will be appreciated by young film enthusiasts, and considered one of the filmmaker's best. This film, which was a failure, is also the story of a failure, that of *On est au coton* and of Quebec cinema. It is the sarcastic denunciation of the "new deal" of commercial film.

Arcand will soon pay the price. Telefilm Canada will turn down his *Maria Chapdelaine*. He will be obliged to direct commercial television series, *Empire Inc.*, *The Crime of Ovide Plouffe* and commercials. Before, he would still have managed to subvert the system, as he did by writing the *Duplessis* mini-series for Radio-Canada. An example of how Arcand never loses sight of the true value of cinema, for which he has fought since the sixties and the Quiet Revolution.

9
"THE SALVATION ARMY, OR WORSE, PROFESSOR AT UQAM"

"**I** am not volontarist, I'm assailed with doubt. I don't know who I am. I'm contradictory, but persevering and hard-working." In this reflection shared with Minou Petrowski on the radio broadcast *Paroles de stars*, in 2001, Arcand is referring to his doubts at the time of the controversial release of *Stardom*. He could have said the same thing in the mid-seventies after the launching of *Gina*.

The 1975 release of this third dramatic feature ends in bitter failure. For *Gina*, there will be no Cannes Festival. In Quebec, though the audience response is quite positive, the critics are harsh. Today, as if it were still a fresh wound, Arcand recalls the great disappointment expressed to him by Patrick Straram. To add to these difficulties, the NFB is in the process of dismantling. Remote-controlled by the new co-production policy, private industry takes Hollywood for its model and produces "Québécois films" such as *City on Fire* and *Quest for Fire*. The first dark period of Arcand's career has begun. "I saw myself knocking at the door of the Salvation Army or worse, becoming a professor at UQAM (Université du Québec à Montréal)."

At the beginning of 1975, Arcand seems to be going in circles, as if his filmmaking career were heading for a dead end. As he says of *Gina* in *Le Devoir* of January 25, 1975, "the dancer [Gina] is a marginal character, filmmakers are marginal characters." Curiously and contrary to

Réjeanne Padovani and Arcand's other scripts, *Gina* was not based on reading. "I've stopped thinking, it's been a while now. I won't even read books on theory. It's a kind of dumbing-down process. I'm in a period of creating stories and don't want to come out of it. I let myself be invaded by increasingly irrational things; I feel if I express them in the form of ideas, I'll kill them." However, as we have seen, "no reading" did not mean no research on deviant criminal groups. As for the part of the script dealing with the team of documentary filmmakers, Arcand simply referred to his own experience from *On est au coton* and its highly publicized political censorship. The filmmaker watched his ghosts file by.

Some of Arcand's cinephile friends were puzzled by *Gina*. Of course, the film contained beautiful moments, moving scenes about a documentary film that is fighting to survive, but the finale with its warring criminals seemed overdone, as if the film itself were giving in to the kind of commercial movie clichés that it set out to ridicule and denounce. Almost ten years after its release, film students viewed *Gina* and came away dazzled and moved. Thus, at last the film was discovered in all its beauty and rigour, all the astonishing parallels it draws between attacks on culture and the violence inflicted on workers, as well as that of deviant subgroups. In 1998, in *24 images*, Gilles Marsolais publishes a new review of *Gina*, which he says "did not, in its time, receive the critical and audience response it deserved in terms of its significance in the works of Denys Arcand [. . .] a *film d'auteur* that brings us real pleasure as long as we let ourselves be thrown off balance."

But the film did not meet with this kind of appreciation in 1975, in spite of several good reviews when it was presented at the Festival de Paris. The failure of *Gina* burnt Arcand's bridges in terms of funding for future productions. In 1987, in retrospect, Arcand confides to Louis-Bernard Robitaille in *La Presse*: "My pretext was that cinema was in a state of crisis, which was true, but the fact is, maybe I had nothing to say at the time." For the time being, Arcand lived in obscurity. There is a revealing detail that emerges from one of the interviews he did for the book *InnerViews* (1975). In the end of the interview, Hofsess asks Arcand: "What are we coming to? Next we'll be discovering sex." Arcand replies, "That too." But Hofsess does not believe him.

Arcand perseveres in the face of his post-*Gina* blues. If he is on the blacklist for private industry, he will work for institutions instead: the

Confederation of National Trade Unions (in Quebec, the CSN), the NFB and Radio-Canada. In 1976, he directs a short film for the CSN on the hospital workers' labour struggle: *La lutte des travailleurs d'hôpitaux.* "I got a call from a guy I met while shooting *On est au coton:* 'The hospitals are on strike. Would you agree to make a film that we could broadcast on Télé-Métropole next week?' I've never made a film so quickly, a political message from the CSN to denounce working conditions in Montreal hospitals. I had to choose an institution quickly—it was the Hôtel-Dieu de Montreal, where I landed in a real serpents' nest. The Marxists controlled the union and were very distrustful of the CSN. The administrators all belonged to *En lutte* and another grouplet. They weren't sure of my allegiances; they wanted to know what ideological category I placed myself in. I had to manoeuvre very carefully while making the film so it would satisfy the union federation, which was Québécois and vaguely leftist, as well as the enraged militants who controlled the union. I shot the film in two or three days, edited it in two, and it was on the air seven days later. The film describes the daily life of the most humble hospital employees, the ones who work in the basement laundry, taking in linen that comes down the chutes stained with blood and excrement, and others who prepare meals or clean the rooms." Few people remember this film, but Pierre Falardeau does, and he discussed it in an interview for Radio-Canada on February 11, 2004, calling *The Barbarian Invasions* cynical, bourgeois cinema, colonized cinema. In the seventies, says Falardeau, Arcand made films to defend hospital workers whereas now "he shits on them like Premier Charest and Prime Minister Martin."

The same year, 1976, when the embargo on *Coton* is lifted by the NFB, Arcand writes a script called *Nesbitt's Trip* for CBC Toronto. A producer from CBC, Robert Hershorn, wants to shoot films in English by Quebec filmmakers Francis Mankiewicz, Claude Jutra and Denys Arcand. Arcand proposes *Nesbitt's Trip*, written in collaboration with Jacques Méthé, assistant director on Arcand's two previous dramatic features. The screenplay is completed in August.

Nesbitt's Trip is one of Arcand's first unproduced screenplays, which luckily he put away in his filing cabinet instead of throwing it out, as he did with the scripts for *Seul ou avec d'autres* and *Jusqu'au cou.* Its main point of interest is that it is the first drama in which he addresses the themes of suicide and death. In the eighties, he will return to the sub-ject in four different projects: *La femme idéale* (April 1991), *La Vie éter-nelle* and *Dernier amour* (October 1991) and *C'est la vie* (1993–1994). These themes reappear in *The Barbarian Invasions* at the turn of the new millennium. Thus, it took over twenty-five years of adjustments and sheer determination to tackle the subject and bring his character to the point where he could "enter into death with eyes wide open," take charge of his passage down the Styx between life and death.

"The people at CBC Toronto were horrified; they thought *Nesbitt's Trip* was dreadful. I don't know what they were expecting, maybe lumberjacks dancing a jig or something like that. The project came to a halt. It was the first time I had broached the subject of suicide, a subject that's always haunted me. I think about it very often. I think it was Camus who said: "There is only one philosophical problem, sui-cide." The problem is whether to keep living or not. What's more, seven of my friends have committed suicide, that's a lot.

When I really started to think about the subject, later, in the beginning of the eighties, I met with a specialist in Sociology at the University of Toronto. I told him I knew seven people who had killed themselves. He was flabbergasted, because that's very rare. There aren't a lot of people who have so many close friends who have committed sui-cide. In sociological terms, that makes me a candidate for suicide. Now, with *The Barbarian Invasions*, I've finally managed to make the film I wanted to do on the subject."

Nesbitt's Trip is Arcand's first screenplay in English. It is the story of a rich fifty-six-year-old banker who lives in Beaconsfield. One morn-ing, when driving in his Cadillac to his office on rue Saint-Jacques in Montreal, Ross Nesbitt meets Sylvie, a young woman of twenty-five who is hitch-hiking. A kind of unemployed hippie, a wandering soul. She is on her way to Quebec City to stay with friends.

The banker and the girl start talking about their lives, their trav-els and their work. For some unexplained reason, Ross decides to drive his passenger to her destination, passing through Contrecœur and Sorel, where there is a high concentration of industrial sites. Then he drives through Gentilly, passing its nuclear site, and through Saint-Pierre-les-Becquets, Deschaillons, Lotbinière (across from Les Grondines, on the other side of the river, he observes), all the way to Quebec City. The film unfolds as a long dialogue between the two protagonists during the journey. This unusual duo talks to the point of exhaustion about the flamboyant and rapid modernization of Quebec, its triumphant industrialization, the relation between wealth and political power, all while driving along the Saint Lawrence River through a series of small communities. An intellectual and philosophical road movie.

Sylvie has said that she'd like to go to Malbaie and Ross decides to take her there after a fine meal at the Quebec Hilton. This time, he goes by way of the North Shore through Sainte-Anne-de-Beaupré, Saint-Tite and Baie-Saint-Paul, finally landing at the *Auberge de nos aïeux* in Éboulements where the couple spends the night. In a cross-cut we see Nesbitt's family and office colleagues in a panic. The banker has disappeared, cannot be found; the police are called in. We cut back to Charlevoix. After letting Sylvie off in Malbaie, Nesbitt drives to Cap-à-l'Aigle and parks his car at the end of a long pier. He drinks champagne and then kills himself with carbon monoxide in his beautiful car. A little boy discovers the body.

Nesbitt's Trip, written in the mid-seventies and rejected by the CBC, already contains numerous characteristics and themes that will be developed by Arcand in the following decade, first in his script for the *Empire Inc.* series, in *The Decline* and *Jesus of Montreal*, and even later, in the 1980s, in works on death and the ephemeral nature of female beauty. Here, the meeting between the rich world of finance and the beauty of the young woman takes place on a background of despair.

This twenty-four-hour Buñuelian journey is Ross Nesbitt's way of putting off his suicide and taking stock of his professional, family and sexual life. He has lived coddled in a world of decadence. He has a love-hate relationship with his wife and has not developed emotional ties with his daughter and son, now in their twenties. He takes a bitter view of the collusion between money and political power. In the restaurant on top of the Hilton he even refers to chapter four of the Gospel according to Saint Mark, when Jesus is taken to the mountaintop and offered wealth, glory and power by Satan. This prefigures the top of Complexe Desjardins as it appears in *Le confort et l'indifférence*, the summit of Mount Royal and the office tower of the modern Satan in an Armani suit in *Jesus of Montreal*. Moreover, the dialogue-based screenplay in some ways foreshadows the "racy conversations" of *The Decline*, which will appear almost ten years later. In *Nesbitt's Trip*, concludes Arcand, abundant conversation serves to camouflage the true subject. It takes a genius like Chekhov to make characters have a dialogue with each other while the true subjects of solitude, despair and death are evoked between the lines.

In September of that same year, 1976, Arcand proposes an idea to the NFB for a film on the economy of tourism, for co-production by Canada and Mexico. He intends to follow a group of *Tabarnacos*, Québécois tourists, to Acapulco and at the same time draw a portrait of the economic infrastructure of tourism. The goal of the script is to represent tourism as a "closed economic system, a self-sufficient circuit that the traveller-tourist does not leave and whose entire economic activity boils down to transfers of credit within different departments of the same company. [. . .] Tourism is one of the faces of imperialism. For example, steaks for all the Hiltons in the world are bought in Kansas City and shipped by Pan-Am. The same goes for Holiday Inn soaps and Sheraton towels. The natural tendency of these companies is to limit their contact with the local market as much as possible." In conclusion, "tourism is very expensive for the countries who are its victims," and "a great number of the tourists themselves have the aberrant peculiarity of being proletarians in their own countries who, while visiting a foreign country, turn into pitiless agents of imperialism." The project goes no further, for the entire Canada-Mexico co-production program is cancelled.

In 1977, Arcand works on several projects at once. He is writing the script for *Duplessis*, a Radio-Canada television series to be directed by Mark Blandford, and for *Le confort et l'indifférence* for the NFB. It is interesting to read the writer's evocation of *Duplessis*'s success, as told to Michel Coulombe: "At that time, I lived in the country. The nights that *Duplessis* was on, I played basketball with a group of phys-ed teachers in Donnacona, thirty kilometres from Deschambault. Driving home at night, I passed through villages where, through the windows, I could see families gathered around their television sets watching my program. I have to say, I was quite moved. I think that was when my father stopped thinking of me as a failure. The magnitude of *Duplessis*'s success overwhelmed him."

Written with the help of historian Jacques Lacoursière, the series includes seven episodes: *Les comptes publics* (1936), *L'Union nationale* (1939), *L'échec* (1939), *La retraite* (1942), *Le pouvoir* (1948), *Herr Kanzler Duplessis* (1952) and *La fin* (1959). It is a gigantic script, "the equivalent of a PhD thesis," as Arcand says. Some scenes absolutely had to be cut. In other places, dialogue was removed or shortened. Several scenes were not shot by Mark Blandford, usually because of lack of time, for example, in the fourth episode, scenes having to do with culture: André Malraux's visit to Montreal, references to Doctor Bethune, Paul-Émile Borduas in the Automatistes' studio, the signatories of the *Refus global* Manifesto, Duplessist censorship of the film *Les enfants du paradis*, not to speak of images of Madeleine Parent in prison. In the sixth episode, they cut a scene in which Hilaire Beauregard, deputy chief of the Quebec provincial police, explains to Duplessis his strategy for breaking the Louiseville strike, and another in which the Quebec premier boasts about his influence over the clergy and the Vatican. Finally, in the last episode, they take out an allusion to a sex scandal involving the wife of Daniel Johnson, which had not been broadcast by the media, thanks to the intervention of Duplessis.

In spite of resounding public and critical success in 1978, the series is quickly targeted by an ultraconservative group headed by the Jesuit Jacques Cousineau (who had been ecclesiastic consultant for *Séquences* magazine when it demolished *Champlain* and *Ville-Marie*). The pressure group included Victor Barbeau, Robert Rumilly, Jean-Marc Brunet and Yvon Dupuis. Cousineau had already denounced *Duplessis* as an attack against the Quebec Church. He convinced the protesters to file an official complaint with the CRTC on the basis of the following arguments: "The work of an unhealthy imagination has distorted the attitudes of certain characters to the point of near-perversity, laying them out in an atmosphere of morbid fantasy and fiction. [. . .] The undersigned feel that the Radio-Canada Corporation did not provide a balanced service with the series, that the series in itself did not contribute to the development of national unity or express the reality of Canada, particularly of Quebec, and that finally, the Radio-Canada Corporation did not respect the law on radio-television broadcasting" (*Le Droit*, May 9, 1978). The CRTC and management for Radio-Canada are shaken by the gravity of these attacks.

The series is not re-broadcast as planned—yet another blow for Arcand. He remembers the emergency meeting at Radio-Canada. The director of programming, Jean-Marie Dugas, summoned Lacoursière, Blandford and Arcand. "The network administrators begged me to admit that I had written falsifications or lies. I answered them: 'Everything is true, everything is authentic.' They were thunderstruck."

There were no immediate consequences, definitely not as far as *Mackenzie King* was concerned. There was some question of Arcand working on the project with Mark Blandford, but in the end he was not included. Moreover, the hugely successful *Duplessis* was not re-shown on Radio-Canada, except once in the 1980. It was not until 1996 that the series received public tribute at an event on the theme of political censorship, organized by the Fondation André-Guérin. Marc Laurendeau led the panel on the *Duplessis* affair, and the series was shown in its entirety.

Arcand's relations with television go back a long way. At Collège Sainte-Marie, he participated in the pilot for *Premières armes*, produced by Radio-Canada and hosted by Gérard Pelletier. As a university student, he applied to Radio-Canada for work, as well as to the NFB. He could reasonably expect to see his first short historical films broadcast on television, which was customary at the time. In 1966, when he left the NFB, Arcand started writing for the téléroman *Minute, papillon!* It was also for television that he would write *Nesbitt's Trip* ten years later, in 1976. Thus, it is not surprising that he agrees to write *Duplessis* for Mark Blandford and Radio-Canada, as well as the script for *Les gens adorent les guerres* (*People Love Wars*), the fourth episode of *Empire Inc.* At the end of the seventies he is indirectly involved in the television adaptation of *Maria Chapdelaine*. He directs *The Crime of Ovide Plouffe* at the beginning of the eighties, and in the 1990s, the television adaptation of *Les lettres de la religieuse portugaise* (*The Portuguese Nun's Letters*) as well as *Joyeux calvaire*. Arcand is one of the few Québécois film directors who has never looked down on television, though in general contempt of television among filmmakers is sovereign. (This attitude is apparent, for example, in the comments made by dozens of filmmakers published in the program for the 1988 *Rendez-vous du cinéma québécois*.) Arcand clearly expresses his views on the television machine when accepting his award from the Association des réalisateurs de télévision in

1990 (see "Selected Readings"). He also discusses the subject at length in *24 images* (1982) and in the *Globe and Mail* (1984), emphasizing that he belongs to a tradition of filmmakers who work for television, including Ingmar Bergman, Ermanno Olmi, Paolo and Vittorio Taviani. He might have added Rossellini, whose *The Rise to Power of Louis XIV*, the film he so admires, was made for French television.

Roger Frappier, at that time a producer at the NFB, begs Arcand to do a film on the Quebec referendum of 1980. In the autumn of 1976, the Parti Québécois, led by René Lévesque, triumphed in the general elections and Frappier, also a member of the executive committee of the Association des réalisateurs et réalisatrices du Québec, immediately sent a telegram to Premier Lévesque: "We have a deep, necessary and passionate desire to participate in the most immediate way in the irrefutable proof of Quebec identity. [. . .] It is the first time that we have fought to wrest Quebec cinema from foreign economies and ideologies knowing that we will be able to work *with* the government *for* our society." A referendum on Quebec sovereignty-association is on the agenda. Arcand lets himself be convinced by Frappier to do the film."He brought several bottles of very good wine to Deschambault." On June 16, 1977, he presents his project; on September 8, he begins shooting, and continues on a sporadic basis until May 22, 1981. At the end of the process, Arcand writes to Jacques Leduc in *Format cinéma* how spent he feels, both physically and intellectually, as he emerges from this adventure. He is also at the end of his rope in terms of his sovereignist and political convictions.

The shattering release in 1981 of *Le confort et l'indifférence* launches a new volley of criticism. Though everyone, or almost everyone, admires Arcand's caustic intelligence in using the character of Machiavelli in his report on the referendum, the film also provokes the most stinging reviews the filmmaker has received since *Québec: Duplessis et après . . .* , ten years earlier. As usual, the filmmaker has seen it coming: "I knew I'd displease both the Federalists and the Sovereignists. I'm fed up with politics." On January 30, 1982, on the editorial page of *Le Devoir*, Lise Bissonnette devotes a long article to the film, which she describes as "the vengeance of an intellectual wanting to insult the little people who voted NO. [. . .] I will never understand how a filmmaker who dreamed of the YES ended up paying such admiring tribute to his adversaries and sharing the, indeed, very Machiavellian pleasure of contempt. He tells the people they are stupid and cowardly and thinks he is brave."

In retrospect, it is interesting to note that *Le confort et l'indifférence* was Arcand's last "documentary" (or more precisely, docu-fiction, because of the character of Machiavelli). The filmmaker has never returned to this form, which is more political *essay* than documentary, as are all his films of the same type. Though the film has hilarious moments, by and large it deploys a cold and implacable vision of human society and the acrobatics involved in its administration. It is also the film in which Arcand most clearly expresses his idea that the destiny of the Quebec people is blocked, that the Quiet Revolution is an epiphenomenon and that societies and civilizations evolve as slowly as glaciers. These were his views at the time he wrote *Duplessis* and *Les gens adorent les guerres*; for Arcand, there is a very fine line between documentary and fiction.

Le confort et l'indifférence spelled an end for Arcand's interest in political themes. As he often said at that time, he had arrived at the finishing line as far as this kind of subject is concerned. In the fall of 1986, he told *24 images*: "if that's the kind of society I live in, there's no point in continuing to preach." In *Copie zéro* the following year he specifies: "No theory, no idealism, no analysis ever totally convinced me. To me, it always seemed that experience was more vast than all those systems, and that it was dishonest to reduce it for reasons of political efficiency. I will never be a good soldier. But on the other hand, I have never known the fraternal joys of militancy and I've always lived in a relative solitude. My 'community' experience is limited to film crews."

According to habit, Arcand reads in preparation for *Le confort et l'indifférence*: Aristotle, Clausewitz, Tite-Live and, of course, Machiavelli. "I had to think, try to situate this event in a broader context, understand what was going to happen before our eyes. I began by reading a few basic texts on human confrontation: Clausewitz on war and battles, *Politics* by Aristotle, Tite-Live on the Roman Empire. I'd read *The Prince*, but not the complete works of Machiavelli." As the filmmaker explains, the film turned out to be completely different than what he had first imagined. Originally, *Le confort et l'indifférence* was to be entirely shot in the Hockeys Canadiens company, which manufactured hockey sticks and was located on the Jean-Lesage autoroute in Drummondville. Arcand thought it would make an interesting nodal point, allowing him to go from the lumberjacks cutting down ash trees to the workers preparing the wood and sending it to the hockey stick factory, and then focus on the manufacture and sales of hockey sticks to the Montreal Canadiens hockey team. Arcand would have liked to examine the workers' reactions to the referendum at every step of the production chain. "A really interesting focal point. But three or four months before the referendum campaign began, the company workers decided to go on strike. I couldn't shoot my film anymore. It was a catastrophe, I was in desperate straits; I was lost. My brother Gabriel gave me the idea of Machiavelli: 'If you're lost, why not reread Machiavelli? If you're making a film on politics, he's essential.' If I couldn't have a material focal point, at least I could construct a kind of intellectual crystallisation with the writings of Machiavelli. We'd shoot all we could of the events of the referendum, and then I'd try to compose the film around the texts. That's the film as it is today. Readings help structure a film. I'm like all intellectuals; when I have an idea in mind, I always start by reading everything there is on the subject. I've done it for all my films, including the dramas. After that, I get down to work. I even did it for *The Decline of the American Empire*; I read everything about divorce, couple relations, statistics, the social state of relations between men and women in 1985. I was thoroughly versed in the subject before I began shooting the film."

Just before the release of *Le confort et l'indifférence*, Arcand meets with another rebuff. Between 1979 and 1981, for producer Pierre Lamy, he had worked on the script for *Maria Chapdelaine* in collaboration with playwright André Ricard. The screenwriters received funding of $15,000 from the Institut québécois du cinéma. The work was done in two phases, which was customary at that time for screenplays adapted from Quebec literary classics: first a six-episode television series and then a feature film. The two versions are different. For the feature, Arcand chose to introduce as main protagonist the author Louis Hémon who is working on his novel *Maria Chapdelaine*. This element does not appear in the television series.

The unproduced screenplay for *Maria Chapdelaine* resurfaced in the Cinémathèque's 1987 monograph on Arcand in *Copie zéro*. The filmmaker claimed he did not have many projects that had not been produced; however, by that time, he had over ten of them, to which many others would be added during the 1990s. Arcand does not remember working on the six television episodes, apparently written by André Ricard alone. However, he has an unforgettable memory of his screenplay, which is highly original in the modest history of film adaptations of classic Quebec novels. Indeed, Arcand's script includes the voice of Louis Hémon, who is writing to his mother about his life in Grand Péribonka, in the Lac Saint-Jean region. Throughout the screenplay, the words of Hémon are taken from the novel itself. This narrative decision means that the story of the novel's composition is an integral part of the film. Never do we lose track of the raw, dark subject of a French novelist, a writer. This is Arcand's way of making literature visible and paying tribute to it. The film opens as follows:

Scene 1

Winter in the great burnt-out woodland area of Lac Saint-Jean. A cart drawn by two old horses slowly approaches. Samuel is asleep; it is Maria who is holding the reins.

VOICE OF LOUIS HÉMON: Madame Félix Hémon, 26 rue Vauquelin, Paris. Dearest Mother, Agriculture is no longer short of hands, for it has mine. On the farm where I'm working, I'm helping clear the land in a part of the country that greatly needs it. Here is my new address: Poste restante, Grand Péribonka (Lac Saint-Jean), the Province of Quebec, Canada. [. . .] What I like here is that manners are simple and devoid of affectation. We go to bed fully clothed so as not to have to get dressed again in the morning, and wash ourselves down on Sunday mornings. The fields have a way of trailing off into the woods, and once you're in the woods, you can go all the way to Hudson Bay. Do not send me too many newspapers, I'm dozens of kilometres away from the post office, which itself is a day's cart-ride from the railroad, and mail gets to me in bundles. I hope this finds you all in good health. Your son, Louis.

Hémon's presence as narrator increasingly asserts itself over the two years that Arcand works on the screenplay. An interim version of 182 pages, dated December 1980, shows that a voice-over has been added for Hémon's character, but only at page 123. At the end of the screenplay, after explaining that he has mailed the manuscript for *Maria Chapdelaine* back to France, the novelist character specifies: "No, the manuscript will not be published here. If you knew French Canada, you would not make such a comical presumption." This remark disappears in the final, 118-page version of February 1981 in which "Hémon's" voice is present throughout the film. His last words are as follows: "Dearest Mother, I'm leaving for the West this evening. My address will be Poste Restante, Winnipeg, Manitoba. My best to everyone. Louis Hémon. P.S.: I've sent my manuscript to your address, but in my name. Please put it in the trunk with my other papers." It is 1913. Louis Hémon will never reach Manitoba. On July 8, in Chapleau, in Northern Ontario, he is hit by a train and dies.

Thus, Arcand constructed this extraordinary script, his dream of an implacable film, biting and naturalistic, anything but romantic. Then came the coup de theâtre. Arcand explains: "Astral Film, which had been denied licensing from the CRTC for a specialized television channel, had to prove itself in the domain of cultural production. The company set its sights on the classic *Maria Chapdelaine*." Jean Lebel of Inter-vidéo, in conjunction with Radio-Canada, gives the project to Gilles Carle. Arcand loses production financing for his *Maria Chapdelaine*, a tough blow for one of the most beautiful screenplays in Québécois cinema.

After this setback, Arcand lets himself be convinced, for the first time, to try writing for theatre (as we will see in the "Intermezzo" chapter in this book). In 1982, he adapts his play *Fin du voyage* into a script that will never be produced but in which it is hard not to see a kind of mock-up for the future *Decline*. The synopsis is five pages long and is dated August 2. "This film would be a comedy on marriage and sexual fidelity, divorce, women's liberation, the ambivalent relations between the French and the Québécois, prostitution, Quebec men's fear of women, hypochondria, cancer, the solitude of thirty-five-year-old women, credit cards and other subjects of current interest." The more developed version of the script introduces two Quebec men, Jean-Guy, an agricultural engineer, and Roger, a sales' representative, as well as a

Quebec woman, Dyane, an English teacher. The trio is at the end of a trip to Paris and the scene is Charles-de-Gaulle airport. There are also three French characters, Nadine, Alain and Véra. On the eve of their departure for Mirabel airport, Roger spends the night with Véra, a prostitute from rue Saint-Denis. The next day, in a boutique at Charles-de-Gaulle, Jean-Guy spends all his money on luxurious gifts, in order to be "forgiven for his trip. Yet he has nothing to be forgiven for: his conduct has been above reproach. However, as he knows, the absent are always wrong." There is an announcement that the plane will be routed through Toronto due to a strike at Mirabel. "Jean-Guy phones his wife to apologize for the fact that the plane has to be rerouted. He also apologizes for the general strike." Having missed a night in Paris with Nadine, who runs the duty-free shop at Charles-de-Gaulle, Jean-Guy spends this unexpected night with Dyane at the Toronto Hilton: "A terrified, grateful, trembling, lost, happy and desperate Jean-Guy." It must be kept in mind that the filmmaker, in writing this project (he does not at all remember whom it was written for), is not far from beginning his "Conversations scabreuses" ("racy conversations"). *La fin du voyage* already resembles a synopsis for *The Decline of the American Empire*.

It has always been understood that Arcand worked on the screenplay for the fourth episode of *Empire Inc.*, but without his name appearing in the titles. The truth is more complex. In February 1980, he finished a complete screenplay entitled *Les gens adorent les guerres* (*People Love Wars*). This unproduced screenplay is of great interest, as it returns to the form of the original *On est au coton*, with its antagonistic parallels between bosses and workers. The story takes place in Montreal during World War Two, and revolves around North Air, one of the war-equipment factories belonging to the millionaire Munroe. The film opens with a documentary shot: "On the walls are posters that urge workers to work harder than ever for the sake of the war effort." Through the development of various related themes, the screenwriter draws a dialectical portrait of wartime, contrasting the forces of money with the factory workers' milieu. The latter milieu is described by French-Canadian soldiers who do not return from the European front, the ones who always find a way to make music. "Even at the front, they always managed to find accordions, guitars, violins, bombardes. And they played for hours. I still remember some of the pieces, *Le reel du pendu* (*The Hanged Man's Reel*), *La ronfleuse Gobeil* (*Snoring Mother Gobeil*). *La ronfleuse Gobeil* was my favourite."

The workers are also trade unionists, both Communist and non-Communist. As Munroe says, "Communists are the ones who produce the most" but who "want control over production," with whom management works things out—or not. Strikes are multiplying all over Canada. Arcand's script also evokes the political context at the time of the alliance with the Soviets in the fight against Nazism, when Duplessis promulgates his anti-Communist "Padlock Law" and has strikers charged by police. Also shown are hospitals that have run out of space, a series of photos of rural Quebec in the forties, and then urban photos of rich opera-lovers. Above all, the screenplay emphasizes the fact that the world loves war because it is a liberation: "War is an opportunity for me. A wonderful opportunity. [. . .] People always say: It must have been hell. But really it's not like that at all. It's true that it's hell. But it's also an extraordinary opportunity. Anyway for us, in Canada. War was what helped me get away from my father. [. . .] For the French Canadians, war was a fantastic opportunity to escape unemployment and misery. It's an honourable way for anyone to escape. Escape from the family you hate, the woman you don't love anymore, the job that disgusts you. Go off to Europe or the Pacific, have adventures you'd never have had otherwise. And if you don't come back, well, too bad. No one cares about life as much as that. That's why wars are so successful. You know, wars are very popular. In fifty years, one hundred years, we'll still be reading novels and seeing films about that war. People love wars. Even those who don't fight in them."

Munroe, the Anglo-Montreal capitalist, "feeds off the blood of the French-Canadian working class," exploits "the people who are neither handsome nor intelligent" and practises bookkeeping as if it were "an art, like surrealist painting." He lives in his area of the city as if it were another city entirely. He divulges the secret of his success: "My secret is that I never trust anyone. Never. I've never thought the government was there to help me, I've never thought the trade unions were there to help me, I've never thought the banks were there to help me. I've never thought anyone would help me. I've always thought there was only one person I could count on. Always. And that person is myself. That's my secret. That's how I became a millionaire." One last aspect of the film to be noted is its violence, comparable with that of *Gina*: to lose a hand at the factory is serious for a manual worker and also for a pianist.

The screenplay's themes and sociohistorical framework call to mind the dialectic developed by Arcand in the first *On est au coton* and in *Nesbitt's Trip*. Arcand explains that the script was not accepted because it was too different from the other texts in the series and didn't tally with the style of the whole.

It is during this period that Jacques Benoit proposes an original script idea to Arcand, called *Les journalistes*. According to its author, the film-maker liked the text, but the project went no further. Meanwhile, as a change from direct documentary and Quebec current events, Arcand dives into his personal life for inspiration—a rare occasion. In 1982, a project is launched for a series of films revolving around a house on Carré Saint-Louis, the mythical square that was home to the poet Nelligan, Pauline Julien, Gérald Godin, Gaston Miron and a whole string of artists. Arcand writes a screenplay for the series, entitled *1960. En mai nos amours*. It is the story of a night in the life of a student and takes place at the same period as *Seul ou avec d'autres*. The half-hour text is to be part of a series created by Andrée and Louise Pelletier, called *La maison du carré Saint-Louis*. The object of the series is to tell the story of a house on the square, from its construction as a bourgeois dwelling at the turn of the century until the 1960s, when it is trans-formed into a rooming house and hideaway for young lovers. The proj-ect goes no further for the moment but is picked up again in 1985 and restructured into six one-hour episodes. Several directors express inter-est in directing the episodes—Gilles Carle, André Brassard, Claude Jutra, Denys Arcand, Aimée Danis and Francis Mankiewicz. Arcand writes his own script; the others are written by Andrée and Louise Pelletier. The last version of *En mai nos amours*, dated August 11, 1986, is co-signed by Arcand and the Pelletiers.

The story is a comedy based on Arcand's personal memories of his last days at Collège Sainte-Marie. The story takes place in May 1959, when the young man, Jean-Guy, is still living with his parents. In his father's car, the student goes to pick up his sweetheart at the Marguerite-Bourgeoys convent school. Their plan is to spend the night in a rented room in the house on Carré Saint-Louis. But very quickly, the student comes up with numerous pretexts to flee. He phones his mother on the sly to tell her he'll be home late, and finally abandons the young woman, saying that he has to go work at the student newspaper. Back at his parents' home, the young man eats a piece of his mother's good raisin pie and tells his parents that he has been to see *Hiroshima, mon amour*, a "film on the atomic bomb, very interesting, part of the French new wave." The mother expresses concern. "I thought I read somewhere that there's nudity in that film." "Not really," replies Jean-Guy. Arcand would still like to see the *Maison du carré Saint-Loui*s project picked up again and brought to term, which there is occasionally question of doing.

Almost ten years after writing *En mai nos amours*, Arcand works for a time on *C'est la vie*. These are the only projects in which the film-maker refers so transparently to his childhood and youth in descriptions of Deschambault and his teen years in Montreal. Also in these scripts, we discern the Arcand who admits to *Elle* magazine in 1987 that he has always felt more at ease with men than with women. With women, he says, he always has the impression that he is under surveillance.

In the beginning of the 1980s, there is a change in Arcand's personal life. Soon he will leave Deschambault and become a Montrealer again. He and Édith de Villers separate in 1982, just as he is beginning to shoot *Empire Inc.* for CBC and Radio-Canada. Johanne Prégent is working on script continuity for the production. The two become a new couple and will last for almost ten years, until *Jesus of Montreal*.

Filmmaker Johanne Prégent started out with a "so-so" intellectual and cultural education during the leftist seventies at UQAM. It was a time when, so the joke goes, there were more strikes than courses and seminars. In the film industry, Johanne Prégent first works on costumes and then as a camera assistant. She meets Arcand when she is doing script continuity for *The Crime of Ovide Plouffe*. Arcand confides that Johanne Prégent, like Édith de Villers, had a great influence on his films. "No doubt I did," says Prégent, "but it's difficult to say exactly how. When I met Denys, he was coming out of his long documentary period; his first dramas still showed the influence of this tradition. *Empire Inc.* was his first big television series. I think that among other things, I helped him become aware of the importance of the artistic dimension of film, the mise-en-scene work with the actors, because he had the tendency to fix on the actors' faces, which is not a fault, of course. I helped him become aware of the whole artistic dimension of the image."

Arcand becomes involved in *Empire Inc.* at the instigation of Mark Blandford, executive producer for the series. Starting in the winter of 1982, Arcand directs parts II, V and VI, and Doug Jackson has been working on parts I, III and IV since late 1981. In the titles for the latter episode, Arcand's name appears along with that of Douglas Bowie, though only a few fragments remain of his original text *Les gens adorent les guerres*. In an interview with Nathalie Petrowski in *Le Devoir* on February 20, 1983, Arcand explains that he wants only to direct apolitical episodes because "I'm getting fed up with politics." Disillusioned, almost bitter, he continues: "I'm like a whore. [. . .] I don't have the soul of an apostle or a missionary. After *Duplessis*, no one expressed interest in seeing me move onto something else . . ." And then his *Maria Chapdelaine* was confiscated: "Our main problem here is that Quebec culture is run by civil servants who don't give a damn about creation. [. . .] Filmmakers are not encouraged, not stimulated, not recognized."

In the commissioned *Empire Inc.*, we may discern a number of details that bear the Arcand signature. In the second episode, there is a short opera scene in which a vocalist sings the Countess's cantilena from Mozart's *Nozze di Figaro*, the melancholy "Dovè sono i bei momenti"; there are also several Strauss waltzes played on the piano. In the fifth episode there are some very beautiful shots of a working-class street and the pond on Île Sainte-Hélène, and others taken from the promenade on Mount Royal looking down over the city.

In 1983–1984, Arcand works on a feature project on Émile Nelligan, initiated by Aude Nantais. The project is granted $20,000 for script development by the Institut québécois du cinéma. Aude Nantais, Jean-Joseph Tremblay and Denys Arcand are to write the script; Arcand is to direct. His film treatment proposes several interesting approaches to the subject: "What fascinates me about Nelligan's life story is that it allows one to imagine how a person's country can drive him mad. And God knows that Quebec (like many other little provincial, backward countries) has had this effect on many people who see themselves as 'artists.'

Through the story of Nelligan, I see the faint outlines of those of Borduas, Hubert Aquin, Claude Gauvreau and many others. [. . .] The only film I can think of that comes close to what I have in mind is Peter Watkins' *Edvard Munch*. Like Watkins, I envisage an intimist film, resolutely removed from the usual style of 'period films.' It could be shot in 16 mm with a lot of close-ups, in an evocative and rather claustrophobic style." The project goes no further. After the refusal of *Maria Chapdelaine*, Arcand suddenly turns away from tragic Quebec subjects with miserabilist undertones. The subject of Nelligan in particular horrifies him to the point of nausea, partly because he thinks the young man was a mediocre poet who wrote not even four interesting lines. *Nelligan* will be made years later and released in 1991, a feature written by Aude Nantais and Jean-Joseph Tremblay, directed by Robert Favreau. This *Nelligan* is diametrically opposed to Arcand's view of the subject. Arcand would have depicted Nelligan as mad, a tragic victim of his family and the society of his times, locked up on his father's orders at Saint-Jean-de-Dieu, an asylum in east Montreal where he was even castrated to neutralize his sexual impulses.

Also in the first half of the 1980s, Arcand does script consulting and bread-and-butter jobs in television and advertising. For five years, he is a reader for Telefilm Canada and is often asked for his advice. Besides *Nelligan*, he works on *B.L.A. Finance* (Robert Ménard, Donald Pilon, Donald Lautrec), *Baie James* by Louis Saïa, *Petites violences et grande douceur* (Laurier Bonin and Claude R. Blouin), and three versions of a single project, *L'oncle maternel*, *Caractères imprimés* and *Ma sœur, mon amour* by Suzy Cohen, as well as *L'amour scorpion* by François Floquet.

He explains that while he does not earn a great deal from this work, lesser-known screenwriters benefit from the sponsorship of an experienced filmmaker when their projects are examined by the funding institutions. It also gives them a chance to improve the quality of their writing. He admits that more skilled and experienced screenwriters do not need this kind of sponsorship whereas the others, the ones who need help, usually don't go any further. "Often, I didn't dare say no to friends and acquaintances, or others who needed support for their grant applications. Today I stay away from that kind of request. I hardly do any script consultation anymore."

But once in a while, his opinion is required for important projects, such as Harold Pinter's film adaptation of *Remembrance of Things Past*. Consulted in 1993, Arcand refers to Pinter's script as "a great book" ("I hesitate to call it a script," he says), calling it "supremely intelligent and amazingly faithful to the original work." In spite of the screenplay's many qualities, Arcand firmly maintains that Proust's masterpiece cannot be adapted for the screen. In his opinion, Pinter is trapped by his intention of doing so and that his script is more novelistic than dramatic. Following the principles of Aristotle's *Poetics*, Arcand firmly believes that a film depends most of all on a dramatic framework. But Proust was no dramaturge, he says; his ambition was to evoke the slow passage of time, and he does so with rare mastery, a complex, even tortuous use of the French language in his phrasing and punctuation, all of which are things that a camera cannot capture. An image cannot register an odour or capture the way the mind works to recall a colour. Arcand will use these arguments in his paper for a 1995 conference on film and literature in Bologna. This text is included in the "Selected Readings."

"*The Crime of Ovide Plouffe* was my consolation prize for having *Maria Chapdelaine* taken from me! It was a commission and I worked on it in the way one performs a technical exercise." The idea of making an American-style sequel to the classic *Les Plouffe* (*The Plouffe Family*, based on the novel by Roger Lemelin) comes from Denis Héroux and Gilles Carle. Since the early eighties, Carle has specialized in superproductions adapted from Quebec literary classics, in a mixed-genre formula combining a television series and a feature for theatrical release. According to this formula, *Les Plouffe* appears in 1981 followed by *Maria Chapdelaine* in 1983. This first triptych ends with *The Crime of Ovide Plouffe*, a sequel to *Les Plouffe* written at top speed by Roger Lemelin and published in 1984.

Ovide Plouffe is a strange hodge-podge, composed of six television episodes, the first of which are shot by Carle in 16 mm, the last two by Arcand in 35 mm and spliced together to make the film version. Arcand's shoot runs from July 19 to October 15, 1983. In 1984, the *Globe and Mail*, which scorns this hybrid formula, finds Arcand a little embarrassed by having to present "his" film in Toronto. Today the filmmaker concludes: "Denis Héroux, who claimed he couldn't find a dollar to produce one of my scripts, hatched a plan to make a sequel for the film *Les Plouffe*. A mongrel project. Héroux had air time to fill on Radio-Canada. He had a contract in pocket even before Lemelin started writing his new novel, which is first and above all commissioned by a producer! An abominable novel! I never worked as hard as I did on that film, to achieve a result that was neutral at best. It was a much more difficult exercise than making a good film from a good script. It's the only unpleasant shoot I've ever done. Luckily Johanne Prégent was there. Everyone was just doing it for the money. A sordid business! Sheer hell!"

As for Johanne Prégent, she says that Arcand put all his sensibility and determination into shooting *Empire Inc.* and *The Crime of Ovide Plouffe*: "Denys never does anything lightly, whether it's a TV series or a commercial. When he accepts a project, it's to direct it and do a good job. I always found it odd how he called himself lazy, which he isn't at all. He's very contradictory. Yes, *The Crime of Ovide Plouffe* was a commission, but it wasn't without interest. He put all his energy and all his soul into the shoot, not as much as for one of his own films but almost. He had a lot of fun making this film and working with the author." Arcand himself likes to recall a comment made by Jean Carmet during the shoot, "It's not the first bad film we've had to make and it won't be our last. So we might as well have fun." Still, Arcand feels it was his worst film experience. "I didn't have my usual team; I was like a foreigner on the set. I was dying of boredom. The worst shoot of my life."

A number of Arcand trademarks can be discerned in the script: inserts on opera and the vocalist Yvonne Printemps; a scene with a vendor of plaster relgious statues, a sort of foreshadowing of the sequence with Father Leclerc in *The Barbarian Invasions*; and finally, Ovide Plouffe's lecture in Paris about the historical friendship between the Montagnais and the first French colonizers in Canada, and how the Iroquois hated them.

Starting in 1983, Arcand will also direct several commercials, as he describes in his speech entitled "Filmmakers and Advertising." Unlike many Québécois filmmakers, who for the sake of their image mention only the films they make as "artists," remaining silent about bread-and-butter work in advertising, Arcand talks abundantly and with pride on the subject. He is always learning about film, no matter what he has been commissioned to do. Let us recall that he considered his first short films with the NFB as "film school." Similarly, offers from Radio-Canada, commercial made-for-television-movies such as *Empire Inc.* and *The Crime of Ovide Plouffe* and work in advertising all provide an unexpectedly fertile terrain for the development of screenwriting skills, experimentation with new filmic techniques and mise-en-scene. These productions, he emphasizes without batting an eyelid, are also good opportunities to make money and keep yourself alive.

In 1983, after the release of *Le confort et l'indifférence*, Roger Frappier sets up a work group at the NFB that will allow a certain number of filmmakers to develop collective film projects. Tahani Rached, Léa Pool, Denys Arcand, Jacques Leduc and Pierre Falardeau participate in the workshop. This "band of five" will gradually develop *Haïti-Québec*, *Anne Trister*, *Le Déclin de l'empire americain*, *Trois pommes à côté du sommeil* and *Octobre*. There is a lot of poker being played in Quebec film in the mid-1980s.

In this workshop framework, Arcand conceives his most emblematic film, a sensational coup, a miraculous success both nationally and internationally, an all-time triumph for modern Quebec cinema to date. This period strongly contrasts with the one following *Gina*, the decade of Arcand's "crossing of the desert," the only time he sincerely and profoundly doubted his abilities as filmmaker and felt he had run out of ideas for *films d'auteur*. But we may recall that at that time, Arcand also produced two powerful works: the screenplay for *Duplessis*, an exploit until then unequalled in the entire history of Radio-Canada television series, as well as *Le confort et l'indifférence* at the NFB, the filmmaker's finale in the documentary essay genre, his *Finis coronat opus*. Also during this period, he writes five solid screenplays: *Nesbitt's Trip*, *Maria Chapdelaine*, *Les gens adorent les guerres*, *La fin du voyage* and *1960: En mai nos amours*, not to speak of an astonishing synopsis for his *Émile Nelligan*. For a filmmaker in a state of darkness, powerlessness and doubt, this is quite a list of accomplishments. And that is not to mention his first foray into writing for the stage, with two plays and the synopsis for an opera.

The project for *Conversations scabreuses* (*Racy Conversations*) is dated September 6, 1984. "Four women arrive at a country house where four men are waiting for them. The dinner is delightful and the themes discussed earlier that afternoon are taken up by the group as a whole. Everyone lies. Male solidarity is invincible. Female complicity is triumphant. Hatred flashes beneath the smiles and jokes." This is the matrix for what will become the first version of a film entitled *The Decline and Fall of the American Empire*, written between November 1984 and February 1985. It opens in a gym at the physical education centre at the Université de Montréal, to the sounds of a baritone trio, the *Eurydice* trio of Haydn on an air by Gluck.

In this first version, the young woman student whom Pierre falls in love with, and who works as an erotic masseuse, names several examples of major violence in history: 40 million Amerindians killed between 1525 and 1750; the religious wars in France; half the population of London dying of starvation in 1850; the Punic Wars and sixty thousand deaths in Cannes in a single day. Pierre replies: "The history of humanity is a horror story." These pieces of dialogue, which were cut from *The Decline*, reappear almost word for word in *The Barbarian Invasions*. Also in the first drafts we find allusions to friends who have committed suicide. One shuts himself in the garage and turns on his car engine; the other goes to the grounds of a convent and shoots himself in the mouth with a 12-gauge shotgun; a third one runs into a highway pillar at 110 miles an hour; another simply lies down on his kitchen floor and turns on the gas; a fifth hangs himself with a nylon stocking in a cupboard; the sixth throws himself off the Jacques-Cartier bridge and the seventh from Place Ville-Marie. And then there is the surprising detail of a poem by Auden on beauty and death, "Lay your sleeping head, my love," which opens a window on the future screenplays of *Beautiful* and *Stardom*.

The Decline ends with the Haydn trio. The second version is produced in May and June of 1985, followed by a third at the end of the summer. The film is shot in the fall and comes out in the summer of 1986, a triumph. It is released only a few months before Horace Arcand's death on Thursday, November 13, at noon. The Arcand *pater familias* passes away at his home, at 122 rue Pointe-Lauzon in Deschambault, the house he had built after returning from Montreal, where he would spend the rest of his days. Through the big window, the "Queen's Pilot" tirelessly contemplated the river he knew so well.

INTERMEZZO

THE LITTLE THEATRE OF DENYS ARCAND

As in Jean Renoir, we open with the rising
of a miniature curtain, red and gold.

For Denys Arcand, the passion for theatre goes back to
Deschambault and the games of the Arcand children,
playlets and little adventures with costumes, makeup and
props. It also goes back to the young Denys's "role" of incense bearer in
church, playing as he would on stage with the censer as his prop. His
obsession develops in a more clear and conscious manner at Collège
Sainte-Marie in the mid-1950s. Arcand has a particularly strong memory of the first professional play he attended, Shakespeare's *Twelfth
Night*, a Theatre Club production directed by Jean Doat with sets, costumes and makeup by Alfred Pellan. And then there is the following
savoury anecdote, worthy of Alexandre Dumas: the students discovered
an underground passage, nicknamed "the catacombs," that led from the
college to the adjacent Gesù theatre in the basement of the church of the
same name. "We entered the theatre without paying; we were there all
the time, for all the plays of the Theâtre du Nouveau Monde (TNM) and
also the Theatre Club, by Molière (including *Le malade imaginaire* with
Guy Hoffmann) and Shakespeare, *Ubu roi* and lots of other plays . . ."
Once in a while, the young Arcand helps out as a stagehand.

Hence, in the cultural life of the young Arcand, the theatre
becomes a choice setting for artistic expression. Moreover, Arcand's

entire film career is constructed as a kind of "little theatre," as in *Le petit théâtre de Jean Renoir*, the last film made by the great French filmmaker and one of Arcand's favourites, especially the final sketch with Françoise Arnoul. Indeed, Renoir's title could also be applied to the work of Denys Arcand, in view of the passion for theatre that is revealed in and through his films. For this singular title is not only a reference to the original matrix of cinema but also to the space in which the dramas of the human species and its civilizations unfold. Like Ingmar Bergman, Jean Renoir possessed an uncanny instinct for producing pure cinema from the arts that preceded and nourished it: painting, music, poetry and especially theatre, the synthesis of all the arts. For example, *Le carosse d'or* (*The Golden Coach*) starts in a theatre, in the middle of a production of Prosper Mérimée's *Carosse du Saint-Sacrement*, and yet we are never *in* that theatre because filmic elements devour and transfigure the devices and simulacra of the stage. The same goes for Renoir's *Le petit théâtre*, a full-length film composed of four sketches of varying lengths. It opens with the filmmaker standing next to a tiny theatre made of red and gold cardboard. The filmmaker himself announces: "Ladies and gentlemen, here is my little theatre. On this miniature stage, I have the honour and the pleasure of illustrating for you several anecdotes that I find amusing and that I hope you'll find entertaining." In this testament film, Renoir achieves a synthesis of Belle Époque theatre, opera and song, and modern realism à la Pagnol, all of it cast in a triumphant filmic language.

Denys Arcand is one of the rare Quebec filmmakers to have accomplished this kind of metamorphosis. His passion for theatre is especially evident in his films—in which he also occasionally acts—and in his exceptional talent for dialogue. His dramaturgical structures employ the unities of time, place and action of neoclassical French theatre. The influence of theatre asserts itself in his work in film and television, though from time to time, he also makes a foray onto the stage.

The epithet "little" is anything but pejorative. It simply designates the reduced dimensions of the performance space in question. Arcand's theatre is made on the scale of Quebec or Montreal, as the Gospel according to Saint Mark, a text that Arcand likes very much, contains "a little apocalypse." "Theatre" also refers to the fact that a filmmaker practises his art in public, whether during the production process or while accompanying his films after their release. Press conferences and interviews are part of the art of self-performance and the presentation of works. A filmmaker is an actor, the way in Shakespeare the world is a stage on which each person plays his or her little role and then leaves, as W.G. Sebald often reminds us.

While a student, Arcand sees an incredible number of plays, by Beaumarchais and Shakespeare but also De Musset, whose *Lorenzaccio* he is lucky enough to see with Gérard Philipe in the lead role. In *Le quartier latin*, he writes reviews on several performance events and plays: a touring production by the Comédie-Française, the Royal Ballet of Denmark, Kleist's *The Broken Jug*, the comedy troupes Les Cyniques, the Joyeux Carabins and the Bozos (with Clémence DesRochers), *Le barbier de Séville* in which Geneviève Bujold makes her début, Shakespeare's *Richard II* ("an excellent performance"), *Les trois coups de minuit* (*The Three Strokes of Midnight*) by André Obey, as well as portraits by André Dubois, Monique Lepage, Stéphane Venne, Gilles Vigneault, the Winter Carnival and the Bleu et Or choir, not to speak of plays at McGill University's Moyse Hall, such as *Doctor Faustus* by Christopher Marlowe.

Arcand also acts in several productions: *Murder in the Cathedral* by T.S. Eliot, Hochwalder's *On Earth as in Heaven* at Collège Sainte-Marie and *Twelve Angry Men* by Reginald Rose at the Université de Montréal. André Brochu remembers the Hochwalder play, presented in 1958 by the two classes in Rhetoric. "Denys played a majestic bishop, an adversary of the Jesuit State in Paraguay. He played him with the necessary roguish dignity and arrogance. At the end of his confrontation with the provincial priest, in front of the visitor of the King of Spain, in a very mannered way he drops the hand he extended to be kissed. This conceited gesture delighted the students, who were as amused by all this unction as the actor himself was, and also the Jesuits in charge of the production. For them, you couldn't overact the role of this representative of the high clergy, the enemy of controversial 'reductions.'"

In his first year of university, in the spring of 1961, Arcand acts in *Twelve Angry Men*, by the American playwright Rose, while continuing his theatre workshops with Gilles Marsolais. The play is directed by Marc Laurendeau, who will soon become the director of Les Cyniques and perform his monologue "La soirée de culte" in the film *Seul ou avec d'autres*. The Reginald Rose play deals with the harrowing deliberations of a jury that must decide the fate of a young man from a disadvantaged neighbourhood who is accused of murder. It was later adapted for the famous film of the same name. The Université de Montréal production, performed at the Theâtre du Gesù, seems to have been well received. A critical summary written by Stéphane Venne, in the student paper for March 7, praises Juror number eight, played by Denys Arcand, noting flexible movements, firm voice, impeccable diction and speculates: "Mr. Arcand possesses the necessary talent to make a career of theatre."

It did not turn out that way, though we can well imagine that Arcand might have considered going into theatre as an actor, director or playwright. At the end of the seventies, he tries his hand at writing plays and in the eighties, an opera libretto.

In the beginning of 1990, he directs his first professional stage production at the Theâtre de Quat'Sous, the *Lettres de la religieuse portugaise* (*The Portuguese Nun's Letters*). As for acting, he dismissed this option early in life, as he explains in his short essay "On Being an Actor," which is included in the "Selected Readings." He does not think he has the physique for this profession: "I thought I was too tall, my head too big, my nose too long, my voice too deep. For theatre you have to have a flexibile body, which I didn't have. I was clumsy, awkward."

This will not prevent him from giving into the temptation to act, once in a while—ten times in all. Over the decades, he has been seen or heard in a number of films, including *The Barbarian Invasions*. He did the voice-over for *Seul ou avec d'autres*, *Québec:Duplessis et après . . .*, *On est au coton* and *La lutte des travailleurs d'hôpitaux*. On the sound track for the ONF production *Duplessis*, it is his voice we hear interviewing Gisèle Trépanier, who reads aloud from "the voters' little catechism": "What do you mean by marasmus?—We usually take 'marasmus' to mean the phase of languish and wasting that precedes death." Arcand appears as an extra in a promotional short for the fifth World Film Festival in Montreal, made in 1964 by Gilles Carle; in a 1966 film by Jean-Claude Labrecque, he plays the lead role of movie-lover and film-reel messenger who risks everything to get the films to the spectators. In Gilles Groulx's *Le chat dans le sac*, he even plays one of the stuntmen, replacing Barbara Ulrich at the wheel of his sportscar, an MGB that no one but himself was allowed to drive.

Later he briefly appears in Michel Brault's *Le temps perdu* (1964), in Jean Pierre Lefebvre's *Mon œil* (1966) and, the same year, in an IMAX film directed by Colin Low for the Quebec Pavillion at Expo. In 1967 he appears in *C'est pas la faute à Jacques Cartier* by Georges Dufaux and Clément Perron, and plays the lead in Jacques Leduc's feature drama *Nominingue . . . depuis qu'il existe*, as we have already seen. In the seventies, he appears in his own films, *La maudite galette* and *Réjeanne Padovani*, but also in another film by Lefebvre, *On n'engraisse pas les cochons à l'eau claire* (*Pigs Are Seldom Clean*) and *La tête de Normande St-Onge* by Gilles Carle. In the following decade, he appears in Jean-Claude Lauzon's *Un zoo, la nuit*; in *Jesus of Montreal*, playing a judge; in the sketch by Patricia Rozema, *Desperando,* in *Montréal vu par . . .* , Arcand flies in the sky over Montreal on the arms of two charming young women. In 1992, he acts for Jean-Claude Lauzon once again, in *Léolo*, and in Mireille Goulet's *Les malheureux magnifiques*. Later he appears in *Littoral* (*Tideline*), Wajdi Mouawad's first feature. A surprise: in *The Barbarian Invasions*, Arcand gives himself the role of a Mafioso-type trade unionist, a caricature for the benefit of those who have for years reproached the filmmaker for having abandoned politically committed filmmaking in favour of navel-gazing and hedonism.

At Collège Sainte-Marie, paradoxically it is theatre that led Arcand to film. At the Université de Montréal in 1961, for *Seul ou avec d'autres*, Denis Héroux recruits Arcand mainly for the purpose of having him direct the actors' improvisations. Hence, Arcand's first film experiences are theatre-related, a kind of metamorphosis or subversion of this artistic domain. Later, having chosen filmmaking as a profession, Arcand constructs his filmography with the help of various parameters borrowed from the dramatic arts. Before you do anything, the filmmaker repeats, you have to go back to the sourcebook for Western drama. When young screenwriters come to him for advice, Arcand tells them: "It's very easy, just read the *Poetics* of Aristotle, it's all there. It's relatively simple: you have a hero facing a challenge who heads towards the climax, the catharsis at the end. In modern terms, that's what's in the screenwriting recipes of Robert McKee and Syd Field, or the films of Arnold Schwarzenegger. But Aristotle is hard for young people to understand. This ancient Greek work has become unreadable."

In the words of writer Yvon Rivard, a friend of the filmmaker and one of his tennis partners, all of Arcand's cinema can be understood in terms of Greek philosophy: "Just as he doesn't improvise in tennis or golf, in film he is someone who has learned and mastered the rules of dramatic art, be it from Aristotle or from going to see the great classics of theatre. That's where his strength comes from, his ability to take charge of a narrative, his sense of formula and scene organization."

Other parameters of Arcand's films are derived from theatre as well. The mixing of genres, for example, very common in Shakespeare or Molière, is consistently practised by the filmmaker, something that many spectators and critics find disconcerting. Comic elements are combined with dramatic and tragic ones, taking on a number of forms: suppressed irony, humorous passages, jokes and caricatures, even buffoonery. In *Réjeanne Padovani*, the solemnity of the Gluck aria, *I lost my Eurydice*, gives way to a parody of the opera *Carmen* by the drunken musician and singer; the chaotic seduction scene with the mayor's wife, the meal of the gluttonous minister, grotesque moments such as these serve as counterpoints to the tragic murder of the Mafioso's ex-wife. In *Gina*, the music of "Oh, Canada" at the end of the programming day precedes the rape of the dancer; at Dorval airport, mariachi melodies played for the benefit of tourists accompany the dancer's escape from Quebec. In *The Decline*, as in *The Barbarian Invasions*, the outlandish and ridiculous punctuate plots that are eminently sad and tragic. The same goes for *Love and Human Remains* and *Stardom*, in which the melancholy rock-ballad and the arias of Verdi and Weber lend a background of gravity to comic scenes whose irony is nonetheless tinged with anxiety and bitterness.

Arcand also uses the famous rule of three unities, time, place and action, the cornerstone of French neoclassical theatre. "We've invented nothing. It is the fundamental rule of story structure that goes back to the dawn of time or to the Stone Age storytellers. Good directors are extraordinary storytellers, even in daily life." The actions and stories of Arcand's films always take place in a very limited time frame: a single night in *Réjeanne Padovani* and *The Decline*, a few days in *Gina* and *Jesus of Montreal*. Moreover, to tell a story in a condensed manner while keeping the spectator on tenterhooks requires an acute sense of dialogue. Dialogue must be honed with concrete, daily and local images that also have an aura of universality. The great strength of Arcand's dialogue is that it resembles theatrical dialogue.

Arcand's greatest film tribute to the theatre is *Jesus of Montreal*. Its pretitle sequence is an excerpt from a stage production of Dostoevsky's *The Brothers Karamazov*, the scene of Smerdiakov's suicide. The itinerary of Daniel Coulombe/Jesus consists of subverting the Passion of the Gospel, turning it into a passion for theatre. The source of Coulombe's great anger is not some form of religious mysticism but simply *people's contempt for actors*, which he cannot accept. It is this situation that leads the actor René Sylvestre to say that "acting in the passion play is dangerous." Theatre is dangerous, a strange sort of sanctuary, a world of superstition and fear of bad luck. For example, one must never utter the word "rope" or say the title *Macbeth*, the latter being a cursed play whose main character must be referred to as "the Scot."

Jesus of Montreal also teaches us a great deal about how Arcand directs actors—one need only observe Daniel Coulombe. First, Arcand respects and likes actors; he has full, almost absolute trust in them. Here we may recall another anecdote featuring Jean Renoir. Just before shooting a scene, before saying "camera" or "action," the director would take off his hat as a sign of respect for the actors who were about to play the scene. Arcand shows this kind of respect to the actors on his shoots. He is not at all "directive," and even less dictatorial; on the contrary, sometimes he even forgets to say "action" and the first assistant does it for him. Daniel Coulombe tells his fellow actors: "Act with restraint," that is, without show, without projection, always interiorizing, whether or not the scene contains dialogue. The only exception is when the scene calls for caricature and burlesque. Then Arcand asks the actors to pull out all the stops, enlarge their characters' traits to the point of excess. Otherwise, as in general his films are sad and melancholic, the filmmaker's instructions to underplay persuade the actors to become almost like statues, reminding us of how ancient Greco-Roman theatre or neoclassical French tragedy is described: actors in hieratic poses and costumes that leave as much room as possible for dialogue; lighting that is almost always natural daylight; little or no scenery, as in Shakespeare's time.

It was not until the Romantic period in the nineteenth century that stages filled up with "scenography," elaborate costumes, projected voices, ultradramatic acting, and with the advent of electricity, increasingly studied lighting effects. Arcand, on the other hand, has adopted the style of classical theatre, which is part of what makes his cinema so complicated and disturbing, despite its outward resemblance to melodrama or téléromans. Dominated by pure classicism, this cinema is a far cry from modern romantic realism. It tends towards purity of line, a stripped-down style that verges on abstraction. It is a cinema that is enveloped, like its subjects, characters, dialogues and silences, in a kind of intellectualization based on ancient parameters. In this sense, Arcand's filmmaking resembles that of Pier Paolo Pasolini—it's a cinema of risk, a dangerous cinema that inspires respect and sometimes admiration but is often difficult to grasp in its anachronistic classicism. In this archaic simplicity, there is a will to transform the banal into the mysterious, light into darkness, and a Buñuelian or Sebaldian way of loading the dialogue with quite heavy meanings so the author never falls into the verbiage of the téléroman, as Arcand explains in *Copie zéro*.

At the end of the seventies, Arcand decides to take the plunge into theatre by way of writing. In December 1979, Arcand writes *Un peu plus qu'un peu moins* or *La fin du voyage*, a sketch for the comedy *Les sept péchés capitaux* (*The Seven Deadly Sins*), created in Quebec City in 1980, starring Rémy Girard, Marie Tifo and Yves Jacques. Still in 1980, at the request of actor Michel Côté, he writes *Petite variation sur un thème de Claire Brétécher*, which is part of a show entitled *Mousse*, a sort of female version of *Broue*. The sketch is unsuccessful and Arcand is asked to withdraw it, which he does gracefully.

The first of the two plays is a comedy on sexuality. This is the text that Arcand will later turn into a screenplay, as mentioned earlier. The play is thirty-two pages long. The setting is Charles-de-Gaulle airport in Paris. Two Québécois men, Jean-Guy and Roger, are waiting for their Air Canada flight to Montreal. While Roger, a recent divorcé, gets drunk to erase a long night with a hooker from Pigalle, Jean-Guy, the faithful married man, chats with Nadine, a saleswoman at an airport boutique. Though he is innocent as a newborn and has not allowed himself adventures of any kind in Paris, he buys all sorts of presents for his children, his mother-in-law and his wife, "to be forgiven." He is going through a purification phase, has quit smoking and goes jogging every morning. As for his wife, she's tried every diet and attends a plethora of courses. "All the courses are very popular. My wife is always learning something. She's taken courses in folklore, pottery, leathercraft, photography, Chinese cooking, flower arranging, introduction to women's issues, jazz-ballet, physical fitness." Jean-Guy narrowly escapes having to respond to Nadine's invitation to stay an extra night in Paris. Faced with what looks to him like a mass of complications, he decides to get on the plane and return home instead.

In Arcand's second play, *La fin du voyage*, a nine-page sonatina on a theme from Bretécher, the tone is caustic and foreshadows the depiction, in *Jesus of Montreal*, of young actors and their condition. Two young actresses, Priscille and Dominique, are chatting in a laundromat and discover a kind of proletarian passion for the women coming in to do their laundry. They recall their very brief encounters with Planchon, Bourseiller, the Bread and Puppet Theater, Grotowski (whom everyone calls "Grott"), Living Theater, Peter Brooks: "When we were with Grott, we went off to discover a lake in the Carpathian Mountains. We were a totally unlikely group, a Brazilian, two Albanians, Montenegrins, and we walked through the forest in search of a certain lake. For three days we drank the lake water and swam in the middle of the night. And we ate bread. It was . . . MYSTICAL!" And then they rail against the poverty of Quebec theatre, the rotten TNM, the Rideau Vert, Duceppe—totally obsolete. In the end, a woman film director arrives and has them rehearse an ad for Oxydol laundry detergent!

An excerpt from *La fin du voyage* was presented in the *Copie zéro* monograph, as well as the synopsis for an opera that Arcand was supposed to develop and later direct with François Dompierre (music) and Jacques Stréliski (libretto). This project was written in 1985, just before the shooting of *The Decline*. Created at the request of the Fondation de l'Opéra de Québec, the work was to be presented during the second summit of La Francophonie, held in Quebec City in the autumn of 1987. In July, Dompierre confirmed that he and his colleagues had been working for a year and almost finished the first act but heard nothing more from Quebec. Thus, this opera never truly existed. Called *Fin de siècle*, "end of the century," it might as well have been called "end of the road" for this dream of a Quebec opera. The story line? "The action takes place today in a Western metropolis. The World Institute of Capitalism wishes to pay tribute to the most capitalistic century in history. To usher out the century in style it commissions the popular composer Nicolas Gauthier to compose a five-minute super-jingle." In an ultramodern recording studio, the composer works with his friend and former companion from the Conservatory, Barbara Morris, a classical vocalist. One night, he dreams that the Quebec government asks him to compose an opera, though "no one writes operas anymore; they're passé because film has replaced lyric drama." In a nightmare, the composer sees himself adapting *Maria Chapdelaine* for opera, or finds himself stuck with another rock-opera. Later, music critics appear in pastiched arias from Handel, Gershwin and Verdi. The musician sees himself as a little boy "wearing a blue chasuble," singing in a choir and being reproached for "being undisciplined and headstrong, and never doing anything the way other people do" and he is told: "an attitude like that will get you nowhere in life."Having been unable to "compose a national opera," Nicolas Gauthier is sentenced to be hanged by three critic-judges, just as the electronic alarm clock goes off, bringing the composer back to his studio, ready to record his jingle. End of opera.

In his 1990 début as theatre director at the Théâtre de Quat'Sous, it is curious and paradoxical that Arcand did not adopt a more classical approach, one characterized by sobriety and hieratical postures. We may recall that he chose this engagement as stage director when his script about death was turned down by Roger Frappier. Significantly, the work in question is one of the most classical texts of French literature, the famous *Lettres de la religieuse portugaise* (*The Portuguese Nun's Letters*), in which five passionate letters become a five-act tragedy, without strictly speaking being a play. The letters are more a metaphor, a dramaturgy of passion for one voice, without dialogue or confrontation in the usual sense. Arcand presents the text as follows: "Five anonymous letters published in 1669 by a bookstore in the Sainte Chapelle in Paris. The author will never be known: seventeenth-century modesty! The most beautiful text in the world about the sorrows of love. Is this the writing of a woman or a man? The debate has lasted three centuries. Does pain have a gender? A text that verges on incoherence, like a plaint of wounded love. A timeless voice that we immediately recognize and that speaks to us of great emotion, seduction and abandonment, gazes exchanged, sublime pleasures and despair, departures, letters, impossible reunions. How not to be touched? This story is about all of us."

In his adaptation and staging, at least if we can judge by the filmmaker's video recording of his production, Arcand takes a number of liberties with the hieratic purity of the original text and distances himself from the finished product. First, he decides to add several scenes with dialogue based on characters who are mentioned in the letters, thus increasing the number of actors, including extras to act as nuns. He adds sound effects using bells and the sound of the sea, as well as period music. He agrees to a realistic-romantic scenography, full scenery and sophisticated lighting. Finally, he allows Anne Dorval to play in a quite extroverted, rather than a restrained and interiorized, fashion, with tears and gesticulations, cries and pathos. In short, starting out with a classical text, the director ends up with a romantic, almost naturalistic production. To recall the expression of an actor in *Jesus of Montreal*, was it "dangerous" for Arcand to stage this play? Whatever the case, some call it a "succès d'estime" and others a failure.

For Arcand, if there is one form of theatre that takes precedence over the others, it is no doubt the one that is revealed on the "stage" of his filmmaking career. The director's greatest role is surely that of himself as filmmaker, a long performance of his own personality and works, acting that is all the more subtle because it does not look like acting. Indeed, when a filmmaker agrees to do interviews, or as they say in the media, "to confide," there is every indication that the object of his task is to convey information and explain his work. But our perception of this exercise changes if we think, even for a moment, that it may only be a game, the filmmaker an actor strutting across a stage or film set.

With Denys Arcand, this theatrical posturing is all the more effective because he is an excellent actor, who moreover has perfect control over the text he has authored. He does not hide this role of actor. In 1989, in *Châtelaine*, he admits: "It's all part of the game!" In *Ciné-bulles*, in the autumn of 2000, he says that the recording of an interview puts him in a "performance situation," like Tina before the eye of the camera in *Stardom*. The filmmaker has also observed, after reading Michael Ondaatje's *The Conversations: Walter Murch and the Art of Editing Film*, that cinema is a craft practised in public, during the production and promotion of one's films. Hence, all of Arcand's shoots and interviews become a long play in which he has been acting for almost a half-century. An excellent storyteller, a skillful fabricator, he has produced a torrent of interviews that form the great script of his personal theatre. He is always performing. As far as playing the role of his life is concerned (and "life is a theatre," Shakespeare wrote), Arcand has the physique as well as the mind and heart for the job. He acts. "You have to act. I act the part of a director."

The filmmaker's habit of acting no doubt also explains Arcand's tendency towards dissimulation, hyperbole and even provocation as a kind of "coup de theatre." It is possible that he partly inherited this tendency from his parents. Though his father was occasionally known to reveal fabulous details of his youthful voyages at sea, he remained essentially secretive. "My mother was a bit of a liar," Arcand confides to the television program *Entrée des artistes*, referring, for example, to the way in which she explained her departure from the Carmelite monastery. In the same breath he reveals that he "suffers from the imposter complex." To paraphrase W.G. Sebald (*On the Natural History of Destruction*), we might say that Arcand suffers from the "survivors' tale" syndrome, which arises when a person has experienced a trauma or a break in their life story; their stories are discontinuous, erratic, sometimes fabricated, resembling a novel.

The information that Arcand transmits about his life and work is sometimes random, inaccurate or approximate. It is often fabricated. For example, it is possible that during his adolescence, he did not see *La strada* at the Snowdon cinema but at the Laurie, or that *The Robe* was not playing at the Loew's but the Palace. One cannot make head or tail of it. The narrative of his career and his life are theatrically structured; everything happens in two motions, three movements. Most of the time his vocabulary is decisive, full of sweeping statements and contrasting imagery that produce spectacular effects. Often his affirmations are pointed and peremptory, final verdicts with no possibility of appeal. For example, when replying to certain allusions to the violence of the crucifixion in *Jesus of Montreal*, he comments, unruffled, "The cross was progress compared to impaling." Then there is the following judgment, perhaps the most ironic of his entire career: "The ideal for the civil servants at the NFB and funding organisms is *never* to make films!" Some people find these declarations insulting, like invitations to a duel. It appears to some that the filmmaker runs after his adversary and slaps him in the face, deliberately exposing himself to negative or vicious criticism.

Arcand's films may all seem alike. But they contain many more contrasts, nuances and contradictions than they may at first appear to. If Arcand states in an interview that "the health system is rotten" in Quebec and in Canada, it is presumed that *The Barbarian Invasions* categorically defends this point of view; if today Arcand says that the character of Claude in *The Decline of the American Empire* did not have AIDS, it is seen as contempt for the homosexual community and the impact the tragic epidemic has had upon it; his silence when he is presented with his Oscar is interpreted as a camouflage of his pride as a Quebec filmmaker. Much of the critical and audience response to Arcand's cinema confuses the theatre of his public declarations with the complex content of the films. In this sense, our best course is no doubt to follow the advice of the filmmaker, who repeats that what is most important is to watch and "read" the films themselves. That is where the meaning of his work and thought can be found, far more than in the theatre of his interviews. His true opinions can be found in the texts he has written and in the few in-depth interviews he has done, principally those he has revised himself. As for the rest, his media appearances and discussions, they must be taken with a grain of salt or a touch of humour, or simply viewed as a filmmaker-actor routine.

The tiny red and gold curtain falls.
End of the Denys Arcand little theatre.

PART TWO

HAVE TUX, WILL TRAVEL

I've often wanted to abandon film. I've stuck with it because I've never been able to find another job and because I hate teaching film. Later, after the success of The Decline, *life got easier. I became reconciled to the idea that film was my craft. A way of earning my living, which I still find very difficult, but which I like in spite of everything. I try to make the best films I can. Ones I'd like to see as a spectator. Films in which we hear the voice of an author who is struggling with the contradictions in his own life and who shares all his dilemmas, all his fears and fits of laughter, all his joy, with an eventual spectator whom he considers his equal.*

From an unpublished text,
September 15, 1991

March 2003. For the first time in over half a century, Denys Arcand watches the Ezio Pinza film in which the bass singer interprets Flégier's "Le cor." Afterwards he exclaims: "Is this really the same film? I remembered an opera singer in a tuxedo!"

In fact, the film is made in two parts. First, Pinza is rehearsing, wearing an ordinary suit, and then we see him in concert. When at the end of his aria the singer executes his famous extra-low note that so impressed Arcand, he is indeed wearing a tuxedo. The sound and image that little Denys of Deschambault retained from the film: a daredevil musical feat and a singer in gala apparel.

There is an expression that was once used by vaudeville actors looking for work: "Have tux, will travel." The tux is the counterpart of Rossellini's new suit, ordered from his tailor to go see the banker and borrow money to shoot a film.

10
FIRST RESURRECTION: BLEAK END-OF-THE-WORLD LIGHT

"Filmmaking: pure poker." Denys Arcand responds with these quiet words to the enthusiastic reception of *The Decline of the American Empire*. The film is his sixth dramatic feature, his tenth if we count the scripts he wrote for *Jusqu'au cou*, *Entre la mer et l'eau douce*, *Nesbitt's Trip* and *Maria Chapdelaine*. This colossal triumph, extremely rare for a Quebec film, is Arcand's first major national and international success, which he comments upon with philosophy and humour. "You're only as good as your last film," he says in a paraphrase of Hitchcock's quip, whether a film succeeded or failed: "After all, it's only a picture!"

The Decline travels all over the world. Today, it is known to two generations. What's more, it is one of the rare Arcand films everyone remembers, along with *Jesus of Montreal*. With *The Decline*, Arcand becomes a world-class filmmaker, accompanying his film on a promotional marathon that lasts almost a year and that is interrupted by the death and funeral of his father in Deschambault.

Yet no large-scale success has ever been so ambiguous. First, because it appears to be based on *The Decline*'s reputation as a sex comedy, albeit an an intelligent one, although it is one of the most deadly serious films its author has ever made. "*The Decline*," says Arcand, "is a waiting for the barbarians." The film glows with a light so brilliant, it is as if it were emanating from the resurrection of a filmmaker whose last big success was *Réjeanne Padovani* in 1973, and who has just finished the commercial and banal *Crime d'Ovide Plouffe*. This light-ning-like brightness resembles a burst of Tolstoyan "end-of-the-world light," as Professor Georges Nivat calls it, "a dim, bleak, factitious light, cut off from its source, in which there remains no trace of youth, purity or faith."

On the fifteenth anniversary of *The Decline,* on Télé-Québec, Arcand says he has understood something that was left unsaid in the film, that basically the film is about friendship, not couples' sexuality. "Personally," says Arcand, "I don't see the unspoken values of my films. It's others who point them out to me and make me aware of them." At an even deeper level, underlying the strata of friendship, *The Decline* emanates an archaeology of disintegration—of people, feelings, civiliza-tions and history. In some ways, *The Decline,* like *Jesus of Montreal,* resembles Paolo and Vittorio Taviani's adaptations of Tolstoy. In *San Michele aveva un gallo* (*Saint Michael Had a Rooster,* 1971), based on the story *Divine and Human,* or in *Sole anche di notte* (*Sunshine Even by Night*) adapted from *Father Sergius,* the Italian filmmakers cultivate their taste for decadent beauty, unrealized ideals, aborted revolutions, unspeakable and impossible loves. They depict a godless world in which people are driven to flee the prospect of putrefaction and yearn to res-urrect like Lazarus or Christ, a world in which the phrase from the Bible "Love one another" has become *vain and empty.*

It is especially important to remember that in spite of its great suc-cess, *The Decline* was one of Arcand's most violently attacked films. For example, after its triumph as the opening film at the Directors' Fortnight in Cannes, *Libération* describes it as nothing more than an "America that's discovered sex . . . sad sex, the clumsy release of a bag of hot air, incredibly dry and mechanical, typical of a new standard taste for clean, affected and cultivated cinema." The verdict is delivered point-blank: "Throw cretins to the lions!"

In Quebec, shortly after the film's release in July 1986, a long and bitter polemic is unleashed in the pages of *Le Devoir.* Writer Louky Bersianik charges: "Whatever his intentions were, Arcand has repro-duced the clichés of sexual politics and revived ordinary sexism from beginning to end." Or: "All the talk about the 'degeneration of elites' that accompanies their fall would suggest that these empires (all patriar-chal) are beneficial and should remain standing." Then came the counterattacks. A reader, Victor Levant, wrote: "Saint Louky, think for us. Could you explain the myth of the castrating woman again?" Another letter to the newspaper from Renée Thivierge: "For me Arcand's film is a fresco in which everyone can find a character to identify with. [. . .] You say nothing has changed? Quite the contrary. Through the magic of film, through likeable characters, we think, we speak. You say men are reassured? I think that yet again, they are simply resigned."

Sociologist Louise Vandelac, from UQAM, saw the film as nothing but a remake of *Deux femmes en or* (an erotic populist comedy): "perhaps the first yuppie film of a rising neoconservatism." "Women [. . .] merely serve as scapegoats for the discourse of men. [. . .] The misogyny flaunted by the main protagonists, comforting for some but distressing for most, conceals a much deeper androcentrism." What is ironic in this affair is that Louise Vandelac was offended that Arcand thanked her in the film's titles for her participation in *The Decline*. Finally, in his book *La petite noirceur*, essayist Jean Larose expresses contempt for Arcand: "For a filmmaker like Arcand, to work *inside* the crisis of culture is to represent what separates his own class, the newly educated petty bourgeois (the one which since the Quiet Revolution has laughed at the bad taste of others) from "*les qué-taines*" (the kitsch and corny). In *The Decline of the American Empire*, Arcand has looped the loop of bad taste by bringing his irony down on the milieu that politicized the judgement of taste in Quebec." More recently, in February 2003, an article by Nicolas Renaud appeared in the webzine *Hors-champ*, entitled "Le secret honteux du *Déclin de l'empire américain*: Histoire d'un malentendu" ("The Shameful Secret of *The Decline of the American Empire*: The Story of a Misunderstanding"). The article attacks in advance the film's "sequel," *The Barbarian Invasions*, denouncing the original matrix and describing *The Decline* as "a film that in spite of its qualities has aged very badly and whose wrinkles are impossible to hide beneath its crown. The mise-en-scene is shaky, even nonchalant and without interest." Did *The Decline*, in Renaud's view, have intellectual import? "Isn't it more a case of intellectuality as style? The style is all that is intellectual in *The Decline*." In conclusion, he writes, there is no call for "raising an ordinary film that has had popular success to the ranks of a work by a national *auteur*."

In spite of these jabs, *The Decline* is as much a hit on the international scene as it is in Quebec. In this sense, it is a historical milestone. French-Canadian film had seen other triumphs such as *Aurore, la petite enfant martyre*, which ran from 1952 until the end of the sixties, or *Deux femmes en or* (1970). But these films were unsuitable for export and their success went no further than Quebec. Only Claude Jutra's *Mon oncle Antoine* (1971) succeeded in breaking out of Quebec; adopted by English Canada, it became "the greatest Canadian film of all time." Some of Gilles Carle's films met with success in Paris. *The Decline* exploded all these boundaries, raising Quebec cinema to the ranks of international *cinéma d'auteur*, as well as filling box-office coffers.

Yet the genesis and production of this film were modest, fragile and fraught with setbacks. Almost all the referees' reports were negative, describing it as a film "for intellectuals," or "for a handful of spectators." Arcand always maintained that he was working on a "little film" that would run for a few weeks at movie theatres. He is unequivocal about it in the text he wrote to present the film at the opening of the Toronto Film Festival in 1986 (see "Selected Readings"). Johanne Prégent has another view. "I never thought it was a little film and I wasn't alone. I was quite a she-wolf during this period, when I was Denys's companion. You couldn't attack him, I might bite. I was very protective of him with his producers. I got angry at the readers' reports. I remember very well having defended and believed in the screenplay. I was like a fanatic. My feeling is that Denys, even if he didn't foresee the great success the film would have, did not think he was making such a small film as that. If he'd been perfectly honest, he'd have admitted that it wasn't just a small film. He believed in this film too fundamentally and fought too hard to make it the way he had envisioned it. The entire team was committed to that project. You can't be sure of what Denys says; he contradicts himself from one day to the next. He invested great energy and a lot of heart in *The Decline*." For Johanne Prégent, who worked as continuity person on the film, Arcand was making an essential, very important work. The shoot was magical, sheer bliss at every level, not just because of the harmonious atmosphere but also because of the contemporary subject matter, which in spite of its male chauvinism spoke to both men and women: "A subject which, at the time, had almost never been addressed in Quebec film. Rarely had such intelligence and refinement of thought been combined with so much humour."

Written over 1984 and 1985 from the synopsis for *Conversations scabreuses* (*Racy Conversations*), with an investment of approximately $30,000 from Telefilm Canada, *The Decline* is shot in the autumn of 1985. No fewer than twenty-six scenes were dropped from the script during shooting. These include such details as the stealing of Alain's big Simon and Schuster atlas, or a short hallucination sequence involving the same character: "Alain, lying on his back, rolls on the floor of the apartment. He assumes a fetal position. He opens his mouth as if he were about to shout. He remains mute, and then utters a tiny cry, like a child." In another scene, Rémy explains that love lasts only two years and that after that, "the possibilities are infinite, going from hatred to tenderness"; then he tells young Alain that he knows he'll never be C. Vann Woodward or Fernand Braudel, that he is starting to see the approach of death, that like Wittgenstein he believes we can be sure of nothing except the ability to act upon our bodies. At the time of shooting, these two last pieces of dialogue are given to the character of Pierre. Also dropped at the time of shooting is the sequence in which Pierre explains to Rémy: "Absolute fidelity is death. That's why the apotheosis, for a woman, is when you die. Look at widows: behind the surface grief is an air of sacrifice and sublime contentment. He's dead. He totally belongs to them."

Another remark from Rémy, that appeared in the film adaptation of the play *La fin du voyage*, concerns women who take night courses at university, "hundreds of women taking notes like mad on the succession of Amenophis the Fourth, or who want to learn German, the guitar, tap dancing, shiatsu, primal scream." In *The Barbarian Invasions*, too, the names of the sagely Souvannah Phouma, Souvannoughong or Phoumi Nosavan are evoked with humour. Young people who dislike baby boomers would appreciate the scenes in which Alain and Danielle complain about the advantages enjoyed by the boomers born just after the war. Later, Rémy, who also enjoys the favours of the student masseuse Danielle, confesses to her that he corrected her paper on millenarianism and gave her an A+, deceitfully adding: "That's what's so amazing; you're bright as well as dirty." Towards the end of the script, we read that Claude dreams of having a baby while Dominique confides her conformist desires. She says to Alain, "If you only knew what a soppy, corny side I have—yearnings for babies, Christmas trees, a husband," and tells him, "every morning I wake up in a rage against the university of idiots, the government of cretins and my blow dryer!"

In December, right after the *Decline* shoot, Arcand produces "a rough-draft for a pre-synopsis" for *Jesus of Montreal*: "This film will revolve around the character of Jean-Guy Chrétien, an unemployed actor of about thirty who obtains the role of Jesus Christ in the passion play that is performed every evening for tourists in the gardens of Saint Joseph's Oratory. He will die playing this role. Jean-Guy's trajectory will take us through ad agencies, where we see how they take advantage of actors in difficulty, to the staging of *The Passion* by a retired Radio-Canada tele-theatre director, to the insane emergency rooms of our hospitals, and ending with a techno-medical apotheosis of organ removals and transplants. All this is to say that Jesus must always die and will always be born again. It will also be a reflection on the acting profession, and a meditation on the Gospel in Montreal in 1986, with the money changers of the Temple played by advertising people, Herod and the High Priests played by the Catholic hierarchy, Pontius Pilate and the Romans by the police and the medical establishment. The poor and ill will play their usual role. This could be a tragedy or a comedy, or both." The Société générale du cinéma du Québec provides $15,000 to develop the script.

Roger Frappier, who has left the NFB and founded Les Productions Oz Inc., has set up a new workshop for project development and screenwriting. The collective includes Léa Pool's *Kurwenal* (later *À corps perdu/Straight for the Heart*), Alain Chartrand's *La quête de Ding et Dong* (*Ding et Dong: le film*) written by Serge Theriault and Claude Meunier, and finally *Jesus of Montreal*. In the workshop project description Frappier writes: "A year of writing awaits Denys Arcand, divided between his collaboration on *Ding et Dong* and work on his own script."

But this year of writing will not occur in 1986 or the year after. First, because editing for *The Decline* continues until the spring of 1986. Though turned down for official competition at Cannes, the film is presented at the Directors' Fortnight in May and is a huge success. It comes out in Quebec during the dog days of summer. So begins the filmmaker's long tour with the film, which will last over a year. He will not resume work on *Jesus of Montreal* until 1988.

The two films are made in close succession, in the same workshop context whose guru and catalyst is Roger Frappier. Thus, as producer, Frappier's career peaks at the same time as those of Léa Pool and Denys Arcand as filmmakers. Frappier, a director-become-producer, has the excellent intuition—in the second half of the 1980s—of bringing together Quebec filmmakers in a collective, reconstructing the kind of creative-competitive group setting that was the heart of Quebec cinema in the sixties. In the 1990s, when Frappier will attempt to play the same card with a new generation of young filmmakers, the results are less convincing.

But at the time of *The Decline of the American Empire*, the formula proves successful. Frappier, who emerged in Quebec film in the early seventies, has seen all the demonstrations and the red barricades, all the bohemian protests in the name of a free cinema, all the shrewdness too, of a Quebec cinema permanently chained to the assistance of a State for whom the private industry, to all intents and purposes, does not exist. In this web of contradictions, the first card played by Frappier was the possibility of production by the NFB, as in the case of *Le confort et l'indifférence*; then he played the card of co-production by the NFB and private industry. Finally, he founded his own film and television production companies and ended up succeeding where Cinéastes associés had failed twenty years earlier in the mid-sixties.

Paradoxically, the great success of *The Decline* went against the founding principle of the workshops. It suggested there was a winning formula that Quebec's *cinéma d'auteur* needed only to follow to earn profits. But *The Decline* was an epiphenomenon, not a golden rule. Another perverse effect of the film's success was that it obliged Arcand, who was relatively unknown on the international scene, to accompany his film and take care of its promotion; this caused a considerable delay in the making of *Jesus of Montreal*. On the other hand, the long tour consolidated his status as director. It also meant he crossed paths from time to time with Jean Lefebvre, an administrator from Telefilm Canada. Lefebvre was director of the festivals bureau, after doing promotion for Canadian films at the NFB. Arcand paid him tribute in the late 1980s: "He's taken care of my films, from the first short films at the NFB in the 1960s up to my most recent films. How can you not like someone who impatiently awaits the closing of the Cannes Festival each year to finally be able to go visit Roman churches? A civilized man is so hard to find these days."

The Decline of the American Empire (a title his distributor René Malo hated, feeling it was too intellectual and scholastic) cost $1.85 million. In Quebec and English Canada, the feature earns several million dollars. It is released in Paris in early 1987, with a total of 400,000 viewers, a record for a Quebec film in France. The film won several awards at festivals: Cannes, Sète, Toronto, Québec, Vichy, Chicago, Rio de Janeiro, and New York. In *La Presse,* in April 1987, Luc Perreault alludes to 13 million box-office receipts on the international market and 4 million in Canada. Another perverse effect: this manna mainly goes to co-producer and distributor René Malo, of Malofilm. This new millionaire has to think about how the receipts are to be shared. Though Arcand has already been paid a flat rate for his double job as writer and director ($50,000 for the script and $75,000 for directing) he is also entitled to 10 percent of the receipts. But how to calculate a film's receipts? Here we enter the domain of "creative accounting," a grey zone in which a distributor can deduct all sorts of costs from attractive receipts. In this case, from an ethical point of view, should the first contract be ripped up and a new one negotiated? Arcand explains that Malo refused to do so, first offering him a kind of consolation prize before agreeing to a more appropriate compensation. The filmmaker learned how to judge his own true market value, and this will not happen again.

While writing *Jesus of Montreal* for Productions Oz in the fall of 1987, Arcand becomes interested in the question of a standardized contract to protect directors. He discusses it in *Lumières*. Still stinging from his unfortunate experience with *The Decline*, the filmmaker supports the idea of a standard contract that, in the context of an increasingly industrialized cinema, would offer "a general framework for negotiations between producer and director. Without one, conflicts will always be resolved in the producer's favour. But having said this, I consider the standard contract to be a bare minimum." This tool makes it possible to recognize a director's rights over his or her works at an artistic level, as well as the need for a minimum pay scale. Arcand agrees to help develop the sample contract with the Association des réalisateurs du Québec, and hopes to see it approved by its members.

It was in the same spirit that four years earlier, he had signed the "Actes de Madère," a "summary of the requirements of directors from all over the world," motions that aim to guarantee "standard and financial rights for all directors." In particular, the Actes recognize that the director (and not the producer) is the author of a work, that she or he has the right not to want it to be modified by another, and also the right to receive "remuneration proportional to receipts from all sales or distribution of the work."

The success of *The Decline* changed René Malo and Roger Frappier, who had become the champions of a private industry. At this time, it truly existed—in their minds and in what they said, if not in reality—because this audiovisual machine was still heavily subsidized by the State. Meanwhile, what had become of Arcand? He often says that glory came to him at the advanced age of forty-five, allowing him to keep a cool head. But one suspects that there is more to it than that. It is the filmmaker's lucidity that has helped him keep his wits about him. A director is only as good as his last film, as he is fond of repeating. Arcand explains his sang-froid in terms of his past experience, of the film domain, which is rife with harrowing contradictions, or of his own fluctuating career. After the triumph of *Réjeanne Padovani*, he took a fall with *Gina*. After *Duplessis* on Radio-Canada, he made a new descent into hell. And was *The Decline* not preceded by *The Crime of Ovide Plouffe*, a commissioned film that Arcand hated doing?

Though he keeps a cool head about cinematic glory and the pomp of the international jet set, there is one thing that *The Decline* will change for Denys Arcand: his status as filmmaker. After *The Decline*, his career will be more comfortable, as well as the prospect of growing older. If he is forced into "early retirement," it will be taken care of. From now on his life will be more a reflection of his consecration as great international filmmaker.

What is most astonishing in the triumph of *The Decline* is the apparent contradiction between a subject that is intimately linked to Montreal and Quebec and the universal resonance of that subject. Here, let us recall the Arcand formula, the Buñuelian subversion of death beneath the surface of a sex comedy in the form of a téléroman. *The Decline* is Arcand's exterminating angel. We must not forget the profound river of melancholy that flows through the film, the total disintegration of the sexual revolution and "flower power" of which the last part of the film is symptomatic: in the hours of dawn, when death creeps across the slides of paintings by Géricault and Caravaggio; in the anxiety that grips the characters who stand before the immense fire of Rome at the Empire's end, or observe that the flash of an atomic bomb dropped on the American city of Plattsburg could be seen across Lake Memphremagog.

These disillusioned characters, these Quebecers who are "Etruscans to the Romans," stripped of everything but the warmth of human friendship and the disturbing beauty of nature, feel themselves slipping into an era of shadows, a new and unexpected Dark Age. All that remains is sad music, whose scores must henceforth be protected, played once in a while to keep them from falling completely mute, perhaps for centuries. The film's finale, with the two women from two generations playing the piano side by side, contains the germ of *The Barbarian Invasions,* in which Rémy, in his dying moments, accompanied by a Mozart sonata, murmurs: "Barbarians everywhere . . . the Middle Ages . . . the manuscripts . . . ."

The true subject of *The Decline* once the surface gloss is stripped away—the deceptive, hedonistic and commercial surface of the sex comedy and the college variety evening—is the bitter and sad *postmortem* vision of intellectuals in the face of the Apocalypse. *Jesus of Montreal,* which forms a diptych with *The Decline,* further elaborates this secular and pagan, de-christianized gospel that also contains and camouflages its own "little apocalypse."

Thanks to *The Decline of the American Empire* and *Jesus of Montreal,* Denys Arcand becomes a celebrity. "Have Tux, Will Travel," replaces Arcand's earlier slogan "Have Gun, Will Travel," adopted in the days when he considered his films as works of sociopolitical and cultural observation. Though Arcand's motto may have changed, his political consciousness remains as strong and acute as ever, but it expresses itself in other ways and in other filmic forms. This filmic œuvre, whose flow was often interrupted in the past, now evolves in a continuous and ever-deepening way. This cinema was never meant to be a vehicle of propaganda but was to show the melancholy politicocultural disintegration of our society, especially that of the Quebec nation.

For the time being, what we see on the surface of Planet Arcand seems to be the international jet set. After Cannes, Quebec and France, *The Decline* starts travelling and is nominated for an Oscar. An American remake is even planned. William Goldman, the guru of American screenwriting, is consulted. In July 1987 screenwriter David Geiler finishes his version, *Better Drunk than Enslaved*. It is an unrealizable project, says Arcand, for two reasons: first, American university groups form quite a different sociocultural milieu from those of Montreal. There is no golden tenure in the United States; competition never lets up and teaching positions are tenuous. Second, the American language is unsuited to the banter of love; it's language of sexuality is very crude and does not possess the subtleties of French in this particular matter. Arcand writes about this American interlude à la Paramount and the Oscars in his text *Two Hollywood Memories*.

Tributes continue to pour in. *La Presse* names the filmmaker personality of the year at its gala of excellence. In 1987, Arcand receives an Order of Canada, and becomes president of the second *Mondial de la publicité francophone*. In 1989, *Jesus of Montreal* is received in official competition at Cannes and earns a nomination for Best Foreign Film at the Academy Awards. As a crowning touch, in 1989, the Quebec government grants Denys Arcand its prestigious Albert-Tessier Award for film.

The decade ends in a blaze of glory for Arcand, the first Quebec filmmaker to achieve this kind of international stature. His fans in Toronto, on the verge of ecstasy, will soon be calling him "Denys of Montreal."

11
"DENYS OF MONTREAL"

This engaging title, *Denys de Montréal*, was invented by the Cinematheque Ontario in 1991 for one of the first Toronto retrospectives of Arcand's films. The name is, of course, a tribute to *Jesus of Montreal*, but even more so refers to the captivating presence of the Quebec metropolis in the director's filmography. At a 1995 seminar at Concordia University, Arcand confided to students that Montreal "is what nourishes him."

Indeed, most of Arcand's films take place in Montreal or at least in Quebec, with the exception of *Stardom*; Montreal is a magnet. *Seul ou avec d'autres* is set at the Université de Montréal. *On est au coton* mostly takes place in Coaticook, in the Eastern Townships, but Montreal is the technocratic centre essential to its analysis of the collapse of the Quebec textile industry. *Québec: Duplessis et après . . .* or *Le confort et l'indifférence* travel around "la belle province," but the dramatic heart of both documentaries is Montreal. In the first of the two, was it not in Maisonneuve riding, in the city's East End, that the most heated struggle of the 1970 provincial election took place? In the second film, does Niccolo Machiavelli not live in one of the towers of Complexe Desjardins?

Montreal is not only a setting, location and metaphor in practically all Arcand's films, but it is also the centre of his formative years, the cocoon of his intellectual and artistic training. In Arcand's system of dualism and contradictions, Montreal is the flip side of Deschambault-de-Portneuf, which gradually recedes from his vital space, his intellect and his imagination. Free-thinking replaces anti-intellectual rigorism; nonbelief and secularity replace Catholic mysticism; the life of an artist replaces a conventional profession.

Montreal is the keystone of his early short historical films. Although *Champlain* takes place before the founding of Montreal in 1642, the French cartographer often passes the place where the city now stands while exploring Canadian territory. We learn in *Les Montréalistes* (*Ville-Marie*) that the founder of Quebec cut down several trees on the island that was the site of Hochelaga (an Iroquois village visited by Jacques Cartier) first and then of Ville-Marie, which later took the permanent name of Montreal. Even if *Champlain* mainly follows the explorer's travels through Quebec City and down the Saint Lawrence and Ottawa Rivers while tracing the commercial mythology that is associated with his name, Montreal is already faintly visible as the dramatic nucleus of a kind of historical illusion. But most of all, in *Les Montréalistes*, Arcand shows how the strange politico-Catholic vision of the mystics from the Société Notre-Dame influenced the founding of Ville-Marie. He then describes its metamorphosis into an industrial and commercial metropolis to become the most prominent Canadian city, until the Second World War when it was dethroned by Toronto. Between religious fanaticism and the lucrative fur trade, paradoxically, Montreal grows from the ruins of the Catholic religion into a city of money and vice. Once its place is established, the city will almost always figure in Arcand's films.

In spite of his long years in Deschambault, the filmmaker has the appearance of a confirmed urbanite. Montreal is where he went to college and university and where most of his films are centred. The city permeates his work, inspiring him with the melancholy motifs of past glory, dilapidation and decline; it is also a major pole in the Quiet Revolution. Since the 1960s, it has housed as many Quebec government offices as the "national capital," Quebec City. After making his short historical films, it is in Montreal that Arcand shoots *Volleyball* and *Montréal un jour d'été* (*Montreal on a Summer Day*).

Arcand's first two dramas of the 1970s, *La maudite galette* and *Réjeanne Padovani*, are entirely set in Montreal, which is only logical. Mafias, whether big or small, can only be based in cities; when they move into towns, they are just seedier and smaller-scale extensions of the urban variety. The story of *Gina* is set in Louiseville, a kind of distant suburb of Montreal, where both the filmmaking team and the dancer come from. The film begins in Montreal and ends at Dorval airport. The short film for the CSN, *La lutte des travailleurs d'hôpitaux* (*The Hospital Workers' Struggle*), takes place at the Hôtel-Dieu de Montréal. The Montreal setting dominates *The Decline of the American Empire* and *Jesus of Montreal*. *The Decline* opens at the heart of the Université de Montréal, in its proud and immense Claude-Robillard sports centre, of which Lake Memphremagog, in the Eastern Townships, is simply an extension.

However, it is in *Jesus of Montreal* that Arcand fully expresses his vision of the metropolis as mythology and metaphor. Not far from the Université de Montréal, on Mount Royal, is Saint Joseph's Oratory, a popular pilgrimage site built at the instigation of Brother André. This humble and simple friar of the Holy Cross community, who is recognized as a miracle worker, lived at Collège Notre-Dame at the foot of the mountain in the same institution as Brother Jérôme, his antithesis, a modern painter and *Refus global* sympathizer, a "jazzy brother" as he called himself. Brother André was one of the "four great Quebecers" chosen by Pierre Maheu for his film series at the NFB. Saint Joseph's Oratory is the main setting for *Jesus of Montreal* and gives Arcand a new opportunity to compose his mise-en-scene in "storeys," that is, in terms of up and down, as in *Réjeanne Padovani* (the rich Mafiosi are on the ground floor, the underlings in the basement) and in *Le confort et l'indifférence* (Machiavelli is at the top of a Complexe Desjardins office tower and far below, at ground level, is the swarming Referendum struggle). In *Jesus*, "up" are the gardens of the Oratory and Christ's passion performed along footpaths that mark out the Stations of the Cross; "down" is the metro, the film studios and crowded hospital corridors.

The story of *Jesus of Montreal*, at once simple and complex, involves a group of young actors who are given the task of revitalizing the Passion play, performed every summer in the gardens of Saint Joseph's Oratory. It also shows the difficulties the actors encounter in the worlds of advertising, television and showbiz. Through this web of contradictions, a parallelism can gradually be perceived between the destiny of Jesus, on the one hand, revived thanks to recent historical and archaeological research, his ideal of purity and humanism, and on the other hand, the most glaring problems of modern society, the power of the media and money, health care and the moral misery of the little people, pornography and prostitution . . . .

Jesus of Montreal is certainly a tragedy, ending with a man's death, but the writer-director sees it as "a serious comedy." "I wanted to do a film full of ruptured tones, swinging from madcap comedy to the most absurd drama, a reflection of life around us—fragmented, commonplace, contradictory. A little like one of those supermarkets where all in the same ten-metre aisle you can find the novels of Dostoevsky, toilet water, the Bible, pornographic videos, the works of Shakespeare, photos of earth taken from the moon, astrological predictions and posters of actors or Jesus, while loudspeakers and cathode screens drone away on a musical background of Pergolesi, rock 'n' roll or the Bulgarian Voices." In the introductory text he wrote for the press kit, Arcand adds: "In *Jesus of Montreal* you have the Gospel according to Saint Mark, eau de cologne ads, the Brothers Karamazov, the dubbing of pornographic movies, the Big Bang, the formula for Coca-Cola Classic, Hamlet's soliloquy, the inconvenience of being born in Burkina-Faso, a Roman soldier by the name of Pantera, fascists who take communion every day, organ transplants and Paul Newman salad dressing. In short, everything we cannot get away from!"

Jesus of Montreal is shot between July 24 and September 23, 1988. Few changes are made between the script and the final edit, except for the discarding of a quote from the works of Charles Bukowski inserted at the very beginning of the film: "Peace be with men of good will who cry alone at night." Arcand cuts two sequences in which the penniless Daniel Coulombe goes into a pizza parlour and begs for pizzas with which to feed his troupe. Nor does he keep the entire melancholy sentence from the astronomy film narration: "In a thousand billion years, when the sky is dimly lit by a few old stars that will slowly fade, life as we know it will have lasted but an instant . . . ."

This "Jesus of the human comedy" is the object of numerous Western Christian art works, from painting to statuary, literature to theatre and opera, and since the twentieth century, film. Christ, Jesus, the Gospel, Apocalypse: an inexhaustible archaeological site, a matrix of infinite variation. This philosophical-mystical tapestry shows off its colours to full advantage, becoming a metaphor for a modern world without faith or law, without God and without ideology. Thus, Christian history and religious myth metamorphose into the end of history and barbarian invasions on the triumphant Catholic empire. This is the theme of Leonard Bernstein's delirious opera *Mass*, in which rockers bellow: "I'll believe in twenty gods if they'll believe in me!" In other words, "I believe only in beings of beauty who love me." The young actors in *Jesus of Montreal*, like those in Arcand's next film *Love and Human Remains*, whisper, "I will love whoever wants to love me." We find the same young people in *Jesus Christ Superstar*, or *The Last Temptation of Christ* made by the tortured and anxiety-ridden Scorsese; we see them again in the enraged revolutionaries of Pasolini's *Il vangelo secondo Matteo* (*The Gospel According to Saint Matthew*). *Jesus of Montreal* is also a magnificent cinemascope of Roman and Christian dereliction, that of Quebec Catholicism, clerics and nuns, eschatological visions that augur the end of civilizations, books, films and all music. As the astrophysical sequence in *Jesus of Montreal* suggests, nothing will survive this hecatomb but the music of matter.

The film's reception is, if anything, more fabulous that that of *The Decline*. This time, it is in competition at Cannes and enthusiastically received at press screening, foreshadowing the success of *The Barbarian Invasions*. If the *New York Times* finds the film flawed, it nonetheless identifies Arcand as a leading end-of-century filmmaker, as Daniel Latouche writes in *Le Devoir* on May 26, 1989. In France, *L'humanité* praises a film that "fully deserves the warm response of the journalist audience." "What is touching in this film is that it takes a theatrical approach to its subject, face to face with the spectator who is asked for his opinion on the great question of the world. So Arcand proceeds, while twirling his whip of satire, which remains the most elegant way of achieving the required gravity." However, *Libération* is more skeptical: "*Triste* is born again! Kind of a drag, this *Jesus of Montreal*," concluding: "A paradoxical result; this strange *Jesus of Montreal* with its rather blasphemous content is ultimately a fine act of faith in man."

In Quebec, as Daniel Latouche reminds us, "our critics have all chosen to praise the film to the skies, as if it had become necessary to close ranks," while deploring that *Jesus of Montreal* had to "make do" with the jury prize at Cannes rather than winning the Palme d'Or. Yet it is the first Quebec or Canadian film to receive such a tribute on La Croisette. Latouche concludes: "In private, some of these people had no shortage of good reasons why the film absolutely could not win at Cannes." Meanwhile, the Montreal Mirror affirms that this "gospel according to St. Arcand" is a "splendid film."

While the gospel voices that marked Arcand's youth play a key role in the film, *Jesus* is also his most beautiful and moving tribute to actors. It is worth coming back to this subject for a moment. Johanne Prégent says: "Denys is a master. His greatest quality is his way with actors. He performs miracles. As a director, he isn't directive; he has incredible charm along with a lot of humour and intelligence. The actors aren't even aware of where he can take them with his observation, his attention, his way of coming close to them when he talks. He's the one who taught me not to address actors from a distance. You move, you go towards them, you talk to them directly. In this sense, he's a very great director." In Arcand's castings there are, of course, many actors who are "specialists" to whom he often gives unusual roles, the most transcendent of these perhaps being Luce Guilbault's role in *Réjeanne Padovani*. But what is more striking is the brilliant results that he draws from actors he has radically transformed, such as René Caron, J.-Léo Gagnon, Jean Lajeunesse, Pierre Theriault, Céline Lomez, Roger Lebel, Donald Lautrec, Dominique Michel and, last but not least, Stéphane Rousseau. It is Arcand's personal way of expressing the idea that "the most beautiful face is the human face." From this point of view, *Jesus of Montreal* is a singular agnostic gospel of the life and death of actors.

Jesus of Montreal would also more or less reconcile Arcand and his mother, Colette Bouillé. She had hated *The Decline of the American Empire*, but took a liking to this new film made by her eldest son, her "Denys of Montreal." Yet, as the filmmaker tells the young writer-director Patrick Damien Roy: "My mother told me at the end of her life: 'My life is a failure, my children will not go to heaven.' After the death of Horace Arcand, Colette Bouillé left the house in Pointe-Lauzon, unable to get used to the idea of living there alone for even an instant. She moved into a luxurious residence in Saint-Augustin, the Jardins du Haut-Saint-Laurent, where she lived for about three years. Having undergone an operation for colon cancer fifteen years earlier, Colette

Bouillé died on February 11, 1990, in the Hôtel-Dieu in Quebec City of peritonitis (septicemia) following a hernia operation. This Christian who believed in the resurrection of the entire body paradoxically left her body to science. This gesture is strangely reminiscent of the "after death" of Daniel Coulombe in *Jesus of Montreal*, the donation of his body being a kind of universal eucharist.

Arcand's films of the 1990s, with the exception of *Stardom*, all take place in Montreal. In the beginning of the decade, the filmmaker meets Denise Robert for the first time through *Montréal vu par . . .* (*Montreal Seen By . . .* a.k.a. *Montreal Sextet*). This new feature is a celebration of Montreal's 350th anniversary. It's a kind of pleasant anachronism reminiscent of the "omnibus" films of the sixties and seventies that were so numerous in France and Italy and modelled after *Paris vu par. . . .* Denise Robert is the producer of this first Quebec-Ontario co-production that brings together Atom Egoyan, Patricia Rozema, Jacques Leduc, Michel Brault, Léa Pool and Denys Arcand. Arcand is working on his script on death for Roger Frappier and MaxFilms and does not have time to write another, but he agrees to shoot Paule Baillargeon's script entitled *Vue d'ailleurs* (*Seen from Elsewhere*), which he directs between May 21 and 26, 1991. However, he adds a personal touch by writing the first sequence of the sketch, set in a Quebec delegation to a Latin-American country. The characters refer to Montreal as a pleasant but ugly city where the word "châr" replaces the word "automobile" in the local creole, and where the girls are pretty but lack imagination in bed. The filmmaker ends his mise-en-scene with a few shots of the city during a snowstorm.

Due to a curious and unexpected fluke related to financing, *Love and Human Remains* was shot in Montreal rather than in Edmonton. At the last minute, the Alberta Motion Picture Development Corporation refused to co-finance the production. Arcand had made ample use of Montreal as the setting for *Jesus* and wanted at all costs to avoid using a similar scenography. Instead he sought out places in Montreal that had rarely or never been shown on film and would coincide with the desperate trajectory of the young characters. A closed world, a strange and unusual cocoon, with no sign of family members, suburban bungalows or city houses. A fantasy Montreal that brings to mind Godard's science-fictional *Alphaville,* set in Paris but showing the City of Light from a surrealistic point of view, as it had never been seen before.

Arcand sets his film in a Montreal of expressways and concrete interchanges, lofts in an asphalt desert, little streets in old neighbourhoods revamped in industrial style, that is, in an atmosphere of startling postmodernism. Thus, the filmmaker transforms a typically English-Canadian script and characters into Montreal subjects. But the metamorphosis is subtle, made palpable through a strange and impenetrable urban setting, so that its "Quebecness" appears foreign. Here, Arcand transforms Montreal into a *barbarian* metropolis, which may partially explain why the film was rejected and misunderstood in Quebec. The Montreal of *Love and Human Remains* is no longer familiar. Surreptitiously it has been turned into its own opposite through a kind of organized, and by now well-established, procedure of hybridization. It is also a Montreal of infinite melancholy, a ruin among the ruins of an unrecognizable past.

Arcand keeps to the same approach and point of view when preparing to shoot *Joyeux calvaire* in 1996, a very Québécois and Montreal film, written by Claire Richard this time. The director and his first AD, Jacques Wilbrod Benoit, intend to add to the script a dimension of strangeness via its settings: the statue of Norman Bethune near Concordia University; the façade of the old York Palace movie theatre in a state of advanced decay; the rundown quays of the abandoned port area. This decrepit and decomposing Montreal closely resembles the characters who have become human waste, always moving, with no resting place or liveable home base. Montreal, as Benoit explains, is portrayed as a disaster area.

In *Stardom*, there is only one short sequence in Quebec before the story moves to Paris, New York and London. The film opens in Cornwall, Ontario. The snow, the expressways and the skating rinks of this little Ontario backwater are the same as the ones found in Quebec. Montreal does not appear in the film, though it did in *Beautiful*, the first version of the script, written in 1995 and rejected by Alliance. The Montreal pole of the story disappears in the second version, *15 Moments*, which develops the theme of beauty as seen through the kaleidoscope of television media, and is primarily set in the United States and Europe.

The "Montrealist" geocultural configuration of Arcand's films is contradictory, as is apparent in "Montreal," the only text the filmmaker has ever written about the city, which appeared in a special monograph called *Montréal, ville de cinéma* (1992). In this short essay, included in "Selected Readings," Arcand asks himself why he likes this "anonymous and grey city."

Unlike most Quebec artists and intellectuals of the Quiet Revolution generation, Arcand has never worked or studied in another country, except for rare and brief trips to France and Scandinavia to shoot the historical documentaries, and to New York, Paris and London for *Stardom*. Quebec has always remained his "beat" and Montreal his unique centre of interest and the immutable setting of almost all his films. Though his roots are in Deschambault, the setting of much of his life and career is Montreal. *The Barbarian Invasions* is a recent illustration of this phenomenon, as well as Lake Memphremagog (also seen in *The Decline*), which itself serves as a kind of country annex for a motley group of confirmed Montrealers.

Most of all, Montreal is the matrix and cocoon of Arcand's education and intellectual life. It is in Montreal that he first discovers libraries and bookstores, film, theatre and music, which he studies for more than ten years, and is first introduced not only to sports but most of all to writing, history and film directing: "I've always defined myself as an intellectual. At Collège Sainte-Marie, my teachers were Jacques Brault and intellectual Jesuits; at university, I did courses with Maurice Séguin and Michel Brunet, also intellectuals. Most of my friends are academics, writers and researchers. I spend my life reading philosophy and essays. I don't think anti-intellectualism has ever been among my failings." Yet one of the most essential and little-known facts about Arcand has to do with his status as an intellectual. He is, of course, well known as an artist, but far less as an artist-intellectual.

It is a complex issue, he explains, especially in North America. In the United States, there's a long tradition of anti-intellectualism. American writers always pretend to be something else. Faulkner raised horses; Hemingway was a fisherman and boxer. Anything so as not to say "I'm an intellectual" because America was made by cowboys, farmers and *coureurs des bois*, not by intellectuals. In this sense, Quebec is part of America; it has developed contempt for the intellectual, who is often qualified as a "fairy" or a parasite. A lot of filmmakers and writers present themselves under false tough-guy façades. Pierre Perrault was first a fisherman, a hunter. Anything to assert an almost insane virility so as not to be accused of intellectualism. Filmmakers wasted years scraping down houses, fixing up campers and mixing cement when they should've been reading, seeing theatre and ballet. They should have developed their intelligence rather than becoming do-it-yourself experts. For his whole life, Horace Arcand considered his eldest son Denys a failure. To try to justify himself in his father's eyes, the filmmaker had to prove that he could work with his hands, "because in the intellectual world, which was foreign to him, I was never going to make it or be right."

Traces of anti-intellectualism may also be detected in the distinction some Quebec filmmakers make between "creative" professions, such as writing and directing, and noncreative ones, such as civil service jobs in arts administration, teaching and criticism. Jean Pierre Lefebvre calls these professionals the parasites of cinematic creation. As Arcand has often taken both groups to task, one may wonder if he has not (if only unconsciously) been contaminated by anti-intellectualism, in the same way he says a person who has become agnostic or atheist remains marked by his former religion. When asked about it, he replies it is impossible to be both artist and analyst on the same film, though one always remains an intellectual. "Sophocles hadn't read Freud," he says. In *Oedipus*, the Greek playwright does not explain why the young prince kills his father and marries his mother. To tell this tragic fictional story, he calls upon his unconscious, his *daemon*. Because of this "demonic" possession to which artists are subject and because they are not trustworthy, Plato goes so far as to banish them from his Republic. We will have to wait twenty-four centuries for Freud to analyze the meaning of this Greek tragedy and bring the "Oedipus complex" out of hiding. One cannot, in the same work, both create and analyze characters; they have their own logic and lead their author by the hand, fed by their progenitor's unconscious mind. The same person cannot write both *Oedipus* and *Essays on Psychoanalysis*. In any case, few writers manage to do it. Proust is a rare example. In *À la recherche du temps perdu*, suddenly there is a whole chapter of reflections on music and painting, and then the narrator picks up the magic thread of his story again and leaves for Venice with his mother . . .

The first encounters between Arcand's films and the critics were not easy, especially when it came to *Objectif*. Published during the sixties, this Quebec film magazine was, or wanted to be, the antithesis of the Catholic *Séquences*. First, it assassinated *Seul ou avec d'autres*, creating tense relations with the filmmaker, who felt completely despised by the reviewers. The magazine ignored his other films of that period, the historical documentaries. In a text he wrote for *Parti pris,* in the April 1964 issue on the NFB and Quebec cinema (included in the "Selected Readings"), Arcand takes *Objectif* to task, saying that new Quebec cinema is not being helped by its critics "who want to put Quebec cinema in a perspective that is too vast for it." Arcand still reproaches this clique of critics for modelling itself upon the *Cahiers du cinéma* and espousing an ethereal view of cinema, worshipping great foreign filmmakers while taking a condescending attitude towards the films being made in Quebec.

In film criticism, Arcand makes a distinction between journalism and critical essay. To the same degree that he appreciates those who practise the essay form, journalists or weekly film critics get on his nerves, because they write too quickly, are satisfied with the "loved it/hated it" approach or criticize the film for not having "said it all" about its subject. For Arcand, journalism is not high intellectual activity. Upon his return from Cannes in June 2003, on Marie-France Bazzo's radio program, he lashes out against "rotten" French criticism. Like a number of French filmmakers before him, he attacks a system of reviewing that is enclosed and ensnared by the policy of *auteurs*; reviewers condemn a film even before seeing it in order to make their mark and because, in any case, certain filmmakers have been labelled for once and for all. For example, Arcand is convinced that *The Barbarian Invasions* got negative reviews in *Le monde, Les Cahiers du cinéma* and *Libération* because the media have him pegged as a bad filmmaker. But then again, this is not always the case, because during the sixties and seventies these same publications praised Arcand's first films, *Réjeanne Padovani,* in particular. It was only after *Gina* that they changed their tune. But Arcand also takes an ironic view of his uneasy relations with film reviewing. For example, on receiving the prize for Best Foreign Film in Hollywood on January 10, 2004, awarded by film critics for the North American television networks, the author of *The Barbarian Invasions* declared, all smiles: "This award puts me in an awkward position. Today you've shown such impeccable taste, I'll never be able to say a word against critics again!" To everyone's delight, Clint Eastwood repeated Arcand's words later, when receiving his lifetime achievement award.

Also on the subject of criticism, Arcand greatly regrets having reviewed certain Quebec films of the 1960s. This is why he has for so long disowned his articles in *Parti pris*. However, his system of criticism, more akin to essay writing than to journalism, is solid and unassailable, maintaining that a work is interesting to analyze only insofar as it relates to the economic, political and cultural domains of a society. Some of these reviews have been included in the "Selected Readings" in this book.

What to think of all this? Denys Arcand has certainly not been contaminated by Quebec anti-intellectualism. On the contrary, he is one of the rare filmmakers who unreservedly claims the status of intellectual artist and has done so since his final years at Collège Sainte-Marie. He denounces laissez-faire intellectual attitudes, is militant about the need to "suppress all kinds of idle rambling and combat *prêtrisme*," or the conservatism of "spiritual nourishment based on cadavres," Thomas Aquinas or Bossuet, Péguy, Claudel. Throughout the year of 1959, in the newspaper *Le Sainte-Marie*, Arcand deplores that "81.2 % of college students have never been to a music recital," that "few have access to the Fathers' library," that most college students are uninterested in extracurricular activities, which are "anti-bourgeois by definition," allowing [students] to "step out of their slippers and into their skates," which leads to "a higher awareness" and which in spite of "the fetter, freely accepted, that is momentarily imposed, ensures a later and complete liberation from the college student's regular activity."

At the Université de Montréal, the intellectual herald continues to write in a similar vein, denouncing the "general intellectual laziness of students" with regard to activities of artistic expression (*Le quartier latin*, November 7, 1961). In the numerous articles he writes over his two years of studying for his *licence* in history, he staunchly defends theatre, concerts, film, books, song and the lucid and destructive madness of Les Cyniques. Arcand's youth and formative years will pave the way for a lifetime of declarations in favour of intellectual activity over checked-shirt populism and the manual tasks it holds dear.

Nonetheless, the filmmaker is inhabited by a kind of *daemon* that creates a conflict between a clearly affirmed intellectual life and a kind of wariness about certain intellectual occupations. It is all very well to insult the civil servants in charge of film financing, but when one understands how the game works and agrees to live and work in an industry that is necessarily state-supported, one also has to get used to respecting its finicky rules. Arcand's reservations about the professions of teacher and critic are perhaps related to anxieties he once had that he may have to make a career as one or the other. The profession of film teacher in particular has always seemed to him nightmarish. Other nightmares include writing-related anxieties such as writers' block or slowness to produce, though these are things that all writers have to contend with. Film reviewing or teaching have their own form of performance anxiety and nightmares. In spite of all his denials, many people feel that Arcand could have made a good critic or an excellent film teacher.

Montreal is not only the physical setting, past and present, of Arcand's films and his intellectual career, from *Seul ou avec d'autres* to *The Barbarian Invasions*. The city is also a metaphor for the destiny of Quebec itself, as analyzed by the historian Maurice Séguin, a point of view espoused by Arcand. A modern city that is big enough to accommodate many modern and universal developments, this metropolis is also too small, a shadow or "summer kitchen" for big American "megalopolizes" and their major universities. Rémy's haunting bit of aftersight is only too true; after graduating from Berkeley, had he been American, he would not have vegetated in a "a province of hicks." Montreal, in the hands of Arcand the playwright, is the setting for a tragic scene, for unresolvable and irresolute destinies.

As he describes in his commentary for *Les Montréalistes/Ville Marie*, the city is the site of a brutal and singular telescoping of past and present. Seen through the eyes of Arcand, it is as if these historical, antagonistic extremes were two sheets of cellophane placed on top of one another, with their colours and designs contrasting but also aligned. "As Montrealers, we are as much products of 1642 as of today. Are we?

A rare occurrence in history: Montreal's origins are mystical. Nothing would be easier than to forget it, for strangely enough, what was termed religious fanaticism in fact made Montreal into the business capital it later became for New France." Montreal is the essential setting for Arcand's imagination. "Life in Montreal is quiet for most people. They seem to like it that way. Me too."

With the major success of *The Decline of the American Empire* and *Jesus of Montreal*, Arcand seems to be on top of the world. However, the1990s will build a new bonfire of the vanities. The most cruel and humiliating decade of his career is about to begin.

12
HUMAN REMAINS

For Arcand, the new decade opens on a bittersweet note. After the death of his mother in February 1990, he starts work as director on his first professional theatre production. *Lettres de la religieuse portugaise* (*The Portuguese Nun's Letters*) is a cruel and ardent epistolary tale about the desert of a convent life and an exacerbated passion. Dating from seventeenth-century France, it is told in a woman's voice but written by a man. The next year, Arcand writes the comedy *Vue d'ailleurs*, a sketch from *Montréal vu par . . .* a businesswoman's love affair, a romantic elegy preceded by a comical prologue set in a Quebec delegation in a foreign country. The general scene is all the more disorderly because Quebec has just experienced its biggest psychodrama since the Quiet Revolution. In the spring of 1990, the Meech Lake Accord on the inclusion of Quebec and its specific rights in the Canadian constitution ends in dismal failure, followed on June 24 by the biggest nationalist demonstration that the province has ever known. It eventually leads to the second referendum on sovereignty-association in 1995, which almost succeeds.

Arcand starts work on his new feature on death, a tortuous project that he has great trouble finishing, chipping away at it for over two years before finally abandoning it. He also becomes involved in two film projects in English, which will also prove problematic. But in the middle of it all, a major event occurs in his personal life, the adoption of a child. Smiling, he explains on the program *Entrée des artistes* that he has agreed to become a father because the little girl is beautiful and bad-tempered! "For my entire life I've lived with women who have these characteristics. If I succeed in raising my daughter well, my life will have been a success."

At the professional level, in spite of the triumph of *The Decline of the American Empire* and *Jesus of Montreal*, the nineties will be one of the darkest times in the career of Denys Arcand, perhaps even darker than the mid-seventies, after *Gina*. Though he is renowned and esteemed all over the world, several factors conspire to make him a kind of black sheep in Quebec, shouted down by part of the intelligentsia and critical community and more or less ignored by the public.

His two previous films having travelled to dozens of countries, he is honoured in New York, Paris, Cannes and Hollywood and also paid the highest tributes in Canada and Quebec, yet by many he is considered suspect, suddenly uninteresting, and even to be avoided. Insults and harsh reviews start to pour in, not to speak of the violent and hateful "editorial" of Pierre Falardeau, published not just once but twice.

What is Arcand being reproached for? To give the short list: for being a disenchanted baby-boomer, for having lost his social and sovereignist conscience, for having sold out to the great federal Canadian whole, for flirting with theatre instead of continuing with film or continuing to make films but without writing his own scripts, for making commercials and working for television, for working in English, even for moving to Toronto, a fact the media reports without having verified it. Arcand seems to be one of the "human remains" that will later capture his attention when he attends a performance, at the Théâtre de Quat'Sous, of the Brad Fraser play *Unidentified Human Remains and the True Nature of Love*, produced by André Brassard (*Des restes humains non identifiés and la véritable nature de l'amour*).

The release of *The Decline of the American Empire* marks the turning point. In August of 1986, in the magazine *Allure*, Richard Martineau deplores "a cretinism that is all the more alarming because it is dressed up as culture and good taste. After the beatific smile of the silent majority, move over for the belly laugh of the big-mouth minority, the depraved winks of the conscientious objectors and for the uncomfortable but different decline of the Quebec elite."

In May 1989 comes another volley of negative criticism, this time from the cultural weekly *Voir*, founded and edited by Jean Barbe. Even before he has seen *Jesus of Montreal*, Barbe comes out with two surprising articles attacking the film and its author. "You have to admit, it's a little sad to see this nostalgia about God coming from the same people who cheerfully dumped him a few years back. Morals have gone by the boards, young people don't want to be torch-bearers for worn-out causes, computers are incomprehensible, television is no picnic. Before at least there was sex, but now . . . Might as well replace the lost scents of sex with the old beaten track of religion. One almost gets the feeling that Arcand has stopped living, that all he has left is the memory of his old beliefs and ideas. Sometimes cynicism has the appearance of surrender, of comfort and indifference. Come to think of it, maybe *Jesus of Montreal* talks about real problems after all." Later when Martineau succeeds Jean Barbe at *Voir*, he continues indefatigably in this anti-boomer vein, playing it over and over like a broken record until 2003 and *The Barbarian Invasions*, which he reproaches for the same reasons—after admitting he "loves the film"! In past times, people loved something and then burnt it, in that order, and in an orderly fashion; today, it seems they burn what they love at the moment they are loving it.

In 1987–1988, Arcand receives from the Société générale du cinéma du Québec (SGCQ) a grant of $9,259.26 to develop a project entitled *Summer Love*. Unfortunately, the filmmaker has no memory of the synopsis to which he gave this English title. It may have been an embryonic version of *Stardom*, or perhaps a vague recollection of a summer love in Deschambault with a young woman from Ontario, a subject he developed a few years later in the unproduced script for *C'est la vie*. All that is certain is that *Summer Love* belongs to one of the shadow zones in Arcand's œuvre, and that the project was never developed.

The attacks directed at the filmmaker do not prevent him from receiving a number of honours. In 1990, he is made a Chevalier de l'Ordre national du Québec and a member of the Academy of Great Montrealers. He is the second filmmaker, after Norman McLaren, to receive the latter distinction. In his acceptance speech he remarks: "When we talk about culture, we generally think of the oldest forms of expression, literature, painting, music or theatre rather than cinema, which, because if its origin, is often considered as a somewhat unrefined form of popular entertainment. Thus, you allow me to accept this honour in the name of all my confrères and conseours in Quebec film, who along with myself have helped make Montreal known all over the world." Though with no intention of striking a sour chord in this pleasant evening, Arcand takes the opportunity to denounce the fact that "Montreal is the city in which culture is most heavily taxed in the world," and that the City considers the Cinémathèque québécoise building as a commercial establishment no different from a shopping centre or downtown skyscraper. Finally, he issues a warning against politicians who declare in speeches that they are proud of Quebec culture and suggests they be reminded that "we, the artisans of this culture, pay Montreal taxes that are approximately three times the amount the city pays us in grants." The next year, France decorates the filmmaker with its Médaille des Arts et des Lettres; the Festival du cinéma québécois in Blois organizes a big rétrospective of his films; Serge Losique's World Film Festival in Montreal presents him with a bronze plaque; Cinematheque Ontario presents its retrospective *Denys de Montréal*.

It doesn't stop there. In 1992, he receives the Canada Council's Molson Award. "I am very happy to share this tribute with Professor Charles Taylor, to whom I am greatly indebted, for it is thanks to his famous *Hegel* that I been able to claim upon occasion, to a few naive souls, that I understand the slightest thing about *Sein*, *Dasein* and *Fursichsein* in *The Phenomenology of Mind*. I wanted to make this confession." In 1994, several events occur: the world première of the original version of *On est au coton*; the retrospective and *Leçon de cinéma* at the Festival de Namur; and a retrospective at the Museum of Modern Art in New York. Arcand is named president of the *Rendez-vous du cinéma québécois* and comes back for a second year, the hundredth anniversary of cinema, for which he writes this very brief preface: "Cinema will prove to have been the art form of the twentieth century. An exemplary product of the industrial revolution; cousin of the sewing machine and the phonograph, cinema will probably not survive the century in which it was developed. Its electronic progeny have already commenced their work of patricide." In 1995, Arcand receives his honorary doctorate from the Université de Montréal and a Governor General's Award for the Performing Arts in Ottawa.

But all is far from calm. In 1992, a provincial-style scandal breaks out, called "the Rockies of Denys Arcand." The Acadian singer Édith Butler and Arcand appear in commercials promoting the beauty of skiing in the mountains of British Columbia. Later, without their knowledge and consent, their faces are used in federalist propaganda spots for Canada 125. All hell breaks loose, as this letter to *Le Devoir* suggests: "What has got into Denys Arcand? Can he be so naive as to believe that this 'tourism' campaign for Canada's 125th anniversary is apolitical? Has he quite simply crossed over to the federalist camp? Could he have possibly sunken into comfort and indifference?" In *24 images*, Yves Rousseau calls his article "The Comfort and Indifference of Mr. Canada 125," maintaining that "the affair of Denys Arcand and the Rockies is twisted, the very image of his protagonist [. . .] when Machiavelli does figure eights on the slopes of Jean Chrétien." As a rare exception, the filmmaker writes a letter to the newspapers and explains: "As a result of I-don't-know-what kind of mishaps and manoeuvres, and without my ever being consulted, these spots were incorporated into a vast federal government advertising offensive. So in spite of myself, I was transformed into a propagandist for national unity. [. . .] With no illusions, I would like to inform all those who may happen to be interested that Canadian unity is the last thing in the world that I worry about, and that next winter, like many Quebec skiers, I will probably be in Austria or Colorado, it has fewer consequences."

We have yet to mention the prose of Pierre Falardeau, the Québécois "Père Duchesne," who flogs the same old dead horse in his diatribe in summer 1992 in *Lumières*, the organ of the Quebec film directors' association (Association des réalisateurs québécois). The polemicist lights into fellow filmmaker Denys Arcand, in a text entitled "La soupane and la marchette" ("The Gruel and the Walking Stick"). In this pseudo-political column, before getting around to the subject of Arcand, he comments on the recent death of author Roger Lemelin: "At long last! What a piece of dirt. The rats will end up dying too." Later, while tearing strips off the creator of the *Plouffes* and *The Crime of Ovide Plouffe*, Falardeau does not neglect to mention that Arcand worked with Lemelin on the adaptation of the latter novel. Finally the pamphlet describes the sad fate of Quebec artists and intellectuals living in a "climate of spinelessness and premature senility [. . .] in the country of Mother Plouffe, that old bitch." How sad it is to see how the creative milieu has enclosed itself "in formalism, aestheticism, mannerism, decoration and time wasting [*enculage de mouches*]." In this country where "heroes quickly tire and young wolves age prematurely," where there may be a predisposition to cowardice and failure, the crowning touch is a full-length portrait of Arcand: "The Great. One of our two geniuses who weeps for his Rocky Mountains in the commercial for 125, like a lowly Elvis Gratton, a *sous*-Jean Chrétien, the dove of Barcelona. This is sad. And completely pathetic. He looks stupid with his Order of Canada medal. Arm in the wringer. And pants down. What will he defend next? The honorary presidency of the Calgary Stampede or speechwriting for the Governor General?" A man exposed, ready for old age "with his walking stick, his bowl of gruel and hernia bandage to hold his pretty medal."

Arcand, dumbfounded and saddened by these accusations, talks them over with their author who seems to regret or be embarrassed by them. Yet three years later, when Falardeau publishes his book *La liberté n'est pas une marque de yogourt* (*Freedom Is Not a Brand of Yogurt*), he reprints the text without batting an eye or taking account of Arcand's statements in *Lumières*, *Le Devoir* and *La Presse*. This accusation will survive so well that, again in 2000, when *Stardom* comes out at the Toronto Film Festival, Martin Bilodeau will also allude to "certain unfortunate associations" from Arcand's past, such as "the commercial in which he appeared, singing the praises of Canadian unity" (*Le Devoir*, September 8, 2000).

The 1990s bring many changes in the filmmaker's personal and professional life. The beginning of the decade is marked by his separation from Johanne Prégent and then from Roger Frappier, with whom he has worked since the end of the seventies.

While Arcand is directing *Jesus of Montreal*, Johanne Prégent has also started directing films. She has already made *La peau et les os* (1988), a docu-drama. Soon she will proceed to fictional features, with *Blanche est la nuit* in 1989 and a short drama in 1990 called *On a marché sur la lune*. The couple separated at the time of *Lettres de la religieuse portugaise*. During this period, she is busy writing the script for *Les amoureuses*, her second dramatic feature. Written in 1990–1991 and released in 1992, the film tells the story of a couple's breakup.

Hence, the professional relationship of Johanne Prégent and Denys Arcand, which began as a relation between a director and script supervisor, became a kind of friendly competition between two writer-directors. Johanne Prégent believes that Arcand was a little startled by this. She feels that, in a premonitory way, the *Les amoureuses* script inspired the breakup: "Not in the sense that it was autobiographical, that it told our story, but because I used my world, my friends, my couple life for inspiration, the way one continually does in writing drama. I always wanted to write and direct my films, and that wasn't going to change because Denys Arcand was at my side with all his experience. What became disturbing and difficult is that all of a sudden, I had to deal with reports to Telefilm, to producers, to reviewers, as he did. Denys saw me going through what he had gone through, it got to be too difficult for him. *Les amoureuses* depicts characters who still love each other but who can no longer live together."

The situation at that time was not helped by the relative failure of Arcand's first foray into theatre directing with *Lettres de la religieuse portugaise*. Johanne Prégent talks about Arcand's anger and bitterness. He himself remembers mixed reviews, neither raving nor incendiary about his mise-en-scene. "It's a work full of mystery," he emphasizes. "They may be the letters of a woman in love, reworked by the anonymous author who received them. It is true to life in its bursts of passion, its sudden leaps from one subject to another, the reversals of the character, who loves, hates, rejects, desires, et cetera. A surprising, fascinating text; a mysterious work."

The next year, his film work is limited to directing *Vue d'ailleurs*, a sketch written by Paule Baillargeon, for *Montréal vu par . . . Six variations sur un thème*, shot in May. This episode describes a story told by a middle-aged woman, the astonishing tale of a passionate encounter during a Montreal snowstorm at the time of a business meeting. The woman tells the story to a young woman, but it is meant for her husband, who is listening from a distance. The man concludes: "I knew the story, but I'd never heard it before." While working on this short film, Arcand is intensely occupied with other things. He confides to *Lumières* that he is dreaming about another film, the synopsis for the future *Stardom*. Over 1991, he primarily works on a new dramatic feature for

Roger Frappier. He has received a grant of $3,504 from the Société générale des industries culturelles du Québec and a project development grant of $75,000 to write the script for *La vie éternelle*. Thus Arcand is wrestling with his film about death, with "dark thoughts about death that haunted him," as Johanne Prégent says. Three different drafts of the screenplay exist, each with a different title: *La femme idéale*, *La vie éternelle* and *Dernier amour*. Frappier is not convinced by the project.

In your childhood, did you go to catechism? The answer to this question reveals what generation you belong to. In the Catholic religion in Quebec during the 1940s and 1950s, the end of childhood was marked with the ritual of Holy Communion. It happened at the age of seven, "the age of reason," at a big ceremony in the parish during which the parish priest, from the pulpit, read out the marks received by the children in their catechism exam. The exam required that the child understand (or rather, be able to recite by heart) the "little" *Catéchisme* "of the provinces of Quebec, Montreal and Ottawa, approved April 20, 1888 by the archbishops and bishops of these provinces and published by their order."

This ritual of instruction was called "going to catechism," and consisted of taking special classes from the parish priest based on this little Bible. As Denys Arcand shows in *Québec: Duplessis et après . . .*, apropos of the *Voters' Catechism* of Maurice Duplessis, the catechism that prepared children for their first Holy Communion was a collection of questions and answers. For example: "What is a mortal sin?"—A mortal sin is one that destroys the sanctifying grace of the soul and brings everlasting death and damnation upon the soul. Or: "What is impurity?"—Impurity is an inordinate seeking of the pleasures of the flesh."

The catechism also taught that after death there were certain places for the soul to go: heaven, hell and purgatory. That does not include limbo, a kind of no-man's land, a zone for children who have died unbaptized or a stopping place for the souls of the just before the coming of Jesus and the eternal entry into heaven. While writing almost three thousand pages of screenplay, Arcand is in a kind of limbo, a space that is real but also in the middle of nowhere, heaped high with stillborn projects and unproduced or rejected scripts—his film on death from the first half of the 1990s is a particularly revealing example.

The first version of this script, *La femme idéale*, dated April 10, 1991, is 173 pages long. The opening scenes: titles over a long tracking shot of a crowded hospital corridor; the cancer of a certain Henri Martin, literature professor at Collège Maisonneuve in Montreal, a former student of the Jesuits whom we discover at the hospital reading the *New York Review of Books*; confusion about the patients' names due to the new computer system; a patient greedily watching television. On the small screen, an interview with Marc Peralta, a rich and famous writer who believes "success is the natural consecration of talent." Later, Professor Martin tells his students that he will no longer be giving his course for reasons of illness. The story of his hospitalization is punctated with suicides. Before the opening titles, an elderly man, an Auschwitz survivor, throws himself from the sixth floor of a stairway— "we see his body pass, we can even see his closed eyes and the peaceful expression on his face"—a transparent allusion to Primo Levi's suicide in Turin, in 1985; in the other suicides we recognize the death of Claude Jutra, who throws himself off the Jacques-Cartier bridge, and that of Hubert Aquin in the grounds of the Villa-Maria convent in Montreal. Another man kills himself with the exhaust pipe of his car at the end of a pier, as in *Nesbitt's Trip*, after drinking one last glass of Johnnie Walker Black Label and listening to a cassette of John Coltrane. Another man, who in adolescence was Freudian and then existentialist, a Marxist, Maoist and hippie Buddhist, a man with "a bad reputation and a good reputation," disguises his suicide as a car accident.

Gradually, Peralta will help Martin be discovered, publish his out-of-print books or unpublished manuscripts and make him famous too. He finds him an ideal wife, an ex-prisoner, and most of all arranges a serene end for the professor-author, surrounded by friends. Martin tells them, "I am extraordinarily priviliged to have had people like you around me"; he can enter into death with his eyes open, like the Roman Stoics. This reference is highlighted by the reading of a letter from Seneca to Lucilius: "How could he be afraid, when he hoped to die? When we do not have the courage to die, life is slavery. No one has power over us once death is within our power."

This Martin, who "has made a new life for himself in frivolity and vanity," amuses himself by lying during televised interviews, by playing the peacock with his "ephemeral success and seduction of the mass-media." An intellectual nourished on Wittgenstein, Plato and Kant, he believes that "especially since Hegel, a philosophical system of whatever kind is simply a cultural production, the same as a work of literature or music." He is also the hedonist, who on a tennis court marvels at the physical beauty of two professional women players.

For this difficult project, Arcand assembles a reading committee composed of Jacques Brault, Yvon Rivard, Johanne Prégent, François Ricard and Gabriel Arcand. The third version of the script, entitled *Dernier amour*, is 174 pages long and is completed "at Sainte-Adèle, October 9, 1991, on the feast day of Saint-Denis." The main character, now called Thomas Bessner, teaches literature in a college; Marc Peralta is still a famous writer who will make Thomas a fashionable and prosperous author, which a college teacher could never be. He arranges a gentle death in which Thomas will be surrounded by friends. The letter to Lucilius is shortened at the end, but nonetheless includes the same sentence of farewell: "The time has come for us to part, for me to die and for you to live. Which of us has the better lot, no one knows but the gods." The music over the closing titles is Tammy Wynette's "Stand By Your Man." We see the professional tennis players again, in slow motion.

The second version of the script, called *La vie éternelle*, cannot be found at MaxFilms, Roger Frappier's company. According to its author, this version, finished at the end of 1991 or in the beginning of 1992, is quite similar to the other two, except for a few details. In 1992–1993, Arcand writes a new version of his film on death, called *C'est la vie*. He even refers to it as a fourth version. During a press conference, he announces the title and specifies that he has written eighty pages of the script. This new work is quite different from the previous three. First, it remains in handwritten form (all of Arcand's other scripts are typed), which means that it remained unfinished and never made it to MaxFilms. "It is absolutely unknown," the filmmaker emphasizes.

The story of *C'est la vie* revolves around the death of its protagonist, but it takes place in a whole other context from that of the other three scripts. This time it is set in the author's family milieu and includes flashbacks to his childhood in Deschambault. It is the second time that Arcand has so transparently made use of autobiographical elements. As the script has already been referred to, here we need only point out how it differs from previous versions. For the first time it concerns the death of a father, a retired Saint Lawrence river pilot named Adrien, and his relations, past and present, with his children, particularly his famous architect son Éric. Éric goes to the hospital to bring his father back to his home by the river. When his father dies, Éric is abroad and only gets back in time for the funeral, at which the village choir sings a *"Dies iræ."*

For some time, Éric has been separated from his wife, the woman who calls him "the man of her life." He occasionally sees young female friends. He travels a great deal for his work and "no longer knows what to do with his money." Relations between son and father are tense; there are two epic quarrel scenes, full of shouting and vociferation. Adrien dies without fully reconciling with his eldest son. In the hospital "they shake hands, a little ceremoniously." In this version of the script, Arcand kept the scenes depicting the suicides of Hubert Aquin and Claude Jutra. He specifies that Jutra's body was found on the riverbank, near Deschambault. The scenes from childhood include the mass attendants at church, Éric's tennis lessons with his mother and his hockey lessons with his father, and finally this beautiful sequence in flashback: the seven-year-old Éric sits on his father's lap at the wheel of the family car on a little country road. It is summer. Adrien is teaching his son how to drive. "Don't look at the hood, look into the distance. You have to look in the distance when you drive." "Okay," says Éric, who is concentrating very hard. Today when he rereads the script for *C'est la vie*, Arcand says that he would like to go back and rework it.

While work on the script stalls, Arcand falls in love with Brad Fraser's play at the Théâtre de Quat'Sous. He tells Frappier that he would like to direct it as a film. The producer buys the rights at the end of 1991. Arcand supervises Fraser's work on the screenplay. He shoots the film between September 20 and November 26, 1992, and edits it over the winter of 1992–1993. *Love and Human Remains* premieres in September of that year at the opening of the Toronto Film Festival. However, it is not released in Montreal until March 18, 1994. Frappier was hoping for a big North American launch but the project aborted, not without turbulence. After the film's test screenings in the United

States, the producer asked Arcand to re-do the ending. The new scenes are shot on July 3 and 4, 1993.

"Relations between Frappier and myself had become tense," explains Arcand. "He doubted my script about death, whose success at the international level to him seemed uncertain. Perhaps wrongly, I felt that Frappier was too ambitious, carried away by success. Throughout the production of *Love and Human Remains*, he seemed irritable. For example, he didn't like the work of the DOP, Paul Sarossy (Atom Egoyan's regular cinematographer); I liked it. He couldn't stand the acting of Ruth Marshall. After his test screenings in the United States, he insisted that I change the ending. I now regret having done so. Meanwhile I received Robert Lantos's proposal, from Alliance. I accepted."

At that time, I was writing an article for the London publisher of *Auteur/provocateur*, and at the end of the winter of 1992–1993, Arcand gave me permission to view the original cut of *Love and Human Remains*. In my article I describe the final sequence as follows: "In the film's brief and magnificent epilogue, a moment of high NFB purity, the waiter-actor David decides to return to the stage and start his life over. In the great empty theatre, peaceful and radiant as a new earthly paradise, the fat producer asks the young man if he has anything to say before his audition. 'Yes,' answers David, 'I love you.' 'What?' 'I love you . . .' Here is all of Arcand, condensed into a few seconds, a critical mass about to explode: the peace of the theatre and the theatre-within-the-film, of art. I love you, art and music, the only human cry which continues to vibrate, waiting for an echo." When the book came out in 1995, the editor had to write a note explaining that this scene had been changed.

This was the most important difference between the script and the film. Other changes were made during the writing process. Arcand explained that he had supervised the work of Brad Fraser, notably in structuring the original play for film. But clearly, he also altered the content and even the style of the play. In *Voir Québec*, the filmmaker explained that he had had to contend with two elements that seemed to him problematic. The first of these was the author's gory imagination. "In the first version of the script," says Arcand, "the young women's murders took five minutes each because their entrails and eyes were torn out, et cetera." Then there was the matter of Fraser's gay militancy, his "illustration and defence of homosexuality." Moreover, Arcand had to scramble to keep track of the film's physical geography because Fraser's script broke away from the "unity of place" and moved around from one setting to another.

Love and Human Remains is a dramatic comedy about two young friends and flatmates, David (Thomas Gibson), a cynical actor, and Candy (Ruth Marshall), a literary critic. The former has left his profession to work as a gay prostitute, the latter dreams of a great heterosexual love but in the meantime agrees to detour to a lesbian relationship. A childhood friend, Bernie (Cameron Bancroft), turns out to be a serial killer and commits suicide, whereas another young man, Kane (Matthew Ferguson), who hoped to become David's lover, ends up joining David and Candy in a tender and moving trio of friendship that will convince David to return to the stage. Another characteristic of this film: as much as the original English version is interesting, the Quebec version is monotonous and boring, which worked against its distribution to francophone audiences. Contrary to what was reported, Arcand did not supervise the film's postsynchronization.

In 1993, Arcand's separation from Frappier begins, after more than fifteen years of working together. It is not the only separation in Frappier's career: his assistant Pierre Latour has left to establish his own distribution company; since 1988 and her film *À corps perdu*, Léa Pool has been working with Denise Robert at Cinémaginaire. Yvon Rivard believes both men were deeply affected by the professional separation. At the time of the breakup on December 7, a curious and unexpected article appears in *La Presse* following a press conference called by Frappier. The article's title affirms that "all was well" between Frappier and Arcand. Rumours have begun to fly and not only about *Love and Human Remains*, shot in English and according to the media "with Toronto money." It has also been learned that Arcand has signed a contract with Robert Lantos of Alliance Communications to provide a film in the next five years and not shoot any other. The subject has not yet been chosen; Arcand can take his time. Yet the filmmaker emphasizes that he is still working with Frappier and MaxFilms on "a project we're going to do later" entitled *C'est la vie*, of which eighty pages have already been written—a kind of *Fanny and Alexander* based on memories of his Deschambault childhood and set in motion by the death of his parents. Indeed, Arcand explains, he wanted to do a film on death, but after three years opted instead for a film on his relationship with his mother and father.

Significantly, during the press conference, Frappier never mentions that Arcand has written three different versions of a film about death. This seems to confirm that he has no intention of producing the film. Yet as early as 1991, Arcand declared to *L'Express* in Toronto that two versions of this script had been thrown out. Also in the December 7th press conference, the delayed release of *Love and Human Remains* is explained. Frappier does not yet have all the answers about the North American launch, which is "still at the discussion stage." The Montreal release might even be moved up, ahead of the American one. Not a word is said about the changes to the final sequence. In spite of the denials, it is clear something has upset the so-called unchanged collaboration between the producer and his famous filmmaker. The relative failure of *Love and Human Remains* in 1994 does nothing to improve this state of affairs.

Separations and regrets: Arcand has known a few of those over the course of his career, though by temperament he is a model of fidelity to his friends, a quality which is not unrelated to his training in the "collective workshops" of young Quebec cinema. Starting with his films at the NFB, for many years he worked with Alain Dostie on camera and Serge Beauchemin on sound. Indeed, Arcand worked with Beauchemin on all his films from *On est au coton* up to and including *Le Confort*. He explains that their collaboration ended through a kind of fluke. However, this was not the case with Alain Dostie, who was a kind of alter ego for Arcand from the time of *Coton* until the three episodes of *Empire Inc.* when things started to grow sour. It was like "a real lovers' quarrel," says Arcand. After *Empire Inc.* the cameraman would no longer work with him, except in the case of a few commercials and the televised version of the *Lettres de la religieuse portugaise*.

Since *The Decline of the American Empire*, Guy Dufaux has been director of photography on all of Arcand's films, except for *Love and Human Remains*. For that film, Arcand chose Paul Sarossy, with whom he had worked on *Montréal vu par . . .* Another crisis. "Dufaux's feelings were hurt," says the filmmaker. "It's strange how closely these conflicts resemble passion; the ties between a director and his director of photography are like those of lovers." The filmmaker continues, "I also think of my professional relations with my brother Gabriel. While shooting *The Decline*, he became difficult on set. To make his role of a macho punk credible he said he had to hate the other characters. A few years ago, he even told *Elle Québec* that *Jesus of Montreal* was a "Social Credit" (*"créditiste"*) film! Our relations are difficult."

The release of *Love and Human Remains* makes waves in several places, starting with Quebec. The film is well received at its première at the Toronto Film Festival in September 1993, but in both Quebec and Canada its theatrical release is delayed. Frappier's fantasy of a North American launch is abandoned and the film comes out in the spring of 1994. Though some defend it, wholeheartedly or with reservations, certain influential critics, like those from Le *Devoir* and *24 images*, are dead set against it. Bernard Boulet, writing for Le *Devoir*, sees it as "a film with an artificial climate that leaves us cold, or worse, indifferent." As for *24 images*, the magazine feels that the film cannot be viewed as part of "Arcand's œuvre" but as a producer's film made by a filmmaker "who is no expert in mise-en-scene," who has given up his native language, his documentary experience and history training. Alain Charbonneau concludes: "Maybe Arcand is getting stuck in the drama of all Quebec filmmakers who meet with success: making films that are increasingly well made, but more and more removed from us, his audience."

However, *Love and Human Remains* is defended in *Voir* by Georges Privet, who sees it as a game that allows Arcand to "explore his favourite themes again: the duo of comfort and indifference, of the empire and its decline, love and its remains." This does not prevent the film from bombing, though later in the same year it is very warmly received by both critics and audiences in Australia and Austria. In Bologna, Italy, Arcand is stupefied to discover that young people have adopted it as a cult film and recite its dialogue by heart. The following year the film receives mixed reviews in both Washington and New York. In France, several years later, it passes almost unnoticed.

Quebec film students were amazed and disturbed by *Love and Human Remains*. I have rarely seen young people follow a film with such intensity and write analytical papers with so much concentration, without noticing the time go by. This film went straight to their hearts and they dissected it, writing to the end of their exam time and even beyond it.

Shortly after the Montreal release of *Love and Human Remains*, Arcand is given a very special opportunity to revisit his film *On est au coton*, when the André-Guérin foundation organizes a retrospective of censored films. This organism was created in 1991 with the mandate of protecting and developing the greatest possible freedom of expression in all the audiovisual domains. On the last evening of one of its programs on censorship, June 19, 1994, the original version of *On est au coton* is screened. It is the film's "premiere" almost twenty-five years after its making, the premiere of a film that is not supposed to exist. The NFB does not recognize its existence, for the director himself removed all the scenes of Edward F. King, director of Dominion Textile. Thus, the first version of *On est au coton* emerges from the shadows. To use the words of Sebald again, the condemned feature film "emerges out of nothing like the shadows of reality," as when the dead become visible.

During the 1995–1996 administrative year, in conjunction with Cinémaginaire, Arcand obtains from SODEC (Société de développement des entreprises culturelles du Québec) a development grant of $12,000 for a script called *Critical*. The same year he also receives $25,000 to write the script for *Beautiful*. This time, the filmmaker vividly remembers the project. With Denise Robert, he intended to make a film on cultural critics, a comedy inspired by the British horror film *Theatre of Blood*, with Vincent Price, in which a washed-up Shakespearean actor murders, one by one, the critics who disparage his acting. Arcand explains that in this film, he particularly wanted to describe the phenomenon of "junkets" offered to Canadian and Quebec film critics. On trips to Hollywood that are paid for by distributors, critics attend advance screenings of films they provide with abundant and widespread media coverage. Arcand's project for *Critical* developed no further.

In early 1995, Arcand receives what he terms a flattering proposal. Joan Fraser, the new editor of the Montreal daily *The Gazette*, invites him to be one of a pool of honorary contributing writers. Arcand declines the invitation, saying that his mode of expression is the screenplay and that he does not want to bore his fellow citizens by holding forth on various subjects. He prefers, he says, to keep his ideas for scripts. Several months before, in a 1994 interview when *Love and Human Remains* comes out, Arcand did not hide the fact that he was working on a new film on beauty and superficiality, the project announced in 1993, another film in English. In November 1995, in the Ottawa newspaper *Le Droit*, the filmmaker says that he will soon have an answer from Alliance about the script, *Beautiful*. What the public will not know until later is that the Toronto firm categorically rejects the project, without appeal. Another Arcand script in the trash.

This time Denise Robert is involved in the project, though not yet as producer. Before moving to Montreal and founding Cinémaginaire in 1988, Denise Robert was unfamiliar with most of Arcand's work. "I was brought up in Ottawa, in an anglophone culture, far from his films. The first of his features that I saw was *The Decline of the American Empire*, at Cannes. I was excessively puritanical; the film shocked me because I couldn't believe people could throw their values out the window like that. Then I saw *Jesus of Montreal*, which I loved." She first worked with Arcand on *Montréal vu par . . .*: "A one-of-a-kind experience. I also had a long working relationship with Léa Pool. She first came to see me at Cinémaginaire with her project *À corps perdu*, based on the novel *Kurwenal* by Yves Navarre. Roger Frappier was supposed to do the film and then decided not to. I fell in love with Léa Pool's script. I work with filmmakers if I believe in their universe, if I feel capable of taking them further in their creative process. My career as producer was already established before meeting Denys Arcand; I was already working with writer-filmmakers like Léa Pool, and I produced Robert Lepage's *Le confessionnal*. Later; Arcand proposed shooting a script by Claire Richard, *Joyeux calvaire*."

After the twisted circumstances of *Beautiful*'s rejection in 1996, it is not surprising that Arcand and Cinémaginaire decide to do *Joyeux calvaire*. Shot between April 8 and May 3 that year, the film comes out on November 28. Denise Robert explains that Arcand is bound to Alliance by exclusive contract to direct a feature film. If he can shoot *Joyeux calvaire*, it is because it is for television and not, a priori, for theatrical release. Commissioned by Charles Ohayon of Radio-Canada, the film is based on Claire Richard's project about the endless itinerancy of two tramps who are friends. Jacques W. Benoit, first AD, describes how on every day of shooting, he scouted for locations with Arcand and art director Patrice Bengle. The sites chosen evoked "a city in ruins, Beirut from start to finish, a postnuclear city," to allow Arcand, with his surrealist sensibility, to make this story of itinerancy into "a Buñuelian outing."

Surprisingly, Benoit is convinced that the *Joyeux calvaire* script was written by the novelist Réjean Ducharme, Claire Richard's partner. "If the critics had known that, they wouldn't have had the same opinion of the film." Was *Joyeux calvaire* really written by Réjean Ducharme? Arcand says, "I don't know what the exact influence or participation of Réjean Ducharme might have been, I don't know him. He must have done critical readings for the script. I know he supplied the anecdote of the prostitute who goes down into what is called 'a manhole' to join the workers under the street. He also proposed putting the word '*calvaire*' in the title or calling the film *Le chemin du calvaire*. I finally opted for *Joyeux calvaire*."

Denise Robert is very proud of the film, made with a small team of ten who drove around in an old bus that had been used by Elvis Presley during his final tour in the seventies and now belonged to an old hippie in Toronto. "I don't know either how much influence Ducharme might have had on the script, which is based on a diary Claire Richard wrote for fifteen years while working as a volunteer with the homeless in Montreal. But when you live with someone, they certainly influence you in some way."

The reception of *Joyeux calvaire* is generally quite good. *La Presse* writes that the film "manages to avoid miserabilism, and do more with less." Pierre Demers, in *Factuel*, praises the implicit parallel that Arcand draws between itinerancy and Quebec cinema. In *24 images*, Yves Rousseau writes a very positive summary, highlighting the beautiful gravity of the parallels that are drawn between the decaying city and death. *Ciné-bulles* offers two reviews with opposing points of view: André Lavoie is happy to see Arcand return to "a precision of tone comparable to that of his scathing fictions of the seventies," whereas Paul Beaucage finds that "the director is once again bogged down by modest and conventional aesthetics that are disturbing to no one." The moral of the story: "Denys Arcand would have had to take a stand to convince us that what he was saying is true." The *Globe and Mail*, which regrets the little attention the film receives in English Canada, praises the author's "quiet respect for the mystery of each human personality" as well as "the subtlety of Arcand's directorial approach." In Quebec, the most virulent attack comes from *L'itinéraire*, the journal published by the homeless, which sees in *Joyeux calvaire* only "crude images" of the reality of homelessness; however, the same paper later publishes a text written by volunteers and workers from Accueil Bonneau, a Montreal organization for the homeless, which defends the film.

"She arrived in Quebec in October 1996, around the time that *Joyeux calvaire* was released," says Denise Robert. "She" is Ming Xia. Ming means "clarity" and Xia means "rainbow over the sunset." Her full name is Ming Xia Robert-Arcand. An event that disrupted the filmmaker's life, leaving a double trace on *The Barbarian Invasions*. First, there is the film's dedication "to my daughter Ming Xia" and then the presence of the little girl herself in a short sequence at the end of the film, the piano lesson given by Louise. Ming Xia listens attentively to the sonata by Diabelli. A short nonspeaking appearance, yet a scene which shows an important piece of Quebec's future: three young girls of Asiatic origin; Montreal, and classical music from eighteenth-century Europe. An appealing mixture for brighter tomorrows—or maybe not so bright? "I don't know," says Arcand, "but tomorrow won't look anything like what we've known in past. The massive arrival of immigrants, everywhere in Western countries, is a disturbing event. Will my daughter be excited by stories about Dollard des Ormeaux at Long-Sault or Curé Labelle? I'm not sure. Will the new children really be interested in Mozart or Diabelli? There's a big age difference between my daughter and I, and I tell myself that maybe when she's twenty, she'll want to know something about that man who gave her a home. She'll be able to say, *The Barbarian Invasions* is the image of my adoptive father."

Back to work with Alliance. The script for *15 Moments*, written in collaboration with Jacob Potashnik, is finished in June 1998. Telefilm provides funding of about $75,000. The film is shot between March 14 and June 6, 1999, and released under the title *Stardom* in 2000, six years after Arcand began writing it and almost ten years after the idea first came to him. Though *Stardom* has a number of fierce and passionate champions, few like the film and most do not understand it, poorly grasping the subtle interplay between reality and media-generated images. The decade's end finds Arcand more full of doubt than ever. He wonders if he's made a mistake, if he's succeeded in conveying his subject. What if *Stardom* is nothing but a huge misunderstanding that has not lived up to the promise of the *Beautiful* screenplay? Having cost over $11 million, the film is the very antithesis of *Joyeux calvaire*, which was made for $700,000. These two last films form the most contrasted diptych that Arcand has ever produced.

Thus the 1990s come to an end with mixed results. Four films have been brought to term, certainly, but some consider them to be failures even today. Dark and melancholy films, haunted by death and degeneration. But more than that, five scripts have been abandoned or rejected, a particularly high negative score for Arcand. Of course, it is not the first time in his career that projects or scripts have been put aside, rejected or left in an embryonic state. But it is astonishing that after the enormous success of *The Decline of the American Empire* and *Jesus of Montreal*, so many have been consigned to limbo.

13

THE STARDOM MISUNDERSTANDING

"The mechanics of film fascinate me. I'm never afraid on set or in the editing room. In my filmmaking I'm fearless, it's the opposite of my private life, in which I'm often terrorized," Arcand affirms in *Copie zero,* in 1987. However, more than ten years later, he starts to feel doubt. Denys Arcand has doubts about *Stardom.* "Maybe I didn't succeed in making myself understood," he confirms in *Ciné-bulles* and on *Paroles de star,* a program on Radio-Canada. Today he adds: "*Stardom* is a failure."

The film's history is long and tortuous. Already in 1991, in *Lumières,* Arcand describes a screenplay dream he has had, a rough sketch for *Stardom.* It is an idea that is contemporaneous with his film about death, *Dernier amour.*

I'm writing a screenplay this year and I'm already dreaming about another film I could do in four or five years, if I'm still alive and if my next film isn't a total failure.

I dream of diffuse, imprecise, fragmentary images. I have dreams of dreams. In the morning I write down my dreams of the night before. It seems to me that I'm dreaming more and more, though I've never dreamed much. It seems to me that in this film, there'd be a lot of dream-sequences. I think of two novels by Theodore Dreiser that could be related to what I'd like to do.

[. . .]

There would have to be rock music in this film. Or maybe rap? To do it properly, I'd have to be able to shoot this film in New York, Paris, Milan and Tokyo. It's very extravagant. I'll never have the budget for it. Unless . . . You never know. And besides, I'm very sedentary. Shooting in a foreign country must be hell. I'd have to be able to take a scene from an American TV series and postsynch it in all kinds of languages. A program you'd see all over the world. That must create problems with rights. And then I see a sequence in the desert, with a plane stopped at the end of a runway. Complicated to shoot. It seems to me that the main character would almost never talk. Except to utter a few onomatopoeias. An autistic character. Is it possible to have a character who's defined solely by the people around him? It's not clear how it could be written. It think I'd want to talk about the power of beauty. A power as terrible for the person who possesses it as for those who fall under its influence.

What am I going to do with all that?

In a December 1993 press conference, Roger Frappier announces that Arcand has signed a contract with Robert Lantos of Alliance. A single film to shoot, in English, in a five-year bracket, that is, by 1998. Exclusively. "For the next five years," explains Arcand, "I won't make any other films." In other words, *C'est la vie*, the unfinished screenplay he is writing for MaxFilms, will not be produced until after the Alliance film. Arcand also specifies that he does not yet have a subject for Lantos. The journalist Luc Perreault writes: "It would seem this project is nothing new. After *The Decline*, Arcand met regularly with producer Robert Lantos, at which time Lantos expressed interest in producing one of his films."

In 1994, Arcand announces that he is working on the theme of ephemeral beauty. Over a year later, in November 1995, the filmmaker tells the Ottawa newspaper *Le Droit* that he will soon have an answer from Alliance about his screenplay, *Beautiful*, bearing the copyright "Les Films Denys Arcand."

The Alliance adventure began when Robert Lantos met with

Denys Arcand and told him he wanted one of his films "the way one buys oneself a luxury yacht." He had no subject to suggest and the filmmaker mentioned his project on beauty. "I'll take it," said Lantos, who then asked the filmmaker to choose a producer. Arcand asked Denise Robert to become involved in the project. Robert did not necessarily want to involve Cinémaginaire as co-producer but agreed "to provide Arcand with the tools that will allow him to direct the film he wants to make."

Denise Robert accompanies Arcand to Alliance. "But right from the first meetings," she says, "we sensed that Denys's approach was at odds with that of Alliance. The meeting for the *Beautiful* screenplay was a catastrophe. The producers found the screenplay completely worthless. Arcand said that even their secretary thought it was bad. Robert Lantos and Alliance refused the new screenplay and cunningly suggested Arcand write a ten-page synopsis for a new version. Everyone hated the heroine's 'politically incorrect' side. Denys was white as a sheet, in a state of shock; he didn't say a word. I did everything I could to defend him, but I could see the project wasn't for us. Denys had lost all confidence in himself. He was unable to write for months."

But making *Joyeux calvaire* a short time later reconciles him with film. He wants to go back to work on his project on beauty. In 1997, Denise Robert and Arcand decide to produce the film, and ask to buy back the rights from Alliance. Lantos agrees. Arcand then joins forces with Jacob Potashnik to rewrite the screenplay, which becomes *15 Minutes*, or *15 Moments*. Cinémaginaire receives a call from Polygram, who would like to co-produce the new script. But the arrival of this powerful competitor makes Lantos change his mind, and he goes back on his decision to cede his rights. Denise Robert and Lantos agree that Cinémaginaire and Alliance will co-produce. Shooting is to begin in May or June of 1998, but is delayed when Alliance is sold to Atlantis, and Lantos leaves to to create Serendipity Point Films. The new shooting date is fixed at September of the same year, and then delayed again. In the end, *15 Moments* is not shot until 1999. It is screened on closing night the following year at Cannes, and at the Toronto and Vancouver festivals. Its new title is *Stardom,* "for a very simple reason," Arcand explains. "While we were editing, we discovered that there was another film-in-progress with the title *15 Minutes*. It was bound to cause confusion." Denise Robert adds: "After a disastrous test screening in New York, Alliance forced us to make cuts of almost twenty minutes, which reduced the heroine's 'incorrect' side and whitewashed the film. Denys agreed to it, he wanted to be conciliatory, but those cuts should not have been made." "Yes, I regretted it," Arcand continues. "I'm a good boy, I don't like confrontation. I agreed to cut the film down. In the original version, Tina showed her cruel and mean side; with the cuts she becomes a little too nice, not ambiguous enough. Luckily there's a copy of the original version in the vaults of the Cinémathèque québécoise."

The first screenplay for this film is one of the most polished that Arcand has ever written. *Beautiful*, or *Full Beautiful* is written in English, a first draft of 191 pages completed on October 24, 1995, with an epigraph of five short quotes on feminine beauty by Keats, Plato, Andy Warhol, Coco Chanel and Freud. It is the story of a young woman from Ontario, Lisa Stojanovitch. The film opens in a psychiatrist's office on Park Avenue in Manhattan where Lisa is talking about a nightmare she has had about three masked men fishing on a frozen lake in northern Canada. Intercut with her description of the dream, the young woman's life story is told in flashbacks. A high school basketball player who wears thick glasses, she is discovered by a beauty-hunting photographer at an amateur fashion show held in a gymnasium. The photographer convinces Lisa to meet with a Montreal agent who will try to find her lucrative contracts as a model and cover girl in Paris, New York, Miami, Toronto, Milan. For a while, Lisa is the mistress of the photographer, Olivier Dubois, and then moves on to a shady businessman, Blaine, who goes bankrupt and becomes a pariah, sinks into a deep delirium and attempts suicide. He dies of a heart attack just as Lisa, after a number of setbacks, finally attains both glory and wealth.

The nerve centre of the screenplay is the city of Montreal, Lisa's home base. She will become known in Quebec through fashion photos shot in an old church to the sound of Gregorian chants, or a jeans factory full of immigrant women workers and deafening noise. We are also treated to sarcastic jokes on "Canadian values" ("neat is a summer camp on the Ottawa river") in chic restaurants and bars reminiscent of *Love and Humain Remains*.

Other recurrent Arcand themes become apparent in this version:

film (screenwriters have no power in Hollywood) and media ("sports, politics, finance, that's all show business nowadays; show business is a complete universe"); a certain Mathieu, met on an airplane, says he was a hippie in 1968, a Marxist in the seventies, an anarchist in 1982, and is now an ecologist with monarchist Catholic leanings. "I used to like workers, poor people, immigrants, blacks. I can't stand them anymore." This screenplay also makes reference to the high incomes of certain artists, Mozart, Picasso, Monet, and the fact that "poor countries have never produced great artists." Beautiful music is woven into the text, Strauss waltzes, Weber's *Freischütz* chorus.

The beauty profiteers see Lisa as a kind of idiot with an eight-word vocabulary. Her beauty is a marketable product that has depersonalized her ("Who am I? Never thought about it, really"), a mask for emptiness. The screenplay emanates a profound melancholy. It is basically a film about death, because in the media beauty has no content, has become an icon, a kind of metaphysical abstraction. Beauty can only be used in this way in a ruined world that draws a lavish and seductive curtain over putrefaction. Beauty has become a kind of makeup for cadavers. In this film, fashion and the media are instruments for the perversion of beauty, but remain in the background, even more than in the following version, *15 Moments*, later renamed *Stardom*.

Arcand resumes work in 1996–1997, this time writing in collaboration with Jacob Potashnik, a writer-director whom he greatly appreciates. Potashnik particularly helps him write the English dialogue. In the new screenplay, the dramaturgical geography is modified. The centre of the film is no longer Montreal but New York. Though the story remains the same, that is, the short-lived career of a young woman and the commercial exploitation of her beauty, the approach is different. The screenplay glitters with a thousand and one television screens, proposing a film within a film, a multimedia maelstrom, electronic acrobatics. One huge channel-surf. A kaleidoscopic structure, the shaping of the subject through the language of media to the point where meta-language prevails in the narrative discourse, lending it all a more distant and incisive quality than that of the more classical *Beautiful*. *15 Moments* takes us to the heart of the "beauty machine," which is a death-machine. The film this script proposes is less about the dismantling of television and mass media, in the style of *Network*, *The China Syndrome* or *To Die*

For, than a realistic description of a life diffracted through the prism of media images. As Arcand remarks to journalist Mathias Brunet: "The camera is not reality. The lens distorts the image and the microphone distorts the sound." Or, in the words of the television spot featuring Andre Agassi: *Image is everything.*

The screenplay's prologue is explicit: "Our narrative is built on televised images. Our challenge is to tell the story of the rise and fall of Tina Menzhal through an exploration of how television identifies, absorbs, exploits and finally abandons those people who for a brief moment fall under its relentless, insatiable, unblinking eye." The continual presence of television icons is reinforced by the fact that hip video filmmaker Bruce Taylor shoots a documentary about Tina, which we see in black and white, a documentary within the fiction, reminiscent of *Gina*. With a mocking detachment Bruce sets out to film "the *Zeitgeist*, the superficiality of our time." "Superficiality never killed anybody," he philosophizes. "You know, I'll take Warhol any day over Lenin or Heidegger or Pol Pot or you name them."

Arcand drops a number of scenes from *Beautiful*: the two suicides based on the deaths of Claude Jutra and Hubert Aquin, photo sessions in the church and the jeans factory staffed by immigrant workers, the Strauss waltzes. He also makes more substantial changes. Young Tina does not play basketball, but hockey. Her father, Marek Menzhal, was a key player in the North American major leagues. He comes from behind the Iron Curtain, from Brno in the former Czechoslovakia, and has abandoned his wife and two children. Tina laments the loss of her father ("I'm walking around with this hole in my heart"), though is reminded that when he was teaching her to play hockey, he constantly scolded her, chiding her for not moving quickly enough or for being afraid of going into the corners of the rink—in short, for being worthless. Here we are reminded of a scene in the *C'est la vie* script, when the father shows the young Éric how to play hockey. Choosing this sport for his film gives Arcand the chance to draw a portrait of jet-set hockey star Steve Bourque of the New York Rangers. It also allows him to set part of the action in Cornwall, Ontario, in icy winter landscapes, a leitmotif he used in his historical short films, in *Québec: Duplessis et après . . .* and in *Gina*.

Five men stand out in Tina's brief and dazzling trajectory through the world of modelling and the jet set. After Bruce Taylor, the video film-maker who first discovers her, there is Philippe Gascon, a French photographer from Montreal, and Barry Levine, an upmarket restaurateur. In New York, Tina meets René Ohayon, superagent, and finally the Canadian ambassador for the United Nations, Blaine de Castillon. Blaine and Levine are driven to madness and self-destruction by their passion for Tina. The three other men are dandies who keep their cool. Taylor embodies *Zeitgeist*. Gascon recites Baudelaire during an exhibition of his erotic photos. Ohayon devotes his entire career to "recognizing talent," which he says is "an art in itself." "Remember, Tolstoy was a runner-up for a Nobel Prize for literaure. Tolstoy! *War and Peace*? He lost to a diminutive French poet, Sully Prudhomme." Ohayon also cites the public's failure to recognize future superstar Céline Dion in a photo of a slightly chubby teenage girl. The philosophical discourse on beauty is pursued from time to time, for example, on ABC's *Nightlife* when a certain Dr. John quotes Plato on the subject.

In terms of music, Arcand keeps the chorus from Weber's *Freischütz* for the fashion show, but replaces a Strauss waltz with one from Verdi's *La traviata*. In *Stardom*, Arcand continues the practice of inscribing his films with musical signs and symbols, most of them from opera, whose harmonies resonated in earlier films such as *Réjeanne Padovani*, *The Decline of the American Empire* and *Jesus of Montreal*. In fact, this practice may be traced all the way back to *Les Montréalistes*, in which Purcell set the tone that was carried through to later films in the music of Gluck, Handel or Pergolesi. The musical sign inscribed in *Stardom* is the Verdi of *La traviata*. In spite of appearances, *Stardom* is not only a film about television, but a Canadian *Traviata*. The film's beginning and finale, based on the sad waltz of Verdi's opera (the famous "Libiamo," a drinking song), serve as pillars for a very precise filmic structure and determine the architecture of the whole.

The main theme is established from the opening sequence at the Cornwall Arena, a reverse tracking shot of Tina in the middle of a group of young woman hockey players who are skating around the rink before the game begins. The choice of music is significant: the "Libiamo" from the opening scene of the Verdi opera, in which Violetta (*la traviata*, a girl or woman "gone astray") is hosting a luxurious dinner party. The melody is joyful on the surface, but melancholy in its depths, foreshadowing the death of Violetta. The second time the director uses this theme is at the end of the film. After a hectic, hypermediatized life of glamour, Tina has married a doctor from Cornwall. She is pregnant, standing alone behind a big picture window in her luxurious suburban home. The waltz has grown sad, disenchanted, discordant, now played by a small string ensemble. The young woman has fallen back into anonymity and the dullness of a small Canadian city. The former hockey player is on the threshold of total defeat. Her trajectory has ended in the insignificance of marriage and maternity, at the portals of dreary death.

In *La dame aux camélias* (a novel published in 1848 and adapted for the stage in 1852), Marguerite Gautier, the protagonist of Alexandre Dumas *fils*, is a girl from a poor background. Her only quality and only chance of social success is her great beauty. A bourgeois notices her and buys her from her parents. In Paris he makes her a courtesan, who passes from a rich banker to an even richer millionaire. She is adulated, elegantly dressed and lodged; she holds receptions and banquets, appears in theatre boxes and at the opera. In *Stardom*, Tina has affairs with several men; her beauty is magnified by the media (the theatre boxes of today) and maintained by the mercenary sponsorship of haute couture and television. This *"dame aux camélias"* of the year 2000, on the basis of her physical beauty alone, has become a high-class prostitute of television networks. The only destiny of a *traviata* is to be seen, contemplated, gaped at from head to foot by the voyeuristic society that "keeps" her, and views her in much the same way as the media. The myth of *la traviata* is told by an intellectual, a novelist and playwright. Today, Alexandre Dumas *fils* would be a screenwriter and filmmaker. And what would the mythic life of Marguerite Gautier have been if Dumas had not made a novel and a play about her, if he had not for a second time dragged her out of the relative anonymity of Parisian mansions? It is he who transformed the young woman from a fleeting player in society life of nineteenth-century Paris into a great universal and metaphorical figure. The dynamic continues to be developed in *Stardom*. Arcand does a metaphorical reading of Canada and today's world in which everything can be bought: beauty, art, romantic feelings, fame—all pass beneath the bulldozer of money and through the gigantic meat grinder of the media.

Thanks to the film within the film, Bruce Taylor's conspiratorial wink in the direction of the invisible filmmaker, also thanks to Tina's final gaze at the director's camera, accompanied by a Mona Lisa smile, Arcand is telling us: Make no mistake, beyond the self-satisfied gaze of the media, I am the one who chooses to film all this, to be both accomplice and distant observer, and above all be in love with this young beauty, with her triumphs and her reverses of fortune. It is I who magnify this beauty with film writing (the novel and theatre are dead), it is I who, at the very last moment, pull the lost girl out of the wreck to cast her back into anonymity, silence, marriage and pregnancy. I am the one who, like a character in an Edgar Allan Poe story, closes the lid on a face and body walled up in a Cornwall-tomb.

Arcand has no illusions about what he films, no more than he ever was. His distant observation, creative, meditative and critical, is derisive and disillusioned, profoundly melancholy. What Denys Arcand may be telling us in *Stardom* is that filming beauty is difficult. In his hands, film is painfully transformed into a mirror and a bonfire of the vanities.

Stardom, as Arcand explains to the weekly newspaper *Voir*, "is a fairytale intercut with television." The character of Tina, he explains again in the magazine *Clin d'œil*, a beautiful young woman who is both an accomplice and a victim of the media, becomes "a deer paralysed in the headlights of a car." And as he had already explained in 1990 to *Cineaste*, at the time of *Jesus of Montreal*, today "Satan is someone dressed in an Armani suit." Here, we cannot help but think of Pasolini's testament film *Salò*, completed the day before he was murdered in 1975. Pasolini does more than merely show bodies. He shows them as carriers of spirit and culture, of barbarity and civilization. With this filmmaker, ideologies are no longer pure abstractions, but spirituality inscribed in bodies, sexes, faces. Bodies and feelings, hearts and minds co-habit, are one and the same. Judaeo-Christian culture separated them, Pasolinian materialism reunites them: "the natural is not natural," the human body is not only corporeal, sex is not only sexual, they must not be reduced to objects. This point of view can also be applied to *Stardom*. In a civilization that makes bodies into marketable products, sexual relations become a metaphor for their commercialization by power and the media. This is the source of Pasolini's disenchantment in *Salò*. His clinical and surgical descriptions express his disillusionment about a crypto-Nazi-fascistic reality that vilifies the human body, feelings, spirit and culture. In this sense, *Salò* heralds the globalized totalitarianism of today, that of pornographic images of body-objects. The same ethics as in *Stardom* can be read in the films of Catherine Breillat and in Michael Haneke's *The Piano Teacher.* .

There is no doubt that during the long and very costly *Stardom* saga, for Arcand, *Joyeux calvaire* came as a kind of relief. Not only because of its subject, the homeless, but also because the film is made in Quebec French, set in Montreal and made on a limited budget, the very antithesis of the superproduction with Alliance. It is interesting to note that the Buñuelian itinerancy of the damned in *Joyeux calvaire* is set in the shadow of a statue of Norman Bethune (late of the Chinese Revolution), that of a ruined movie palace or of Montreal skyscrapers, looming on the horizon. In other words, it takes place in the shadow of money and the degraded gold of *Stardom*'s world.

"Film is money. Money kills," Yvon Rivard remembers Arcand telling a novelist who wanted to become a screenwriter. And as the filmmaker remarked at the release of *Le confort et l'indifférence*, "it's wealth that's destroying culture and the social fabric." For example, Denys Arcand was on the board of directors for the Société des auteurs, compositeurs et dramaturges (SACD) when the Cinar affair was revealed, and was witness to its turmoil. Until 1999, Cinar was the biggest and most lucrative private audiovisual production company in Quebec and Canada, a model of savoir-faire and achievement, often cited as an example. The SACD discovered that government funding agencies had paid a million dollars in royalties to phantom Canadian partners for scripts that had actually been written by Americans. In Canada, only Canadian citizens are eligible for screenwriting grants. The scandal was enormous. In the summer of 2001, Cinar's new administration decided to reimburse a handsome sum to Telefilm Canada. As reported by Sophie Langlois on Radio-Canada television, Cinar returned $2.6 million to the federal organism for overpayment of financial assistance. Confirming the reimbursement and allowing it to be understood that the case would not be taken to court, Telefilm's spokesman and director François Macerola states: "We are putting an end to a painful episode that was damaging to the milieu, to the Cinar corporation and the entire concept of public investment. We're moving on. We're turning the page!" As the journalist Jean-Claude Leclerc writes in *Le Devoir* on

March 22, 2004, "Even the most disillusioned members of the public were quite surprised not only that the Cinar affair could happen at all, but that it led to nothing that could be called a sanction."

For Arcand this is an example, more obvious than most, of a certain form of corruption that is endemic in the funding system for private film and television. "I'm used to living with this kind of corruption, which is all around but not extensive enough to make us stop everything and demand a Crown inquiry. Canada is a semihonest country. A percentage of grants to the audiovisual industry are circulated among friends of the party and a certain number of production companies. The Cinar case was a big deal, but I know of other companies that do the same thing, though not so flagrantly. From the moment an industry is state-supported, there's corruption, strings pulled, friends in power." It was different in the days of the NFB, when filmmakers worked "for the Queen," were poorly paid but got a fixed yearly salary, and corruption was impossible and nonexistent. But Canadian political power decided to dismantle the NFB and fund private industry, which itself had to come to grips with co-production and globalized film distribution, as well as complex and confidential systems of private accounting. "It's called creative accounting. Over the years, I've gotten used to living with this system. I expect it's part of human nature; that's what cinema has now become."

Arcand concludes his assessment. *Stardom* is the product of a large-scale production-distribution, involving not only Robert Lantos and Serendipity Point Films, but both Alliance's Toronto bureau and its film division in Los Angeles, not to mention a Paris co-producer, Philippe Carcassonne. Its $11-million budget is quite substantial for a Canadian film and enormous for a Quebec filmmaker. Arcand admits: "I was completely lost in this milieu, a world of practice requirements that were unknown to me, such as the lists of name actors whose responses to the script you had to wait for, agents to be consulted, test screenings in the Village in New York, threats of court proceedings, distributors who demand cuts, et cetera. I had to struggle along in this milieu—I, who don't like confrontation but want to work in pleasant conditions, in a spirit of harmony and family feeling. I don't have the ferocious combativeness of Oliver Stone or Martin Scorsese." Considering the context, it is not surprising that Arcand feels completely snowed under by *Stardom*. He can only fight back in indirect ways, such as making sure the producers cannot change the film's editing. Hence, "Everything was bad on that film; I fought with demons from start to finish. I'm not cut out for that type of cinema, those types of production conditions. I won't be going back to fight in that sort of milieu in future."

Ths *Stardom* script is the first Arcand has written that is not centred in Montreal or Quebec. One of his colleagues, filmmaker Paul Tana, felt Arcand had lost himself in *Stardom* and should not have set his story in New York and Paris. "You could have told the same story in Montreal and, as the poet Blake said, find the universe in a grain of sand." With *Stardom*, Tana was convinced that Arcand had lost sight of his "grain of sand."

Another difficulty of *Stardom* is that the story is a reflection on the ubiquity of television images and is largely told through the language of the image. Arcand found it difficult to convey this message. If he has doubts about the film, it is due to this and not because he feels he made a bad film. On the contrary, he is happy with *Stardom*, which was painstakingly planned and constructed with great refinement. It questions the hegemony of the image at the dawn of the new millennium. In this sense, it may be likened to *Gina*, from the mid-1970s, another relative failure that questioned the role of cinema and ironically denounced the ascendancy of the commercial image to the detriment of the documentary and reflective image. We may recall with *Gina* Arcand deplored the death of a certain kind of cinema. Since that time, he has often repeated that his kind of filmmaking is dying.

In 1996, while he is struggling with his script on beauty and the media, he writes to Adriana Schettini, a journalist for *La Nación* and Buenos Aires correspondent for *Lumières*: "Filmmakers can no longer keep the attention of young people who continually 'zap' between images on their televisions. That's why cinema is dead. *Films d'auteurs* are still being made, but fewer and fewer of them in every country. Cinema was born with the twentieth century and will die with it." And then in 2000 when the film came out, he answers the questionnaire in *Cahiers du cinéma*, in a file called "The State of Film as Viewed by 50 of the Planet's Filmmakers": "There are only two types of filmmakers, Americans and Others, who can be Swedish, Persian or even occasionally Québécois. Faced with this sorry state of affairs, some of these wog filmmakers try to disguise their works as American films. Such efforts greatly amuse the citizens of the Empire. Not only do the Americans impose their cultural products on the entire world but also excel in siphoning the wealth of nations."

In *Stardom*'s production conditions, Arcand almost lost control of his *cinéma d'auteur*. He managed to save his film, but swears he will not work in such conditions again. "Money kills," he says, and he knows what he is talking about. Throughout his career, he has scrupulously examined the financial state of Quebec cinema and made a point of honour of scrupulously respecting his production budgets, never exceeding them. Gilles Messier, one of his golf partners and also his accountant, remarks that despite his great generosity and availability, Denys Arcand is very economical. His friends like to call him "El Cheapo," borrowing the expression of humorist Guy A. Lepage. He is especially economical in his filmmaking, by staying within his production budgets and also showing an acute consciousness of what Quebec cinema is capable of achieving with the means at its disposal. "The industrial answer is not a solution for Quebec," Arcand explains in *Lumières* in 1988, "it is to make *films d'auteur*, modest films that could prove very accessible to the international market." Throughout his career, Arcand has been interested in, and has explained his views at length on the relation between economics and culture, both in the past, "when money did not have the power of life and death" and in the current period, starting in the 1980s, when "the profession became more structured and more directly related to money." The more money is available, the more tangible its presence on the screen. That is another good reason to retain creative control of one's film work and never underestimate the importance of careful thinking before shooting and editing begin.

To launch the film, Arcand writes a short text of introduction:

> Plato said: "Beauty is a beautiful girl." Freud said: "Anatomy is destiny." Warhol said: "In the future everybody will be world-famous for fifteen minutes." *Stardom* is about the face of a girl reflected on seven billion screens around the planet. The images are opaque, enigmatic and meaningless. The girl keeps her secret while the idiots fill their screens with sound and fury.

The film does not do well in Quebec—reviews are negative or mixed. Juliette Ruer, in *Voir*: "a film that disturbs no one, light and very perilous." John Griffin from *The Gazette* maintains that "Stardom is a shallow look at shallow people." Jean-Philippe Gravel, in *Ici*, believes that the film "gets lost in the clumsy orchestration of its parodies," Christian Côté, in *Le Droit*, that it is an "average work, a comedy of noxious superficiality." Even harsher are the judgments of Martin Bilodeau in *Le Devoir*, or André Roy in *24 images*. The first writes: "*Stardom* has all the elements of a great unsubtle farce in which the filmmaker denounces the lack of culture and the voracity of world media with a series of self-satisfied winks." The second commentator alludes to the "decline of Denys Arcand," a film whose "devices cancel out all critical vision" and reveals "a distressing misanthropy and stupefying narrow-mindedness, the author's vision constantly overdetermined by a cynicism that belittles and betrays each character in no time flat."

Philosopher André Baril takes the opposite point of view: "An abrasive and funny film with a thousand different levels, a thoroughly riveting strip of dreams." His arguments in favour of the film are inspired by Freud: "Today's society, as opposed to those that preceded it, seeks narcissistic forms of love to the detriment of subject-object complementarity." In consideration of the universal fascination with feminine beauty, the essayist deduces: "By presenting a genesis of this fascination, Arcand creates a critical distance which allows us to see how the image industry succeeds in determining production on the basis of conspicuous consumption, and not on the basis of people's needs or any kind of collective project. Throughout the film, Arcand presents the enigmatic power of feminine beauty, reminding us to what degree the emotional force of basic narcissicism eludes us still as it eluded our ancestors." In conclusion, "*Stardom* clearly shows that it is because human beings are pulverized by their passions that it has proved so difficult to establish a just society. *Stardom* integrates Freud and unveils with humour and intelligence an entire chapter of the human comedy, while taking a discerning look at the forms power takes today."

Shortly after the film's release, in July 2000, the most hateful article that has ever been published about Arcand is published in *Le couac*. This lampoon is one of a series of columns by Victor-Lévy Beaulieu (VLB), entitled "Du fond de mon arrière-pays." The title of the article is

"Le cul du Québec" ("The Ass of Quebec"), in which the writer starts out by denouncing the journalist Robert Guy Scully: "You boast about your Franco-Ontarian roots while cheating on our holy mother, Société Radio-Canada, with a nice Liberal Jew by the name of Robert Rabinovitch." The writer then attacks Denys Arcand and his film *Stardom*, "yet another film set in the world of fashion." VLB reproaches the filmmaker for having been chosen Personality of the Week by *La Presse* in light of his recent statements in *Le Devoir* (May 23, 2000). In naming three examples, VLB practises the art of the truncated and convoluted quote, a literary strategem that perfectly illustrates the proverb, "He who wants to drown his dog accuses it of having rabies." Comparing Arcand to Robert Guy Scully, VLB concludes, "It is a great mistake not to recognize that Denys Arcand is just as perverse, not to say a thousand times more decrepit [than Scully]. [. . .] With people like them around, you don't make a country, you just want to plant bombs." It may be recalled that this same author, VLB, was also the satisfied publisher of the *Duplessis* screenplay by Denys Arcand in 1978.

The mixed reactions to *Stardom* do not prevent the filmmaker from receiving his fair share of tributes. In 2000, the Writers' Guild of Canada presented him with their award for best script. He was named "Personality of the Week" by *La Presse,* and the following year, honorary president of the Festival de cinéma panaméricain in Quebec City (second edition). He took advantage of the opportunity to once again drive his message home. First, that almost all movie theatres in the country are owned by two American super conglomerates, and the films on offer in Quebec are determined in New York and Los Angeles. Next, that an event such as the pan-American film festival is the only "window on the Americas" that exists outside the criteria of the international media industry, and finally that American independent production is the first victim of this industrialization process.

After *Stardom,* by applying himself to another film, Arcand turns his back on the mixed blessings and double-edged sword of the hegemonic tendencies of the Canadian-American production context. In 1993, he refuses an invitation from Hollywood to direct *Sleepless in Seattle* because he does not like the original screenplay. With *The Barbarian Invasions,* he returns to the world of his Quebec "grain of sand," though not forgetting that no matter what one says or does, cinema is and always will be a mirage, hocus-pocus. After all, when only a child, he understood that even religious and pious films could be erotically enticing, given a glimpse of thigh or an on-screen kiss. In the burst of light indicating the exact moment of Rémy's death in *The Barbarian Invasions,* a shimmering film image appears: Inès Orsini in the role of the saintly Maria Goretti, walking into the sea and raising her skirts, her thighs bared. Cinema, light. A new "bleak end-of-the-world light."

14
SECOND RESURRECTION: THE TWILIGHT OF THE GODS

What will "lyrical death" be like?
François Ricard

In the old days, the priests at the classical colleges were fond of quoting Latin phrases from the pink pages of the Larousse. One of them was: *Bis repetita placet*, an excerpt from the *Poetics* of Horace. "Things which are repeated are pleasing." This cameo from Arcand's days at Collège Sainte-Marie could have crossed his mind at the triumphant release of *The Barbarian Invasions*, a kind of encore, a repetition of the success of *The Decline of the American Empire* and *Jesus of Montreal*.

Though no doubt Arcand desired this great success from the bottom of his heart, he remained cool-headed throughout the production process. To those who repeated that the script was extraordinary, the shoot and rushes showing excellent results, the final product brilliant, Arcand replied: "Wait and see. Until it reaches the audience, you never know. I just hope to make a good film."

After the mix was completed in March 2003, several weeks before *The Barbarian Invasions* was launched in Montreal and at Cannes, Arcand agreed to take a critical look at his new film. He began by specifying that the word "barbarian" is derived from a Greek word referring to foreigners, that is, those who do not belong to the Greek culture. The word was later used by the Romans to designate those who were not part of the Empire. We live under the reign of the American Empire. Those who do not want to or who cannot be part of it are barbarians; they do not think in the same way, have a different social organization, religion and world view. The word is not pejorative. To be a barbarian is neither a quality nor a fault, it simply means that a person belongs to a foreign physical and cultural space.

With *The Barbarian Invasions*, Arcand comes to the end of a work he has been developing since the mid-seventies, beginning with his script *Nesbitt's Trip*, about a suicide. Later, in the early 1990s, he will attempt to tackle the subject again. "We make the same film over and over, in different forms. As we get older, the subject becomes more concentrated, synthesized; we deal with the same theme with greater density." Here again, the characters from *The Decline* and *Jesus of Montreal* expose their anxieties and their state of upheaval. For them, Arcand emphasizes, the European civilization born with Dante, Chaucer and Montaigne has come to an end; it began to die during the twentieth century and finally expired in the twenty-first. We thereby find ourselves plunged into the complete unknown. Painting ended with Andy Warhol, theatre with Samuel Beckett. Playwrights Gilles Maheu or Robert Lepage do "shows," performances, as they call them, not plays. After Berg or Schoenberg, where to go in music? John Cage presents the listener with four and a half minutes of silence, a work entirely devoid of sound. The entire structure of civilization has been abolished and its young people, in the eyes of Rémy and those of his generation, seem like barbarians.

Despite the love they discover for one another, they no longer have anything in common. However, this next generation is capable of showing Rémy how to die. His son Sébastien, though a barbarian, is an organizational genius. A London banker who earns a million a year, he knows what strings to pull to make administrations, staff and unions serve his interests. Unlike his father, he does not believe in the collective good. He is an individualist who trusts only his own powers and the money at his disposal. Nathalie is a heroin addict; she lives with death every day. She slowly brings Rémy to envisage and accept his own death. She is far wiser than him. Between them, the quasi-suicidal young woman and the demon of logistics make Rémy's death the gentlest that one could ever imagine.

And then, at the end of the film, the third generation appears, that of the immigrants. They arrive from everwhere, explains Arcand, they are coming out of the woodwork: "Now the most common name at the Montreal School Board is no longer Tremblay but Nguyen. It's very different from the way things were before. Same thing in Paris; Arabs and blacks everywhere. In the Club de Soccer de France, there are only two whites. Miami is a Latin-American city that resembles Caracas or San José. The entire infrastructure of Los Angeles is Spanish speaking. In the last shot of the film, with the music of Diabelli, the two teenage girls at the piano are Vietnamese; they take music lessons from an elderly nun and another lady, both of whom are Québécoises. My own daughter appears in this scene. She is Chinese, born in Yangzhou. I'm not sure that Quebec legends really interest these young girls. Last year, Louis Lortie told me he was worried because all the people he sees at concerts now are elderly. What will be the future of this new youth? I have no idea, and I won't be around to see it. I know that this future will look nothing like what we have known. I think we're headed for a new Middle Ages."

"I wanted the film's dedication to be 'To my daughter Ming Xia' because there's a huge age difference between us. I was fifty-five when I adopted her and I can't be sure I'll be there in her life for long. I told myself that if I'm no longer around when she's twenty, maybe she'd want to know more about the man who gave her a home. This film will make a good portrait. I'm fairly happy with it; it may be the best thing I could have done on the subject." In making the film, Arcand tried to come to terms with his own death, in the way that all good philosophy is said to teach us how to die. It is yet another way for Arcand to express his "absolute love" for his daughter Ming Xia, as he put it in his interviews with Mathias Brunet. What a lot of ground has been covered since our interviews for *Copie zéro*, in 1987, at which time the filmmaker repeated that he planned to spend his entire life without children, that he did not really like working with children because, in general, this kind of character leads to an infantilization of the film.

In early spring of 2003, Arcand is pleased with *The Barbarian Invasions* but waits for the verdict of critics and audiences before allowing himself to rejoice.

In May, the extraordinary occurs, putting the lie to the title of the Old Italian melodrama, "miracles only happen once." In Quebec, film critics are unanimous for once, calling *The Barbarian Invasions* "very good" and even "a masterpiece." Then comes the triumph at Cannes, the award for best screenplay, and the Best Actress award to Marie-Josée Croze. *La Presse* names Denise Robert and Denys Arcand personalities of the week. At the opening of the new session of the Quebec National Assembly, members voted that congratulations be extended to the the film and all of Quebec cinema. In fact, besides being a popular film that has already fulfilled its expectations for 2003 at the box office, *The Barbarian Invasions* has become a staple film, a flag bearer, a reference in discussions on health care, history, medicine and intergenerational relations. It appears this "good film" also serves as a kind of metaphor in the Quebec sociocultural landscape. Even Roger Frappier quotes it as an example. Several of Arcand's film titles are used as buzzwords: a journalist for Radio-Canada, talking about the War in Iraq, wonders in all seriousness if the "decline of the American empire" has not begun. A headline in *Le Devoir* declares that "poor countries are *au coton* [fed up]." Such results, Arcand admits on his return from Cannes in June, inspire "great relief and happiness." Speaking of Arcand's career, Édith de Villers feels that "his trajectory represents a way of intensely living the greatest passion of his life, cinema, of maintaining constant fidelity to what he is and loves, an insatiable curiosity and a strong sense of careful and well-done work."

This glory is a happy turn of events, all the more wonderful because it crowns a film the director has laboured over for years. Arcand, though he is greatly satisfied by the exceptionally good reviews and the enthusiastic audience response, is not inordinately surprised by its success. He has seen it before, with *The Decline of the American Empire* and *Jesus of Montreal*. As for the fact that *The Barbarian Invasions* has become a staple film, the filmmaker explains it in terms of the rather modest quantity of films made in Quebec. This, he says, is the advantage and disadantage of living in a small society. When there is a hiatus or drop in production, we complain about impasses and crises that don't exist, because we're working. When suddenly a film has a lot of success, we think it's a renaissance, which it isn't. But then, concludes Arcand, "We've never seen the U.S. Congress vote to congratulate

Martin Scorsese. If my film hadn't done well, it would have been hard for me to get to do another feature. I might have had to go back to working for television. Now, I can easily decide what features I'll do in future. The deal has changed. At a psychological level, it's also gratifying to have so many people thanking you, even people who don't often go to films; it's like an electrical current going through you and an encouragement to make other films. Gilles Jacob, the big boss of the Cannes Festival told me: 'We're here to give you energy.'"

There are two versions of *The Barbarian Invasions*—the Quebec version and the international version. The latter was suggested by the French co-producer, who wanted to cut down on certain Quebec particularisms. The French distributor, though without making it a requirement, requested a ten-minute shorter version to increase the number of daily screenings. Arcand tried it out at Cannes, and everyone was happy with it, including his friend Piers Handling, director of the Toronto Film Festival, and the people at Miramax, the film's U.S. distributor. "For me, the Quebec version is my film in its entirety. I'm very happy with it. It includes the slow parts, the parts that wander, the comedy scenes that border on bad taste, but I like it. The shorter and more efficient version gets to Rémy's death more quickly. I don't know what to think of all that. The two versions exist. The original negative will be stored at the Cinémathèque québécoise. When the film comes out on DVD, there could be room for both versions. Time will tell which is the better. Art's repertoire is full of works with more than one version: Mozart's *Don Giovanni*, Bruckner's *Fourth Symphony*, et cetera."

The film's second version, for international distribution, was projected at the opening of the 28th Toronto Film Festival, on September 4, 2003. Nothing essential from the longer cut is changed, and most of all, it gets right to the film's main subject. However, that does not mean we are unaware of a few losses. As the film's editor Isabelle Dedieu explains, three characters are dropped from the new cut: that of the first enraged ex-mistress (Sophie Lorain), the bad-tempered nurse (Micheline Lanctôt), and finally, Pierre's mistress (Macha Grenon). All are secondary but striking presences. The role of the second ex-mistress (Sylvie Drapeau) is suppressed except for one final shot. The role of the television-addicted patient, Duhamel (Denis Bouchard), is considerably reduced, Arcand having eliminated the scene of his recriminations against Vidéotron cable and the Société générale de financement du Québec.

Elsewhere, the filmmaker took the liberty of making a few short-cuts: Louise and Gaëlle in Rémy's apartment; the melancholy image of Rémy's departure from the Université de Montréal; and especially the short sequence at the end of the film in which the three young girls practise the Diabelli sonata in front of Louise, representing the "third generation" after the baby boomers and their children. Arcand greatly regrets the disappearance of this sequence shot. He also removed several other brief shots that take place after Rémy's death: Pierre and his wife in the country house; Claude and his companion; the farewell scene with Stéphane and Gaëlle at the airport. The French co-producer wanted the film to end with Rémy's death. Arcand did not yield to this request, but kept none of the postmortem sequences, other than Sébastien's departure from his father's apartment, and the plane taking off at Dorval airport.

It may be recalled that after his first edit, Arcand removed the entire scene with the third ex-mistress, the Québec minister of culture (Suzanne Lévesque), as well as the sequence in which Rémy reads the *Memoirs* of Saint-Simon to Sister Constance. The changes made between the Quebec version and the international one say a great deal about the filmmaker's ability to comply with the demands of producers and distributors, yet without ever compromising his will to orchestrate the movement of his film through continual reduction, tightening and pruning. The essential, always the essential.

Monique Fortier talks about this method, referring to the need to find the "particular rhythm of a sequence" and strike a balance in the movement of the film as a whole. Monique Fortier, who edited *Ville-Marie* at the NFB, later worked on three of Arcand's dramas, *Empire Inc.*, *The Crime of Ovide Plouffe* and *The Decline of the American Empire*. Paradoxically, these are the only fictions in her filmography, which primarily consists of work in documentary. "In both cases," explains Fortier, "the job of the editor is to give rhythm and meaning to a footage. With fiction, you don't have to look for the film's structure and build it—the script does that for you. But in documentary, the editor has to actively look for the film and its structure. The artistic reality of fiction film is built from a multitude of fragments, facets of this reality, using several different moments from a single timeframe. Fiction continually plays with time. This play allows the editor of fiction to find, in the director's choices, the points of emphasis she needs to unfold the particular rhythm of the sequences and the film. In this unfolding, this rhythm sought and found, the editor of fiction finds all the freedom she or he needs for editing to be a pleasant experience." Monique Fortier concludes: "In working with Denys, I believe I found a kind of balance that is difficult to define. It's there or it isn't. Denys's profound intelligence, his often surprising sensitivity, his good temper, make working with him a constant pleasure. Might as well say it—we love Denys!"

Isabelle Dedieu worked as editor on three of Arcand's films, *Jesus of Montreal*, *Stardom* and *The Barbarian Invasions*. She edits documentary films for television and dramatic features and has worked with Alain Cavalier, Francis Girod, Samy Pavel and Dominique Delouche. The first part of her job, during shooting or after, is to make a first assembly, a rudimentary film whose first screening is always a bit of a shock and that, among other things, reveals the film's most flagrant errors: repetitions and overloaded scenes, faulty construction, nonessential elements. A kind of marble block from which Arcand says "everything must be removed that is not Michelangelo's David." This copy also makes it possible to see the film's "spinal column."

If in editing a documentary, the editor, in a sense, creates a script, in drama his or her work consists essentially of finding the filmmaker's main idea and point of view, and highlighting the story's best features. You can do everything in editing; it's an emotion- and sensation-driven craft. While working on a film, you find its rhythm by trying out different choices, which takes a lot of time, it is true. Since the advent of digital editing (AVID), unlike in the old days, when you worked for hours at a time physically handling pieces of film, now editors are carried away by a kind of frenzy, with less room for reflection.

With drama, it is the author/director's intended meaning that prevails. In this case, the editor's role is to understand and reveal the initial idea and the true logic of the film. The editor's own inventiveness, creativity and sensibility come into play. Thus, editing is not, first and foremost, a matter of rules and techniques that must be respected. The editing room is a magical place, where the alchemy of images bubbles away. The editor is the film's first spectator, its first outside viewer. It is a craft that has a lot to do with sewing, the lacemaker's "fine hand."

For *Jesus of Montreal*, the editing was quite simple. It followed the chronology of the script and did not allow for too many inversions. *Stardom*, however, was a little more problematic. Viewers had to be able to understand that they were entering the world of television, and then leaving it at the end. But the audience did not quite grasp the subject of media reality, and wanted to be able to identify with the character and her youth and beauty. *Stardom*, which did not require many inversions in the editing process, is a film that appeals to the intelligence of spectators, demanding that they enter into a system they must decrypt. A more complex editing was required by *The Barbarian Invasions*, whose construction was a veritable jigsaw puzzle. There were numerous possibilities of inverting the order of sequences.

Moreover, it is a film that passed through two different stages, first, during the editing of the original Quebec version, transformed from a first assembly of two hours and thirty minutes to a one-hour-fifty-three-minute rough cut. Dedieu finds the latter version more complex and rich, alternating between comedy and dramatic comedy, which naturally implies varying rhythms, such as a slower pace in moments of drama to allow the emotion to unfold. Also in this version, Arcand's "unnecessaries" prove in fact to be necessary. The French distributor requested that the film be reduced to under one hour and forty minutes, the story focused on the death of Rémy and ended right after. The new version changes all the rhythmics and the structure of the film, for each re-edited sequence affects the organization of the whole.

"It's wonderful to edit with Denys Arcand," Isabelle Dedieu comments, "as his work as a filmmaker is built on a process that goes from writing to directing, from shooting to editing. Arcand resembles the great couturiers who know how to design the clothes and also cut the fabric. His method of supervising the editing is a direct extension of his temperament: calm, thoughtful, cheerful. He knows exactly what he wants but is open to what an outside sensibility can bring to the work, and his editing is guided by emotion. To me, he is a model of humanity, intelligence, humour, and open-mindedness."

The importance Arcand attributes to editing comes from his long hours of observing Gilles Groulx in action, not to mention the fact that earlier in his career he did the editing on three of his own films,

Montreal on a Summer's Day, *Volleyball* and *Gina*. The all-important work of editing, while possessing distinctive attributes, is also closely linked to previous phases of film production and relies upon the script. However, there is a crucial stage in the process, preproduction, which is hardly ever talked about and which marks the beginning of the real film. Casting, meeting the actors, locations scouting. How exactly is a film's physiognomy determined? It depends on the film, Arcand explains. For example, in the case of *Jesus of Montreal*, even before the script was written, he asked Lothaire Bluteau to confirm that he would play the lead. But this is a major exception. In general, the filmmaker starts his preproduction work when he is halfway through the scriptwriting process. He gives a version of the script to two key readers, Guy Dufaux, director of photography, and scenographer François Séguin. Then discussions begin, sometimes still a little undefined—there are still six months of screenwriting left—but the face of the film is starting to take shape. Again for *Jesus*, Dufaux travels to Europe, visits a lot of museums, investigates different representations of the crucifixion, their geometrical lines and perspectives; Séguin does the same in Montreal, and then one day comes up with the following reflection: "We need red earth." For *The Barbarian Invasions*, what is most important is to find a hospital. Lachine's is empty and serves the purpose very well. The costume designer Denis Sperdouklis gets involved, shortly concluding that in this kind of hospital, white is not used because it gets dirty and stains too easily. The little team often goes through the building looking for appropriate settings, Rémy's first room, his new room, et cetera. Arcand takes a lot of photos and sometimes drops by the hospital alone to look around and reflect.

While participating in a 1995 seminar at Concordia University, Arcand explains that even before he starts a film's preproduction, he always has a little stock of places and actors "in the bank." It is also clear that his work with his first assistant directors is an extension of his method of reading and researching to enrich his characters and his story. In this regard, his "work standards" are followed and shared by others. Lothaire Bluteau wants to read everything on Jesus, too. He even joins the Saint Joseph's Oratory library. He spends so much time there that the priest who takes care of the library leaves him the key.

Once the actors have been chosen, Arcand proceeds to the next two tasks: first, a collective reading of the script, usually at his home, without any acting but simply to go through the script, talk about it and ask questions so it will not have to be done while shooting. Each actor has his or her own method. Rémy Girard works from instinct, never asking questions, everything comes out on set; Dorothée Berryman arrives with dozens of questions about her character that will help her obtain the best possible results. The next task consists of making the characters come to life. For Marie-Josée Croze, a first attempt to play her junkie character with jeans and multiple earrings falls flat. Arcand has the actress and the costumier Sperdouklis meet a young woman heroin addict the director knows whose image is anything but punk. Their observations go into making Nathalie a hieratic, enigmatic character, intellectual, beautifully dressed, the one who will become "the guardian nun of the manuscripts." Arcand also made a point of changing the actress's hairstyle to reveal her splendid eyes.

For Sister Constance, another angel of death and an important figure of whom unfortunately little is said, Arcand conceives the character of a gentle, kind woman as he did in *Jesus of Montreal*. Johanne-Marie Tremblay laughingly protests that Arcand sees her as a saint. To create this character, the filmmaker met with a sister of the Grey Nuns order who travels every morning from the west end of the city to the Hôpital Notre-Dame to accompany patients in the last stages of illness. The sister also provided the screenwriter with descriptions of hospital thefts, generally perpetrated by employees protected by their trade unions.

Stéphane Rousseau had to be transformed with British-style made-to-measure clothes with real buttonholes, and all-cotton tailored shirts. His hairstyle had to be changed, his long hair cut, all in the name of creating the elegant, cold and troubling character who astonished everyone who doubted Arcand's decision to give this role to a stand-up comic.

Arcand would always like to take three to four months for preproduction. But as Telefilm financing agreements are settled at the beginning of the summer and principal photography must be completed before winter, the shoot has to be organized in a very short time. But Arcand is also counting on a more long-term kind of preparation, his ongoing work of investigation and research with which to enrich this filmic reality. Arcand affirms, again in the Concordia seminar, that if he involves his director of photography from the beginning of the process, it is because a sort of love affair is established between himself and this key professional. Generally, in preproduction, as during shooting, editing and mixing, Arcand has always adhered to one main principle: "Never try to be better than your team."

Some feel that *The Barbarian Invasions* repairs the "errors" that Arcand committed by shooting in English and making so-called flops, such as *Love and Human Remains* and *Stardom*. In short, people are satisfied that he has "become Québécois" again, after falling prey to what is called the Toronto or international syndrome. But that is to forget that this film provokes a number of different reactions; its triumph does not mean that opinions are unanimous. This phenomenon can first be noted in Cannes, where some see it as a "hopeful film," whereas its director calls it a "sad film." Denise Robert, in her interviews, often emphasizes that "it is the first of Denys's films in which we can see a ray of hope and perhaps a slightly brighter view of the future. Fatherhood has brought him the wisdom of hope. If he had not had his daughter, it would have been a different film." Yet Arcand had already clearly explained that the "Buñuelian lightness" he likes to use as his inspiration consists of "not taking yourself too seriously," whether in expressing emotion or in denunciation. The smile and the laugh, as he explained, again in *Copie zero*, have a diabolical quality for someone like himself, "a very amoral individual." This philosophy holds true in *The Barbarian Invasions*: the generations are reunited but the bond between them remains fragile. For Arcand, we have entered a time of darkness. Once again, the light that emanates from this film is that of a modern, Tolstoyan type of resurrection or a Wagnerian twilight of the gods.

The first negative reviews come out at the time of the Cannes Festival. First, a salvo from a British newspaper, objecting to the screenwriter's incorporation into his film of a television monitor image of the attack on Tower 2 of the World Trade Center. Next come the reactions of *Libération*, *Cahiers du cinema* and *Le Monde*. The latter sees the film as merely "a sitcom whose dialogues and script got the vote of the champions of a cinema of entertainment and convention." All that *Libération* retains of "these very talkative barbarians" is "a flatly photographed object, with outdated découpage. Old school." Finally les *Cahiers*: "a tiresome editorializing sitcom," a "total dud." Luc Perreault in *La Presse* quotes a French critic colleague as describing *The Barbarian Invasions* as "ultralibral at the very least, and perhaps even Le Pen-ist"!

In Quebec, after the initial euphoria has subsided, voices of discord can be heard. Yet again, the two phenomena exist side by side. The attacks are as unflagging as ever, and some are more sly and convoluted than usual. In an opinion piece published in *Le Devoir*, Daniel Couture deplores the praise the film has received: "The degenerate Romantic aestheticism, in other words, the 'subjective appeal' of the discourse, has become the sole criterion of its value." Some critics like the film, even love it, *but. . .*! Hence, *24 images* which in spite of two articles full of praise, dogmatically repeats that *Love and Human Remains* and *Stardom* were failures. Though Richard Martineau, in *Voir*, says he likes the film, he cannot resist the temptation of making a few attacks on the "boomers."

As for Robert Lévesque, he writes in *Ici* that once upon a time, or so he believes, there was an excellent Arcand, but that as of *The Decline*, a sort of post-Arcand emerged, one who no longer made "caustic cinema but money-making movies. His cinema was nonconformist, his movies were conventional; in this new one, you can smell death, not because of its subject matter but in its manner and style. These *Barbarian Invasions* miss their target just as they get lost in a dialectic which, beneath the surface of the professed cynicism, is completely reactionary in nature." Jean Larose, true to his own analytical logic, hates *The Barbarian Invasions* as much as he did *The Decline*, which he condemned so energetically in the not-so-distant past. "A film about death that doesn't take death seriously," he tells *Le Devoir*, a film full of sentimentality, "a curious combination of nihilism and sentimentalism," revealing a "kind of commitment to reducing the spectator to despair" using the style of the téléroman and melodrama, moving away from tragedy. Jean Larose remarks that the funerals of great Quebecers Maurice Richard, Riopelle and Dédé Fortin were grotesque, just like the death of Rémy in *The Barbarian Invasions*: "Because all ritual has been abolished, we seem to be unable to derive any symbolic national legacy from these deaths." Josée Legault's opinion piece in *Le Devoir* underlines "the difficulty the characters of the *Invasions* seem to have in identifying with Quebec." She denounces these baby boomers who consider the dream of an independent Quebec as youthful folly, who include sovereignism in their list of old "isms," such as Maoism or Marxist-Leninism; she is bitter that the film represents Yves Jacques' character as sponging off a good and generous Canada, or Rémy's son "living comfortably abroad" and looking down on Quebec as a "province of hicks." For Josée Legault, the last Arcand is "*Comfort and Indifference,* take two," recalling the words of Pierre Bourgault who died June 16, 2003: "My personal comfort versus sovereignty."

On the cover of its summer 2003 issue *Ciné-bulles* magazine unexpectedly features a photo from the successful comedy *La grande seduction* (*Seducing Doctor Lewis*) and then devotes three articles, mostly negative, to *The Barbarian Invasions.* Éric Perron's editorial, "Le cinéma québécois va-t-il vraiment bien?" ("Is Quebec Cinema Really Doing Well?"), denounces Hollywood-style marketing and policies based on box-office performance. In lumping together films such as *Séraphin, The Barbarian Invasions* and *Mambo italiano,* the chief editor wonders if this trend might not end up "sacrificing cinema on the altar of profitability," while recognizing that Arcand "is still getting by in spite of the system."

André Lavoie's article revisits *The Decline,* taking an antiboomer stance and decribing *The Decline* as "not an intellectual film but a film on Quebec intellectuals who are so 'open' to the world that they've lost the map." The article expresses regret that Arcand has undertaken to "repudiate the past and shelve the political dimension," falling into a kind of yuppie populism with the kind of ingredients "that have made local crowds come running since 1969, when Denis Héroux decided to undress the little Québécoise in *Valérie.*" The critic especially objects to the fact that young people, "silent and slightly stunned before the cynicism and bitterness of their elders," have been portrayed by a filmmaker who is incapable of really grasping who they are. As for Jean-Philippe Gravel ("Denys Arcand, d'un *Déclin* à l'autre" ["Denys Arcand, from One *Decline* to Another"]) also denounced the American-style ("*à la barbare*") film launch, leading to the manufacturing of consent in favour of *The Barbarian Invasions.* The author misses the days of Arcand's politically committed documentaries, pointing his finger at the "Europhilic culture" of the hip intellectuals, the film's woolly ideology, the filmmaker's lack of a point of view, his depiction of youth as conservative rather than champions of a dynamic antiglobalism and enlightened anarchy. A case in point is Rémy's contempt for his son Sébastien, prince of the Barbarians.

The misunderstanding has lasted since *Le confort et l'indifférence*, when Arcand abandoned his fervour for an "independent, socialist and secular" Quebec, to use the terms of *Parti pris*. He has not been forgiven for giving up his dreams, and is reproached for having changed, for having become an "other." Trade unionist Gérald Larose, on Radio-Canada, emphasizes that in the past, the filmmaker defended textile and hospital workers: "He was Left then, now he's in bed with the Right." Yet in spite of the transformations in his career, there have never been *two* Arcands, just one, who might have taken for a credo this powerful reflection delivered by Roland Barthes at the Collège de France: "Better the deceptions of subjectivity than the impostures of objectivity. Better the subject's Image-repertoire than its censorship."

Arcand has been consistent throughout his career and in all his filmography. He has evolved, to refer to the interesting expression of Pierre L'Hérault, from a more visible and exteriorized form of distancing to an "interiorized form of distancing." After his bigger portraits— economical, political, social—Arcand chose to examine his life and the lives of those around him, artists and intellectuals, biological and artistic families, lovers and friends. The terrain to be explored has changed but not the political and philosophical vision of Quebec and Quebecers. Already in 1972, he affirmed loud and clear that he considered the documentary as being "something other than a combat weapon," a tragic and personal view of the world of labour, society and politics. In 1973, he repeated to Robert Lévesque: "My cinema is not mobilizing, it is despairing." He has always clearly stated, without nostalgia, that he suffered from the loss of religion, the coherence of the family, even the loss of his NFB "family." For him, creativity springs from "a pathological lack of love; the only reason for which one does this profession is to be loved." In the book *Auteur/provocateur*, he insists: "I make films for myself and my friends. When I work on a screenplay I do not think about the broad symbolic interpretations of the film. I deal only with 'micro-problems.'"

What has been apparent since *Gina* is the greater role of sexuality in his films. It has moved to the foreground, whereas in his first three fictions it hovered in the background, though was evoked in a somewhat caustic manner. Arcand has long been interested in the subject. In the January 19, 1961, issue of *Le quartier latin*, he defended *Lady Chatterley's Lover*. One of his most suprising essays, published several years later in *Parti pris* is called "Cinema and Sexuality." The question becomes omnipresent starting with *Nesbitt's Trip*. Arcand pursues it in the unproduced script *La fin du voyage*, which precedes and anticipates *The Decline*, then in the script on death, and in *Love and Human Remains*, *Stardom* and *The Barbarian Invasions*. Two other unproduced scripts, *En mai nos amours* and *C'est la vie*, contain an autobiographical dimension as far as the subject of sexuality is concerned. The mother's attitude towards sex is very rigid; for her, nudity is ugly; she fears that her teenage son has seen naked lovers in Alain Resnais's *Hiroshima mon amour*. Later, Colette Bouillé will hate *The Decline* for its treatment of sexuality. However, sighs Arcand, "You don't make films for your mother." Going even further back are Arcand's memories of erotic revelation in religious films seen in childhood.

Moreover, the writer-director defends the idea that the writer or filmmaker must address all aspects of love and sexuality. The filmmaker reveals all points of view and all aspects of passion: that of men and women, of young people and the elderly, homosexuals and heteros. He is a kind of demiurge of androgyny, a Flaubert who proclaims: "*Madame Bovary, c'est moi!*" The filmmaker constantly repeats that his characters reflect different aspects of himself, different parts of his contradictory personality and his inexhaustible search for deeper understanding.

At the Toronto Festival, Denys Arcand is celebrated in a number of film publications. The magazine published by Cinémathèque Ontario, a division of the Toronto International Film Festival Group, announces a more or less complete retrospective of Arcand's works for its autumn 2003 programming and includes a judicious article by Bart Testa, "Before *The Barbarians*, the Films of Denys Arcand." The critic refers to a "small body of key films" that comprise the filmmaker's oeuvre, which constitute "an incomparable project in North American cinema." Denys Arcand, Testa maintains, "was the first, and today remains one of the only, completely postcolonial Canadian feature filmmakers. Only an artist as self-aware, paradox-loving and deeply pessimistic as Arcand could recognize how extraordinary and ironic that accomplishment is, given the ideological and material history of Canada and Québec." *Cinemascope* magazine describes the ritual-assisted suicide as "an occasion staged with maudlin solemnity and maximum autumn chill, an elegy not so much for a dying playboy, a lost dream of nationhood or even a brokered generation's ideals, but for the end of laughter." Matthew Hays's article in *Montage*, "Close-up on Denys Arcand," begins with this brief portrait, accompanied by an illustration by Jacquin Oakley: "His handsome face is often lit by a welcoming smile that bespeaks a Gallic charm. Though his demeanour seems easy, Denys Arcand is an intense man who can often be seen gesticulating with his hands." *Take One* maintains, "*The Barbarian Invasions* is his best film in years, proving once again that as an astute observer of the human condition, Arcand has few peers." Critic Rick Groen for *The Globe and Mail* feels the opening film for the Toronto Festival manages to avoid the usual banality of sequels.

On the evening of the opening gala, Arcand strides down the red carpet of Roy Thomson Hall and faces the wall of media as if playing a scene from *Stardom*. He casually extracts a little disposable camera from the pocket of his tuxedo and starts photographing the photographers and cameramen. "It's for the Sundance Cable channel," he explains with his Buñuelian smile. The *Globe and Mail* calls him the doyen of Quebec filmmakers, and the Ontario media says he is the most famous Canadian film director ever. Arcand is a good sport. After all, it is the second time, along with *The Decline,* that he has opened this festival, as well as being honoured at two other gala evenings (for *Jesus of Montreal* and *Stardom*). His presentation of *The Barbarian Invasions* recalls that of *The Decline* in 1986—the text is published for the first time in the "Selected Readings." The director declares: "How to motivate actors during a shoot? By telling them we have to make the Toronto Festival, preferably opening night at Roy Thomson Hall. If that evening's audience likes the film, it's bound to be a success in the theatres."

Next to speak is Denise Robert, who has become Canada's #1 producer. Only days before, on September 2, she received the Montreal World Film Festival's Great Prize of the Americas in a sad and empty little theatre at the Parisien movie complex. This evening, in Toronto, dressed by Chanel, she glows in the thousand lights of the road to Hollywood. She announces that the *Invasions* will soon be opening in France on four hundred screens, the equivalent of a film of *Harry Potter* calibre. In the same breath she adds that in the Miramax test screenings for the film's U.S. release the following December, the film scored high in the satisfaction ratings and that several American film industrials are already dreaming about the Oscars.

The first speech on opening night is delivered by Piers Handling— luckily, it might be said, for the posterity of Quebec cinema. The bright and lucid Toronto festival director, emphasizing that Denys Arcand is a friend, introduces the author of *The Barbarian Invasions* as an outstanding "Québécois" filmmaker, responsible for creating the most extraordinary films the country has produced. He admits to having been perplexed and apprehensive upon hearing Arcand was making a "sequel" to *Le Déclin*. Today he says he is pleasantly relieved: the characters of the *Invasions* clearly portray the current social context of Quebec, representing its past, present and even its future. Handling's comments are particularly relevant in light of the fact that the English-Canadian media, starting with the CBC, persist in presenting Arcand as a great "Canadian" filmmaker and Marie-Josée Croze, named Best Actress at Cannes, as one of the top "Canadian" actors. As Daniel Louis explains, these stipulations must be viewed in the context of Telefilm Canada's new policy of box-office performance-based funding. Canada and Quebec are merged in the federal organism's accounting, though most box office receipts are from Quebec-made films (*Séraphin*, *The Barbarian Invasions*, *Mambo italiano*, *La grande séduction*), whereas English-Canadian films continue to trail behind in the theatres. Given the context, it is ironic to see Arcand become once again, and reluctantly, the epitome of Canadian film, when thirty years earlier he had fought against the Etrog Canadian Awards and their will to merge Quebec film into the great Canadian whole.

Meanwhile, independent filmmakers from the journal *P.O.V. Point of View* express opposition to the federal policies of assistance to film and video. The government agencies are not only reproached for making significant cuts in grants to television productions, but especially in taking neoliberal views on the issue of support and reinforcement of the production-distribution industry and its increased competitive capacity on the international market. Policies like these lead directly to the negation of Canadian cultural content, for example, when Telefilm Canada chooses to encourage producers and distributors with strong box-office track records.

Paradoxically, English Canadians, before their own wailing wall, praise the "Quebec model" for films that in the past few years have managed to move away from demagogy and show equal favour to *films d'auteur* and commercial comedies or television series. This model, so highly praised by the voices from Toronto, is exactly what producer Denise Robert has managed to put into practice. She manages to score just as high at the box office with a comedy such as *Mambo italiano* as with a *film d'auteur* such as *The Barbarian Invasions*. With this model in mind, English Canadians continue to search for parameters that will help them strengthen the Canadian content of their film and television productions while increasing revenues.

A certain Canadian-American sensibility emerged during the press conference with the filmmaker. The media wanted to know more about his views on *The Decline of the American Empire*, about the attacks from certain "barbarians" and his opinions on euthanasia. Arcand repeats that he is in favour of elective death, but that during his lifetime, he is unlikely to see it legalized in Canada as it is in "some other civilized countries." He also expresses his belief that wars and conflicts will not subside, that one will break out in every decade of the century. In short, as he declared to Peter Howell, in Cannes, for *Take One*: "The first [attack] that succeeded, 9/11, struck at the empire's heart. It's the first of many more to come. I feel more and more out of sync with today's reality. The constant acceleration of life and the media roar are repulsive to me. I believe that countries are a vanishing species." A good reason to retire? "You never know. Buñuel did his best films when he was seventy."

In Paris, on December 8, 2003, Arcand is awarded the Prix Henri-Jeanson in recognition of his film career as a whole. This indicates the esteem in which Arcand is held in the French film world, in spite of several harsh critics. The award was presented to "an author whose insolence, humour, and dramatic power perpetuate the memory of one of French cinema's most famous screenwriters and 'dialoguists.'" Previous recipients of the award, since 1997, include Robert Guédiguian and

Jean-Louis Milési, Agnès Jaoui and Jean-Pierre Bacri, Dominik Moll and Gilles Marchand, Bertrand Blier and Michel Blanc. Arcand tells Jean-Pierre Tadros, of *Ciné-TV multimedia*: "When I went to see *Fanfan la Tulipe*, in 1952, at the Cinéma Champlain on rue Sainte-Catherine Est, I could not possibly have imagined that fifty years later I would receive the Prix Henri-Jeanson, named after the dialogue writer for this film." The next day, at the SACD (Société des auteurs and compositeurs dramatiques), escorted by Jean-Charles Tacchella, Arcand meets a hundred young film professionals who address him as a great international filmmaker, a master they venerate for his technical and artistic qualities. Questions and exchanges relate to his screenwriting method, his choices of mises-en-scene, not to mention certain elements of his film's subject. For example, one filmmaker says she is struck and moved by the scene between Nathalie and Rémy at the hospital, in which the boomer is shaken by the young woman's advice to forget the past and learn to look death in the face. Arcand explains that he cannot take credit for this dialogue but borrowed it almost word for word from the ancient Seneca in his "Letter to Lucilius." Moreover, it is a quote the filmmaker has had for a long time in his screenwriting notes. In *The Barbarian Invasions*, Arcand appropriates it and puts it in the mouth of the angel of death.

Arcand is very proud of having received the Prix Henri-Jeanson, awarded by his peers through a company founded by Beaumarchais to defend his royalties for the *Barber of Seville*. He is also pleased that young filmmakers see him as a film director, period, rather than a "Québécois film director": "As far as the directors I like are concerned, I don't consider them to be national artists. A filmic œuvre does not have to be emblematical. The connotation of 'Québécois film director' or 'Canadian film director' has always really gotten on my nerves. In Toronto, these connotations are connected to issues of English-Canadian nationalism, which has trouble asserting itself and evolving."

By early 2004, Arcand can already make a first assessment of his film's reception the previous year. He says he is very touched that in France, his film has become one of the most popular films made in French, that it has drawn more than 1.5 million spectators in that country since opening on over four hundred screens, surpassing even the success of *The Decline*, and receiving four nominations at the Césars: "My film was warmly received. I have received a lot of letters from the French, thanking me and saying they were moved. I even received one from the mayor of Paris, another from President Chirac."

In Brazil, *The Barbarian Invasions* is a great success, shown in parallel with a new release of *The Decline*. The same goes for Italy. The film is given a warm but more modest welcome in Germany and Spain: "I did most of the big American cities, but also places I didn't know, art cinemas in Atlanta, Georgia or Dallas, Texas. Most of the spectators knew four or five of my films. I was amazed and touched by this; I didn't know it existed outside of New York and Los Angeles. In Philadelphia, the house got to its feet to tell me they hadn't voted for Bush, contrary to what was said in one of the film's dialogues: 'Change your script, we're Democrats!' All very pleasant." On the other hand, in English Canada the film bombed—"The English Canadians are hopeless!" About this last fact, Denise Robert specifies: "*The Barbarian Invasions* earned $1 million in box-office receipts in English Canada."

If we were to retain a single metaphorical image from *The Barbarian Invasions,* it could be that of the protection and conservation of a very precious object. An icon with two facets: the preservation of books, the protection of a child.

Books occupy an important place in the life and career of Denys Arcand. Let us recall the numerous readings he usually does in preparation for his films, whether documentary or drama. He finds a way of making fun of this type of research in the 1992 edition of *Projection: A Forum for Film Makers*. Before shooting, he essentially says, he does a mountain of research that lasts for months, sometimes years. Research includes skiing in the Alps, the Rockies, the Andes, even sometimes deep-sea diving in the Dead Sea, or off the coast of Belize or the Philippines. Sometimes he also needs a pass to Wimbledon, or a box at the opera in Salzburg. He always arranges to be accompanied by a Thai masseuse, an Italian mezzo-soprano or a group of statuesque beauties. "A private airplane would probably be required, and a yacht would be nice also. At this moment, I cannot reveal the exact nature of the research itself, but since the film is not going to be distributed and the budget is unlimited, why are you worrying?"

During a press conference April 15, 2003, in Montreal, the filmmaker quotes Olivier Rolin's novel *Tigre en papier* as being one of the good books that have been written about "our red years." In his interviews with Michel Coulombe, Arcand takes pains to explain the solitary phase of writing, a period of reading, research, investigation and inquiry, providing him with a healthy change from the times he practises his art in public during the production and promotion phases. We may also recall his anecdote about the Flower Power of the sixties and seventies, when many artists retreated to the country. To appear more earthy and not too intellectual, these people spent an incredible amount of time renovating and restoring. "They'd have been better off reading more!" For Rémy, the intellectual who has spent his life in books, nothing that could be more "barbaric" than the fact that his son Sébastien has never read a book in his life. This remark of Rémy's makes us think of another, one of the harshest pieces of dialogue in the script for *15 Moments*, unfortunately cut from the final version, when Tina says: "Don't hate me because I'm beautiful. . . . Hate me because I've never read a book in my life."

For Arcand, one of the traits of our barbarian civilization is that given the confused state of our systems of education, the seventeenth century cannot be taught, even in schools in France. Students no longer understand or are concretely able to read Racine, Bossuet, Pascal; they no longer understand the words. When one of his friends, a teacher of French literature, explains that Madame de Montespan had ascendancy over the king, students understand that she lived upstairs from the king. There's no point in even mentioning Greco-Roman literature. "Young screenwriters have a terrible time understanding what's being discussed in the *Poetics* of Aristotle. We're heading for a new Dark Ages. All we can do under the circumstances is to protect manuscripts, because for centuries we will no longer be able to read them. That's what happens at the end of *The Barbarian Invasions*: Rémy's apartment is covered wall-to-wall with books. Nathalie becomes their keeper, like a monk in the Middle Ages. She will be able to transmit them to someone else. I hope that humanity will manage to perform this work of conservation, for CDs, Mozart, or Ezio Pinza singing 'Le cor,' which will be discovered later, during a new Renaissance age."

André Brochu remembers Arcand at university: "He was an incredible reader, as I discovered when we shared an apartment in

1962–1963. He read more quickly, and retained what he read better than I did. His ability to synthesize information was remarkable. Instead of getting lost in shades of meaning, he went straight to the main argument and stuck with it. That allowed him to discuss what he'd read with firmness and clarity. His liking for clear ideas led him to express positions that could seem simplistic but were hard to argue with, as if he positioned himself outside of the usual rhetoric and spelled things out: the unavoidable truth, the obvious, in the best sense of the word." Arcand is intractable and insatiable when it comes to books. When, for example, he talks with Mathias Brunet about the question of money and material comfort, he names as his first concern: "an armchair and books."

At the design pavilion at UQAM, in May 2003, to accompany the release of *The Barbarian Invasions*, the department organized a little exhibition of mock-ups for the film's poster. Not surprisingly, some of these show the scene in which Rémy is holding the book *Les malheurs des temps* ("The Misfortunes of Time"). Arcand explains that he kept this book, the choice of art director Patrice Bengle, because it is so well suited to the character of Rémy. Elsewhere, Rémy confides to Nathalie that he also regrets not having written a book like Primo Levi's *The Periodic Table*. At the end of the film, when Nathalie visits Rémy's apartment, the first thing she does is look through the deceased professor's library. Let us recall the four close-ups: *The Gulag Archipelago, If This Is a Man*, Cioran's *History and Utopia*, and finally *The Diary of Samuel Pepys*. Books suited to the character of the historian Rémy: "Solzhenitsyn and Levi, because they are essential works on the great massacres of the twentieth century, written by witnesses, survivors. The Pepys is an amazing book, a ten-year diary of life in seventeenth-century London. The Cioran, because I like his twisted mind, similar to Ionesco's, and that strange Balkan world, a book that points out, for instance, that bronze statues are made of despots and bloodthirsty men, never good and generous men."

These books, shown from very close up, were shot at Arcand's home; they belong to his personal library. Martin Lebel, assistant cameraman for the second team, shot these images under the direction of Nathalie Moliavko Visotzky. This crew also did the nature shots of Lake Memphremagog. Lebel often says that in his eyes, Arcand is one of the great Quebec directors and intellectuals; after shooting in the director's library, he went to buy himself a copy of Primo Levi's *If This Is a Man*.

This anecdote from the shoot gave me the idea of asking the filmmaker if I could visit his library. He willingly agreed. The visit helped me to better understand the essence of what the Arcand wishes to protect and pass on. What follows is a guided tour, in the company of the director.

Here is my library. It's very small. I buy a lot of books each year. But I'm not a keeper; I only keep the books I'll go back to one day. My criterion is: will I reread this book, or will I need to refer to it for my work? I keep the ones I want to consult. The others I give away to café-libraries and to whoever wants them. It's a big problem giving books away. Public libraries and hospitals don't want them anymore; they haven't got the staff to take care of them. But I'm incapable of throwing a book in the garbage. It's a kind of sacrilege.

So I try taking them to whoever wants them.

First section—is this significant or not?—history. *L'histoire universelle* in the La Pléiade edition. *The History of the United States*, *The History of Private Life*. Obviously, Gibbon's classic *The History of the Decline and Fall of the Roman Empire*. Or *Fatal Shore*, the history of Australia, by Robert Hughes, an absolutely fantastic book. And then *Histoires du Canada*, *L'histoire du Québec* by Linteau, Durocher, Robert and Ricard. It continues with classics of history: Tacitus, Suetonius, *Lives of the Twelve Caesars*, and then, out of order, *Inside the Third Reich*, by Albert Speer, Hitler's architect. Reference books, which I may need at any time.

Below that, the second section, theatre. Fairly classical: Molière, Racine, Corneille, the complete works of Chekhov, Goethe (*Faust*, the second *Faust*), all of Ibsen, all of Shakespeare in different versions, in the original and in French translation, the American David Mamet, Strindberg, the authors of the English Restoration: Congreve, Farquhar, somewhat esoteric playwrights.

Section three, books on film. *Memoirs* by Michael Powell, absolutely delicious. *Laterna magica* and *Images* by Ingmar

Bergman, of course. Luis Buñuel, *My Last Sigh*, his memoirs. The big biography of Howard Hawks, the correspondence of François Truffaut, the classic *The Cinema According to Hitchcock*, a must. Published editions of my own scripts. Tarkovski's *Journal*, sublime, very, very beautiful. And books on the American studios, stories about film shoots, like *The Devil's Candy*. Also *The Devil Made It*, Peter Bogdanovich's book on American directors. And then a pretty good book by Satyajit Ray, the Indian director, *Our Films, Their Films*, an essay on film.

After that, the essays. All kinds of essays, from John Kenneth Galbraith, *The New Industrial State*, to Herman Hesse. Sometimes a little esoteric, like *The Queen's Throat*, about the love of divas among homosexuals. The author wrote about Callas in particular, we share that love. The biography of Hemingway. What else? *The Empire of Fashion* by Gilles Lipovetsky. Philippe Muray's *La fin de l'histoire*, *The Lyric Generation* by François Ricard about the baby-boomers, *Language and Silence* by George Steiner, also quite beautiful. *The Coming Dark Age*—it's one of my favourite themes—by an Italian engineer, Roberto Vacca. And then some random things. Criminal stuff also, for example, the story of Paul Bernardo and Karla Homolka, the Ontario murderers. *The Right Stuff*, by Tom Wolfe, his essay on the astronauts, a classic . . .

Fifth section, philosophy. I'm not very well versed in philosophy, but I've got a few classics, Aristotle's *Poetics*, Albert Camus, all of Cioran, Machiavelli's *The Prince*; Herbert Marcuse's *One Dimensional Man*; Ludwig Wittgenstein; Jean-Marc Piotte, *Great Thinkers of the Western World*, a nice summary, a good reference book. Plato, most of his *Dialogues*.

The sixth section is fiction. Lots of novels. All the short stories of Raymond Carver, who I like a lot. Bowles's *Distant Episode*, Albert Cohen's *Belle du Seigneur*. Dostoevsky, of course. More modern novels like *The Name of the Rose*. Franz Kafka. Nothing very original. Detective novels, the spy novels of John Le Carré. *The Man Without Qualities* by Robert Musil; George Orwell, *1984*. Classics. Edgar Allan Poe, all of Proust, of course. Our common friend, W.G. Sebald. Voltaire, the novels and stories. Quebec writers like Mordecai Richler, *Barney's Version*. Tom Wolfe, *The Bonfire of the Vanities*.

Below that, section seven, memoirs. I've got a lot of books of memoirs, I find them fascinating. Pablo Neruda. Simone de Beauvoir's *Letters to Nelson Algren*, very beautiful. The correspondence of Mozart; V.S. Naipaul, his voyage through the Muslim countries, very interesting, from the Middle East to the Far East. Samuel Pepys; the *Memoirs* of the Duc de Saint-Simon, obviously. Solzhenitsyn, Andy Warhol's *Memoirs* (fascinating, that one), the journal of Stefan Zweig.

After that, in section eight, I've got religious stuff. Missals and prayer books, I like them a lot. Sometimes I use them for reference in my films. I find them quite interesting.

A very small poetry section, the ninth, in which we find Saint-John Perse, Dante, Baudelaire, of course. And look at that! I don't know what it's doing with the poetry, but I also have the complete collection of *La bonne chanson* by Abbé Gadbois, in which he gathered all the folkloric songs of Quebec. And here's a prop I kept, the Michel Brunet book from *Le déclin*, with a false cover.

In section ten, a very small collection on sports, books I find fascinating, written by American football players or other books on sports, skiing, et cetera.

I have a separate section for books I haven't read yet, ones to read next summer: Victor Hugo, *Things Seen*, Greek tragedies I absolutely want to reread. The biography of Gabrielle Roy, the short stories of Chekhov, the complete works of Montaigne, which I reread in fragments. There you have my provision of books for the summer of 2003.

Certain books have been accumulating for a very long time, they're there for good. The missals, for example, I didn't exactly buy them last week. I've also got a very big *Webster's*. I use it because I read in English a lot and occasionally write in the language. A cabinetmaker friend made me a little stand to put it on, because it's huge. Next to my worktable, my dictionaries, including a quotations dictionary, very practical. Et cetera. On the same shelf, books and documents for the film I'm doing, which I need while I'm writing the script. That's the work-in-progress section. Some of these books, I won't keep, I'll give them away.

That's it. We've visited my entire library.

Denys Arcand's attachment to books shows itself in another way. Sometimes while putting together his research, he limits his readings to a few specific works. While we were preparing *Copie zéro* dossier in 1987, he read with enthusiasm Simone de Beauvoir's essay, *Must We Burn Sade?* While preparing the present biography, we discuss W.G. Sebald—all his works, *The Rings of Saturn, The Emigrants, Vertigo, Austerlitz, On the Natural History of Destruction.* When he explains his attachment to two books by Primo Levi, we have a better understanding of why he included the first suicide in his unpublished script on death. For it recalls the death of the Italian writer, who threw himself from the top of the staircase in his apartment house in Turin. "Turin, a cursed city, haunted by ghosts, where Primo Levi and Cesare Pavese took their lives."

The protection and conservation of precious books is a major obsession throughout *The Barbarian Invasions.* And the idea does not stop there: films, too, must be conserved, as well as musical recordings and radio archives, for as long as possible before the final disintegration, when the Sun incinerates it all.

This protective enveloping of the books of civilization is coupled with an even more important and all-encompassing gesture, the love of children. If Rémy manages to convince his son Sébastien to appoint Nathalie heir to his entire library, it is because the history professor deeply loved his child, protected him from death. This act of rescue can be summed up in a single image: that of the child in his father's arms. In *The Barbarian Invasions*, a major reversal occurs in the drama when Louise tells her son Sébastien: "When you had meningitis when you were three, your father held you; he rocked you in his arms for forty-eight hours without ever letting you go, without even sleeping, so death couldn't get you." It is this memory, this luminescent image that will convince Sébastien to take care of his father's death and *in extremis* tell him that he loves him.

In the preface for the published version of his screenplay, Arcand writes: "We make films to dream an ideal death, to erase reality. I never told my grandfather or my mother, and certainly not my father, how much I loved them. I should have." The initial script for *The Barbarian Invasions* was called "Father and Son." Today Denys Arcand confides: "I really loved my father. I adored him. He was a wonderful man, gentle, strong, kind, very present, though not extraordinarily affectionate physically. I remember the few times he took me in his arms or that I was in his arms as a child—he was sturdily built, with very strong arms—as being the moments I've felt safest in my entire life. Safe in my father's arms. Since he's been gone, I miss this sense of safety and I try to give it to my daughter by holding her in my arms and telling her that there, no one can do her any harm."

"My father is stronger than the police," children used to say. Stronger than the police, stronger than death.

15
LYRIC SPACES

une 25, 2003. Denys Arcand celebrates his sixty-second birthday, already glowing from the great success of *The Barbarian Invasions*. At the same time, he can celebrate a film career of almost forty-two years. What road will unfold before him, as in the final image from Chaplin's *Modern Times*?

In his most recent film, he picked up where he left off in his portrait of Quebec today, this time depicting with lyrical brushstrokes the twilight of the Quiet Revolution. He could always continue in this vein. Whatever the case, he has successfully renewed his filmmaking passport and will not have to go back to working in television. This is not something that happens every day in a film industry as small as Quebec's.

Does he still dream of making a film about his father and his childhood in Deschambault? Or has he set his sights on that long cherished utopia, the dream of doing theatre or directing an opera? For the filmmaker, the theme of the new millennium may be opera; or he may alternate between film and opera, as many directors do in Europe, and as François Girard does in this country.

As we come to the end of this professional biography, in the months following the launching of a dazzling film, it may be of interest to follow Arcand into a few spaces that define the scope of his most recent work and also provide us with a few "leads" as to what his next project might be. Not surprisingly, for Arcand these zones of exploration are musical spaces.

Whether he is resting his melancholy gaze on half a century of Quiet Revolution in Quebec, the love/hate reviews of his work, the numerous awards and tributes he has received or his trip to Russia where he meets the ghosts of Tolstoy and the gulag, the same recurrent themes resurface, the same music we have heard throughout his films. After visiting these spaces with him, we may not be too surprised to see Denys Arcand emerge once again upon the shores of a mysterious and subtle hybrid of opera and film.

Quebec Space

"I have a love-hate relationship with Quebec," Arcand confides in a 1993 interview with Michel Coulombe. Indeed, though since the early seventies he has considered the Quiet Revolution an epiphenomenon, he nonetheless made it his project to do "a big portrait of Quebec today" with a series of documentary and fiction films. The two attitudes are not necessarily incompatible, but definitely indicate a state of tension between "realism and observation" on the one hand, and on the other hand, the dream of a country. This is not a cynical view, as some have said, a remark that even the filmmaker himself finds hurtful, but the view of a director who sees himself as a "despairing ethnologist."

He acquired this way of viewing Quebec in the early sixties through the teachings of historian Maurice Séguin. In the *Copie zéro* file, in the late 1980s, Arcand clearly summarizes this theory and methodology for the analysis of Quebec history. "Séguin affirms, in the main, that the Québécois were too numerous and well organized within a border to fear immediate disappearance, but at the same time, neither powerful, rich nor organized enough to achieve independence and form their own country. So we were condemned to a kind of eternal mediocrity, wavering between disappearance and self-assertion, neither here nor there. I see nothing happening today that would allow me to contradict this view, and I find it very disturbing." Quebec as it was after the Conquest is one of the keys to understanding Quebec today. Arcand was also influenced by Marcuse, an author whose dark vision of social and political life he abundantly quotes in *On est au coton*. "I'm not a doomsday prophet saying the end is near," he tells *Cineaste*, in 1986, "but there's an element of that."

Though a member of the "lyric generation" described by François

Ricard, one cannot say Denys Arcand belongs to the cohort of "joyful mysteries," to borrow the name of a form of rosary recitation practised in Quebec Catholic ritual. He is more of the "sorrowful mystery" cohort, and according to Jacques Brault's description, one of the tormented members of his generation. Fortunately, Arcand's ineradicable pessimism ("I'm an eternal pessimist," he tells *La Presse* in 1994, "I've always felt guilty or in the wrong") is counterbalanced by his determination "not to take himself too seriously." Still, Jacques Brault notes the persistent fantasy of suicide that he shares with other young people of the same generation.

Death has haunted the filmmaker since childhood. He lost a number of his friends to suicide. "I've always wanted to deal with this subject in my films. I managed to do so in *The Barbarian Invasions*, along with the idea of euthanasia as a solution, an idea that must be fought for, in the face of social inertia, the minister of justice, lawyers, and everyone who believes their life belongs to God, the king, the government. As with abortion or the death penalty, with this issue it will take centuries of struggle to change anything. I'm sorry, but my life does not belong to Prime Minister Jean Chrétien!"

Arcand has managed to avoid the dizzying allure of suicide's black hole by working incessantly. Bohemian in appearence, and seeming on the surface to be somewhat *farniente*, he is actually a glutton for work, a taskmaster when it comes to himself, a kind of workaholic. Filmmaking has kept him alive by giving him a trade with which to earn his living, but has also saved his life. His political consciousness, informed by the tragic theories of Séguin, drives him to question himself and the people around him, to take stock of personal experiences that are deeply rooted in Quebec. The filmmaker has always remained moored to Quebec, both to its reality and the myth it represents. In *This Magazine*, in 1974, when he is asked whether he is interested in subjects such as the struggle of the Palestinians, Arcand replies that he does not have a close enough knowledge of the phenomenon and that he prefers to stick with subjects he knows intimately. Yet Arcand, while Québécois, is a kind of foreigner in his own country. In *Ciné-bulles*, in 1986, he comments that he has never felt integrated either in Quebec or Canadian cinema. His "sorrowful mystery," illuminated by multiple readings on western civilisation, bears the imprint of numerous personal wounds.

He returns to the idea of loss as a kind of leitmotif: loss of religion, the family, *collège classique*, the founders at the NFB of the first Quebec cinema, the masterpieces of international film.

In October 1993, in an unpublished letter, Arcand clearly expresses his views on Quebec society and explains what he means by its "lack of real scope." His view is "merely the observation that there are societies too small demographically, too poor economically and too weak politically to achieve the critical mass (as the physicists say) that is necessary for growth. That has nothing to do with the individual possibilities of a particular artist." The filmmaker goes on to name a few examples. Georges de La Tour and Cézanne were French, Vermeer and Van Gogh Flemish. Their talents were eventually recognized, albeit belatedly. But try to name an Albanian, Roumanian, Finnish or Serbo-Croatian artist living at the same period.

There were no doubt remarkable individual talents in those countries, but history has forgotten them forever and probably with reason, for their respective societies never allowed them to fully develop. "For me, art is indissociably linked to economics and politics. There are probably a lot of children born with remarkable gifts for music all over the world, but only the Austro-Hungarian Empire could have nurtured the talent of Mozart, Haydn and their successors. When I went to the Cannes festival with my first film, *La maudite galette*, I stayed in the same hotel as a rookie American filmmaker called Martin Scorsese. I honestly thought our first films were on a par with each other. Since then, the director of *Mean Streets*, borne along by American wealth and dynamism, has been able to realize his full potential. I have only been able to develop a fifth of mine. He was born in New York, I in Deschambault. It's not his fault nor mine. That's just how it is. That's all."

After *Le confort et l'indifférence*, Arcand does not abandon his sociopolitical awareness but rather, ceases to focus his films on the world of politics. In *Le Soleil*, in 1982, he says of *Le confort*'s cruel and desperate tone, "It is my tone in life." Never will he make epic cinema, for his filmmaking style is that of an essayist and not a novelist. Moreover, he incessantly tries to "deflate the tendency to romanticize," and sees himself as a kind of bum, a punk, a teenage iconoclast. But in fact, there has only ever been one Arcand. He has applied the idea developed by Pierre L'Hérault: to remain clear-sighted before his subjects does not only mean viewing things from an exterior, scientific perspective but also knowing how to use a more inward form of distancing. And constructing his films' narratives as a kind of "spasmodic storytelling, moving back and forth between fiction and reflection, between the inability to forget the original wound and the impossibility of giving it a definitive meaning." In the work of Arcand, the ethnographer's gaze cohabits with the expression of the shadow zones of the characters and the world. After *Le confort*, the specific and limited sphere of politics no longer interests him, but that does not mean his sociopolitical consciousness has disappeared. In *24 images*, in 1989, he clearly explains that he is not on the side of *Salt of the Earth*, but of Buñuel the iconoclast and anarchist.

What does he think of the half-century that has passed since the beginning of the Quiet Revolution in Quebec? "We had a long way to go and we haven't made much progress. These days, when *Séraphin* is the most popular film in the history of Quebec cinema, and producers and distributors still favour projects such as *Le survenant* and *Aurore, l'enfant martyre*, how are you supposed to talk about "modern Quebec" and "progress"? After Duplessis and the Church, Quebec woke up to a world without structure; young people were thrown into a state of confusion from which they haven't yet recovered."

For Arcand, film helped make up for this loss, filled the void left by the old religious structure that no longer existed. We are still too close to the events of this revolution; historians have not had time to examine it from every angle, they are unable to take an exact measure of its impact, it is too early to learn anything from it. Of course, the filmmaker was concerned with the question of Quebec independence, up until *Le Confort et l'indifférence*. "After that, I didn't say the struggle had ended or the project was no longer valid. It was a personal decision to no longer deal with the subject and move on to something else. Alain Resnais's film *La guerre est finie*, written by Jorge Semprun, left a strong impression on me. He said that for the old Spanish Communist revolutionaries, the war was over, that Franco had won and they had to wait for him to die. The new Spain, yet to be born, would have nothing to do with the Spain of civil war. I've always been afraid of fighting losing battles, of becoming bitter and living a painful existence, telling the same old stories over and over again."

The leading lights of the Quiet Revolution, the filmmaker explains again, defined themselves as the accoucheurs of the new Quebec, and brushed Duplessism aside as a period of great darkness. Yet everything that happened during the Quiet Revolution had been in the works for a long time, for example in the *Refus global* manifesto of 1948, a thoroughly modern document. There were no cataclysmic events in the sixties that radically changed everything. We remained Québécois, with the same old mentalities and the same atavism. It so happened that people saw salvation in the State apparatus, saw it as a way of gaining access to big capital and industry. The Quebec State had to be built. Hydro-Québec, the Caisse de dépôt et de placement. Jacques Parizeau, Bernard Landry, and others constructed this apparatus as a collective last hope. A strong and directive State was built, which tried to control almost everything, leading to today's disastrous consequences in hospitals and the system of education. A lot of defrocked clerics became provincial civil servants. Yesterday Jesuit Superior, today deputy minister of education. Mentalities change much more slowly than governments and social structures. In history, changes happen very slowly, people progress at the speed of glaciers. That often makes us impatient."

André Brochu, whose trajectory through this torment paralleled Arcand's, through to the demise of *Parti pris*, also sees the collapse of Quebec's religious empire in the sixties as a major event. The arrival of television in the 1950s, the freedom to travel and often study abroad, the emergence of a secular culture of science and technology were all factors that led to the disappearance of an order of values whose main reference was God. Gone was the "life given over to constant prohibitions, the impossibility of real self-assertion; gone was religion as a formidable reservoir of clichés and the repetition of rituals." In this sense, "secularity is doubtless the most obvious acquisition of the Quiet Revolution."

Love/Hate Space

Today, at a more personal level, what strikes Arcand most is the aggressiveness expressed towards his work and himself. "I hadn't realized how much I am hated. A journalist from the *Nouvel observateur* commented on it, asking me if I had any idea of where this kind of aggressiveness comes from." The filmmaker is now aware of the extent of the phenomenon, which has existed since the beginning of his career. The ancient Romans might have called this chapter "*De Odium*," or use terms such as "*malevolentia, inimicitia.*" It is a complex phenomenon. "Some people hate me. It's incomprehensible. A mystery I try to live with. This phenomenon must be elucidated."

The *prêtrisme* type of hatred, feverish and undivided, has been expressed since the beginning of Arcand's career on the pages of *Séquences* or by Jesuit commentators such as Jacques Cousineau and Marc Gervais. In other cases, hatred for Arcand is the flip side of adulation, which partly explains the director's wildly fluctuating career. The examples go both ways. Jacques Leduc shoots down *Seul ou avec d'autres* in the journal *Objectif*, but later, at the NFB, becomes Arcand's friend and admirer. During the sixties, *Objectif*, though the antithesis of the "*prêtriste*" *Séquences*, seems to hold Arcand's films in contempt, refraining even to comment on the first documentaries. Then, having denounced Arcand for years, *Séquences* opens its doors to him with *Le Déclin* and *Jésus de Montréal*. However, in other instances, Arcand is first passionately loved and then pushed into the bonfire of the vanities he is accused of having ignited. After a rising curve that lasted until *Réjeanne Padovani* comes the condemnation of *Gina*. After the triumphs of *Le Déclin* and *Jésus de Montréal*, *Love and Human Remains* and *Stardom* are rebuffed.

Similarly, after the initial praise has subsided for *The Barbarian Invasions*, come doubts and second thoughts, rejections, even hostility. In *Le Devoir*, Odile Tremblay praises the film when it is first released, but six months later, when Arcand refuses to sign the declaration of "Twenty-five Quebec filmmakers" protesting the policies of Telefilm Canada, she calls the director "a fine gentleman spoiled by the system, who refuses to bite the hand that feeds him."

Today Arcand explains: "I agree with the objectives of the manifesto and its resistance to box-office mania. However, I find the proposed remedies inadequate, the suggested solutions not the right ones. To take away producers' performance-based funding envelopes and leave it all up to the civil servants is, in my opinion, a poor strategy, suicidal. At the moment, the civil servants from Telefilm Canada are completely obsessed with the box office; they wouldn't be good judges for deciding which projects will get funding. That's how it worked in the past and filmmakers never stopped complaining. I'd have liked to discuss the text with other directors to see if amendments could be made. Denis Chouinard, who was my contact for the manifesto, told me it was impossible. So I refused to sign. For example, I'd have liked to go into why the text does not mention the fact that the performance-based envelopes go to producers and exclude directors. I'd also have liked to emphasize that because Telefilm wants to apply the same policies in both English Canada and Quebec, it creates confusion. There should be two rigorously different policies, as if there were two countries involved. You can't mix them up."

Arcand is also the object of renewed attacks of hatred. "The *Village Voice*, in New York, calls me an 'asshole'!" Indeed, critic Michael Atkinson, outraged by the "opportunistic" use of the videos showing the attack on the WTC and by Rémy's refusal to be treated in the United States for fear of being strangled by Mahometans, as he puts it, finds Arcand bigoted, his dialogues often infantile, concluding: "Shear away the film's pretensions, and it's a soap opera for assholes." "In France," Arcand continues, "I can understand that people are sectarian and the camps insult each other, the way they did in the nineteenth century in the battle over Victor Hugo's *Hernani*. But after Cannes, abominable articles were published, written in a kind of delirium." In Paris, *Libération* expresses the view that the decadence shown in the film "is also that of the director," that his finale "consecrates the return of the Catholic repressed"; *Le Monde* thinks that by bringing together the characters and actors from *Le déclin*, Arcand shows "less patience than Alexandre Dumas."

In Quebec, the crown of excommunication comes from the monthly publication *Le couac*, a kind of Quebec version of *Le Canard enchaîné*, dedicated to the practice of "chauvinistic *sans-culottisme*." Even at the time of *Stardom*, the paper compared Arcand to a cynical mummy exhibited in film festivals for the sake of chic. This time, the paper concludes his last film shows "a Quebec with a majority of cretins ('*ti-Counes*'), ready to be bought and unable to rouse themselves for the sake of a cause," and that he describes the Quebec people, who are degenerate in his eyes, "the way a snob looks at a piece of snot on the tablecloth." And then the article's author, trade unionist Michel Rioux delivers his *ad hominem* climax: "It's been a long time since Denys

Arcand has lived in Lower Town. Falardeau still lives there. No doubt there's a connection."

Arcand is most often reproached for what people call his cynicism and contempt for people or characters, places and peoples, demonstrations and causes. He defends free-thinking that rejects all the "isms," including *indépendantisme*. With his curious intellectual posture, he always seems slightly off to the side or above the melee, and to emanate a zest for contempt and disdain. His love of mixing genres and species, his Machiavellian observation from a timeless and inaccessible sphere at the top of Complexe Desjardins, his way of describing the film director as "God the Father," all these aspects of his free-thinking appear to be unacceptable in a society bent on maintaining a consensus. "Free-thinking," recalls André Brochu, "was a slogan aimed at getting the Jesuits worked up." To borrow the words of Philippe Olivier, referring to Maria Callas: "Her personality and appearances provoked the hatred of some. Here on earth, it has never been a good thing to be different from other people. Even less so to be *too* different."

Hence, it is customary to attack Arcand without restraint after praising him to the skies. For scandal and success bring their share of satisfactions and even delights, but rarely or never do they bring quiet sympathy and unconditional admiration. In the wake of all the awards and honours, a debate explodes in Quebec over *The Barbarian Invasions,* called "neoliberal, anti-unionist and reactionary" by Gérald Larose on Radio-Canada. What a contrast there is between this alternation of love and hate and the deference Arcand is shown outside of Quebec, for example, in Toronto, New York or Paris—sometimes in Montreal too. For example, critic Dimitri Katadotis in his 2003 annual wrap in the *Hour* calls the *Invasions* "a work for the ages." André Baril, in *Le Devoir*, speaks out against "the cream pies thrown by the moralists," the ones who accuse Arcand of taking "a cynical, neoliberal and anti-unionist view of the world." For this author, "the very great richness of *The Barbarian Invasions* is to have presented, for a second time, a Quebec personality that in no way resembles the severe Séraphin of Claude-Henri Grignon, or the immature Elvis Gratton portrayed by Falardeau, but who, like these personalities, has lived submerged in the culture of survival. From *The Decline of the American Empire* to *The Barbarian Invasions,* Arcand gives life to a being who has broken with a past determined by conservative values and a colonized mentality, a being who has embraced modernity." Baril comments that "the film's ambiguities and Rémy's awkwardness may be hiding a renascent, not to say a combatant humanism," that "the film in its entirety shows the limits of technical and financial power," proven by the dialogue between mother and son, and the latter's generosity towards the young woman in leaving his father's library to her, an inheritance of "human knowledge, which forms subjectivity in the modern sense of the term," "a fabulous sequence that evokes the potential freedom of the beings who will create the twenty-first century." Finally, André Baril quotes the French philosopher Denis Collin: "Speaking of politics, it has to be admitted that Denys Arcand spells out a few truths we find painful but which explain why everywhere, the Left is beating a retreat."

"Arc de triomphe" Space

At the end of February 2004, in the final days of a particularly cruel winter, Denys Arcand comes to the end of a cycle of honours never before received by a Quebec filmmaker. Significantly, he has received several awards from critics' and screenwriters' associations in New York, Toronto and San Diego, as well as from festival audiences in Sudbury, Valladolid, Winnipeg and Toronto. As much a winner in Paris as in Montreal and Hollywood, warmly received in Brazil, Japan and Australia, the writer-filmmaker has garnered an armful of awards, decorations and trophies. The French State names him a Commandeur des Arts et des Lettres "for his work and contribution to the dissemination of culture," receiving the Prix Henri-Jeanson, the Prix Lumière, three Césars, five Jutras, with an Oscar as the cherry on the sundae. Italy presents him with a statuette of Donatello's *David* for best foreign film. The Cineteca di Bologna presents a retrospective of Arcand's films, and the filmmaker is received at the Palazzo Vecchio in Florence, Tuscany, because his script celebrates the collective intelligence of the Renaissance, and also mentions a wine of the region, the castello banfi "Excelsius." Moreover, the newspaper *Il Messagero* had already specified in December 2003: "The new barbarians' are not the Arabs but us, Westerners." Toronto adds six of the top Genie Awards to this list of honours. In Montreal, Denys Arcand is named Laureate for the 37th Annual Gala of the order of merit association of Université de Montréal alumni. McGill University presents him with an honorary doctorate in Literature.

After a year of screenings in numerous countries, the creative accounting report shows that *The Barbarian Invasions* has earned $35 million, a first for a Quebec film. The author of *The Barbarian Invasions* sees his film and career recognized and celebrated. Tired but happy, the filmmaker admits that since May 2003, he has been living on an artificial planet, parenthetically, but that all has ended as well as it began.

It may not seem so at first, but in these televised performances of kitsch, cash and illusion, Arcand is rewarded for the singularity of his art and thought. This complex and controversial Québécois director has just obtained the first international victory of a small cinema, thereby raised to the ranks of the greatest and most universal. It is a landmark: the image and sound of the entire universe, found in the grain of sand that is Quebec.

Arcand's stubborn insistence on talking about himself, against the backdrop of the economics-politics-culture triad, his enigmatic smile in the midst of a dark and desperate world, his insistence, too, on never wanting to sacrifice freethinking to the diktats of money and commerce, his way of treating tragic subjects through forms associated with popular entertainment: all these are qualities that we associate with Arcand but which tomorrow may be turned against him.

After this rowdy procession of critics and audiences has passed, its shouting and applause mingled with a few furious voices in a long-held bass line, the filmmaker can finally say he has achieved the grace to which he long aspired: "From now on, and until the end of my days, I can make all the films I want, the way I want to and at my own rhythm." He is at the top of his class in Quebec cinema, yes, but also an iconoclast and nobody's fool: docile on the outside but with a mind of his own . . .

Siberia Space

In autumn 2003, Arcand was almost labelled yet again, this time as a "Canadian federalist," when he agreed to join a cultural and scientific delegation to Russia, organized by Governor General Adrienne Clarkson. "I hesitated to accept this invitation, for all kinds of reasons having to do with politics, and also because State visits aren't my kind of thing. But when I learned I could visit one of the gulag camps from the Soviet period, a subject that fascinates me, I couldn't refuse."

A three-helicopter cortège from the Russian airforce took part of the delegation under the Arctic Circle in western Siberia, at seven in the morning on September 28, forty minutes from Salekhard. Here, at the ends of the earth, in an environment that could not be more hostile to man, the remains of a railroad could be seen on the immense taïga, abandoned railway ties and rails. The cortège set down close to an abandoned hard-labour camp, the former Construction Camp 501. Eighty thousand prisoners passed through the camp between 1947 and 1953, half of whom perished there. A haunting, unimaginable place. One day, Stalin had the idea of constructing a railroad in this region to convey Siberian petrol from Tomsk to a port on the Arctic Ocean. But the dictator did not know that you cannot build a railroad on permafrost, because the ground is in constant movement. However, no one dared speak out against this Kafka-esque enterprise. Ten thousand prisoners were brought to Salekhard and then forced to march two hundred kilometres further north and build the camp, surrounded by barbed wire. At the death of Stalin, guards opened the doors of the camp. Since then it has remained in a state of abandon. Rundown wooden shacks can still be seen, cooking utensils and cauldrons. . . . No one had visited the camp until two years earlier, when the president of Iceland insisted, putting pressure on the government, so that the history of the camps would be remembered.

"For me, this visit was a terrible shock. I consider *The Gulag Archipelago* to be one of the most important books of the twentieth century, making Marxism indefensible, at least in my eyes. I could see, touch the prisoners' wooden bunks, in this hostile region where there are only two extremes: minus '50-degree cold in winter and swarms of mosquitoes in summer, a thousand times more than in Canada. This project of Stalin's is beyond comprehension, and so is the bloodthirsty madness of condemning so many human beings to horror. Almost all the other Russian gulag camps have been destroyed. Only a few remain, to be made into memorials like Auschwitz."

Several days earlier, on September 24, Arcand had visited the Tolstoy house and museum in Moscow. Later, during the preview screening of *The Barbarian Invasions* at the Moscow Writers' House, an elderly man with a white beard asked Arcand a question in reference to Tolstoy's *The Death of Ivan Ilyich*: "Do you believe that under the effects of heroin, it is possible the protagonist did not see the light after his death?" Arcand replies that he does not know, but he is very touched by this question because before starting to write his script, he had made a point of rereading the Tolstoy story and remembered it ended as follows: "What death? There was no fear because there was no death. In place of death there was light. What joy!" During this trip, Arcand was able to meet with journalists and audiences at *The Barbarian Invasions* preview screenings, at Dom Kino in Saint Petersburg and Moscow. It is interesting to note that Russian critics see the feature as a "sad" rather than a bitter film, a film made by a lucid intellectual, whose discourse is humane and who made a point of shooting a close-up of Solzhenitsyn's *The Gulag Archipelago*. "Arcand," one critic writes, "is the last humanist of today's cinema." A cinema that is blocked, adds the filmmaker, now that all his director-heroes are dead, Fellini and Visconti, Buñuel, Kurosawa and Tarkovski. In another interview, the filmmaker explains that his inspiration is Chekhov, particularly the comedies, which are only comedies at the surface and tragedies in their depths.

Melancholy Space

Arcand's intellectual world, a world of regret, lack and emptiness, was enriched during the production of *The Barbarian Invasions* by the works of W.G. Sebald. The filmmaker comments that Sebald's books are neither novel nor essay, but hybrid postmodern works. Narratives of journeys and trajectories, illustrated with Polaroid photos, old and recent; they are works of memory, an absolutely fascinating kind of incantatory narrative. Sebald died in 2001, in a senseless accident, a head-on collision. What this writer talks about is very obviously the end of a civilization. Born in Germany, he spent his life in England as a university professor. An emigrant and foreigner, he turns incessantly to the motherland, the *Mutter*, the "Pale Mother" of filmmaker Sanders-Brahms, the distintegrated Germany. Searching for his family, his past, his culture, he is the writer of a world that has become ephemeral, just like beauty. That is what constitutes his tragic charm. In love, there is always a representation of the ideal woman in our heads. And then, Sebald takes a relativistic view of history, which seems to him like theatre or a mental construct. "In a similar spirit," continues Arcand, "I have never wanted to make historical films. All historical reconstruction is a fraud. In Hollywood, John Ford did not make Westerns about the nineteenth century, he was looking at the America of 1946. Reality changes so quickly and so do mentalities. During my childhood, when I went to midnight mass in Deschambault, the road wasn't cleared, people travelled in horse-drawn vehicles. I feel as if I'm talking about *Kamouraska*, a mythical time. I realize that I'm going to have a lot of trouble explaining this world to my daughter, in making her understand how my Grandfather Bouillé thought. Trying to transcribe these worlds in films seems to me completely illusory. To reproduce Versailles, in film today, is to film the Hall of Mirrors, wonderful costumes, characters with teeth. But normally, at that time, no one had teeth anymore by thirty. George Washington had wooden dentures. Still, in spite of what Sebald thinks, there are documents that remain, objects for the study of *slow history*, those studied by the French school of Interwar history, like *Le journal d'un bourgeois de Paris* during the Hundred Years' War or *The Diary of Samuel Pepys*. These documents are cross-sections that give us a brief glimpse of the past. But it's mysterious and complicated, difficult to make films with this kind of material."

Next-Film Space

In the past, Arcand has toyed with the idea of adapting a few favourite books to screen. Among these are short stories by Raymond Carver, like the ones adapted in Robert Altman's *Short Cuts*, or others impossible to adapt and make in Quebec, such as Tom Wolfe's *The Bonfire of the Vanities*, a sociological novel describing the New York world of high finance in the eighties and nineties, or *The Remains of the Day* by Kazuo Ishiguro, "a superb novel that takes place in a very short time, in a single setting, during an international conference held in a castle." Passing reveries, dead souls.

What kind of film projects is Arcand dreaming about at the end of 2003? In the vaults of his imagination he has several ideas that have been stored there for decades: a slapstick comedy à la Laurel and Hardy about Utopia, destruction or deconstruction; the completion of *C'est la vie,* a portrait of his father and his childhood in Deschambault; a sports film, about hockey; a study of the phenomenon of groupies, touched upon in *Stardom*. In 1993, for the *Projections 2: A Forum for Film Makers*, in answer to the burning question, "What will cinema be after the milennium?" Arcand writes: "Cinema after the millennium? Universities are full of people worrying about the next millennium. My only concern is my next film. In this country (Canada), it is still almost impossible to get a decent soundtrack on a picture, let alone properly printed titles. So any futuristic daydreaming seems a little ridiculous. Maybe if I lived in Los Angeles, I would see things differently. And besides, I always try to resist making bold predictions. Ten years ago the most feared sexually trans-mitted disease was herpes, and four years ago the main threat to democracy was the massive power of the USSR. The main characteristic of the future is that we don't know anything about it."

Yvon Rivard shares the following reflection on the subject of Arcand's next films: "I recognize the exceptional quality of *The Barbarian Invasions*, its great variety of registers, but I wouldn't be ready to call it Denys's masterpiece and therefore the end of his cinematic oeuvre. I tend to see it more as a work in which emotion, as in *Jésus de Montréal*, is increasingly present. Emotion always comes from an awareness of time, an anticipated relationship with death. Until now, Denys used his training as a historian to address that whole reality of time, which enabled him to relativize and see things from the moralist's point of view, to see in every human being a little theatre of derision in which the history of humanity plays itself out, relying on friendship to lessen the weight of solitude." Rivard believes Arcand will develop this reflection on time in future films, allowing the dramas of passion and illusion to play a lesser role. This, Rivard believes, could be done very well in the film the filmmaker has had in the works for years, the one about his childhood on the Saint Lawrence River or—why not?— a film on sports. "What's more, those two films could be one and the same, because in both sports and childhood, we are whole in our experience of the moment, with a quasi-physical perception of time. In short, I wouldn't be surprised if we discovered a more silent and reserved Arcand, one we occasionally catch sight of in his films and in life, and who could, using his camera, explore the border zone between child-hood and death with great finesse."

Opera Space

To the surprise of some, *Love and Human Remains,* through the prism of Brad Fraser's script, revealed a tragic "no future" vision of the youth of today. Yet, as he told *L'Actualité* in 1994, in this despair Arcand saw "an almost poetic attitude," a lyrical attitude. This reflection takes us directly to the melancholy realm of opera, the riveting music that has figured in Arcand's films since his early days at the NFB. While working *Auteur/provocateur* in 1993, we talked at length on the subject of sound design and music in his films. It was the first time he had spoken on the subject in such a systematic manner.

His first historical short films, for example, employ a very original stylistic matrix of audiovisual collage in which ancient and contemporary sounds collide. For instance, the soundscape of *Champlain* is comprised of musket fire, elegiac texts from the colonization era in the seventeenth century, funeral music by Purcell (*Funeral Music for Queen Mary*), and noisy contemporary sound sceneries punctuating commercialized images of the founder of New France. In *Les Montréalistes* (*Ville-Marie*), cranes demolish churches, choirs sing the "Hallelujah" chorus or *Chantons à Dieu,* the music interspersed with the sound of muskets or the sepulchral silence of the sisters of the Congrégation Notre-Dame. Finally, in *La route de l'Ouest* (*The Westward Road*), Arcand interweaves the voice-over and its melancholy commentary with old organ music, ancient Scandinavian and Gaelic songs and Renaissance choirs.

Later, for *On est au coton,* he creates a soundtrack that is a kind of industrial symphony: long silences intercut with the whispers of women workers, wracking coughs and the machine-gun "fire" of a typewriter pounding out quotations from Marcuse. The only music during the epilogue is that of a military band, à la Buñuel. Another brass band will play at the end of *Québec: Duplessis and After* . . . . If one views *On est au coton* paying close attention to the rhythmic structuring of images and sound, it less resembles a documentary report or manifesto than a tragedy in music. "Yes," says Arcand, "this film is first and foremost a subjective view of my own discovery of the world of labour. I've never made anything but highly personal films, and have never made claims for any authenticity but my own, which includes the way I look at history. People's blindness before the closing of the textiles factories is a tragedy, especially for the workers who are the victims of this fatality, who live it on a daily basis, it's under their skin, inside their lives . . . ." The infernal noise of these factories is a leitmotif in the film; the filmmaker turns it into a kind of contemporary music, a kind of audiovisual opera. Arcand was marked by the *musique concrète* of composers such as Pierre Schaffer and Pierre Henry, as by the works of Varèse and Schoenberg, modern music that seemed to him ontologically inseparable from cinema. Right from his first films, the director's approach has been quite the opposite from live sound. For his second full-length documentary, on Duplessis, he makes clever collages using the pompous, thundering speeches of the election campaign, constrasting with whispering voices reading historical texts such as *Le petit catéchisme des électeurs* or the Durham Report.

The dramaturgical matrix of Arcand's films is Greco-Roman tragedy, reformulated through the seventeenth-century French tragedies of Racine and Corneille. This form establishes as its premise that death is imminent, inevitable, as in the concept of *fatum*. According to the old *Dictionnaire latin-français du baccalauréat* by Bornecque and Cauët, used in the classical colleges, *fatum* may be translated as oracle, destiny, cruel destiny, misfortune, death and cadavre. In classical French culture of the seventeenth century, it is believed that tragedies were performed by the actors in a sort of declamatory and rhythmic *parlando*. On these foundations, Lully, Charpentier and Rameau constructed and consolidated French opera as "tragedy in music." Arcand's films are constructed from rhythmic cells as in music, creating a curious mixture of *tragédie en musique* and modernism, at once fascinating and disturbing, and also quite rare. For modern audiovisual opera is not necessarily derived from as ancient a model as tragedy, but is based on romantic drama, which Arcand has always made a point of avoiding. All Arcand's films, both documentary and fiction, could be described as tragedies in music.

This goes to explain the filmmaker's fascination with voices. His goal in writing the dialogue for the *Duplessis* series, *The Decline* or *Jesus of Montreal,* or Machiavelli's lines in *Le confort et l'indifférence,* was to create captivating experiences of the spoken word, dramatic music for voice. That is what leads him to say that the voice of Jesus is like the echo of the Big Bang. As a child he knew the gospel by heart and could recite from it; he sang in the choir of Collège Sainte-Marie and the church choir in Deschambault. The singing of his village choir can be heard on a number of occasions in *Quebec: Duplessis and After* . . . . He specifies in *Positif*, in 1987, that he organized the finale of *The Decline* as a *marivaudage* reminiscent of the last tableaux from Mozart's *Nozze di Figaro*.

In the films of Arcand, innumerable references can be found to opera and other music: Gluck and Pergolesi can be heard in *Réjeanne Padovani* through to *Jesus of Montreal*, Handel and Mozart from *The Decline* to *The Barbarian Invasions*, Verdi and Weber in *Stardom*. Even the popular music in *La maudite galette*, *Gina* and *Love and Human Remains* acquires the accents of the crypto jazz-rock operas favoured by Tom Waits.

In the life and career of Arcand, opera is the object of both love and hate. As a child, he loved it because of his father's friend, the tenor Raoul Jobin, and also because Horace Arcand himself listened to the Saturday opera on the radio. We can imagine the child, safe and sound in his father's arms, rocked to the cantilenas of *La Gioconda*, *Don Carlo*, *Carmen* or *Simon Boccanegra*. We imagine him at the home of his Grandfather Bouillé, entranced by the makeshift cinema provided by his uncle Antoine Roy and by the sound of the horn "in the evening, deep in the woods," as interpreted by Ezio Pinza.

In his years at the Université de Montréal, he still loves opera. But he changes his tune, or at least alters it, in the beginning of the seventies. In the context of the social and political struggles of the times, it is not well viewed to be so fond of a type of music and performance that are so closely associated with the bourgeoisie. Arcand says he is seduced by the Québécois fascination for opera, but in *La Presse*, in 1973, he declares it is a decadent art that illustrates "the decomposition of the ruling classes," that he used opera in *Réjeanne Padovani* "in spite of himself." The same year, in *Cinéma Québec*, he explains that opera is made for rich people, that it is an "art form of the European élite, imported to America."

However, this set language will disappear in the eighties, when the movements of the extreme Left dissolve and operatic art undergoes a revival in France and other places in the world. A few opera jokes and references to the enchanting Yvonne Printemps appear in *The Crime of*

Ovide Plouffe. One of the sequences in Episode II of *Empire Inc.* takes place at the opera. We could argue that these are nothing but commercial films and commissions, but at the end of the decade, in *Copie zéro*, the filmmaker reaffirms his fondness for opera and reveals, by authorizing its publication, the concept for a three-act opera called *Fin de siècle.* Created in collaboration with François Dompierre, the project never materialized. Since that time, Arcand has openly admitted that he dreams of being invited to direct an opera one day. He repeats it in *Auteur/provocateur.* He saw Mozart's *Lucio Silla* performed at the Theâtre des Amandiers with the famous mise-en-scene by Patrice Chéreau and says that to this day, he has not yet recovered from it.

On the fourth day of shooting for *The Barbarian Invasions*, Wednesday, September 11, 2002, during a pause while a shot is being set up, we smoke together in the little room Arcand is using as an office. We talk opera. He has been invited by the Canadian Opera Company in Toronto to direct one part of their upcoming production of the Ring Cycle tetralogy. He refused, he says, because he has no great liking for Wagner. He would prefer to do a production in Montreal, a simpler, more intimate work like a baroque or classical opera, *Cosi fan tutte*, for example. But so far, Montreal has not proposed anything. In Quebec, there is no comparison with what is offered to filmmakers in Europe or Toronto: Daniel Schmidt, Werner Schroeter, Werner Herzog, Coline Serreau, François Girard, Atom Egoyan . . . Arcand sighs: "Province of imbeciles!" The history of film directors doing opera mises-en-scene goes a long way back, to Eisenstein and Pabst, but most of all to Visconti in the 1950s. My own memories of opera-cinema include *La damnation de Faust* at the Palais-Garnier in Paris in the mid-sixties, directed by Maurice Béjart; later, the new production of *Faust* by Lavelli at Opéra-Bastille, Gluck's *Iphigénie en Tauride* at the Palais-Garnier under the direction of Lina Wertmüller, and especially Robert Wilson's *Madama Butterfly* at the Bastille. But also one by Egoyan in Ottawa, *Elsewhereless* by Rodney Sharman, and Stravinski's *Œdipus rex* by François Girard in Toronto. Not to mention Corneille's *L'illusion*, an "experiment" by Giorgio Strelher at the Odéon, an opera in which the entire theatre becomes the stage. Of course, Béjart, Lavelli and Strelher are not film directors, but their opera mises-en-scene are for the most part influenced by cinema, using fluid lighting and transitions.

Arcand is pleased to let me talk about my great fortune in seeing the *Barbiere di Siviglia* directed by Coline Serreau at the Opéra-Bastille, a Maghrebian Rossini that becomes "Coline Serreau's storming of the Bastille," whose spirit has much in common with her film *Chaos*. Incidentally, this director has recently made an *18 years later* sequel to her *Trois hommes et un couffin* (*Three Men and a Cradle*) of 1985. Her mise-en-scene of Rossini's *Barbiere* is wonderfully intelligent, a serious comedy ruled with humour and conspiratorial winks, taking us back to the lyricism, both tender and removed, of the film *Qu'est-ce qu'on attend pour être heureux?* Serreau's great "find": imagine a Sevilla shaped over centuries by Arab culture, Spanish aristocrats and bourgeois, materially and culturally crossed with the spirit of Maghreb. The director has no illusions about opera. As Rosine knows how to make use of the codes of masculinity, Serreau does not render this *Barbiere* to the letter but captures its spirit and dares to revitalize it by setting it in a France that believes itself threatened by Arab immigration. Serreau is not afraid of this culture; she does not believe that women will always remain veiled and submissive. Her liberated Rosine makes one think of the film *Inch'Allah dimanche* by Yamina Benguigui, or the passions of Michèle Rakotoson and Malika Mokeddem, writers whom I met in Abidjan in May of 2002 at a conference on literature and cinema. The finale presents a kind of future, at least an *image* of a future in which palm trees shoot up in a desert oasis to the final chords of Rossini's opera. For Arcand too, it is in opera scores that his new film idea has taken root.

EPILOGUE

Denys Arcand has no illusions about opera either. For a long time one might have thought his dream of directing an opera was a sort of closing of the circle, a return to that lyric space of childhood, curled up in his father's protective arms listening to the broadcast from the Met. In *Réjeanne Padovani*, after the Gluck aria, the mayor's wife asks the *padre padrone* Vincent if he likes opera. After a weighty silence, the Mafioso replies: "My father was an opera lover. Saturday afternoons, he listened to the Metropolitan Opera. It was sacred." For Arcand, could opera be a kind of new pact for the future, which would finally realize an earlier one made at the Mozart evening in Parc Lafontaine in 1960: to leave behind cinema and the other arts, and submerge himself in music?

"I don't think so," the filmmaker replies. "I'll probably never direct an opera. Really, I don't think I'll ever work anywhere but in film anymore." The proof: already, amidst all the tumult of travel and awards for *The Barbarian Invasions*, a new film idea germinated. The film will be made in Quebec, in French, according to the production scale and conditions of Canada and Quebec. A subject formed, an embryonic project now firmly lodged in the scriptwriter's imagination.

It is the story of a fortysomething civil servant, whose life reminds us of that of Musil's *The Man Without Qualities* or Gabrielle Roy's *Alexandre Chenevert*. This clerk for the State, servant of public affairs, nurtures wild dreams of becoming a writer or an opera singer. His daily life is gorged with delirious dreams. With a friend, on a kitsch West Indian backdrop, he sings the duet *Au fond du temple saint* (the "Temple Duet") from Georges Bizet's *Pêcheurs de perles*, while contemplating an entrancing goddess of beauty. This dream woman sings his name, Jean-Guy, her voice fading into that of his wife, who is roughly waking him: "Jean-Guy!" Another time, the civil servant imagines himself in the role of Arturo in the magnificent and melancholy opera by Vincenzo Bellini, *I Puritani*, singing the cantilena "*A te, o cara, amor talora* . . . ."

This man's world is a strange combination of reality and fantasy, in which the banality of his conjugal life and the ups and downs of a modest existence collide with social nightmares of epidemics and terrors, bizarre rituals and festivals straight out of a somewhat tacky Middle Ages. Slapstick scenes are mingled with musical imaginings and raw realism. A film unlike the ones that come before it, with a lot less verbiage and discussion, and more silence and music. Exasperated, Jean-Guy flees, leaves everything to hide away in an isolated cottage in the country. Nearby is a retirement residence. At the end of the film, the civil servant finds himself at the old age home. There he meets the old priest from *Jesus of Montreal* and *The Barbarian Invasions*, who intones this reflection borrowed from Jack Kerouac: "In the end, all you can do is pray for everyone in silence." In the end, this anonymous servant of the State, the Québécois without qualities, slowly peels vegetables.

This project outline waits on the table in the Arcand workshop. What will become of it? His will to do this film is unshakeable, but it is always possible that something else will come up to supplant it. Time and material conditions will tell. For do we really know where time will lead us when it is not fixed in a book, a script, on a canvas, a disc or on film?

Abidjan, May 2002
Montreal, April 2004

DENYS ARCAND: SELECTED READINGS

In the classical colleges of Quebec, before the Quiet Revolution, there were very few libraries, except in some of the wealthier institutions. And even those left something to be desired. The study programs for Greek and Latin or French literature were structured around two or three dictionaries, grammars and a few manuals of carefully selected texts. These anthologies were called "selected readings." They served the double purpose of providing short excerpts from literary works and a few quotable phrases of prose or poetry with which one could display one's "solid general culture." The censored selected readings that were in circulation in Quebec had often been put together by Belgian or French networks that had been issued an *imprimatur* by their superiors to publish such works.

I thought of using the form of these old-style anthologies to present a "best of" selection of Denys Arcand's writings. However, in this case, there is no trace of the Jesuit "Index" or censorship. Nor is there any intent to eliminate pages here and there, the choice of works having been solely determined by the amount of space available. For the filmmaker's writings are numerous, as his bibliography attests. Besides numerous film projects and scripts, they include reviews and essays, speeches and acknowledgements, tributes, revised interviews, presentations of his films, et cetera. They cover a long period, from 1958 to 2003. Some have been published; many are still at the typescript or even the handwritten stage.

The writer Jacques Poulin examined some of these pages: "We are struck by three things: first, the serious quality of the writing, which is very polished and disciplined; second, their irony and quirky, humorous details. But their main quality is life. His texts are very lively, and that is a far rarer quality than one might think. Arcand uses concrete images. A kind of formal perfection can be attained without a loss of vibrancy, of life. He manages to do this with ease, which is very much like him."

Other writers heartily agree. Yvon Rivard has praised the screenplays of Arcand, who has the gift of always being concrete and of constructing great syntheses of ideas from small events. François Ricard feels that Arcand's writing reveals "an artist trained in the world of literature and language. Arcand has a perfect command of language. He could have been a writer, an essayist or even a very good novelist. His writing is direct, transparent and precise, full of powerful images. I place him on the same level as artists such as Gabrielle Roy and Milan Kundera, great writers who endeavour to reach the widest possible audience without ever sacrificing their point of view or their own exacting standards."

For Arcand, writing takes place in the shadow zone of a profession he practises in public. It precedes the production and promotion of films; screenplays and other works emerge directly from the artist's solitude.

As he specifies in *Lumières* magazine in 1990, writing for him is an act of animal stubbornness. It keeps him going in times of great difficulty and provides a way of working out fantasies, obsessions and joys. It is also his way of compensating for "the absence of intellectual tradition," a personal form of resistance to the strain of anti-intellectualism embedded in the history of Quebec.

1

This is one of Arcand's very first published texts, which appeared in the College Sainte-Marie newspaper in his Rhetoric year (year six), when Jacques Brault called him "little Voltaire" because of his writing ability. The title "Paideia politeia" can be translated from Ancient Greek to mean "The Education of Youth and Politics."

Le Sainte-Marie, May 2, 1958

PAIDEIA POLITEIA

Antistenes was one of those young Athenians who were said to have received a traditional Hellenic education. Personally, he did not give it much thought, and contented himself with keeping up with current trends. Moreover, when he reflected on the way in which he had been educated, he had no complaints. His childhood had been wonderful: free of all restrictions. Every day was a holiday (*scholê*, from which the words "school" and "école" are derived, means leisure time): nothing to learn, nothing to memorize; no rules, no punishments—freedom. But every good thing must come to an end. When Antistenes was about ten, an old pedagogue took him to a private tutor in the year of the CVIIth Olympiade (the year Adimantus vanquished Glaucon in the cestus event). Antistenes learned to read on a sheet of papyrus, to write on a wax tablet and to count. He was made to memorize passages from *The Iliad* and *The Odyssey*. These remarkable poems greatly appealed to him as books to read at leisure, but as textbooks he heartily loathed them. He believed, as others did, that many teachers had learned the secret of making these wonderful books totally indigestible by analyzing them in class. A little later, he was made to learn geometry. Truth to tell, the scholarly deductions of Euclid left him cold, but he soon learned that geometry was a necessary evil and resigned himself to it.

Like all youths at the time, he was taught by a music master to play the cithara and not the flute, which deformed the facial features. That this was to give him a sense of measure, first physical then moral, for the time being did not interest him in the least. If he touched an instrument, it was mostly for the pleasure of playing a few melodies for himself and setting three or four original paeans or dithyrambs to music, which he found quite pleasant.

But it was the sports ground that provided him with his favourite form of recreation. It was there that his body had developed and there he had attained the kind of physical beauty which so often reflects inner beauty. Moreover Antistenes could, in all modesty, call himself one of the best discus throwers of his own age.

Civic Education

Meanwhile, his social education was accomplished in a most natural way: he watched what his father did, and modelled his conduct on his father's and that of the city leaders. He had many friends, and started to organize little nocturnal banquets at his home, the kind which were the highlight of life in Antiquity. Antistenes believed in the City and its Council, sharing its belief that slaves were an excellent thing and that women should remain at home. Moreover, he would later complete his social education with an obligatory two-year military service. As for his religious education, it was somewhat left to chance, and if Antistenes was not an ardent devotee, at least he recognized the existence of gods superior to himself.

For the moment, his father planned for him to enter a philosophy school the following year, where he would put the crowning touches on his education. Between you and me, he was in much more of a hurry to be admitted to official Dionysian orgies than to be received at the Academy. But a young man does not necessarily say everything that crosses his mind!

When all is said and done, this young man was evolving rather well. He was handsome and lived among physically beautiful people in a city whose architecture was pure of line; he had an innate sense of beauty. He was law-abiding by nature in a city where nothing was hidden and justice was democratic; he had a sense of truth. He was getting ready to enter the City naturally and without effort as his father and great-grandfather had done before him, that is, with no exaggerated notion of grandeur and with the certainty of all reasonable and intelligent people who do not aspire to change the world but to live in Beauty and Righteousness without exclamations or undue ceremony.

Georges-Denys Arcand

2

"A Glenn Gould Concert" *comes from a preface, written in English, for the screenplay* Thirty-Two Short Films About Glenn Gould *by François Girard and Don McKellar, published in 1995. The text was translated by the author.*

I was seventeen in 1958 and I had a friend who was an aspiring pianist. His idols were Arthur Rubinstein and Vladimir Horowitz. One day he confided to me in a conspiratorial tone that a young pianist from Toronto was coming to town the next month. His concert was not going to be advertised in the papers or anywhere else. This artist did not need advertisement, people just knew where and when he would be playing.

One snowy evening in March I took the tramway across town to the old Her Majesty's Theatre. The hall was packed to the rafters with people who looked like they were waiting for the Second Coming. On the bare stage there was a Steinway raised on wooden blocks with an old Persian rug under the pedals and a battered chair hardly higher than a foot-stool.

The lights came down and a very pale twenty-five-year-old man walked nonchalantly on stage with his hands in his pockets. With a self-mocking smile he whispered that by popular request he had just decided to change his program, and that instead of a partita and a sonata he would play the Goldberg Variations. The audience gasped. He then very quickly lowered himself on his old chair, blew on his fingers and atttacked the first Variation at a staggering speed. Now, at that point in my life I had never heard the Goldberg Variations. Listening to them for the first time played live by Glenn Gould is a bit like losing your virginity with Marilyn Monroe: you never entirely recuperate from it. His dazzling virtuosity, his astounding sense of rhythm and his overall intelligence were positively stunning. I sat there with my mouth open, transfixed. I had never before, and would never again in my life hear someone play the piano so well, except maybe Thelonious Monk very late one night in a very smoky club. (But that would be another story.)

[. . .]

How do you explain that the best pianist in the world suddenly stops playing and starts to do strange radio shows exploring the loneliness of people living under the Arctic Circle? What can you say about a world-famous artist who is so desperately in need of human warmth that he is reduced to using the personals section of the newspaper? Physically and spiritually, we inhabit an incredibly bleak country.

3

The Silent Historian *is a tribute to Maurice Séguin, published in an edition of* Normes historiques *followed by testimonies, in* Maurice Séguin, historien du pays québécois *(1987).*

I took courses from three historians: Maurice Séguin, Michel Brunet and Jean Blain. All three were fabulous. After twenty-five years, I still have fond memories of their courses. I was lucky enough to have had masters; not everyone can say the same. And yet, after leaving university, I never saw them again. Today I reproach myself for that.

In 1980, I made a documentary film (*Le confort et l'indifférence*) about the referendum, and out of the blue I got a note from Michel Brunet, at once shrewd and warm, in which he wrote: "You are still intelligent but you are also still impertinent." He invited me to lunch. I meant to accept, but with one thing and another, in the end I never replied. Two years later, one autumn morning on a film set, I learned he had died. He was a man I was very fond of. And now Maurice Séguin's wife tells me on the phone that her husband sometimes mentioned my name. To hear this is rather upsetting.

But what can one write about him? He hardly wrote anything himself. And he was particularly ironic and chilly towards "pen-itives." I find it very significant that our greatest historian was a mute historian. Our history has something inexpressible about it.

I am writing these lines in Rio de Janeiro. Out my hotel window, on the mountainside I can see the Favela de Rocinha, one of three hundred and eighty favelas that cover the hills of Rio, where over two million inhabitants try to survive, that is, a quarter of the city's population. The reality is staggering: three thousand murders per year, over a million assaults, epidemics of infantile meningitis, pollution that surpasses that of Mexico City and Tokyo, army and police with Colt 45s at their belts, right down to the lifeguards, uncontrollable inflation, and I haven't even gotten to Sao Paulo: twenty-five million inhabitants by the year 2000. Here, history is being made. Compared to all that, the agricultural statistics for the Saint Lawrence Valley in the years between 1820 and 1860 seem quite insignificant. Our history is profoundly boring, which might explain why Maurice Séguin was so laconic.

When I was his student, he gave two courses: one on Wednesday evenings and the other on Saturday mornings. He always seemed to get the worst time slots. I often skipped the Wednesday evening courses on nineteenth-century Canada. The subject matter was deadly dull: a population of French peasants quietly trying to survive under the generally benevolent domination of a British governor and merchant elite. No war nor revolution nor dictatorship, no famine would ever break the crushing monotony. The same monotony as today's. The human mind can know no greater drudgery than to read the innumerable petitions of the Scottish merchants of Montreal to the London Privy Council. And yet, Maurice Séguin knew them by heart. Which was how he gave his Saturday morning course on historical norms.

I spent about eighteen years of my life studying, and in all that time I took only one great course. It was that one. There before us was a man who had devoted his entire life to reflecting upon the destiny of colonized nations. And he had succeeded in making his reflections into a system using a set of norms of exceptional rigour and intelligence. His axioms on the tripolarity of societies (political, economical, cultural) seem every bit as brilliant to me today. His courses were on a level with the books of Frantz Fanon and Albert Memmi, who were writing at that time about the decolonization of Algeria.

I would later be astonished to see lightweight thinkers attempt to give Maurice Séguin the reputation of a nationalist historian in the militant or political sense of the term. For the essence of his thought was that the French-Canadian nation was too small and too weak to ever aspire to independence, and also too protected and too deeply rooted to be readily assimilated. Thus, for him, this was a people condemned to perpetual mediocrity until demographic weight and the pressures of the American empire finally relegated it to the oubliettes of history. Maurice Séguin had a tragic vision of our situation. And his thoughts were so disheartening, they may explain his silence.

I remember a polite man, ironic, tormented and extremely secretive. In the winter he wore a beret. My father did too.

4

Arcand's first contract at the NFB, in May 1962, was his report entitled Research Report on the Representation of History in the Films of the NFB. *Here are a few excerpts, never before published, straight from the archives of the National Film Board of Canada.*

It has to be one or the other: either the NFB makes historical films or it doesn't. In the case of the second hypothesis, there is no reason for writing this report. But if, on the other hand, the NFB decides to do a film series on the French Regime period of Canadian history, to my mind it should subject itself to a strict scientific discipline, and all films should be made under the direction of a producer who will make sure they are consistent in their interpretation of French-Canadian history.

[. . .]

From a literary point of view, no truly satisfying *History of Canada* exists at this time. Of course, for several years, the works of professors Frégault, Trudel, Brunet and others have shed new light on our history; but these are works of specialists covering only a few specific aspects of our history, in which most Canadians would be hard put to find a synthesis of their history. As for Lanctôt's *History of Canada*, while it is the most satisfying volume yet to be published on the French Regime, it only covers the period between the Great Discoveries and the institution of the Sovereign Council (1663), and other than that, it is a long way from the new theories of the young French-Canadian historians (Blain, Vachon). It is generally agreed in the history milieu that Monsieur Lanctôt's volume is a new old book. All this is to say that right now it is impossible to find a single book in any bookstore that provides a summary of the major lines of force in the history of the French-Canadian nation. A film series may be able to achieve this tour de force. And it must also be said that film, insofar as it offers the possibility of doing historical reconstitutions, seems to me the obvious choice of medium for "writing" a history that is more lively and passionate than any that can be found in existing books on the subject.

All this leads me to believe that it would be to the NFB's advantage to produce a series of film documents that would, in a sense, provide a synthesis of the history of Canada under the French Regime, and offer television audiences and schools a global view of French-Canadian destiny. This kind of initiative seems to me perfectly consistent with the NFB's new trend towards the "self-observation" of the Canadian people.

[. . .]

II

First, let us examine what has been done up until now by the NFB in terms of historical films, i.e., the series on the Fathers of Confederation. This will help us draw the plans for a future policy.

[. . .]

Here it might be useful to recall that modern historical science is increasingly moving away from the cult of the hero to focus exclusively on documents and social structures. More and more, we are seeing the adoption of American theory (defended here by Professor Michel Brunet), to the effect that it is history that makes great men, and not the other way around. However, the series on the "Fathers" adopts a strangely reactionary attitude insofar as it leads us to implicitly believe that Confederation was entirely forged by the will of Canadian politicians, whereas today it is generally agreed that it was the result of combined social and historical factors far more than a creation of human intelligence alone.

Moreover, this leads us to state a principle of historical science that the NFB, I believe, would do well to respect: history, as such, is far more than just a matter of searching for documents and classifying archives. History is not a series of dramatic or comical anecdotes, it is above all a knowledge of chains of events leading up to the present moment. The goal of this knowledge is to explain the present situation and, to some degree, shed light on future prospects opening up before us at the present time. The rest is simply curiosity and dilettantism. That is, if the NFB decides to make truly historical films, each of these films will have to be imbued with a perspective that aims to explain the current situation of the Canadian people. I feel this absence of perspective is one of the major shortcomings of the Fathers of Confederation series.

III

Here we are before three centuries of history: 1500 to 1763. Let us immediately say that history, which like all sciences is based on rigorously controlled documents, is always part hypothesis or rather, part interpretation. For example, there are several modern "schools" of interpretation on the subject of the French Regime: the Ottawa (Frégault, Lanctôt), Quebec City (Trudel, Vachon), and Montreal (Brunet, Séguin, Blain) schools. However, to say it again: the NFB must choose. This does not mean it has to be partial, quite the opposite; but while scrupulously respecting the facts, and with perfect knowledge of the different theories about these facts, it will have to opt for one of theory or another. One cannot do history without committing oneself to some degree. For one cannot put forward an interpretation of facts while sitting on the fence. Hence, one might think that 1763 definitively condemned French Canadians to mediocrity and provincialization, but one can also think that for French Canadians, 1763 was just a kind of rough patch that did not irremediably determine their future. In other words, one can either consider the French Regime as a failure or a partial success. And it is our overall view of the French adventure in America that will colour the meaning we give particular events. Personally, through my formal training, I belong to the "Montreal school" (Brunet, Séguin, Blain), which in Canadian history is the pessimistic school, the *noire* school. My opinions on how to depict the French Regime on film will naturally be coloured by my allegiance to this school. Its principal theories are too long to go into here, and moreover, this has already been done in numerous volumes, newspaper articles, public lectures and television programs.

So here we are before three centuries of history. It seems that the NFB can devote about a dozen half-hour films to the subject. So what has to be done, in about 360 minutes, is to crystallize twelve or thirteen salient points of this period that are indissociably linked to each other, and lead up to the final failure of 1763, a determining factor in the current state of the French-Canadian nation. What has to be done is to select from this historical period the essential points that could be interesting for film. I've selected thirteen of these, using as my inspiration the diagram created by Bernard Devlin.

1 – The discovery of Canada by the Europeans. The Irish in 880, DeMonts and Champlain in 1604 exclusively.

2 – The Indians and Quebec. Anthropology and geography.

3 – Champlain. A re-evaluation.

4 – Mysticism. The founders of Montreal (dramatization).

5 – The missionary problem and the Company of Jesus. A re-evaluation.

6 – The Iroquois wars (dramatization).

7 – Jean Talon. A study of the most prestigious colonizer of New France.

8 – The fur problem. Studied with regard to the partisans of settlement, the continental vocation of Canada, the alcohol trade, relations with the natives and the negative influence of governmental Catholicism.

9 – D'Iberville and the *coureurs des bois*. The attack of Corlar in 1690 (dramatisation).

10 – Importance of the Canadian woman. Madeleine de Verchères and the simultaneous evocation of other women who played key historical roles: Marguerite Bourgeoys, Jeanne Mance, Marie de l'Incarnation (dramatization).

11 – The English threat: Frontenac and Phipps. Studied with regard to the attitude of the clergy, that of Laval in particular (dramatization).

12 – Sociology of New France. 1713–1744. Social classes. The "Filles du Roi." Slavery. Intellectual life.

13 – The Seven Years' War. The Conquest. Retrospective view of the French presence in America as well as an approximation of the deep meaning of 1763 for French Canadians.

We will now examine these subjects in detail for a more precise idea of how each could be approached.

[. . .]

5 – The missionary problem and the Company of Jesus. The period between 1635 and 1690 was the golden age of missions and the Company of Jesus. For the entire seventeenth century, the Jesuits would work to establish their dictatorship in Canada. We know that from 1635 on, they had schemed in France to have all other religious orders besides their own excluded from the colony, and bar the entry of Huguenots and Jansenists into New France. They were entirely successful. The Jesuit missionaries then began to cross half of the North American continent, making important discoveries and annotating their logbooks with precious remarks on the native "milieu" they frequented, thus gaining control of all the important trade points. In Quebec City, during that time, through scheming or intimidation, the Company's provincial control made sure they kept the Governor well in hand. In 1645, the Fathers founded the Beaver Monopoly,

which they covertly controlled. In 1657, when the "private domain" of Montreal wanted to name the Sulpician Monsieur de Queylus as Bishop of Canada, the Company exerted its influence in Rome and instead it was Laval, a straw man dominated by the Fathers, who was named vicar apostolic of New France. The politico-economical and religious autocracy was so powerful that in 1660, the inhabitants of Canada petitioned the king of France, asking him not to leave them under the Jesuit's religious dictatorship. In 1662, the Fathers attained the height of their power: they punished the alcohol trade with excommunication and the death penalty, and managed to establish a civil tribunal to judge religious offences (blasphemy, adultery, etc.). Even Marie de l'Incarnation protested. It would take men like Jean Talon and Frontenac to partially undermine the Jesuits' power; moreover, their opposition to the Company cost them their careers upon their return to France. French Canada was terribly marked by this dictatorial Inquisition, which was to some degree responsible for the intellectual mono-lithism that for so long would define French-Canadian society. Indeed, if anyone could claim paternity for the colony, it would be the Jesuit Fathers far more than Champlain. Furthermore, this is the opinion of American historian Alexander Riddell in his masterful volume *The Rise of Ecclesiastical Control in Quebec*.

On top of political and economic domination, there was the missionary problem, which is far more complex than one might think. First, there were the missionary-explorers who expended most of their efforts on geographical discov-ery and the fur trade (for example, Father Marquette). There were also mystic missionaries who were absolutely bent on being tortured by the Iroquois. However, statistics clearly show that in anthropological terms, the Indians were impossible to convert. Catholicism is essentially based on an Aristotelian-Thomist mode of thought, that is, a cross between Aristotle and Aquinas, and therefore is deeply inaccessible to peoples who do not possess occidental intellectual con-structs. The English and Dutch preachers had understood this intuitively, and we may suspect that some of the Canadian clergy members, such as Laval and Queylus, when faced with the negative results of the Jesuit missionary enterprise, came to the empirical conclusion that all missionary zeal would be futile unless it was preceded by the total cultural francization of the native population. However, certain missionaries, in spite of all this evidence, continued to penetrate further and further into Iroquois country, to be pitilessly massacred. Psychoanalysts from an American university, using original documents, have studied the private behav-iour of the "Canadian martyrs" and, particularly in the case of one Noel Chabanel, diagnosed obvious symptoms of masochistic neuroses. This is quite dis-turbing. In any case, I think that on the subject of Jesuit dictatorship and the case of the Canadian martyrs, a cinema-interview film including historians, psychoan-alysts, and clerics could be a fascinating and necessary contribution to a re-evaluation of this period of our history.

[. . .]

12 – Sociology of New France. Between 1713 and 1744, the sociological

face of New France took its permanent shape. I feel that a half-hour would be necessary to study the following points: the feudal structures of Canadian society; the social condition of the marriageable women ("filles du roi") sent over on the king's boats to the colony (yes or no, were our grandmothers prostitutes?); slavery; level of intellect ; the first great capitalists (Bigot and Vaudreuil); to me it seems essential that we consider all these factors if we are to understand what happened later, for we must not forget that this society of 1744, which ceased to evolve as of 1763, went into making us what we are today.

13 – The Conquest. This film, after a short examination of the Seven Years' War, could be devoted to a retrospective of French colonization in America, drawing the lines of force of this colonization and explaining the failure of 1763, while clearly showing what the Conquest means to French Canadians and indicating how the future looked to us in the aftermath of 1763. In this last film, we could call on the most prestigious Canadian history theorists to give us their assessments of the French Régime. I have no doubt these assessments would be surprising to some.

[. . .]

5

Another unpublished text from the NFB archives, the commentary Arcand wrote for his short documentary La route de l'Ouest (The Westward Road), *is one of the most beautiful, saturnine texts he has ever produced. It dates from 1964.*

There is no place more familiar to human intelligence than uncertainty. Lost in a cosmos whose laws are unknown to us, confusion and anxiety are our daily companions. For now we know that the ground is always shifting beneath our feet, and what we call science is but a hall of mirrors, revealing only new mysteries.

We are already forgetting our own history, the lives of men who came before us on this earth, and the more we try to dispel the fog that envelops our past, the more unknown isles and unsuspected abysses we discover. That is why the question of Canada's discovery is overshadowed by a sovereign unease.

At what exact moment was this country populated by Amerindians from the West? Who exactly were these Asiatic nomads? In what year did the first European lay eyes on the coasts of Labrador and Newfoundland? Who was this European? A Phoenician navigator who had strayed beyond the columns of Hercules? A strange captain from the fabulous and mystical continent of Atlantis? A Basque or Breton fisherman? An Irish monk? A Viking warrior? Nothing could be less certain, and dreamers may choose their fantasy at will.

Perhaps it all began in Ireland, the birthplace of so many impenetrable mysteries and where so many hypothetical sea voyages began. The Celtic Middle

Ages, with its white-robed monks and eerie monasteries, were well acquainted with the twilight tales of Saint Brandan, Columba and Colomban, great preachers and navigators who had once left their country to spread the flame of the Catholic faith. And in truth it was often said that on their evangelical journeys, many were the new lands they had seen.

When towards the end of the eighth century, Ireland was wracked by multiple invasions, many of the white friars and their faithful boarded their round boats and embarked upon the routes of their legends. And it is said some travelled all the way to Iceland, and continued to live there independently in the service of their God.

But a century later Iceland, that strange country, both polar and temperate, volcanic and glacial, was itself invaded; the white friars took to the sea again, resuming their age-old flight. Did they run aground on some new shore, or were they forever engulfed by the grey undulation of the northern sea? Were they the first to glimpse through intermittent storms the faraway shores of Canada? Some say that it is certain, others that it is possible; some say it is unlikely.

But now our science and imagination must take us back even farther into the slumbering depths of our past, to the days before the Celtic world discovered our most hidden recesses. In the blue fjords of Scandinavia, sagas far better known to us today were about to be forged. Vikings! Natural boatmen on account of their countries' long coastline, in the ninth century these blond warriors would take to the sea again in their superb drakkars and make Europe tremble. Periodically, according to the fluctuations of climate and population explosions, the Norsemen unfurled their sails, raised their oars and headed across the waters towards faraway Edens, places where the women were dark and grapes grew in abundance.

They arrived in waves in search of new spaces, settling there for good or returning with slaves, wine, weapons, gold, fabric, jewels and glass. By 850, they had struck London, Paris, Cadix, Russia, North Africa, Turkey and were about to attack precious Constantinople, the pride of Christianity. In now famous battles they tortured Europe, and on the Dvina or the Dniepr they were feared as much as on the Thames or the Loire.

But though they sailed mainly southward, the West was not unknown to them; they rapidly conquered Iceland, chasing out the white friars of Ireland. In around 981, a Viking captain called Erik the Red, banished from Iceland for murder, set out to sea and discovered in the West a new territory he would call Greenland. Five years later, Captain Bjarni, who had left Iceland to join Erik, was driven off course by a storm in the direction of its fearful coasts in the mid-Atlantic. Seized with an icy anguish, Bjarni, without setting foot on this land-mass, sailed northward and discovered two unknown lands, then a little farther east came upon Greenland and the establishment of Erik the Red. There his adventure caused such a commotion that in 1002, Erik's own son, Leif Ericksson, a.k.a. Leif the Lucky, left Greenland for the territories that Bjarni had seen from afar. Travelling for days across the waters of the North Atlantic, Leif discovered three land-masses: Helluland, the country of flat stones, high plateaux and glaciers, Markland, the country of forest, and finally Vinland, the country of wine. They hauled anchor, carried their leather bags to shore and pitched their tents. They decided to spend the winter in this place and built great houses. Leif Ericksson said: "First we will gather bunches of grapes, then cut down vines and trees to fill our boats." In the spring, they repaired their boats and took to the sea again.

Thus Vinland entered into the Viking tradition. Lief's brother, Thornwald, also came to the land of wine, and the great Thorfinn Karlsefni tried to establish a colony there. But the natives of Vinland, called Skraelings, forced them into many battles and Thornwald would leave his life on the battlefield. Because of all these torments, the Vikings gradually left Vinland, never to return. Instead, they sailed around Greenland, eventually mingling with the Skraelings of Helluland and participating in the formation of what in Canada we call Dorset Culture. The Black Death would soon separate Scandinavia from its colonies, and Viking civilization quietly faded. All that remained were great stone tombs in the form of sailing vessels, bearing testimony to a dormant and solemn grandeur.

On the stones of what far off land might the Vikings have carved their runic characters? . . . No one yet knows. People say Florida, Hudson Bay, Mexico. Conserved in the Vatican archives are memories of bishops who left Greenland for the West to collect tithes in the northern colonies. In 1518, the Mexicans of the Yucatan were still talking about the legend of Votan, the blond man who worshiped the snake-god, and old images of the Mayan god Quetzalcóatl show a white-skinned divinity with blue eyes.

Today bold and restless spirits tirelessly comb the coastline north of Newfoundland looking for traces of Vinland. Every carbon deposit, every unusual stone and mound of earth is examined, and it seems the mark of Leif Ericksson or Thorfinn Karlsefni has been found. But on the sites of the circular camps that once echoed with the ring of metal helmets, sheep now graze, silent and dull-witted. The great wooden houses of the proud warriors are no longer there to serve as backdrops for actors and their grimacing parodies of violent gestures, their ridiculous exclamations for the cinema.

We cannot, in truth, remember these men any more. Goldsmiths with exquisite taste, inimitable sailors, cruel warriors, Catholics who still respected the cult of the snake, they crossed the seas on their ships without cabins, importing coloured glass from Venice for the stained-glass windows of their Hvalsey cathedral in deepest Greenland.

But while Viking culture was dying, further south a new fever was spreading throughout Europe. The flamboyant rigour of the medieval fortresses had become outdated and useless, Luther would burn a papal bull and populations be governed by unique sovereigns, Louis XII, the Tudors, Ferdinand of Aragon, thus reviving the idea of nation, forgotten since the long ago days of the Senatus

Populusque Romanus. Spain without the Moors saw days of glory ahead, then new faces appeared, more akin to Petronius than to Galahad, daring, innocent and cruel men, who thought like Machiavelli that "Men cannot and must not be faithful to a prince who can neither defend nor repress them." In the absence of divine right, princes needed gold. The Chigi family bankers of the pope clamoured for it, the Fuggers, financial backers for the Austrian emporer, had to have it.

The new mercenary armies had to be paid, and the new men, the bourgeois, needed ducats to activate new looms and printing presses. It all had to be paid for, in spices or in gold, but paid for all the same. And the infidels had just taken Constantinople, cutting off Europe's land route to China and the Indian continent, cradle of all riches.

It was then that certain daring spirits took to measuring, in painstaking detail, the world of nature. Up until this time, men had always believed themselves to be the privileged inhabitants of a horizontal earth, where the stars were created especially to light their way. Maps of the world always ended abruptly to the west of Spain. But the earth was round and, it was later discovered, nothing more than a little satellite of the sun. The human race had not yet got over the shock when Darwin came along to tell them they were evolved from a special category of bipeds, then Freud informed them that a good half of their thoughts were beyond their control, and the chaos was complete.

And the mad race did not stop there. Europe scaled its walls and looked westward. The caravel was created, and filled with all kinds of knick-knacks including the compass. After that, it was believed a quick route to the Far East could be found via the West. Flotillas were constructed, armadas of caravels; a number of Italian explorers decided to sail to far-off lands where they would plant the flags of Europe in their earth: Christofo Colombo on behalf of Spain, Giovanni Caboto for England, and Giovanni Verrazano for France. And one fine morning, in the Western sea, from the prow of the Pinta in the flotilla of Admirals Martin Pinzon and Christofo Colombo, Rodrigue de Triana murmured "Terra, Terra." Thus the West Indies were discovered, and with them, the Southern route. The rush began. From all the ports of Europe, expeditions set out for great adventures and discoveries. The Spanish with their épées de Toledo and *The Imitation of Christ*, the English with their songs of Merry England, their short swords and the Oxford Bible.

Whereas for the Vikings, Canada had been just another territory on the other side of Greenland, now people knew there was a planet to be conquered. By very different ways and means, they returned to Vinland.

Giovanni Caboto: Labrador, the east coast of Newfoundland and Nova Scotia, New England.

Gaspar and Miguel Corte Réal: the west of Newfoundland and the Gulf of Saint Lawrence.

Estevan Gomez : Nova Scotia and the Bay of Fundy.

John Rut: northern Labrador and Ungava.

Jacques Cartier: the entire Saint-Lawrence River and its Gulf, all the way to the Lachine Rapids.

In 1590, the coasts of Canada and the Saint Lawrence were known and charted in Europe, fishing on the banks of Newfoundland was organized and fur trade with the Indians began. Then began colonization, the era of Samuel de Champlain. Merchants, missionaries and clerks all headed for the place that was becoming New France; but that's another story.

Discoverers meanwhile searched for unknown spaces to conquer. Their new territories of predilection were Oceania, Africa and the South Pole, where sons of the Vikings and Conquistadors resumed their still unfinished task, as caravels slumbered in mortuary chapels.

For it seems that everywhere on our planet, there are men who feel confined in their immediate environment. These warriors ceaselessly add to the possessions of humanity, and in their supreme pride know there will be no end to their exploits.

6

"Stating the Obvious" *was published in the special issue* L'ONF et le cinéma québécois' (The NFB and Quebec Cinema), Parti pris, *April 1964.*

There is nothing to say about our cinema that any intelligent person does not already know. And there is nothing that can be said or written about cinema that is not merely trivial.

We know very well that the Candid Eye approach of the NFB's French Team provided the only possible outlet for filmmakers who were aware of production around the world and had been given the mission of "presenting Canada to Canadians and to foreign audiences," while at the same time reflecting the opinion of the Canadian government. And we know that the opinion of the Canadian government . . . All they could do was go down into the street and film at random, short of trying out a few timid personal interpretations at the editing stage.

We also know that the skill of cameramen, editors and sound engineers was simply a foil to detract attention from the paucity of emotion and thought in Quebec film, a paucity that is often the result of the work conditions that necessarily prevail within an organism directly attached to a federal ministry. It is also the result of the filmmakers' own inner turmoil. For the most part they are lucid enough to recognize the terrible gaps in their education and thought, and the drawbacks of their situation as French Canadians. But at the same time they are too powerless and isolated to find within themselves the way to reach those lucid emotions that are preludes to decisive creation.

Moreover, these filmmakers are too impoverished to work outside the federal organizational framework, and belong to a people too indigent and too colonized for its businessmen or provincial government to be able to afford the "luxury" of a national cinema.

That filmmakers are indeed colonized is confirmed by two facts. First of all, certain extremely wealthy Canadians, Louis Saint-Laurent and Gerry Martineau, are interested in cinema but are associated with two American distribution trusts which cruelly paralyze all attempts to develop a Quebec cinema. "The *rois nègres*" (we've heard this story before). Next, and this is quite revealing, the first great Quebec feature filmmaker outside of the NFB, Claude Jutra, is backed by an anglophone producer, Robert Hershorn.

It's not that our cinema is doing so badly. Sometimes it wins awards.

For example: "The National Film Board of Canada's most recent film, called: *Bravo! Bravo!*, a *cinéma vérité* study of crowd reactions at a flea fight, yesterday received the *Palme de plastique* at the International Festival of Crépon-les-Tourelles in Lower Syldavia. The festival is held every thirteen years and awards filmic works on the theme of flea fights." Truth to tell, our cinema is in about the same shape as our literature and our painting, awash in an unhappy mediocrity. It keeps telling itself "It won't be long now." Each film director, alone, miserable and most of the time lacking a structure for his thought, struggles with his petty anxieties and talks about "his feature film," in which he is finally going to say it all to the world's face. He is like our writers who are always talking about their famous novel that no one ever reads.

Like everyone here, the filmmaker is alone because collective consciousness is something we have barely learned to recognize. No one helps the filmmaker, certainly not the critics (especially not the journal *Objectif*). These critics wish to place Quebec cinema in a perspective that is too vast for it. They have already come to the conclusion that the NFB French team is made up of *cinéma vérité* theorists. They were referring to Jean Rouch and the others. What a joke! Great theorists are for civilized countries. Here, the Candid Eye is an unconscious lifebuoy for a bunch of poor souls who do not want to sink in the platitudinous waters of Radio-Canada TV drama. And all criticism of Quebec film must take account of the general situation of our nation and the living conditions of its filmmakers. It would be as futile to borrow stylistic points of reference from other cinemas as it would be to criticize *Les Carabiniers* or *Le Petit Soldat* for faulty fabrication. There are works that reflect a nascent consciousness smothered in its sleep, and they must be judged in terms of their level of consciousness and not in terms of the appropriateness, or lack of same, of "slow zooms on quiet seagulls," in the words of Jacques Leduc. There is a time for Lubitsch and a time for Capra, but those are not the times in which Quebec is living.

Canadian cinema does not lack for money or scripts, it is not held back by the limitations of NFB These are all false problems, scarecrows that we erect to mask the real problem, which is serious and deadly: the fate of Quebec cinema (and of all our arts) is inseparable from the fate of French Canada. If our cinema has made progress in the last while, this progress runs parallel to Quebec's new self-awareness. Our cinema of the present time, to paraphrase André Brochu, provides us with a glimpse of what Quebec cinema could be—no longer a cinema of failure but of conquest, in which culture and everyday life would finally intersect. And now that Quebecers have risen and moved forward at great risk, it is true that filmmakers are suspected of fomenting a filmic revolution. I am very afraid that all this will end up hurting a lot of people.

7

This essay, "Cinema and Sexuality," *published in* Parti pris *in the summer of 1964, discusses two seminal Quebec films*: La Petite Aurore, l'enfant martyre (Little Aurore's Tragedy), *a French-Canadian feature that came out in the early fifties, and Claude Jutra's* À tout prendre (Take it All) *(1963).*

Within an alienating situation there exist three possible modes of existence: alienation, revolt and revolution. The road to freedom goes from the first to the last of these situations. Pierre Maheu described this progression in the first issue of *Parti pris*. However, Quebec cinema, like all mirrors of our society (and obviously, like our society itself), has started its march down this road to freedom. If the freedom we seek is social, religious and political, it must also, and most especially, be sexual, for a free and total existence requires an equally free and total understanding of sexual realities.

From this particular point of view, the history of our cinema obviously begins in the most complete alienation. From *Le Rossignol et les cloches* to *Coeur de Maman*, films from the era of darkness are tableaux of sexual aberration, each more disturbing than the last. To explore this aspect, a lengthy analysis of these films would be required, but this is and will always remain difficult to do because copies are rare, often mutilated, and in all cases difficult to obtain. However, such an analysis would greatly stimulate our search for a deeper knowledge of our collective soul. What a royal feast for a psychoanalyst: from little Gérard Barbeau with his soprano voice and short pants, and his good and understanding parish priest to the poor soldier Tit-Coq, who is abandoned by his beautiful-and-pure-French-Canadian-fiancée and gets drunk and sleeps with the bad-and-dirty-Anglo-Saxon-prostitute to the horror of his good French-Canadian-Catholic army chaplain. There on display are all our complexes and our untamed unconscious mind.

I would first like to talk about *Aurore l'enfant martyre*. Though representative, this choice is arbitrary, I know (Guy Coté pointed out to me that other Quebec films no doubt exist that are more maniacal than *Aurore*). However, this film whose success was so great that its very title has become part of our everyday language in Quebec, can give us an approximate idea of the extent of our alienation in past.

The Darkness

Let us start by saying that *Aurore* is a serious enterprise: 35 mm, big camera, arc lamps, artificial sets, professional actors. Thousands and thousands of dollars were invested. This is no "amateur film," filmed furtively on a shoestring. In the credits we find names which in Montreal were once considered the ultimate in good cinematic taste. When I first saw the film I thought maybe it was a cynical work, a huge prank concocted by cruel and lucid individuals who were only interested in making money from the Quebec people (in which case the film's success would still be revealing and its analysis valid). But witnesses from the time assure me that all this was done by serious people who believed they were making a good film. Once we discard the spoof hypothesis, we head straight into nightmare territory.

Aurore Andois, a girl of about ten, lives with her father and mother in a rural region of Quebec. The father is a farmer; the mother is gravely ill and bedridden. A widowed neighbour takes care of the house. The neighbour secretly poisons Aurore's mother to be able to marry the girl's father. Aurore witnesses the poisoning. When her mother dies, she goes to live with her aunt in a distant village. The parish priest convinces Monsieur Andois to bring his daughter back. Having returned, Aurore lets her stepmother know that she is aware of her crime. The stepmother undertakes to systematically terrorize Aurore until she dies under torture. The crime is then discovered and revealed by the neighbours; the stepmother is condemned to death and the father goes to prison.

What must first be said about Aurore is that she is a voluntary victim. Throughout the film, she has dozens of opportunities to reveal her stepmother's crime and tortures to the parish priest, the neighbours and her aunt. At a surface level she keeps quiet (so the film wants us to understand) because she fears her stepmother's reprisals. But objectively, everyone knows this is impossible, that any sensitive person would immediately act to protect a mutilated child. Most of all Aurore remains silent, as she says, "so as not to hurt her papa," so as not to make trouble for her family, and moreover, because the priest, her aunt and neighbours, because her *entire society* tells her that her place is with her father, that children are the objects of parents and owe them respect, obedience and love. Aurore is like Donalda, who remains with Séraphin because he is her husband in the eyes of the priest and the village. The immutable laws of God and society forbid her to leave her husband. Moreover, she does not want to leave him because by doing so, that is, by breaking these superior laws, in her own eyes she would be annihilated for she has never defined herself, or consciously existed, in any other terms but those of religious and social law. For Aurore and Donalda, the only two options are annihilation or salvation. And salvation means accepting the cruelty of the strong. In the works of the Marquis de Sade and the *Story of O*, victims are sequestered in dark chateaux and guarded by menacing servants, which forces them to demur to the masters' will. In the case of Aurore and Donalda, social and religious structures are more than sufficient to imprison the victims. The victims in De Sade and the *Story of O* often end up discovering an essentially masochistic form of sexual pleasure. In the case of Aurore and Donalda, there is no outright sexuality but instead a kind of noxious happiness, a redemptive sense of being in the right. Aurore is proud to be "a good girl" in spite of everything. She is happy to forgive her father who has just struck her on the head with an axe-handle, and when at last she feels she is dying and tells the parish priest of her sufferings, it is with a kind of martyrly pride. She will be a child martyr, or her name is not Aurore! And her determination gives her a clear conscience and a kind of naturalness that is only possible in childhood. The adults want her martyred, and she gratifies them with mute suffering and greatness of soul (in his last book, Jean-Paul Sartre brilliantly observes this sort of two-faced conscientiousness in children who live to please adults).

Naturally, in *Aurore* as in almost our entire culture, the father does not exist. Leaving his daughter in the hands of his new wife, he spends his days in the fields, and is thus completely removed from the drama taking place in his own home. When he is told that Aurore had to be punished because she was disobedient, he believes it and in certain cases even hits her himself "to subdue her." In a sense, we could say that everything that happens to Aurore is solely due to the absence of the father and that the little girl is the victim of the savage world of women, from which males are systematically excluded. The male in question here is the eternal French-Canadian father: stupid, coarse, a good Catholic, honest, quarrelsome, sentimental. He is all that and at the same time he is nothing. Neither sympathetic nor detestable, he simply does not exist compared to the all-powerful mothers. As for the parish priest, the father's perennial substitute, the film unwittingly makes him more dangerous: it is he who by invoking the laws of the family, recommending that Aurore return to her father's home, thrusts her into the arms of the stepmother-torturer. It is also he who, when told of the girl's terrible fate, answers while sipping his orangeade that "he'll take care of it." And indeed, he does take care of it, but too late: Aurore is dead. The most revealing aspect of all this is that the film's authors wanted to make the priest a sympathetic and humane character, but unconsciously and despite the eminently reasonable things they have him say, they make him perform actions that could not be more unfortunate for Aurore. Similarly, in *Séraphin*, the characters talk of nothing but the great and good Curé Labelle, while embroiled in a gigantic historical error that will cost them their lives (the establishment of colonists in the north of Montreal), instigated and directed by the blundering Curé himself.

From a more specifically sexual point of view, *Aurore* contains a scene that is particularly revealing. At one point, two young neighbours of the Andois family declare their love for each other. During the scene, the young girl is scraping a carrot. When she says that she accepts and shares the young man's love, she holds the carrot out to him and he nibbles it, then the girl puts the carrot in her own mouth. Once this little game has ended, they fall into each other's arms and shyly embrace, the kiss hidden from the camera by a big rustic straw hat that fills almost the entire screen. In other words, at a symbolic level, we are faced with overt sexual energy (the symbol of the carrot being quite clear, I think), but as soon as this energy moves to the level of consciousness, that is, when the two protagonists stand and embrace each other, the camera is unable to follow the gesture to its conclusion, while knowing it is necessary, and hides the kiss behind a straw hat. The same scene shot by Minnelli or Cukor would have been full of guile and depraved winks at the spectator, but in *Aurore* there is none of that. We are up to our necks in alienation, in which the actors, filmmaker and spectators all instinctively sense emotions that are as troubled and vague as they are unavowable.

Further proof of this alienation can be found in the very nature of the tortures Aurore is made to suffer. Everyone knows that everywhere in the world, so-called educators, or anyway the ones responsible for children, have always taken pleasure in striking them on the buttocks. This form of torture, while generally representing no danger to the victim's health or appearance, provides the torturer with a pleasure that many a convent superior and prefect of discipline would describe as delicious. De Sade himself and the author of *The Story of* O never tired of pulling up the starched skirts of their beautiful heroines and discussing at length the merits of different kinds of whips. Thus, we might expect to see a few good spanking sequences in *Aurore* seeing as half the young women of Quebec have been through the experience. However, it is quite the contrary. Poor Aurore! Her head is thrust in nettles, her scalp is burnt, she is pushed downstairs and hit on the head with an axe-handle, made to swallow soap and drink dishwater. Her neck and shoulders are lashed, the palms of her hands burnt, but never do we see the slightest hint of white skin or pink thigh. I do not believe I am mistaken in observing a suppression, at the visual level, of a known and recognized reality. And this suppression is revealing.

There are many other things that one could say about *Aurore*, for example, the fact that her last name is Andois, a name which does not exist in French Canada. Hence, the film could not be more rooted in our milieu, but at the same time, the fact that the family is called "Andois" removes it from our universe, making it possible for the spectator to withdraw at any time from the drama unfolding before his eyes, which both confers a mythic value on the characters and renders them harmless. (Moreover, we might draw a parallel between these considerations and Nathalie Sarraute's reflections on the first names of André Gide's characters). And how not to mention the electric organ music (cocktail lounge style) heard throughout the film? The theme music, which notably accompanies the torture sequences, is a melody called *Le Rosaire*. In watching *Aurore l'enfant martyre*, we become aware that we still have a long way to go.

However, little by little, like our society, Quebec cinema has emerged from its sexual nightmares. There was Guy Borremans' *Femme Image*, with its esoteric-poetic eroticism à la Lo Duca, but at least, for the first time, we saw a naked woman in a Quebec film. I can remember film clubs in the old days where we projected *Femme Image* with Witches of Salem expressions on our faces. *Kronos* by Denys Saint-Denis was the same style of film. Then there was *Seul ou avec d'autres,* in which we painfully tried to liberate ourselves through sophomoric humour. Recently, there was *A tout prendre*, which I would like to say a few words about.

The Light

With Jutra's film, we appear to be a long way from the Andois family. The main character is Claude, a bright young film director, appreciated by the beautiful people in Montreal, a friend of François Truffaut. The film tells the story of his affair of the heart with a Montreal model called Johanne. Does this mean we have finally left the ancestral farms and rural churches behind? Have we arrived at the great liberation Quebec has awaited for two centuries? Have we emerged from the dark cave where Donalda and Aurore moaned like Choephores? I'm terribly afraid that we have not. In spite of the modern architecture, the Italian shoes, the volleys of "Ciaos!," our infantile and troubled soul is still omnipresent. The scenery has changed and there is no lack of lucidity, but as psychoanalysis has discovered, simply to recognize a complex is not the same as to cure it. The road from alienation to revolution is long. In *À tout prendre*, only the first hints of revolt are visible.

To start with, I said "Johanne." But Johanne who? Naturally, models are often known by their first name only. The same was true of certain actresses in past. A woman can have reasons for wanting to be called by her first name only, yet it seems to me that something strange is going on here. The ads say: "A film starring Johanne." There on the screen, in the middle of the action, the word "Johanne" appears. Over the course of the film, we see only a few images of her work, a single meeting with a former lover (a superficial meeting, what's more), and a long confession about her unhappy childhood. Not a word is said about her present state, her woman friends, her recent past, her husband, her former way of life—nothing. It's all a mystery. The film's publicity, which is full of detail about the lives of the filmmakers and actors, does not say a word about her except to call her the "all-beautiful," unnamable, indescribable, indefinable, etc. She does not exist outside of her relation to the film. She is not *a* Johanne, she is *the* Johanne. Moreover, she is black. In the beginning of the film, we believe she is Haitian. Then we learn that she is Québécoise. A black Québécoise. This characteristic removes her even further from reality. She's foreign but comes from our own milieu; her colour makes her "different," "special." She says it herself: "You're like the others, you love me because I'm different, I represent something exotic . . . ." Claude answers: "I love you because you are you." But that's just it. "You" is black, and has no family name, and that's how the film wants it to be. And she understands this ambiguity perfectly: she is denied an identity of her own and instead one is made for her, a portrait as abstract as the film's poster in which she is reduced to an essence, a stylized black woman. The cinematography deforms her image through soft focuses (like a Giacometti, said *Time*) or freezing her in still photos. It ceaselessly attempts to rationalize her, make her a "work of art" in the most basic sense of the term. But we know that works of art are lifeless. If the film were more profound, it would end with the death of Johanne. Jean-Luc Godard follows in the footsteps of Edgar Allan Poe in *Vivre sa vie* when he realizes he is killing the woman whose very soul he seeks to extract through his endless photographs. Thus, Johanne can no longer dance or show herself off and flirt with a spontaneous pleasure. She can no longer be born in Haiti, where stately blacks work together in the fields, reaping the crops in perfect harmony, she can no longer be simply embarrassing and get herself pregnant like an ordinary laundry worker from New Toilet System. There is no point in being surprised when Claude and Johanne separate. Claude leaves to travel to far countries and revealingly, the images of these far countries where he goes to live are the very ones evoked by Johanne when she talked about Haiti, the place she was never born. Claude has left in search of his dream visions of black harvesters. He failed to perceive Johanne as an essentially distinct and autonomous other, perpetually different from the photographic projections that he would like to make coincide with her. And this refusal to coincide is not called the feminine mystique or the mystery of Johanne, it is called existence, the real itself.

Let's go a step further. Why can Claude not have a valid love affair except with this strange Johanne whom he wants to make even stranger? For there are "garden variety" Québécoises all around him. Indeed, he sleeps with two of them. First there is Barbara, a salesgirl in a jewellery store. Hardly anything is said of her except that she is a pleasant partner. All this with a slightly biting humour that is without great tenderness. Next there is Monique, an actress. Here the film seems to want to prove that the hero sleeps with this young woman with pleasure and in a carefree manner. However, an extremely awkward scene transpires. Jean-Claude Labrecque's camera, which is usually so delicate around women, remains frozen in a corner of the room, observing in an almost voyeuristic manner Monique's painful undressing. A single camera angle, no movement; the entire scene is imbued with a nerve-wracking tension that flagrantly contradicts the filmmaker's intentions. Even in the editing, in dazzling shortcuts and in spite of his famous virtuosity as an editor, Jutra fails to erase the painful and flagrant awkwardness of the scene. Hence, at the cinematic level as from a psychological point of view, *À tout prendre* fails to approach real and everyday women with any kind of tenderness or satisfaction. In that sense the film's hero is like a lot of French-Canadian men in their thirties who are cultivated and sensitive and who systematically require black, yellow or red women, in any case "foreigners," for their heady affairs. This indicates, it seems to me, an unconscious refusal on the part of these men to coincide with their collective self, as well as an unquenchable thirst for self realization via a mythic exteriority that may have something to do with the general situation of our people.

The impossibility of achieving an "everyday kind of sex life" no doubt has something to do with an unresolved oedipal complex. For obviously in À tout prendre as elsewhere the father is totally absent. So absent that he is never actually seen on screen, though he is mentioned a few times, whereas the mother, as always, crushes the film with her power. A power that, in this case, is accentuated by the solid and measured acting of Tania Fédor. The strange mother-son relationship depicted in À tout prendre is clearly typified in the sequence where Claude goes up to his mother's bedroom, and through tricks of editing, as in L'éternel retour, seems to climb the same staircase several times, moving higher and higher towards his goal.

But whereas in the Cocteau film, Jean Marais is going up to Madeleine Sologne, his love, Claude in À tout prendre is going up to his mother. It is also remarkable that Claude, who cries out for freedom throughout the film, when overcome by difficulties and forced to make a decision thinks only of seeking refuge with his mother and a priest. Thus it is not surprising that the film seems to make a claim for homosexuality. In any case, our literature claimed this right with Jean-Charles Harvey before the last war. Nothing very new or immoral in that. The question that remains is to what extent homosexuality can be considered a solid form of sexual activity, and in what way its practice could be linked with a special state of self-affirmation, considering the general context of our existence and its influence on artistic expression.

À tout prendre, like most of our works of art (from Alain Grandbois to Borduas . . .), is the story of failure and escape. However, via the themes of homosexuality and abortion, it introduces our cinema into the world of revolt. Still, revolt is no easy matter; it is learned slowly and takes a while to jell. Revolt does not happen simply because one wants it to. Thus Pierre Patry, who wanted to include a nude sequence in his last film, says that he was obliged to remove the sequence during editing for purely aesthetic reasons. I believe him, but then again, why was it this particular scene that failed? Certainly not because of Patry's technical crew, who were no doubt remarkably efficient, as usual. I'm much more inclined to believe this indicates, as does the Monique sequence in À tout prendre, how the Canadian film director comes up against very steep and specific walls from the moment he decides to sexualize his cinema. For the fruits of the flesh are generally savoured in conditions of freedom and we are still a long way from the ease of Mizoguchi.

But both À tout prendre and Trouble fête end on an unmistakable note of lucidity. And from the moment our filmmakers manage to forget their mommies for long enough to serenely undress their neighbour called Yvette Tremblay or Yolande Beauchemin, in broad daylight with a well-focused wide-angle lens, then we, like Jean Renoir, will be able to envisage a cinema that is at once free and fiercely national. A cinema of joy and conquest.

8

Again for Parti pris, *in September 1964, the young filmmaker dissects a staple film of new Quebec cinema,* Le chat dans le sac *by Gilles Groulx, who was a master for Arcand.*

I certainly have no intention here of writing a review of Gilles Groulx's film, no more than it is the intention of *Parti pris* to start doing exegetical texts on cinema. However, given the film's significance in our cultural milieu, and given that *Parti pris* is openly mentioned in the film and that the director of the journal appears in the film, it seems appropriate to make a few comments about it.

In relation to his film, I have already quoted to Gilles Groulx the following words from *The Imitation of Christ,* Book 3, chapter 20: "Often, it is a small thing that makes me downcast and sad. I propose to act bravely, but when even a small temptation comes I find myself in great straits. Sometimes it is the merest trifle which gives rise to grievous temptations. When I think myself somewhat safe and when I am not expecting it, I frequently find myself almost overcome by a slight wind." Indeed, what defines the hero of *Chat dans le sac*, is his great weakness and indecision. Within himself he experiences situations of complete ambiguity: dilemmas of the one versus the many, of action versus meditation, of the social versus the individual. This young man, intelligent and honest , refuses to be a "social" man in order to preserve the sacredness of the individual. Though believing in the cause of French-Canadian nationalism, he retires to the country to reflect upon the subject while bombs are exploding and arsenals being raided. Finally, even the woman he loves leaves him and still he remains immobile, in complete and attentive solitude. I think one could say that Gilles Groulx is a philosophical filmmaker.

But his philosophy is not at all Byzantine or Thomist. It is not a mental game, a collision of logical notions cleverly supported within a moral sophistry. His philosophy is essentially gnostic, in the sense that it constantly calls upon a theology, an all-encompassing world view. There is nothing more foreign to Gilles Groulx than the notion of Will; he perpetually seeks a gnostic structure, a Kabbala, which takes the place of his free will and envelops him in total "Understanding." In a way, *Le Chat dans le sac* is an Eastern work. It should therefore come as no surprise that the film is a kind of interminable conversation in which the values of the individual versus the forces of society are constantly being weighed, as well as the need for social revolution for French Canadians, the difference between action and agitation, etc.

But things become difficult when the same film seems to be looking for a solution to these problems. Within a Gnosis, minds should not seek a solution in the strict sense of the word, but try to seek appeasement in complete immobility and silence in relation to those problems they judge to be insoluble. At the opposite pole from the gnostic attitude is the other possibility, commitment, the philosophy of action, which is not based on finding a solution to existential problems but on a will to action that is itself based on an approximate calculation of life's values. Indeed, the dilemma of the one and the many, the social and the individual, will never be resolved. Two possible attitudes may be adopted in relation to them, action or contemplation. The yogi or the police superintendent. Gilles Groulx has a choice to make, as all men do. And with *Le chat dans le sac* this choice is simply posited, not fully lived. But the choice has to be made, and quickly, for as Barbara so rightly says in the film: "He who hesitates is lost." More than one man of intelligence has destroyed himself this way. For life presents us with ambiguities that we must not know how to solve, the human condition itself being ambiguous and multifaceted. The problem is to keep this ambiguity in mind and close one's eyes, smiling, or go ahead and act regardless. The notion that all human acts are multifaceted should not provoke morbid hesitations and futile standstills as in the case of Cicero, for example. On the contrary, it must lead to total immobility or indeed total action, both attitudes illumined with raw lucidity and smiling irony, as in the case of Lucretius or Julius Caesar. So the journal called *Parti pris* was founded because we chose action, without looking back, not because we were convinced the cause was perfect or bound to succeed, but rather because upon sincere reflection it seemed that an option requiring one to take a position, a *parti pris,* was grounded in quite solid values.

In the end, it seems that *Le chat dans le sac* merely represents a step in the inner process of Gilles Groulx and that soon his work will take its definitive shape. As *Parti pris* has already written of André Laurendeau: questioning cannot take the place of wisdom. But for the time being, Gilles Groulx, though he always displays remarkable intellectual rigour, remains standing in that kind of troubled light alluded to by Lawrence Durrell when he wrote of a friend: "He thought and he suffered a great deal, but he lacked the strength to dare, which is the essential condition for any kind of undertaking."

9

Few are aware that Arcand, in his full-length documentaries at the NFB, wanted to do a third film to follow On est au coton *and* Québec: Duplessis et après . . . . *Dated June 1970, the project was called* Les terroristes. *It was refused and remained in limbo for over thirty years. Here it is, an unpublished ghost, risen from the tomb.*

Terrorism is a set of violent actions whose goal is to provoke terror. There may be a number of these actions, ranging from kidnapping and ransoming to murder; however, the cornerstone of terrorism is dynamiting or plastic bomb attacks.

The terrorist situation is one of violent opposition to a political regime, a social structure, an ethnic group, or all three. Most essentially it is the opposition of a MINORITY within a country's population. And it is precisely this minority position that excludes the possibility of democratic action, for example within the framework of an official political party or through a mass revolutionary organization.

It is generally agreed that terrorists are either the avant-garde of a future revolutionary party (Michel Bakunin or Serge Nietchaiev in Russia, in 1870), or the rearguard of a regressive movement (the KKK in the U.S.A. or the O.A.S. in France).

This minority position explains the use of terror. It makes it impossible for those concerned to seriously contemplate taking power. And at the same time, for ideological reasons, it is impossible for them to tolerate the existing power. Terror is the only way out and is resorted to in the hope of creating chaos and at least preventing the powers-that-be from peacefully enjoying the situation (e.g., the incidents of dynamiting in Montreal after the elections of April 29, 1970).

Hence, we understand that provoking terror has no specific objective. It is not a question of seizing such and such a village or building or taking such and such a military position for "x" amount of time, as in guerilla warfare; its only goal is to psychologically destabilize the adversary.

In other words, all powers or a party who depend or want to depend upon the support of a majority are automatically opposed to terrorism, even if their reasons and methods of opposition may differ from one another (i.e., Jérôme Choquette and René Lévesque).

It may be noted that the orthodox Marxist Left is as categorical in its condemnation of terrorism as the bourgeoisie. "We sincerely believe that terrorism is of negative value, that it by no means produces the desired effects, that it can turn people against a revolutionary movement, that it can bring a loss of lives to its agents out of proportion to what it produces" (E.C. Guevara, *Guerilla Warfare*, Random House, 1961, p. 93).

Stalin obviously went further and ordered the shooting of all known terrorists who had made attacks against the Tsarist regime, notably Iakov Blumkin, executed in 1929.

Indeed the only moderate-to-large scale political movement that does not dissociate itself from terrorism (except, for special reasons, Arab nationalist parties) was anarchism. This was probably due to the influence of Bakunin's thought and the libertarian ideology inherent in his actions (on this subject, see the film project of Hubert Aquin).

So, cut off from both Left and Right, terrorists are in a desperate situation. Moreover, history offers no examples of situations in which terrorism did, in fact, succeed in destabilizing a regime enough to make it fall. Even in Algeria, where Arab terrorist cells had the tacit and practical support of the F.L.N., these same cells were completely annihilated by French security forces at least a year before the country's liberation. The Algerian war was entirely won by the classic Maghrebian guerilla, and the popular demonstrations in the big cities, two phenomena that are totally distinct from the terrorism of Alger and Oran.

It may also be noted that in the Chinese and Cuban revolutions, to name only two, there were almost no occurrences of terrorist acts. This is because terrorism, due to its clandestine and mainly urban action, is in an extremely vulnerable position, even if it arises from a political situation in which a majority of people would be in favour of terrorism. "The suburban guerilla must be considered as situated in extremely unfavourable ground, where the vigilance of the enemy will be much greater and the possibilities of reprisals as well as of betrayal are increased enormously" (ibid., p. 30). Indeed, all clandestine action gives rise to denunciations and torture, two anti-terrorist weapons for which there is almost no possible response. Especially because of its minority political situation and its urban tactical situation, terrorism only needs to be IDENTIFIED for its defeat to become inevitable. During the Chinese and Cuban revolutions, everyone knew who Mao Tse-Tung and Fidel Castro were, but this did not curtail their actions in the least. Whereas as soon as Ali-La-Pointe was identified, the French paratroopers had no difficulty in blowing him up in the casbah of Alger. The same pattern is as applicable to Vietnam as it is to Quebec.

Thus terrorism appears to be a dead-end street for those who take that route. And yet, our hypothesis in presenting this film project is that terrorism will exist in North America for many years to come. The reason is that there is no blueprint for anyone who wishes to work towards transforming an advanced industrial society such as ours, which is not the case in underdeveloped societies or ones that are approaching industrialization. Obviously militant trade-unions, citizens' committees, political education movements and popular demonstrations represent exploratory attempts to do so, but we are well aware that in relation to society as a whole, these activities remain extremely fragmentary. They do not emerge from any coherent ideology and represent no serious possibility of succeeding, except perhaps in a very long time, ranging from 25 years to a century or even more. Thus we understand that among the "protesters," there are some who think, as J. Maynard Keynes does, that *in the long run we are all dead*, and want to accelerate the course of history. And we think that our society's tolerant and repressive unanimity, as well as the total absence of a proletariat, in the Marxist sense of the word, will drive many of these impatient and desperate individuals to plant dynamite all over the place.

Indeed, if, as we have tried to show here, the terrorist position is one of desperation, it follows that this position is generally adopted by desperate beings. All the ex-terrorists we have met put a great deal of emphasis on their personal state of mind at the moment they planted bombs: an often disturbed state of mind, in some cases aggravated by temporary psychological imbalance. However, it is certain that our society will continue to produce such individuals (on this subject, see the vaster project on the subject by Louis Portugais).

We feel that since we are going to have to live with terrorism, we might as well film it. First, because conspiracies of silence have never helped anyone. And also because it's time we knew what we were talking about when we talk about terrorism. And we talk about it a lot.

The film we are proposing would be a one or one-and-a-half hour documentary for television and the community circuit. It would be done in 16 mm and would attempt to reply to certain basic questions:

1 - who were and who are the terrorists of Quebec?
2 - what are their methods, weapons and objectives?
3 - what is their ideology?
4 - how is the special anti-terrorist brigade organized?
5 - what are the methods of this brigade?
6 - what is the job of Léo Plouffe, in charge of explosives?
7 - what are the future perspectives for terrorists, as for police?
8 - what historical lessons did the Algerians derive from their terrorist experience?

If we are submitting this project now, even before the completion of *Duplessis* (of which it is the prolongation), it is because we believe that research for such a project will take a long time and that we will have to take great care in choosing the people with whom to collaborate. It is not that the research in itself is complicated, but in order to do it well, it is important to establish a relationship of trust between the filmmakers and the persons concerned. And that could take several months of casual meetings before work can begin.

10

It is sometimes forgotten that the first version of Gina *was presented to the NFB under the title* Les Jarrets noirs *in April 1972—another interesting unpublished text, belonging to the archives of the Cinémathèque québécoise. Here are its highlights.*

Saturday, July 31, 1971, a gogo dancer named "Gina" arrived at the Motel "Les Pins" in Vallée-Jonction, in the Beauce region. The motel owner had recently hired her for a week through the "Hôtesses de Québec" agency at the corner of rue Saint-Jean and rue Saint-Stanislas in Quebec City. The Motel Les Pins is a huge building on highway 23, built in the middle of the forest. It includes a motel, a restaurant, a tavern, a bar-salon and a dance hall that can accommodate 1,200 people.

On Saturday night, "Gina" gave her first show at 9:30. Around ten o'clock, twenty members of the "Jarrets noirs" biker club of Sainte-Marie-de-

Beauce entered the premises. They wanted to force "Gina" to sit with them. She refused. Up until midnight, it appears there were several verbal exchanges between the bikers and the dancer. Shortly after midnight, the bikers left. "Gina" finished her show.

At around 3:30 a.m., "Gina" retired to the motel room that had been made available to her by the owner, according to the terms of her contract. At five o'clock in the morning, fifteen members of the "Jarret noirs" broke down the door and burst into the room. One after the other, they raped her.

At eight o'clock, Sunday morning, August 1, "Gina" made a long-distance phone call from the motel restaurant to someone in Quebec City.

At around two o'clock on Sunday afternoon, two luxurious American cars drove up in front of the Motel Les Pins. Five men get out, Jacques Ti-Caille Vaillancourt of Quebec, Guy Marchand, Pierre Bouchard, Marc Georges from Montreal, Marc Fournier from Quebec and Douglas Sykes from Giffard. They all headed to "Gina's" room and remained there for some time. Around four o'clock in the afternoon, they made a few local phone calls. They left the motel with "Gina" at around six in the evening, after eating in the restaurant. "Gina" assured the owner that she would be back in time for her evening shows.

Meanwhile, on an abandoned country road behind Sainte-Marie-de-Beauce, the members of the "Jarrets noirs" biker club were getting ready to spend a quiet evening with their girlfriends in an isolated barn they had made into their headquarters. At ten in the evening, the barn doors were thrown open and Vaillancourt, Marchand, Bouchard and the others burst in, armed with baseball bats. A battle ensued. Some of the bikers managed to flee into the woods. Gas was sprinkled throughout the barn, which was then burnt to the ground.

"Gina" never returned to the Motel Les Pins.

[. . .]

This news item has fascinated me for six months. It contains such a concentration of violence that it seems almost exemplary. Especially because this was premeditated, willed violence. These astonishing events seem to me so significant that I would like to research them in depth, with the aim of eventually writing a script for a full-length dramatic feature based on the subject. The fictional angle seems to me the only one possible in this case, due to the insurmountable legal and human complications that a documentary approach would entail.

However, an eventual fiction would not simply be a matter of "changing the names of places and persons in order to protect the innocent," as the old disclaimer goes. We must not neglect the hypothesis that research will take us further towards characters and facts that do not appear in the above-mentioned events.

I would like to apply to this situation the research methods of Truman Capote when he wrote *In Cold Blood*. The contacts I have had with some of the story's protagonists give me reason to hope that in this case, the use of such methods would be possible.

11

Arcand wrote this text as a preface for his first dramatic feature La maudite galette. *It is a kind of manifesto in which he outlines the ideas he will apply in all his later dramatic films. The piece dates from 1972.*

La maudite galette is a false action film. It is a "deconstructed" action film. Starting with a fairly sordid news story that took place in the small-time Montreal underworld, and while scrupulously respecting the phenomenology of the action, we wanted to invest the screenwriting with a reflection on the value system and social structures inherent in the characters' behaviour and the events that transpired. Indeed, it seemed to us that most films of the "action" genre are grounded in the social positions of the dominant bourgeoisie. Even when filmmakers consciously wish to move away from these positions, too often it seems that by using a form of filmic expression normally associated with the dominant line of thinking, the initial intentions are ultimately negated on screen, however worthy they may be. Thus, our objective in doing this film was to present an anecdote, in appearance conventional and consistent with the norms of commercial film, and to subvert these appearances in the staging, the cinematography, the sound recording, acting, sets, etc. Essentially, we wanted to make a film that would ring both false and true: true in each of its details but false as a whole, because we wanted to distance ourselves from the norms of conventional film. We hoped this dichotomy would produce a kind of malaise in the spectator, difficult to identify at first, caused by our modification of the filmic language itself. We wanted this malaise to provoke fertile reflection. All this is to say that we hoped to make a film that was insidiously subversive, for Quebec audiences anyway.

That was why we told ourselves while shooting that what we had to make was what Americans call a "B picture," that is, a film especially made to be shown in double features in second-rate movie theatres. A film whose titles no one reads, a film people watch while drinking soda and whose meaning would essentially be subliminal. Unfortunately, at least in North America, television has killed this type of film, so we were pretty much condemned with *La maudite galette* to make a film with a cinematic vocation, that is, an artistic film, which was not our initial goal.

But once a film is finished, it has a life of its own, independent from its makers. And in the end, things are probably better that way.

12

This bittersweet pamphlet, called Deschambault or the Country, *was written for* Le Devoir, *and published on October 28, 1972.*

Even a mildly perspicacious observer will have noticed by now that the country is very "in" among intellectuals, especially filmmakers. The directory for the general union of film workers reads like a voters' list for the rural electoral ridings. It is understandable that in their line of work, exhausting and highly technical, filmmakers need the quiet of fields in order to recuperate. And there is no need to quote Paolo Soleri to know that big cities are doomed to more or less imminent death.

That is why I have chosen to live in Deschambault, in Portneuf county. Out my window, I can see the majestic waters of our beautiful Saint Lawrence, ploughed up by oil tankers and Chris-Crafts with 110-horsepower Mercury motors. During my walks on the shore, I see silvery fish gently floating, belly up, while I deeply inhale the odour of sulphuric acid from Domtar in Donnacona and the Bathurst plant in Cap-de-la-Madeleine. On a calm evening, you can hear the distant song of the Gentilly nuclear power station and its malfunctioning cooling system. Sitting on my verandah, I am gently rocked by the rumble of nearby national highway No. 2, the hum of Mustang Mach IIs driving to the strains of "Big Daddy," the roar of semis driving to Sept-Îles at 80 miles per hour and the harmonious chords of Voyageur bus air brakes, while closer by, Honda mini-bikes plough up my flowerbeds with gusto, accompanied by a quadrille of Lawn-Boys.

In the starry sky, 747s start their descent towards Dorval, waiting for the Concordes headed for Sainte-Scholastique, while the helicopters from the Valcartier forces base frolic overhead.

The long winter evenings are cheered by the croon of Bombardier T.N.T. skidoos beneath my window, and if I go out, it is to soak my snowshoes in a bath of calcium blue. Unfortunately, some evenings the snowstorms are so violent that everything goes quiet and the countryside sinks into a chilling silence. Fortunately, I can run to my T.V. set and be instantly connected to universal culture and civilization by Lise Payette.

And what about that good country food that revives both body and soul? The apples with D.D.T., cherries laced with Malation, plums with Captan, radishes with Diazinon. And I haven't even mentioned the extraordinary culture shock caused by Portneuf pizza, Cap-Santé Chinese and Les Grondines hot chicken. There is no point either in going on and on about the intensity of human exchange and authentic cultural life of the Quebec *terroir*, from the bowling alleys of Saint-Casimir and the broomball tournament in Saint-Basile to the Royal Theatre of Donnacona, where you can see Gungala, Goddess of the Jungle.

I will conclude with a quotation from philosopher Paul Paré, "The country's the same as the city, it's just not quite so bad." Since all Quebec film directors, if they want to stay alive, are condemned to being content with the "not quite so bad," I'm sure my choice is understandable.

In 1974, UNESCO asked Denys Arcand to write a contribution for a special issue of Cultures *entitled* Le Cinéma de l'histoire (The Cinema of History). *His article is called* The problems of making historical films. *Here is the conclusion.*

The subjects of certain films may be "historical" in the sense that the characters represented on screen lived in a bygone era, but still, they exist only on film and all analysis of their existence, in the end, only sheds light on a cinematic reality. Similarly, a study of the painting "Aristotle Contemplating the Bust of Homer" would tell us nothing about ancient Greek civilization but reveal a great deal about seventeenth-century Dutch culture and how the Dutch at that time saw the ancient Greeks. Indeed, an obvious characteristic of all works of art with historical subjects is that they reveal more about the point of view of their creator and his times than they shed light on the past. The hundreds of American Westerns that have been made will never tell us anything about American Indian civilization, except for the way in which this civilization was perceived by American directors at the time they made these films.

The same can be said of all those "epic" cinema scenes in which we see Caesar's Roman army marching along in formation with identical boots and helmets, though the most basic knowledge of archaeology tells us that all Roman soldiers wore armour and carried individual weapons, and that the military march was a Prussian invention of the nineteenth century.

In this sense, a study of popular films with historical subjects can give rise to a number of interesting reflections, precisely because this kind of film is really a form of mass entertainment and is extremely revealing of popular culture. For example, an in-depth examination of French films dealing with pre-revolutionary subjects would indicate this era is depicted in a very positive way and that the excesses of Versailles, the King's suppers and the charms of life at Court, are absolutely not depicted as odious manifestations of a repressive dictatorship. We could even conclude that ideas such as those that prevailed at the time of the French Revolution, though apparently well established, have still not been assimilated by popular culture. And when progressive critics claim that French cinema is essentially bourgeois, we could argue by showing them that their national cinema, in certain ways, is not even bourgeois but is still royalist. However, let us remember here that this type of cinema is extremely costly. To make and distribute it requires enormous amounts of capital, and it is quite possible that the holders of this capital have a vested interest in making us believe history is nothing but an eternal recommencement, and that a people's well-being is in no way linked to social progress. Again on the subject of French cinema, it is quite revealing that one of the only truly progressive historical films to be produced in France, Jean Renoir's *La Marseillaise*, was made under the Front Populaire government before

World War Two. We may also note that with films of this kind, the quantity of money available is in some sense directly responsible for the film's quality (at least from a technical point of view) and thus for its success with audiences.

But cinema is an art and if, as such, it presents us with a certain view of the world, no matter how up to date this worldview may be, it can still be based on a theory of history. It is at this level that cinema and history can and should intersect. Not at the level of scientific practice or didactic method, but at the level of speculation and the philosophy of history. And here cinema will claim to be nothing more than the expression of a filmmaker's (or several filmmakers') personal vision. The film's main interest will lie in the depth, clarity and power of this vision, not in the historical reconstitution itself. A film's accuracy in relation to the real past is of no more importance than the extravagances of Caravaggio in his biblical paintings. It is of little importance whether Ivan the Terrible's followers were really the way they were portrayed by Eisenstein. More interesting is the how the filmmaker represents the evolution of Russian nationalism, and the value he gives it.

From this point of view, cinema can go a long way. One of the most highly evolved examples is certainly *The Rise to Power of Louis XIV* by Roberto Rossellini, which broaches the very complex subject of the weakening of seventeenth-century French nobility in favour of the King's personal power. The entire meaning of the film is based on a theory of history, approved and defended by Rossellini.

It is within this perspective that the dilemmas of filmic creation must be resolved. A strictly historical point of view in no way helps us choose between a tracking shot and a pan, because history, as such, offers absolutely no criteria for the codifying of values within the filmic communication system. But on the other hand, a dynamic worldview, an illumination (the mystery that is the source of all acts of creation) allows for and even imposes a logic of expression that knows whether to choose the tracking shot or the pan, according to the laws, always circumstantial, that govern its own dynamism.

Hence, we could probably say that the way for a filmmaker to combine cinema with history would be to make films based on an awareness of history. The more deeply this awareness is explored, the more certain the value of these films will be.

14

The Rigour of Sport *was first published in* La Gazette de Lausanne, *in the beginning of the 1980s, and again in the journals* Format cinéma *and* Liberté *in the same decade. Arcand revised it slightly for Radio-Canada in October 1995. The following is a translation of the version the filmmaker read on the radio documentary* Denys Arcand: Un portrait pour la radio *in February 2004.*

My job is to make films, so every day I find myself steeped in a world where fraud reigns supreme. I regularly escape into sports to recover the pleasures of rigour that my work continually denies me.

In my profession, everything is a question of opinion and fashion. Ten or fifteen years ago, the German director Wim Wenders was extremely popular. In all the world's great cities, the *beaux esprits* went on and on about *Paris, Texas* or *The Wings of Desire*. Two weeks ago, with my very own eyes, I saw one of the biggest English film distributors fight with an Italian producer for the right to remove the name Wim Wenders from a film poster, saying it was synonymous with total failure.

Numerous critics call the dance films by Spanish director Carlos Saura sheer masterpieces. Yet my friend Bernard Gosselin, a remarkable documentary film-maker with whom I shared a brief and intense passion for a Madrid dancer thirty years ago, maintains that Carlos Saura is a nobody. Several years ago, I saw Woody Allen's *Annie Hall* and had a good memory of it. Then I read the memoirs of Luis Buñuel and learned that he found *Annie Hall* lamentable. I felt like an idiot.

The situation becomes even more complicated when it comes to my own films. The newspaper *Libération* and the magazine *Les Cahiers du cinéma*, both published in Paris, France, said all my films were pathetic and that personally, I'm a cretin. However, the newspaper *Le Monde* the magazine *Positif*, also both published in Paris, have always found my films very interesting and thought I was a pretty nice guy. Some people love my documentary films and don't think much of my dramas. Others take the exact opposite position. A well-known New York reviewer claims that I'm a remarkable director but an awful screenwriter. On the other hand, some fastidious publishers are intent on publishing my screenplays, convinced they represent the most successful part of my work. Personally, I love the films of the Quebec director Jacques Leduc, but when I go see one, there are never more than twelve people in the theatre. It's all a great mystery.

On a tennis court, there's never any mystery. Boris Becker's serve is not a question of opinion. Whether you like it or not, the ball is going to come at you at a speed of 220 kilometres per hour. You have less than half a second to try to start your return. Boris Becker doesn't ask you to love him. He cares very little for the opinion you may have of him, and your perceptive comments about German expressionism do not particularly interest him. All that interests Boris Becker is whether you can return the ball or not. As you are not able to do so, he's the one who is going to win the game. And the whole idea is to win. It's simple, precise and beyond dispute. It's so much beyond dispute that sports commentators, convinced that we attach great importance to their judgments, are often reduced to imagining virtual matches between Boris Becker and Rod Laver or Pancho Gonzales. They quibble about the comparative merits of Miguel Indurain and Eddy Merckx. They wonder if Maurice Richard could have outplayed Raymond Bourque. They have opinions on all those things. Anything to escape the implacable law of sport.

In sports, I know who I am: a golfer with a handicap of fourteen, an "old-timer" hockey player, a category-four tennis player or fifteen-thirty, depending on what classification system you're using. I know this very exactly, and the people I play with know it too. We sportsmen are generally pretty humble. Too many coaches have told us too many times to "play within our means," as the expression goes.

Our bodies have irrevocably taught us that we are not in the same league as Muhammad Ali or Martina Navratilova. The body is a better learner than the mind. I have no idea of my value as a filmmaker. Depending on my mood, sometimes I find myself pretty good and at other times totally worthless. Sometimes I meet artists whom I find pretty seedy-looking yet I see in their eyes that they feel superior to me. Who is wrong? Who is right? We'll never know. If it were tennis, we would know right away. And to make it all more complicated, in art there is always the possibility of posthumous glory, as the ghosts of Stendhal and Van Gogh attest. Sport knows nothing about posthumous glory; it does not even know elderly glory. Success in sports belongs to youth, and its glory is immediate. One day, while playing in what is commonly called an industrial hockey league, in overtime I scored the goal that won my team the championship. The minute that followed this goal was the most intensely jubilatory moment of my entire life.

Yet in my profession, I have received a good many awards, and very prestigious ones at that. I have been decorated several times and in different countries. A number of famous institutions have honoured me with retrospectives of my films. But I admit that none of these tributes have given me as much utter delight as the set I won against the junior tennis champion of Florida. How to describe the pleasure of catching a touchdown pass, half-blinded by the setting sun at the end of an autumn afternoon? There are no words to describe the harmonic perfection required to hit a golf ball beyond 275 yards.

Compared to these pure and absolute pleasures, making films resembles an interminable sinking into a sticky quagmire. Particularly here in Quebec, because of the economic conditions of film production. In countries where cultural activity is partially or entirely subject to capitalist laws, the box office, sales and ratings impose a kind of logic, counterfeit though it may be, on film production. But here, where everything ultimately depends on government grants, we publish, film and produce for stage or the airwaves, anything, in any way and at any price, according to the changing opinions of our civil servants in charge of culture. All of which reinforces the sensation that everything is arbitrary and generally unreal, and perhaps it is also why poor Québécois filmmakers, standing in front of the mirror when the day is done, end up imagining that with a little more encouragement they could have become Kurosawas. At the top of the Val d'Isère ski run, only a dangerous schizophrenic, and one who will not live for very long, could imagine himself to be the equal of Mélanie Turgeon.

In competitive sports, there is no place to hide, that's why I don't like jogging, physical fitness, cross-country skiing or canoeing. I want sports that can be measured. I need them. They provide me with small certainties, points of reference that reduce the daily sensation of being cut adrift. And when on the tennis court I lose the first set at zero, and my legs and eyes tell me that I'm too old to play serve-and-volley, I can always console myself by saying that my last script is frankly pretty interesting. And later, at the first screening, when I tremble with fear, I comfort myself with the prospect of going skiing two weeks later, knowing that then, I'll really be alive.

15

The NFB and Quebec Cinema, *March 6, 1981, a letter from Denys Arcand to the Festival/Symposium on the NFB, translated by the filmmaker.*

Dear Friends,

It is very difficult for me to write coherently about the films I have made. At the outset, I didn't have the conscious intention of becoming a filmmaker. When I left university, all I knew was that I thought I'd be happy to be hired by a big daily newspaper, or by the CBC, or the National Film Board. I also like theatre a great deal, but I didn't consider it a viable choice for a livelihood. I had also thought of going into the Department of External Affairs to become a career diplomat. Another idea I had was to go to Berkeley to do a doctorate in History. By chance, I got hired by the NFB and became a film director. This occupation came easily to me and still does. I have always worked honestly, and my films have always been well received by the audiences for whom they were made, as well as by my colleagues and the critics in Canada and abroad.

The difficulties I experienced with the administration of the NFB arose, I think, partly due to the rather special way that I view society, and also because of the very nature of the Board, which is a governmental body that finds it extremely difficult to underwrite strongly personal points of view. This is especially due to the fact that the NFB, unlike the CBC, is not a Crown corporation but a government service directly under the wing of the Secretary of State. Theoretically, the NFB is the voice of the Canadian government. So one can imagine the kinds of dilemmas that sometimes arise.

As for speaking about my films as a whole, I am unable to do so. I can certainly see, in retrospect, that one could read a certain logical development into the progression of these films, and that certain themes obviously recur—my fascination with political phenomena, my concern for the struggles of the working class, my interest in a certain image of women, etc., etc. I am not really very interested in reflecting on this, however. Each of my films constitutes a new adventure, even though critics may think I am rehashing the same subjects over and over. I think one should leave to the critics what rightly belongs to them, and I also believe that a certain lack of introspection is necessary in all creative endeavour. I am quite convinced that the approach of the critic is diametrically opposed to that of the creator. I am not saying that the two functions cannot be carried out by the same person but only that they cannot be done at the same time and deal with the same subject.

So you will excuse me for not going further into this question.

Sincerely,
Denys Arcand

16

Sometimes Arcand would write to his filmmaker colleagues at Format cinéma *and* Lumières *magazines and freely discuss his craft. On February 15, 1982, he sent the following missive about his experience of working on* Comfort and Indifference.

Dear Jacques Leduc,

To say something about *Comfort and Indifference* for *Format cinéma* . . . that's a tough one. One generally replies with mechanical answers to the questions of journalists. Other than that, the film will speak for itself. Unless we've completely botched it. In which case even the best explanations . . .

A difficult shoot, as usual. Dragging yourself night after night to church basements, CEGEP gymnasiums, parish halls. The ringing of metal chairs on tiles. Sitting on the floor waiting for Jean Chrétien to arrive. Trying to enter the Liberal Party despite orders from Ryan. Trying to enter the Parti Québécois despite orders from Lévesque. Eating nothing but hamburgers, pizzas and hormone-chocked chicken. Plainclothes cops. All over the place, always. Lévesque's with little *fleurs de lys* in their buttonholes. Trudeau's with little maple leaves and wired earpieces. The Queen of England's with their big revolvers. Giscard d'Estaing's. Commissioner Pavillon. The abominable *barbouzes*, Jacques Chirac's secret police. Very dangerous, those ones! Getting thrown out of Hôtel de Ville in Paris. Never being able to film. People who refuse to talk. Who flee mikes and cameras. In Ottawa, in Quebec City. Everywhere. Knowing that anything important is going on behind closed doors. Never being able to film. Taking notes for hypothetical fiction films you'll probably never make. Politicians who lie and lie. Being introduced by chance to René Lévesque and hearing him say: "What are you doing here? What kind of nasty business are you up to now?" Getting a letter from Charpentier, Trudeau's secretary, telling me the prime minister will unfortunately never, in any place or at any time in the next four years, be able to grant me an interview. Getting sick as usual during shooting. Shooting on referendum night, stunned with fever and bourbon. Heading into the editing room for a whole year with 120 thousand feet of exposed film and hundreds of video reels. Going to the tavern every night and drinking the endless beers bought by the NFB barflies. Weeping over the sorry condition of our cinema. Phoning my wife to tell her I'm coming back Friday and that I'll buy fish on the way. Meanwhile, starting to write the script for *Maria Chapdelaine*. Reading in *Format cinéma* that to work on such projects is copping out on the more urgent matter of examining the present and future. Mentally telling *Format cinéma* to go to hell. Continuing to edit. With France Dubé, editing assistant, who is more and more pregnant the further we progress. Will the baby arrive before the film? Re-working one last sequence with editor Pierre Bernier one Saturday in July at the deserted NFB. Being blinded by the sun when I emerge in front of the boulevard Métropolitain, absolutely drained.

Reading the complete works of Machiavelli in the Pléiade edition, a loan from my brother Gabriel. Finally coming back to fiction filmmaking (after seven years) with Jean-Pierre Ronfard in Renaissance costume. What an excellent actor! What a pleasure it is, after all, this profession of ours, at times. If only we could do it a little more often . . . Jacques Paquet was the gaffer for this sequence. The maple syrup man. He died three weeks ago. I suddenly realize that I've worked with a lot of filmmakers who have died: Réo Grégoire, Hubert Aquin, Marc Beaudet, Pierre Maheu, Gilles Gascon and now Jacques Paquet. May those who wish we'd go to hell be appeased: we won't be around much longer. Meanwhile they will live to be a hundred, I'm sure. But the way we're going, that's not likely to happen to us.

Finally, learning that *Maria Chapdelaine* will probably be a Quebec co-production with Carole Laure playing the lead, and that Mr. Trudeau is going to personally help Sergio Leone shoot in Canada. Apart from that, everything is going very well. I'm the fifth highest scorer in the Career Depression Hockey League of Saint-Marc.

17

"To Be an Actor": *Contribution to a thematic issue of* Copie zéro, *October 1984*

When I was a teenager, I wanted to be an actor. Then my body betrayed me. I grew too tall, my voice was too deep, my head and nose too big, my teeth too long. A person acts with his or her body. Mine sentenced me to playing noble fathers and traitors at the age of nineteen. I realized that this would never change. My body forced characters upon me.

The greatest actors are neither short nor tall, neither fat nor thin; their voice is nothing special and they aren't particularly handsome. They are nothing when they are not acting. It is through their characters that they become handsome or ugly, short or tall. But to do that, you have to have a flexible body, which nature denied me.

What's more, this physical rigidity corresponded to an intellectual rigidity that I was starting to notice in myself. My points of view were logical, my opinions coherent, I wanted complete explanations, whereas a true actor delights in paradoxical theories, esoteric sciences, intuitive arguments. To be able to think like both Hedda Gabler and Célimène, a certain mental vagueness is absolutely necessary.

Even when I was still a teenager, I couldn't stand incompetent directors, the greatest curse of the actor's profession, which simply has to be put up with. All around me I saw pretentious characters entrusting lead roles to third-rate actors whose sole talent was servility, coming up with the most banal kind of staging and giving cretinous directions. I understood right away that at the simple economic level of supply and demand, it would be much easier to work as a director than as an actor. I received confirmation of this wise decision several years later from a newspaper vendor at the Algonquin Hotel in New York, that hot spot of American culture. This remarkable woman asked me if I was an actor. When I said I was a director she exclaimed: "You did the right thing; it's so much more stable!" I might add that I have always believed myself gifted with a quality that is essential in my line of work: an ear, the ability to discern good dialogue from false in both writing and acting. I feel I came by this talent in the same way that others naturally sing on key or dance with perfect rhythm. I don't know if it's a very important quality, but I still cannot help but shudder when I see a director approach an actor on set saying, "Here, you stop and you say to him . . .," and then performing the lines himself. To me, this reduces the profession of actor to that of imitator and shows an atrocious lack of respect. And yet it happens all the time.

I can't stand the expression "to direct actors." I find it repugnant. I've never directed anyone. Being very fond of sports analogies, I might compare my craft with that of a football coach and say that my main role is to choose the players. Half the game is right there, in not choosing the wrong actors and being able to coldly evaluate talent, especially in the case of young actors. You have to measure this talent in terms of temperament. They say the best football players, when they don't go to the stadium on Sunday afternoons, go play football. You have to choose actors who show up first of all to play, not worry about the Venice Festival or write-ups in *Écho-Vedettes*. You also have to like to gossip a bit in order to ascertain the various degrees of cocaine or alcohol addiction, the imminence of conjugal crises, the progress or failure of a psychoanalysis, etc. After that, you have to establish a game plan and keep everyone's spirits up. Certain actors have to be challenged, others coddled, it depends on the individual. But it's never the coach who runs, who is hit, who is injured, who scores. Just as it is never the director whose wrinkles and tears we see. It is the actors who are seen, scrutinized, loved or hated. Without the actor's person, all representation is impossible. That is why they are sacred.

I really like actors. They are beautiful, generous, vulnerable and completely crazy. Generally, I only see them on set. First of all, because I find it difficult to take their emotional intensity for long and also because my relationship with them is compromised by the fact that I can, upon occasion, get them work. In Montreal, the majority of actors are always more or less unemployed. I know actors and actresses of prodigious talent who live off social security payments most of the time. When I meet them, I always feel mute expectations that I can rarely satisfy or silent reproaches that make me feel guilty. It's all very complicated.

18

This speech has a rather special history. It was delivered by Arcand when The Decline of the American Empire *was presented at the opening of the Toronto Film Festival in September 1986. Thus began the film's triumphal journey, though only a few months earlier no one had believed in it much. The text was written in English.*

Ladies and gentlemen, this film originated at the National Film Board in Montreal where my friend Roger Frappier was then a producer. He offered me a contract to write a small personal film. That's how I got the idea of writing about my sex life. It's highly personal and it's limited enough so that we could avoid hiring hundreds of extras and building large and expensive sets. Normal bedrooms would do. As soon as the script was finished it became evident that the Film Board had to look outside for a co-producer. Mostly, I guess, for fear of having to explain to the federal minister of communications why a respectable government agency would dabble in such smut. Especially since that same minister would have to somehow relay the information to John Crosbie, and maybe even possibly to the Ontario Censorship Board.

So we found a co-producer in Mister René Malo, but this meant that the script had to be read by the professional readers of Telefilm Canada and Quebec's *Société du cinéma*. The readers were unanimous: they thought it was the worst script that ever came across their desk. No dramatic action, stuffed with elitist references, unsavoury characters, aimed at no more than two percent of the box office. They could find none of the qualities that they had found, for instance, in *Porky III* or *Meatballs II*.

On a personal level, my faithful assistant director, with whom I had done all my previous films, said that this script was below his personal threshold of acceptability, while underlining the fact that his threshold was remarkably low since he spent the greater part of the year working on American movies-of-the-week shot in Toronto and Vancouver. So we hired a new assistant, who came in saying that his wife had just had a baby and he needed the money. My very own sister said that the reading of that script had brought tears of boredom to her eyes, and though she admitted that writing it had probably been beneficial to me since it was obviously a manifestation of my midlife crisis, she added that shooting it was certainly an extravagant kind of therapy. She suggested the names of a few psychoanalysts. Through all of this, my producers kept faith in me, although disagreeing very violently about most of my casting choices and the title I had chosen. In short, we were heading for disaster when shooting began.

I have been asked to tell a few anecdotes about the shooting. What can I tell you? There was, of course, a lot of coke on the set; the production manager had a sweet deal with the local soft-drink bottler, and there was even some stronger stuff around since the key grip had an espresso machine in his truck. We discovered needles in Dominique's bag and we realized she was heavily into knitting. I saw the sweater she knit for herself during shooting, and it's quite becoming, I can assure you. We went to a few restaurants together, and some of us had a glass of liqueur after dessert. That was certainly a highlight. We had a wild wrap party where a classical guitarist played some Bach, and when some young production assistants put on some louder music to dance to, most of the crew left. That was around nine-thirty.

As soon as this film was finished, we tried to enter it into competition at the Cannes Film Festival in France. It was immediately refused by the festival director, saying that from Canadian filmmakers he had expected large vistas, Mounties, polar bears and maybe some seal hunting for dramatic enhancement, but certainly not bedroom comedies, which belong exclusively to French filmmakers, as everybody knows or should know. The film somehow got into the Festival through the back door, in the non-competitive section, where it won the Critics' Award. Knowing the critics, they were probably drunk or stoned out of their minds at the time.

Or maybe the other films were very bad, or they hadn't seen all of them, or they had a collective temporary mental lapse. And this prize was not really important—who are the critics, anyway? What do they know? Knowledgeable people knew that the real test was the general public. No way were they going to like such a highbrow product.

Then we opened in Quebec, and in one week we broke the standing record of *Raiders of the Lost Ark*, then we sold to twenty-five countries, and Hollywood called me, and suddenly it turned out that everybody had believed in this film from the very beginning. It seems they only expressed objections in order to push me into excellence. I discovered to my amazement how many secret admirers I had had all these years without ever suspecting it. This was a very heartwarming experience.

I even overheard people saying that the success was entirely predictable. Sex will sell. Anybody knows that. A lady this afternoon in the press conference said that this was just a Canadian *Big Chill*, no big deal. Some people are beginning to say that it's a very clever commercial operation. They find the "packaging" quite effective.

And here I am tonight opening this prestigious festival, hoping that you liked this little film, not so much for me or for the five actors who played in it, but mostly for all those people who can spot a sure-fire hit when they see one. Please don't disappoint them. Thank you.

19

Found among the filmmaker's papers Memories of the Directors' Fortnight *is an unpublished text that dates from the end of the eighties.*

I only vaguely remember my time at Cannes in 1973 for the presentation of *Réjeanne Padovani.* I remember losing the address of the cinema where the Fortnight was held at that time, and arriving at the screening just as the audience was leaving. Pierre-Henri Deleau tried to introduce me all the same to those who had not yet left. I believe that the film had been quite well received for I was invited to lunch several days later on the terrace of a big hotel by Claude Mauriac, which greatly impressed me. I was staying in a modest hotel where the owner, having read an article full of praise about me, had my breakfast ration increased from one to two croissants. That was the kind of mark of consideration to which I was sensitive.

Other than that, I saw no other films and met no other filmmakers, though in ten days I met a lot of young women I fell hopelessly in love with, I drank Olympic quantities of alcohol, and consumed industrial doses of drugs, each more hallucinogenic than the ones before. In short, I was young.

In 1986, for *Le déclin de l'empire américain*, again I almost missed the projection, this time because the crowd pressing up against the doors of the old Palais prevented me from entering. I was rescued by Pierre-Henri Deleau assisted by a few policemen.

I spent the next ten days holed up in a room in the Carleton giving interviews. I saw no other films and met no other filmmakers. I fell in love with no one and I drank a lot of fruit juice. In short, I had gotten older.

20

This is an interesting unpublished text that explains Arcand's interest in doing film work for advertising. It's a talk given to a group of businesspeople and filmmakers in Toronto in December 1987 called "Filmmakers and Advertising."

To start off this round table and the discussion that will follow, I have been asked to say a few words about the relationship between film directors and the world of advertising. Like my colleagues here today, I'm a professional film director, and as such I have made all kinds of films, in all lengths and formats. In the past few years, I have made only feature films and commercials, which are the two types of film I find most satisfying, in every way.

There are four main reasons that I do commercials. The first one is money. And I don't think that's anything to be ashamed of. It is certainly for my work in advertising that I make the most money, and unless I'm mistaken, the circulation of money, from the consumer to the producer, is what drives the whole advertising machine.

The second reason is the pleasure of filming. I make films because it's what I like doing best, and for me a commercial is a film. So generally, it gives me pleasure to shoot it. What's more, to deliver a message, as I had to do recently, within the very precise time limit of sixty, thirty or even fifteen seconds, represents a very stimulating filmic challenge. I believe it's essential for a director to film quite often in order to stay in shape. And as features only come along every two years, or at even longer intervals, unfortunately, commercials give us a chance to stay in touch with our craft.

The third reason is that advertising gives me a chance to explore all the latest technical innovations in audio-visual communications. Advertising budgets are often quite high, which allows me to experiment with equipment and methods of shooting or finishing a film to which I would not otherwise have access.

The fourth reason is that shooting commercials also allows me to meet new actors and technicians. The last campaign I worked on allowed me to audition over one hundred and fifty new actors I had never met before, and it is certain I will draw on that wealth of acquaintance one day. The same goes for directors of photography, sound engineers, et cetera.

Now, I would like to be able to tell you there is a fifth reason: that working on commercials gives me a chance to develop my creative resources, use all my talents and my knowledge of film. But unfortunately, this is rarely the case.

And I'd like to complain about this for a moment.

Too often, it seems, directing a commercial is considered to be the simple execution of a concept that has been thought up, written down, and timed to the last second, drawn up on a storyboard and sold to the client, without the director ever being involved in this process. In this case, the director becomes a simple technician and I think it's too bad, because he has an experience of the image, specific to his craft, which the copywriter does not possess, no matter how much of a film-enthusiast he may be.

For example, I remember doing a spot that was supposed to contain twenty-nine shots in thirty seconds. Twenty-nine unconnected shots. I'd told the copywriter that in my opinion, the spot would be totally incomprehensible for the viewer. I was told to mind my own business, that the client had already accepted everything, and to go shoot my twenty-nine shots just the way they were drawn on the storyboard. Which is what I did, and then I went home. Naturally the ad was absolutely incomprehensible and was reworked four or five times, each time to reduce the number of shots. Which of course is what I'd foreseen would happen from the start. But having said this, the production company was pretty happy because it was making a fortune with all the reworking of the final cut.

On the other hand, last summer, while working on a campaign in which I was involved in the actual creative process, while holding auditions I realized that one of the ads they wanted me to shoot was unplayable by the actors; or in any case, its result was disappointing. I suggested to the copywriters that they rework their concept. As there was a climate of trust between us, they immediately accepted and came back with a totally different proposition that turned out very well and was entirely to the client's satisfaction.

My colleagues will be able to give you fifty other examples like the ones I have just cited. For the moment, all I wanted to say is that in my opinion, there must be a symbiosis between the work of the copywriter and that of the director. To me it is essential to achieve this goal if we are to improve the quality of our product. The trio of copywriter, producer and director should be involved right from the start of a project. All directors I've spoken to are absolutely convinced of it. And they are also convinced that current procedure for submissions—or "pitches," as we say in the lingo—has to be changed. Our European colleagues will later be able to talk to us about the situation in their countries, but it is clear that creative people here are not satisfied with the submission procedure.

For me it would be out of the question to go "audition" before a committee and try to prove I can do better than Jean Beaudin or Jean-Claude Lord, to name only those who are present today. Moreover, I don't do better, I do differently. As far as the three of us are concerned, we have different personalities, different styles and different work methods. Outside of advertising, we make very different films.

It seems to me that the decision-makers at ad agencies should, from the outset, be quite familiar with our work so they can choose a director in terms of the style of ad they want to do, and not in terms of a fake contest that nobody wins.

The submission is part of a modus operandi used by big administrations for the supplying of goods and services. To use it in a creative context is an aberration. As for the issue of controlling production costs, it isn't exactly in my line of expertise, but no doubt the producers who are with us today will have suggestions to make on the subject.

I would also like to present a few reflections on the rivalry between Montreal and Toronto in the advertising domain. This subject does not concern our European colleagues and I apologize, but here it is a pretty hot topic and I wouldn't be pleased with myself if I ignored it.

As far as film in general is concerned, Quebec, with about a quarter of the national production, generally walks away with sixty to seventy-five percent of all annual awards from all the national competitive film and television festivals. In the international festivals, the figure increases to nearly eighty percent. In the last five years, Quebec films have also enjoyed a solid reputation abroad. It seems this is rarely the case in the advertising world, where people still fawn over Toronto "creativity."

An anecdote on this subject. Recently, as well as several years ago, I had the opportunity of working on commercials with two of the most famous directors of photography from Toronto. These two men had filmed the most famous spots in all of Canadian advertising. Arriving on set, they both took me aside and said: "You know, I only agreed to work on these spots in order to meet you. It's extraordinary what you do here in Montreal. In Toronto, we always make the same old shit. Obviously, I know you've got fantastic directors of photography here, but if ever an opening comes up on one of your films, please think of me." Need I add that all this was said far out of the earshot of both agency reps and producer, who had to pay colossal salaries to these two unhappy men and who would soon go into ecstasies over the quality of their work. I am the first to recognize and appreciate this quality, though emphasize that numerous Montreal cinematographers could provide a similar quality of work.

All this is to say that there is a certain conservatism in the world of advertising that I sometimes find regrettable. You have to have a very big reputation and a lot of authority to succeed in getting those in charge to accept technicians whom we know to be extraordinarily competent but whose advertising experience is limited. "I want to see his cassette" is the final *pronunciamiento* in the advertising Inquisition.

This attitude is the product of the idea, so often brought up, that advertising and film have virtually nothing in common. "He may be good in film, but advertising is another story" is a phrase I've heard a thousand times over. In my opinion, this idea is false. It's true that the goals and methods are different, but a camera is still a camera, the Kodak film the same, framing the image is framing the image, an actor is an actor, and editing is still subject to the same rules. How to explain that our colleagues in Europe go back and forth between film and advertising without batting an eye (and I will spare you the exhaustive list of all the famous filmmakers of Europe who do this, starting with Fellini), and that in the United States, the most prestigious spots are saved for Mike Nichols or Ridley Scott.

Naturally, in the United States, a certain day-to-day kind of production is taken care of by specialists who do only advertising, but I think this situation is primarily caused by geographical factors, the agencies in New York and Chicago being too far from Los Angeles. In any case, Torontonians' servility to the American model to me has always seemed their most serious fault. I believe it represents a trap that could prove very dangerous for us.

I would like to conclude by wishing all of us, both filmmakers and ad agents, a better mutual understanding, greater trust, a better knowledge of our strengths and limitations, so that more of our remarkable Montreal creative resources can be found more often in our commercials. And I believe that is most likely to happen when we start bringing the professionals together, especially copywriters, producers and directors. Thank you.

21

Acceptance speech for an award from the Association des réalisateurs de television (Quebec Television Directors' Association), Autumn 1990. Previously unpublished.

I thank you for this honour. I am especially touched to be receiving this award from you, the directors. The value of an award is directly related to the qualities of the people from whom one receives it. As you may know, I've won more than my share of awards in the past few years, but the one you are presenting me with this evening touches me in a different way than if, say, it had been presented by journalists or critics, about whom the very least I can say is that I have mixed feelings. There's nothing more pleasant than the acknowledgment of people in the same line of work as oneself, a difficult line of work that only we can really judge.

If there is one message that I would like to leave with you this evening, it is a message of solidarity. I have been a professional director for almost thirty years and in that time, I have gone through almost the entire range of work a director can possibly do. First I directed documentaries for schools at the NFB, and then I directed animation films and short films for the movie theatres. I participated in multimedia shows for Expo 67, I wrote feature film scripts, one year I even wrote a téléroman for Radio-Canada. I directed documentaries for television, I directed documentaries for theatrical release, I wrote a TV miniseries and directed two others. I've often directed commercials and obviously, I've directed "fiction" films. I've worked in French and English. I've worked in all the film formats, from 16 mm to 70 mm, and almost all the video formats, from two-inch Ampex to Betacam. In fact, the only thing I am not familiar with is live television, but I'm sure I could learn fairly quickly.

What I wanted to say with this long enumeration is that for me, despite the technical variations these different kinds of work involve, I've always basically felt I was doing the same job, that of director, that is, of trying to structure a series of images in such a way as to convey information and emotion. While directing a theatre production for the first time this autumn, I again felt I was learning more about my craft.

It is always others, our enemies, who want to shut us up in restrictive categories. From my bosses, my employers, I have heard remarks like: "You've just made documentaries, directing actors is a whole other thing." From the authorities at Radio-Canada I heard: "You've only worked in film, television is a whole other thing." The ad agencies told me: "You've just made *films d'auteur*, commercials are a whole other thing." For them, everything is always *a whole other thing*. They all have the nasty habit of ascribing to us a degree of incompetence as great as their own.

And that's not counting that we are obliged to defend ourselves before journalists who are perpetually alarmed by their own insecurities: "You've only done short films, aren't you afraid of tackling a feature?"—"Aren't you afraid of tackling the character of Duplessis?"—"Your last film was such a success, you must be afraid of starting another?"—"Aren't you scared by a budget of four million?"—"At your age, with your reputation, doesn't it scare you to start doing theatre?" It's as if one were to ask Guy Carbonneau or Stéphane Richer: "Aren't you scared of playing hockey?"

All this to say that as all of us here this evening share the same profession, I think we must show solidarity and be prepared to support each other, we must refuse the false hierarchies that some would like to impose upon us. Directing a feature film is basically the same job as directing the evening news. If you can do one, and if by some chance you want to do the other, there's no reason you shouldn't. I believe we must feel we are part of the same family. And speaking for myself, I feel I'm with family here among you. Thank you.

22

Montreal. *Text included in the Cinémathèque québécoise monograph*, Montréal, ville de cinéma, 1992.

I do not quite understand why I like Montreal. Maybe it's just because I've lived here for a long time and we often end up liking things to which we have become accustomed.

Apart from a few dreary English and Scottish merchants in the nineteenth century, there have never been rich people in Montreal. It's a poor city that has been built up with a compensatory architecture: miniature imitations of Notre Dame de Paris and San Pietro of Rome. It is a city without monuments, without fountains, without museums, without concert halls and without theatres. The theatre troupes, however, are very active, playing in cinemas or disaffected music-halls. There is even one that has moved into an old synagogue and another into a fire station. The parks are few in number and without interest. There's nothing to see or do in Montreal. Tourists are few and far between.

The city is built along a river that we hardly even notice, hidden as it is by factories and rundown warehouses. The houses, built every which way, are small and stone or brick-clad, panelled with wood or with anything at all. The apartments are generally narrow and dark. It is a workers' city.

The climate is abominable: humid and oppressive heat in summer, Siberian cold in winter. The streets are constantly being torn apart by freezing and melting. No famous artist has ever lived in Montreal, nor any great scientist. It is an anonymous, grey city.

On the other hand, Montreal is not a provincial city. It does not have its sights set on any capital. London and Paris are too far away, New York is too different. Montreal is oddly autonomous, maybe because its population is so such diverse in origin. All references to a metropolis have become impossible.

We define Montreal in mostly negative terms. The traffic and pollution are not as bad as elsewhere. Traffic jams are practically non-existent. Violence and poverty are less obvious, social inequality less striking, racism more discreet.

Montreal's only real charm is Montrealers. They are generally peaceful and mild. Without great ambition, they tend to their affairs in a justifiably relaxed manner. The great debates that stir up the rest of humanity have no hold over them. They try to work as little as possible, and they succeed. They loved the 1967 World Exhibition and the Olympic Games in 1976. The most obscure anniversary is reason enough for a party. There is some kind of "international festival" each week.

With neither a glorious past nor a promising future, they are hardly chauvinistic about their city. Their toponymy has been borrowed from Catholic martyrology, and British military or pontifical history (rue de Mentana!)

Life in Montreal is quiet for most people. They seem to like it that way. Me too.

23

Two Hollywood Memories. *A letter to filmmaker friends at* Lumières *magazine, February, 1992.*

The vice-president of Paramount Pictures slowly swivelled his chair to face me: "There's something you have to understand. In this city, we don't make films, we make money. Film is an art practised in Europe and formerly in Japan, and maybe in your country too, I don't know, the only Canadian film I've seen is yours. It's not that we don't like film. On the contrary, we watch a lot of foreign films and often admire them; that's the reason you're here today. But unfortunately our situation does not allow us to make films. We manufacture products. If you clearly understand this difference, you'll have no trouble adapting. Paramount is a division of Gulf and Western (this was in 1987). Every quarter, our president, Frank Mancuso, has to go to New York and appear before the Board, and he has to show a profit, as in the petrochemical sector, the hotel and insurance sectors, and so on. A deficit that lasts more than six months means the president is automatically dismissed, along with all his key associates. Having said this, since we like film, we occasionally try to make one, but only when we've just made a gigantic profit that will allow us to lose a little money without risking too much. For example, at the moment, the profits from *Top Gun*, which exceed the Gross National Product of three-quarters of the countries in the United Nations, might allow us to be a little more daring. I hasten to add, this is an unusual situation. If you clearly understand what I've just explained to you, and you still want to work here, I'm sure you'll manage to do so with no difficulty. Your film proves beyond all doubt that you know your craft, and we're always looking for competent people. If on the other hand you want to make films in the artistic sense of the word, I recommend that you go back to your country and continue to make magnificent films that we will always view with great pleasure, I assure you."

I was at a very "in" restaurant in Beverly Hills with one of the hottest screenwriters. He had just seen one of my films and was analyzing the script out loud. "You know how you could have improved your story?" he said, and fired off two brilliant suggestions which, indeed, would have made my film better. "In future, I'll have to come see you before I shoot anything," I said. He replied, smiling: "I'm always completely available. My consultation fee is three hundred and fifty thousand dollars US per script. Just give me a shout." He winked at me and raised his Cajun martini.

24

Do we know many artists who supported the Philosophy teachers in Quebec colleges when the State threatened to eliminate their courses from the curriculum? Unpublished text, 1995.

The abolition of Philosophy teaching is entirely consistent with our provincial policies as a whole. Is it really necessary to know Plato to be a founder of an aluminum foundry in Sept-Îles? Do we need to study Spinoza to operate a bulldozer in James Bay? Is it useful to be familiar with the works of Leibniz to assemble Chevrolets in Sainte-Thérèse? Is it essential to read Emmanuel Kant to root for the Expos? Can the practice of Hegel help you fill out unemployment insurance forms? Do the ideas of Wittgenstein help you obtain welfare payments more quickly? Sawers of wood and carriers of water don't need philosophy.

25

Paper for a conference on literature. Bologna, 1995.

Milan Kundera apparently said that the sign of a great work of literature was that it could not be adapted to film. And indeed, *Ulysses*, *A Hundred Years of Solitude*, *The Man Without Qualities*, *The Magic Mountain* have all been spared so far. But there are still people mad enough to have filmed *À la recherche du temps perdu*, and even the great Visconti wasted months trying to do adapt this work (so perhaps Jacques Godbout should be happy that his works have never been adapted to film, and Monique Proulx may have cause to worry). Great films are almost always original works. There are no novels called *Citizen Kane*, *The Battleship Potemkin* or *8 1/2*.

Literary language is radically untranslatable to film. Suppose that a novel began with the sentence, "It was very cold in Bologna that spring." How would you film this sentence that takes three seconds to read? How do you film the cold? You can't put in snow, it's not snowing, it's just cold. You can have people shivering, but who? And how? You can't give the impression that they're sick. And how do you say Bologna? A typical view of the old centre-town? But only the Bolognese and people who have been to Bologna will know what city it is. A sign in front of the train station or next to a highway? Not very original. And springtime, how do you film the spring? Flowers? But there are also flowers in the summer. A kind of flower that only blooms in spring? There again, only botanists know what's going on. A sentence that takes three seconds to read requires a clumsy sequence that is at least a minute long, etc.

Cinema has a language all its own, a way of taking possession of the world, a hyper-real and discontinuous vision that constitutes something totally original in the domain of artistic discourse.

What causes confusion is the fact that cinema, like theatre in the old days, is perpetually seeking "arguments," as they say in opera, that is, dramatic structures, unexpected incidents, anecdotes, conflicts, dénouements: elements that abound in works of literature but do not in themselves constitute the essence of these works, which is writing.

This is the origin of the Hollywood axiom: the better the novel, the less successful the film, and vice versa: the more lamentable the novel, the greater the film's chances of being a success. An airport novel, poorly written with a dime-a-dozen story involving just one basic action, is always closer to a good filmscript than *The Brothers Karamazov* will ever be.

Moreover, when we talk about "adapting" something to film, the wording hints at a kind of unconscious contempt for cinema, as if the "work" came first, the supreme work, which of course is literary and must be "adapted," that is, simplified, watered down. It's as if one were asking film to play the role of illustration, in the way that novels in the old days were ornamented with drawings and etchings.

Since the making of a film is a complicated business and requires a lot of money, it is always easier to convince investors when you can show them a novel that already exists, especially if this novel has been successful. A producer, even one who's not very intelligent, will always be receptive to the latest winner of the Goncourt, the Booker or the Pulitzer Prize.

My last film, *Love and Human Remains*, was adapted from a play. A play's conversion to film is always more natural than that of a novel. Cinema is in fact a descendent of the theatre, in the sense that actors have only dialogue with which to express themselves. And in this case, the job has been made easier because the author's cultural references are almost entirely based on American movies and comic books. And in fact, this young man started in theatre simply because for him it was the only option available at the time. He could write scenes from his life and have friends perform them in the garage. Today he has become a screenwriter and eventually wants to direct.

26

Why make films? *Around the mid-nineties, after* Love and Human Remains, *Arcand replied to the following questionnaire. Fragments of an unpublished interview.*

1. Do you ever watch your own films?
Never. My old films don't interest me. It's the next one that concerns me.

2. Why do you make films?
For no reason. Because it's my job. Because I don't know how to do anything else. Because there are people crazy enough to pay me for filming. Because it's a pleasant way to wait for death.

3. If there are no more social structures, what values remain?
We have no more values because we haven't yet reconciled ourselves to the idea that God doesn't exist. Art and love help me live, but that's not a solution that agrees with everyone. We're drifting.

4. How do you explain the great success of The Decline and Jesus of Montreal
Success cannot be explained. It's magic. No one understands it; if they did, everyone would be successful.

5. Is Jesus of Montreal a tribute to Christian principles and values?
Jesus Christ is my favourite historical character. What he had to say is unique and I'm touched by it every day. Catholicism is an organized religion, detestable as all organized religions are.

6. Can you explain the contradictions between the view of love in Jesus of Montreal and that of Love and Human Remains?
It's because I'm not talking about the same people or the same milieu. I see no "contradiction." It's as if you were to compare in the works of Shakespeare (and I'm not comparing myself to him!), the lightness of As You Like It *with the darkness of* Macbeth.

FILMOGRAPHY

DIRECTING

À L'EST D'EATON – 1959. 20 minutes. 16mm. Black and white. *Director:* Denys Arcand and Stéphane Venne. Amateur film (now lost).

SEUL OU AVEC D'AUTRES – 1962. 64 minutes. 16mm. Black and white. *Executive producers*: Georges Lefebvre. *Producer:* Denis Héroux. *Production:* Association générale des étudiants de l'Université de Montréal. *Director:* Denys Arcand, Denis Héroux and Stéphane Venne. *Scriptwriters:* Denys Arcand and Stéphane Venne. *Cinematography:* Michel Brault, assisted by Jean-Pierre Payette. *Music:* Stéphane Venne, interpreted by François Cousineau. *Editor:* Gilles Groulx, assisted by Bernard Gosselin. *With:* Nicole Braün, Pierre Létourneau, Michelle Boulizon, Marie-José Raymond, Guy Rocher, Marc Laurendeau, Marcel Saint-Germain.

CHAMPLAIN – 1964. 28 minutes. 16mm. Colour. *Production:* National Film Board of Canada. *Director:* Denys Arcand. *Scriptwriter:* Denys Arcand. *Cinematography*: Bernard Gosselin, assisted by Gilles Gascon. *Illustrations*: Frédéric Back. *Animation cameras:* Doug Poulter and James Wilson, assisted by M. Fallen and J. Chouinard. *Music:* The Montreal Brass Quintet and Kenneth Gilbert. *Editing:* Werner Nold and Bernard Gosselin. *Commentary:* Gisèle Trépanier and Georges Dufaux.

LES MONTRÉALISTES (VILLE-MARIE) – 1965. 27 minutes. 16mm. Colour. *Executive producer*: Fernand Dansereau. *Production:* André Belleau for the National Film Board of Canada. *Director:* Denys Arcand. *Scriptwriter:* Andrée Thibault. *Advisors:* Gustave Lanctôt and Maurice Careless. *Cinematography:* Bernard Gosselin, assisted by Jacques Leduc, with the participation of Michel Brault. *Music:* The Renaissance Singers of Montreal, directed by Donald Mackey. *Electronic music:* Pierre Henry and Pierre Schaeffer. *Editor:* Monique Fortier. *Commentary:* Gisèle Trépanier and Gilles Marsolais.

LA ROUTE DE L'OUEST (THE WESTWARD ROAD) – 1965. 28 minutes. 16mm.

Colour. *Producer:* André Belleau for the National Film Board of Canada. *Director:* Denys Arcand. *Scriptwriter:* Denys Arcand. *Advisors:* Gustave Lanctôt and Maurice Careless. *Cinematography:* Bernard Gosselin. *Music:* Kenneth Gilbert, Olav Harstad, Sorcha ni Ghuairim and La Société de musique d'autrefois. *Editing:* Werner Nold. *Commentary:* Christian Delmas.

MONTRÉAL, UN JOUR D'ÉTÉ (MONTREAL ON A SUMMER'S DAY) – 1965. 12 minutes. 35mm. Colour. *Executive producer:* Raymond-Marie Léger. *Production company:* Office du film du Québec. *Director:* Denys Arcand. *Images:* Bernard Gosselin. *Music:* Stéphane Venne. *Editing:* Denys Arcand.

VOLLEYBALL – 1966. 13 minutes. 35mm. Black and white. *Line producer:* Guy-L. Côté. *Producer:* Jacques Bobet for the National Film Board of Canada. *Director:* Denys Arcand. *Cinematography:* Jean-Claude Labrecque, Gilles Gascon, Jean Roy and Thomas Vamos. *Sound:* Bill Graziadei, Jacques Drouin, Ron Alexander and Roger Lamoureux. *Music:* Claude Léveillée and Les Pharaons. *Editing:* Denys Arcand.

The same year, Arcand shot images that were presented as clips at the Quebec Pavilion, Expo 67.

PARCS ATLANTIQUES (ATLANTIC PARKS) – 1967. 17 minutes. 35mm. Colour. *Producers:* Jacques Bobet and André Belleau. Produced for Parks Canada, National Historic Sites and Monuments, Department of Native and Northern Affairs. *Director:* Denys Arcand. *Based on an idea by:* Jacques Bobet. *Cinematography:* Gilles Gascon, assisted by Roger Rochat. *Music:* François Cousineau. *Editing:* Denys Arcand, assisted by Pierre Bernier. *With the participation of:* Marie-José Décarie, Jean Décarie and Jérôme Décarie.

ON EST AU COTON – 1971. 159 minutes. 16mm. Black and white. *By* Denys Arcand, Serge Beauchemin, Pierre Bernier, Alain Dostie, Gérald Godin, Pierre Mignot. *Line producer:* Guy-L. Côté. *Producers:* Marc Beaudet and Pierre Maheu for the National Film Board of Canada. *Director:* Denys Arcand. *Research:* Gérald Godin. *Cinematography:* Alain Dostie and Pierre Mignot. *Editing:* Pierre Bernier. The original version from 1970 was 173 minutes.

LA MAUDITE GALETTE – 1971. 100 minutes. 35mm. Colour. *Executive producer:* Pierre Lamy. *Producer:* Marguerite Duparc for Cinak, Les Films Carle-Lamy and France-Film. *Director:* Denys Arcand, assisted by André Corriveau and Monique Gervais. *Scriptwriter:* Jacques Benoit. *Cinematography:* Alain Dostie. *Music:* Michel Hinton, Gabriel Arcand and Lionel Thériault. *Editing:* Marguerite Duparc. *Art direction:* Jacques Méthé. *Main cast:* Luce Guilbeault, Marcel Sabourin, René Caron, J.-Léo Gagnon, Jean-Pierre Saulnier, Gabriel Arcand, Maurice Gauvin, Andrée Lalonde.

QUÉBEC: DUPLESSIS ET APRÈS (QUEBEC: DUPLESSIS AND AFTER) – 1972. 115 minutes. 16mm. Black and white. *A film by* Denys Arcand, Serge Beauchemin, Pierre Bernier, Alain Dostie, Jacques Drouin, Réo Grégoire, Pierre Letarte, Pierre Mignot, André Théberge. *Producer:* Jacques Larose for the National Film Board of Canada. *Director:* Denys Arcand. *Research:* André Théberge. *From an idea by:*

Pierre Maheu. *Cinematography:* Alain Dostie, Réo Grégoire, Pierre Letarte and Pierre Mignot. *Sound:* Serge Beauchemin and Jacques Drouin. *Editing:* Denys Arcand and Pierre Bernier. *Actors/narrators:* Gisèle Trépanier and Robin Spry.

RÉJEANNE PADOVANI – 1973. 94 minutes. 35mm. Colour. *Producer:* Marguerite Duparc for Cinak. *Director:* Denys Arcand. *Scriptwriter:* Denys Arcand with Jacques Benoit. *Cinematography:* Alain Dostie assisted by Louis de Ernsted and Michel Caron. *Music:* Willibald Gluck and Walter Boudreau interpreted by Margot MacKinnon. *Editing:* Marguerite Duparc and Denys Arcand. *Art direction:* Robert Scheen and Louis Ménard. *Main cast:* Luce Guilbeault, Jean Lajeunesse, Pierre Thériault, Frédérique Collin, Roger Lebel, Jean Pierre Lefebvre, René Caron, J-Léo Gagnon, Margot MacKinnon, Gabriel Arcand, Jean-Pierre Saulnier.

GINA – 1975. 94 minutes. 35mm. Colour/Black and white. *Executive producer:* Luc Lamy. *Producer:* Pierre Lamy for Les Productions Carle-Lamy. *Director:* Denys Arcand. *Scriptwriter:* Denys Arcand, with the participation of Jacques Poulin, Alain Dostie and Jacques Benoît. *Cinematography:* Alain Dostie, assisted by Louis de Ernsted, Michel Caron and André Gagnon. *Music:* Michel Pagliaro and Barbara Benny. *Editing:* Denys Arcand with Pierre Bernier. *Art Direction:* Michel Proulx, assisted by Jacques Chamberland. *Cast:* Céline Lomez, Claude Blanchard, Frédérique Collin, Gabriel Arcand, Serge Thériault, Jocelyn Bérubé, Paule Baillargeon, Roger Lebel, Louise Cuerrier.

LA LUTTE DES TRAVAILLEURS D'HÔPITAUX – 1976. 28 minutes. 16mm. Black and white. *A film by* Denys Arcand, Jacques Blain, Ronald Brault, Alain Dostie, François Gill. *Production:* Production Prisma and the Confédération des syndicats nationaux (CSN). *Director:* Denys Arcand. *Cinematography:* Ronald Brault and Alain Dostie. *Sound:* Jacques Blain. *Editing:* François Gill.

LE CONFORT ET L'INDIFFÉRENCE (COMFORT AND INDIFFERENCE) – 1981. 109 minutes. 16mm. Colour. *A film by* Denys Arcand, Pierre Bernier, Alain Dostie, Serge Beauchemin. *Production:* Roger Frappier, Jean Dansereau and Jacques Gagné for the National Film Board of Canada. *Director:* Denys Arcand. *Participating directors:* Bernard Gosselin, Pierre Perrault, Tahani Rached, Gilles Groulx, Jacques Bensimon, Jacques Godbout, Guy-L. Côté. *Cinematography:* Alain Dostie. *With additional images by:* Pierre Letarte, André Luc Dupont, Martin Leclerc, Roger Rochat, Bruno Carrière, Jean-Pierre Lachapelle and Pierre Mignot. *Sound:* Serge Beauchemin. *Additional sound:* Yves Gendron, Claude Hazanavicius, Richard Besse, Esther Auger, André Dussault, Jacques Drouin and Jean-Guy Normandin. *Editing:* Pierre Bernier, assisted by France Dubé. *Actor:* Jean-Pierre Ronfard.

EMPIRE INC. EPISODE II: BROTHER, CAN YOU SPARE $17 MILLION – 1983. 51 minutes. 16mm. Colour. *Executive producer:* Mark Blandford. *Producers:* Paul Risacher and Stefan Wodoslawsky for the Canadian Broadcasting Corporation with the collaboration of the National Film Board of Canada. *Director:* Denys Arcand. *Scriptwriters:* Douglas Bowie and Jacques Benoit. *Cinematography:* Alain Dostie. *Script continuity:* Johanne Prégent. *Art direction:* Pierre Garneau. *Music:*

Neil Chotem. *Editing:* Pierre Bernier and Alfonso Peccia. *Main cast:* Kenneth Welsh, Martha Henry, Jennifer Dale, Peter Dvorsky.

EMPIRE INC. EPISODE V: TITANS DON'T CRY – 1983. 51 minutes. 16mm. Colour. *Executive producer:* Mark Blandford. *Producers:* Paul Risacher and Stefan Wodoslawsky for the Canadian Broadcasting Corporation, with the collaboration of the National Film Board of Canada. *Director:* Denys Arcand. *Scriptwriter:* Douglas Bowie. *Cinematography:* Alain Dostie. *Script continuity:* Johanne Prégent. *Art direction:* Pierre Garneau. *Music:* Neil Chotem. *Editing:* Pierre Bernier and Alfonso Peccia. *With:* Kenneth Welsh, Martha Henry, Jennifer Dale, Peter Dvorsky.

EMPIRE INC. EPISODE VI: THE LAST WALTZ – 1983. 51 minutes. 16mm. Colour. *Executive producer:* Mark Blandford. *Producer:* Paul Risacher and Stefan Wodoslawsky Canadian Broadcasting Corporation with the collaboration of the National Film Board of Canada. *Director:* Denys Arcand. *Scriptwriter:* Douglas Bowie. *Cinematography:* Alain Dostie. *Script continuity:* Johanne Prégent. *Art direction:* Pierre Garneau. *Music:* Neil Chotem. *Editing:* Monique Fortier. *Main cast:* Kenneth Welsh, Martha Henry, Jennifer Dale, Peter Dvorsky.

ALLEZ VOIR – 1983. 30 secondes. 35mm. Colour. *Producer:* Yves Plouffe for Télépro Inc. *Director:* Denys Arcand. *Images:* Nick Allen Wolfe. *Sound:* Normand Mercier. *Continuity:* Marie Daoust. *Editing:* Pierre Des Marchais. *Sponsor:* Le ministère des Affaires culturelles du Québec.

LE CRIME D'OVIDE PLOUFFE (THE CRIME OF OVIDE PLOUFFE) – 1984. 107 minutes. 35mm. Colour. *Executive producers:* Denis Héroux, John Kemeny and Jacques Bobet. *Producers:* Gabriel Boustani and Justine Héroux for the International Cinema Corporation, Société Radio-Canada, the National Film Board of Canada, Filmax and Film A2. *Director:* Denys Arcand. *Scriptwriters:* Roger Lemelin and Denys Arcand, based on the novel by Roger Lemelin. *Cinematography:* François Protat. *Script continuity:* Johanne Prégent. *Music:* Olivier Dassault. *Editing:* Monique Fortier. *Art direction:* Jocelyn Joly. *Main cast:* Gabriel Arcand, Véronique Jannot, Jean Carmet, Anne Létourneau, Juliette Huot, Pierre Curzi, Denise Filiatrault, Serge Dupire. This film consisted of parts five and six of the television series, with minor changes. The first four episodes of the series were directed by Gilles Carle.

EXPORTATION – 1984. 90 seconds. 35mm. Colour. *Production:* Télépro Inc. for BCP. *Director:* Denys Arcand. *Director of photography:* Pierre Mignot. *Sound:* Serge Beauchemin. *Continuity:* Johanne Prégent. *Sponsor:* Alcan.

IMPORTATION – 1984. 90 seconds. 35mm. Colour. *Production:* Télépro Inc. for BCP. *Director:* Denys Arcand. *Director of photography:* Pierre Mignot. *Sound:* Serge Beauchemin. *Continuity:* Johanne Prégent. *Sponsor:* Alcan.

LANCEMENT – 1984. 30 and 60 seconds. 35mm. Colour. *Production:* Télépro Inc. for Publicité Martin. *Director:* Denys Arcand. *Director of photography:* Alain Dostie. *Sound:* Normand Mercier. *Continuity:* Marie Daoust. *Sponsor:* Hydro-Québec.

SIÈGE MONDIAL – 1984. 90 seconds. 35mm. Colour. *Production:* Télépro Inc. for BCP. *Director:* Denys Arcand. *Director of photography:* Pierre Mignot. *Sound:* Serge Beauchemin. *Continuity:* Johanne Prégent. *Sponsor:* Alcan.

SYNTHÈSE – 1984. 90 seconds. 35mm. Colour. *Production:* Télépro Inc. for BCP. *Director:* Denys Arcand. *Director of photography:* Pierre Mignot. *Sound:* Serge Beauchemin. *Continuity:* Johanne Prégent. *Sponsor:* Alcan.

THE DECLINE OF THE AMERICAN EMPIRE – 1986. 102 minutes. 35mm. Colour. *Line producers:* Lyse Lafontaine and Pierre Gendron. *Producers:* René Malo and Roger Frappier for Corporation Image M&M and the National Film Board of Canada. *Director:* Denys Arcand. *Scriptwriter:* Denys Arcand. *Cinematography:* Guy Dufaux and Jacques Leduc. *Script continuity:* Johanne Prégent. *Music:* François Dompierre on themes from Handel. *Editing:* Monique Fortier. *Main cast:* Dominique Michel, Dorothée Berryman, Louise Portal, Pierre Curzi, Rémy Girard, Yves Jacques, Geneviève Rioux, Daniel Brière, Gabriel Arcand.

MARTIN – 1986. 30 seconds. 35mm. Colour. *Producer:* Nicole Giroux, *Production company:* Les Films 24 Inc. for Cossette Communication Marketing. *Copywriter (agency):* Louis Gauthier. *Director:* Denys Arcand. *Director of photography:* François Protat. *Sound:* Dominique Chartrand. *Music:* François Dompierre. *Sponsor:* Telecom Canada. *With:* Claude Gauthier.

RAISON PAYANTE – 1986. 30 seconds. 35mm. Colour. *Producer:* Les Films 24 Inc. for Cossette Communication Marketing. *Copywriter:* Jean-Jacques Stréliski. *Producer:* Charles Ohayon. *Production director:* Mychèle Boudrias. *Copywriter (agency):* Louis Gauthier. *Director:* Denys Arcand. *Director of photography:* François Protat. *Sound:* Michel Charron. *Continuity:* Danielle Kelleny. *Music:* Yves Lapierre. *Editing:* Christine Denault. *Sponsor:* Telecom Canada. *With:* Pierre Curzi.

CHIEN, FLAMME, MELON, NOËL, OIGNONS, OURSON, POISSON, POMME, PROUESSES, RÉVEIL, SINGERIES, SPÉCIALITÉ, VICTOIRE – 1987. Thirteen 15-second spots. 35mm. Colour. *Production:* Les Films 24 Inc. for Cossette Communication Marketing. *Producer:* Nicole Giroux. *Production director:* Michel Chauvin. *Copywriter (agency):* Jean-Jacques Stréliski and Cheryl Reay. *Director:* Denys Arcand. *Director of photography:* Karol Ike. *Sound:* Serge Gaudet. *Continuity:* France Boudreau. *Music:* François Dompierre. *Editing:* Avdé Chiriaeff. *Sponsor:* Provigo.

JESUS OF MONTREAL – 1989. 119 minutes. 35mm. Colour. *Producers:* Roger Frappier, Pierre Gendron, Doris Girard, Gérard Mital and Jacques-Éric Strauss, for Max Films and Gérard Mital Productions, in association with the National Film Board of Canada. *Director:* Denys Arcand. *Scriptwriter:* Denys Arcand. *Cinematography:* Guy Dufaux. *Music:* Yves Laferrière, François Dompierre and Jean-Marie Benoît. *Editing:* Isabelle Dedieu. *Art direction:* François Séguin. *Cast:* Lothaire Bluteau, Johanne Marie Tremblay, Gilles Pelletier, Rémy Girard, Robert Lepage, Catherine Wilkening, Yves Jacques.

LES LETTRES DE LA RELIGIEUSE PORTUGAISE – 1991. 88 minutes. 1-inch video. Colour. *Production:* Daniel Harvey, for Spectel Vidéo Inc. *Director:* Denys Arcand.

Scriptwriter: Denys Arcand, adaptation for the Théâtre de Quat'sous, November–December 1990. *Director of photography:* Alain Dostie. *Sound:* Richard Vigeant. *Editing:* Alain Baril. *Cast:* Anne Dorval, Luc Picard, Johanne Marie Tremblay and Jean-François Casabonne.

VUE D'AILLEURS (a sketch from MONTRÉAL VU PAR ... SIX VARIATIONS SUR UN THÈME/ MONTREAL SEEN BY ... SIX VARIATIONS ON A THEME) – 1991. 20 minutes. 35mm. Colour. *Executive producers:* Michel Houle and Peter Sussman. *Production:* Denise Robert for Cinémaginaire and Atlantis Films. *Director:* Denys Arcand. *Scriptwriter:* Paule Baillargeon. *Cinematography:* Paul Sarossy. *Sound:* Ross Redfern. *Music:* Yves Laferrière. *Editing:* Alain Baril. *Cast:* Domini Blythe, Rémy Girard, Paule Baillargeon, Guylaine Saint-Onge, Raoul Trujillo, John Gilbert, Diego Matamoros.

LOVE AND HUMAN REMAINS – 1993. 99 minutes. 35mm. Colour. *Executive Producers:* Roger Frappier and Pierre Latour. *Production:* Roger Frappier and Peter Sussman, for Max Films and Atlantis Films. *Director:* Denys Arcand. *Scriptwriter:* Brad Fraser, based on his play *Unidentified Human Remains and the True Nature of Love. Cinematography:* Paul Sarossy. *Sound:* Dominique Chartrand and Marcel Pothier. *Music:* John McCarthy. *Editing:* Alain Baril. *Cast:* Thomas Gibson, Ruth Marshall, Cameron Bancroft, Mia Kirshner, Joanne Vannicola, Matthew Ferguson, Rick Roberts.

JOYEUX CALVAIRE – 1996. 90 minutes. 35mm. Colour. *Production:* Denise Robert for Cinémaginaire, in association with Radio-Canada. *Director:* Denys Arcand. *Scriptwriter:* Claire Richard. *Cinematography:* Guy Dufaux. *Sound:* Claude La Haye and Richard Besse. *Music:* Yves Laferrière. *Editing:* André Daigneault. *Cast:* Gaston Lepage, Benoît Brière, Chantal Baril, Roger Blay, Lorne Brass, André Melançon, Jean-Claude Germain, Louise Laparé.

STARDOM – 2000. 100 minutes. 35mm. Colour/Black and white. *Production:* Denise Robert, Robert Lantos and Philippe Carcassonne for Alliance Atlantis Communications, Serendipity Point Films, Cinémaginaire and Cine B Production. *Director:* Denys Arcand. *Scriptwriter:* Denys Arcand and Jacob Potashnik. *Cinematography:* Guy Dufaux. *Art Direction:* Zoe Sakellaropoulo. *Sound:* Claude La Haye and Marcel Pothier. *Music:* François Dompierre. *Editing:* Isabelle Dedieu. *Cast:* Jessica Paré, Dan Aykroyd, Charles Berling, Robert Lepage, Frank Langella, Thomas Gibson, Camilla Rutherford, Joanne Vannicola.

THE BARBARIAN INVASIONS – 2003. Quebec version: 112 minutes; international version: 98 minutes. 35mm. Colour. *Producers:* Denise Robert, Daniel Louis for Cinémaginaire. *Coproducer:* Fabienne Vonier for Pyramide Productions. *Director:* Denys Arcand. *Scriptwriter:* Denys Arcand. *Cinematography:* Guy Dufaux. *Art Direction:* François Séguin. *Sound:* Patrick Rousseau, Marie-Claude Gagné, Michel Descombes, Gavin Fernandès. *Music:* Pierre Aviat. *Editing:* Isabelle Dedieu. *Main cast:* Rémy Girard, Stéphane Rousseau, Dorothée Berryman, Marie-Josée Croze, Marina Hands, Johanne Marie Tremblay, Louise Portal, Yves Jacques, Dominique Michel, Pierre Curzi.

Between 1987 and 2002, Denys Arcand directed commercials for the following companies: Ford Canada. Produced by McCann-Erickson. *With* Louise Marleau • Le Journal de Québec. Les Productions Ronald Brault • Les Ailes de la mode. Les Productions Ronald Brault • Société des alcools du Québec. Produced by Figaro Film. *With* Thierry Lhermitte.

ACTING

1962	SEUL OU AVEC D'AUTRES – Narration.
1964	MONTREAL WORLD FILM FESTIVAL, 5th EDITION – *Director:* Gilles Carle. 1 minute.
	LE TEMPS PERDU – *Production:* National Film Board of Canada. *Director:* Michel Brault. 28 minutes.
	LE CHAT DANS LE SAC – *Production:* National Film Board of Canada. *Director:* Gilles Groulx. 74 minutes. Stand in for Barbara Ulrich.
1966	MON ŒIL – *Production:* Cinak. *Director:* Jean Pierre Lefebvre. 87 minutes.
	LE LABYRINTHE – Films from the NFB Pavilion at Expo 67.
1967	C'EST PAS LA FAUTE À JACQUES CARTIER – *Production:* National Film Board of Canada. *Director:* Georges Dufaux and Clément Perron. 72 minutes.
	MONTREAL WORLD FILM FESTIVAL, 7th EDITION – *Director:* Jean-Claude Labrecque. 1 minute.
	NOMININGUE . . . DEPUIS QU'IL EXISTE – *Production:* National Film Board of Canada. *Director:* Jacques Leduc. 72 minutes.
1971	LA MAUDITE GALETTE ON EST AU COTON – Narration.
1972	QUÉBEC: DUPLESSIS AND APRÈS (QUÉBEC: DUPLESSIS AND AFTER) – Narration.
1973	ON N'ENGRAISSE PAS LES COCHONS À L'EAU CLAIRE (PIGS ARE SELDOM CLEAN) – *Production:* Cinak. *Director:* Jean Pierre Lefebvre. 111 minutes.
	RÉJEANNE PADOVANI
	DES ARMES AND LES HOMMES – *Production:* National Film Board. *Director:* André Melançon. 58 minutes. Arcand did the interviews with police officers.
1975	LA T TE DE NORMANDE ST-ONGE – *Production:* les Productions Carle-Lamy. *Director:* Gilles Carle. 116 minutes.
1976	LA LUTTE DES TRAVAILLEURS D'HÔPITAUX – Narration.
1987	UN ZOO LA NUIT (NIGHT ZOO) – *Production:* Les Production Oz and the National Film Board of Canada. *Director:* Jean-Claude Lauzon. 105 minutes.
1989	JESUS OF MONTREAL

Filmography

1991   DESPERANTO, sketch from MONTRÉAL VU PAR ... SIX VARIATIONS SUR UN THÈME – *Production:* Cinémaginaire and Atlantis Films, in association the National Film Board of Canada. *Director:* Patricia Rozema. 20 minutes.

1992   LÉOLO – *Production:* Les Productions du Verseau, Studio Canal + and Flach Film. *Director:* Jean-Claude Lauzon. 107 min.

LES MALHEUREUX MAGNIFIQUES – *Production:* Les Productions du Verseau. *Director:* Mireille Goulet. 5 minutes.

2003   THE BARBARIAN INVASIONS

2004   LITTORAL – *Director:* Wajdi Mouawad.

BIBLIOGRAPHY
I. DENYS ARCAND: WRITING AND INTERVIEWS

1. ARTICLES, ESSAYS, SPEECHES AND CORRESPONDENCE

"Le scoutisme au collège," *Le Sainte-Marie*, 21 March 1957, p. 6. • "Païdeia politeia. . . . D'après usage," *Le Sainte-Marie*, 2 mai 1958, p. 6. In collaboration with Pierre Ménard. Signed Georges-Denys Arcand. • "Après la cafétéria des élèves . . . Le réfectoire de l'esprit," *Le Sainte-Marie*, 28 January 1959, pp. 6–7. In collaboration with Raymond Levasseur, Marcel St-Germain, Jean Paré and Stéphane Venne. • "81,2% disent: non!" *Le Sainte-Marie*, 14 February 1959, p. 4. In collaboration with Pierre Létourneau, Marcel Saint-Germain and Stéphane Venne. • "Honegger," *Le Sainte-Marie*, 25 March 1959, p. 7. Signed G.-Denys Arcand. • "La kaleidoscopie. Distribution officielle des *Oskor*," *Le Sainte-Marie*, 21 May 1959, p. 9. In collaboration with Marcel St-Germain and Stéphane Venne. • "Liberté-sacrifice," *Le Sainte-Marie*, 14 October 1959, p. 7. Signé Georges-Denys Arcand. • "La glace brûlante," *Le Sainte-Marie*, 14 November 1959, pp. 6–7. In collaboration with Marcel Saint-Germain and Stéphane Venne. • "De tristitia (de la chose triste)," *Le Sainte-Marie*, 30 November 1959, p. 11. In collaboration with Marcel St-Germain and Stéphane Venne. • "Ce qu'ont écrit . . . ceux qui ont parlé," *Le Sainte-Marie*, 28 mai 1960, pp. 6–7. In collaboration with Marcel St-Germain. • "De l'autre côté du mur: nous," *Le Sainte-Marie*, 28 May 1960, p. 3. In collaboration with Claude Lamarche. • "Ce n'est pas qu'une vague. Au cinéma: un nouveau réalisme, une nouvelle stylistique," *Le Quartier latin*, 2 November 1960, pp. 4–5. • "Le Ballet Royal du Danemark," *Le Quartier latin*, 3 November 1960, p. 6. • "Lady Chatterley et nous," *Le Quartier latin*, 19 January 1961, pp. 5–6. • "Nos joyeux carabins. 'Aux tanfaura, ho maurice!'"*Le Quartier latin*, 9 February 1961, p. 2. • "Te promène donc pas toute nue," *Le Quartier latin*, 9 February 1961, p. 4. • "Le Carnaval et les arts," *Le Quartier latin*, 16 février 1961, p. 7. • "Un recueil d'André Brochu. *Privilèges de l'ombre*," *Le Quartier latin*, 21 February 1961, p. 5. • "À la boîte à chansons. Tam taladam dam," *Le Quartier latin*, 23 February 1961, p. 4. • "*La Cruche cassée*," *Le Quartier latin*, 23 March 1961, p. 8. • "La Société artistique. Les activités pour '61–'62," *Le Quartier latin*, 21 September 1961, p. 7. • "Les affreux Cyniques. Cynik habarè," *Le Quartier latin*, 26 October 1961, p. 4. • "And How About You?" *Le Quartier latin*, 7 November 1961, p. 3. • "De l'indécrottable stupidité de nos critiques," *Le Quartier latin*, 5 December 1961, p. 4. • "Lesvaches ries," *Le Quartier latin*, 12 December 1961, p. 8. • "Comment j'ai été réhabilité . . . ," *Le Quartier latin*, 16 January 1962, p. 3. • "Il y a quelque chose de pourri au royaume du recteur," *Le Quartier latin*, 23 January 1962, p. 5. • "Les femmes, la lentille, le clinicien et nous . . . ," *Le Quartier latin*, 20 February 1962, p. 7. • "Ce qu'il nefaut manquer sous aucun prétexte," *Le Quartier latin*, 1 March 1962, pp. 4–5. In collaboration with André Duval. • "Un excellent spectacle," *Le Quartier latin*, 13 March 1962, p. 6. • "Nos vedettes: ce qu'elles disent et ce que nous disons d'elles . . . ," *Le Quartier latin*, 17 April 1962, pp. 6–8. In collaboration with Stéphane Venne and Denis Héroux. • "Recherche sur la représentation de l'histoire dans les films de l'ONF, en vue d'étudier l'orientation future d'une série de films de reconstruction historiqueactuellement en production à l'ONF," Office national du film, May 1962, p. 34 Collection ONF. • "*Richard II,*" *Le Quartier latin*, 20 September 1962, p. 5. • "André Dubois," *Le Quartier latin*, 27 September 1962, p. 7. • "De la nécessité d'un machiavélisme," *Le Quartier latin*, 9 October 1962, p. 2. • "Requiem pour une Monique Lepage," *Le Quartier latin*, 18 October 1962, p. 11. • "Abominables," *Le Quartier latin*, 25 October 1962, p. 6. • "Les Cyniques au grand complet," *Le Quartier latin*, 25 octobre 1962, p. 8. • "Les divertissements," *Parti pris*, vol. 1, no 1, October 1963, pp. 56–57. • "Les divertissements," *Parti pris*, vol. 1, no 2, November 1963, pp. 57–58. • "Les divertissements 2, Bergman l'ingrat," *Parti pris*, vol. 1, no 5, February 1964, pp. 54–57. • "Des évidences," *Parti pris*, vol. 1, no 7, April 1964, pp. 19–21. The text is part of the dossier "L'O.N.F. et le cinéma québécois." • "Cinéma et sexualité," *Parti pris*, vol. 1, no 9–10–11, été 1964, pp. 90–97. • "*Le Chat dans le sac,*" *Parti pris*, vol. 2, no 1, September 1964, pp. 69–70. • "1837 à l'école," *Liberté*, no 37–38 (vol. 7, no 1–2), January–April 1965, pp. 130–39. Theme of the issue: "1837–1838." • "Pour parler du cinéma canadien," in *Comment faire ou ne pas faire un film canadien*, Montréal, La Cinémathèque canadienne, 1967. Arcand's article is integrated in the leaflet "Les cinéastesont la parole," inserted in the middle of the brochure. • "*Volleyball*, film by Denys Arcand," in *Rétrospective du cinéma canadien/Canadian Film— Past and Present*, March 1967. • *Programme cinématographique à l'intention du Centre national des artsdu Canada*, Montreal, National Film Board, December 1967, p. 105 • Hommage à Jean Lefebvre, undated [1970s]. Unpublished. Collection Denys Arcand. • "Points de vue," dans *Cinéastes du Québec 8, Denys Arcand*, Montreal, Conseil québécois pour la diffusion du cinéma, 1971, pp. 10–11. Excerpts from writings and declarations by Denys Arcand. • "Cinéma et sexualité," *Presqu'Amérique*, vol. 7, no 3, December 1971–January1972, pp. 21–23. A republication of the text that appeared in *Parti pris*, no 9–10–11, Summer 1964. • "*Duplessis est encore en vie,*" 8 June 1972. • "*La Maudite galette*. Denys Arcand dit," *Cinéma Québec*, vol. 2, no 1, September 1972, pp. 11. This article was also distributed in the form of a typed memo: "*La Maudite galette* vue par Denys Arcand." • "Deschambault ou la campagne . . . ," *Le Devoir*, 28 October 1972. • "*Parti pris* et après," *La Barre du jour*, no 31–32, Winter 1972, pp. 68–69. • "Je ne rentre plus à l'O.N.F," 19 March 1973, p. 4 in *Contre la censure*, Montréal, Conseil québécois pour la diffusion ducinéma, 1973. Text inserted in a pamphlet denouncing censorship at the NFB, distributed during Quebec film week (Semaine du cinéma québécois) at the Cégep Saint-Laurent de Montréal. It also includes texts by Gilles Groulx, Paul Larose, Robert Lévesque, Pierre Perrault and Luc Perreault. • "Présentation de *Réjeanne Padovani*," December 1973 • "Le film historique: problèmes de réalisation," *Cultures*, vol II, no 1, Les Pressesde l'Unesco et la Baconnière, 1974, pp. 15–29. Theme of the issue: "Le cinéma del'histoire." • "Je me refuse à réfléchir," *Le Devoir*, 25 January 1975. This article, signed byArcand, makes use of comments collected by Robert Guy Scully. • Letter to Donald Pilon and Donald Lautrec. Reader's report for script entitled *B.L.A. Finance (You Don't Throw Good Money After Bad Money)* by Robert Ménard, Donald Pilon and Donald Lautrec, 12 January 1976, p. 6 Collection Denys Arcand. • "Hommage à Pierre Lamy," undated [1980s]. Unpublished. Collection Denys Arcand. • "Portrait deJacques Bobet," undated [1980s]. Unpublished. Collection Denys Arcand. • "Portrait de Juliette Huot undated [1980s]. Unpublished. Collection Denys Arcand. • "Souvenirs de la Quinzaine," undated [1980s]. Unpublished. Collection Denys Arcand. • "Arcand: Duplessis et après," *La 8ème Semaine du cinéma québécois*, 3–12 October 1980. Article created from quotes by Arcand, from an interview with the director • "Lettre de Denys Arcand au Festival/Symposium sur l'Office national du film," Deschambault, 6 March 1981, 1 p. Reprinted in *Format cinéma*, no 6, 19 October 1981, p. 4. • Untitled, 27 January 1982. Letter to Jacques Leduc, published in *Format cinéma*, no 12, 15 February 1982, p. 3. • "La rigueur du sport," *Format cinéma*, no 33, 6 February 1984, p. 1. This text was also published in the *Gazette de Lausanne*, undated, and in *Liberté*, vol. 26, no 2, April 1984, pp. 11–13. • " tre acteur," *Copie zéro*, no 22, October 1984, pp. 24–25. • Foreword for published version of *Le déclin de l'empire américain*, Montréal, Boréal, 1986, pp. 9–10. • "*Le déclin de l'empire américain. Waiting for the Barbarians*," *Canadian Profil canadien*, no 6, September 1986, p. 4. • Presentation speech for the *Decline of the American Empire* at the Toronto Film Festival, September 1986. Unpublished. Collection Denys Arcand. Translation by the author, 2003. • "L'historien silencieux," dans *Maurice Séguin, historien du pays québécois*, Montréal, VLB, 1987, pp. 255–57. • Answer to question addressed to filmmakers: "What is your first concern when you are making a film?" *Les 5es Rendez-vous du cinéma québécois*, February 1987, p. 69. • "Lettre ouverte d'appui," April 1987, 1 p. Arcand supports the struggle of citizens of Les Grondines and Lotbinière against the introduction of Hydro-Québec installations in their region. Collection Denys Arcand. • "Pourquoi filmez-vous? 700 cinéastes du monde entier répondent," *Libération* (hors-série), May 1987. • Speech on filmmakers and advertising, December 1987. Unpublished. Collection Denys Arcand. Translation by the author, 2003. • "Foreword," for published edition of *Jésus de Montréal*, Montréal, Boréal, 1989, pp. 7–8. • Presentation of *Jésus de Montréal* at Cannes, March 1989, 1 p. • "Portrait de Renee Furst," undated [1990s]. Unpublished. Translation by the author, 2003. Collection Denys Arcand • Acceptance speech for award from the Association des réalisateurs de télévision, undated [1990s]. Unpublished. Collection Denys Arcand. • *Lumières*, no 24, Autumn 1990, p. 10. Inside a text by Arthur Lamothe, "Le confort, naître ou ne pas naître," a photo taken by Arcand, accompanied by a caption he wrote himself. • "Retraite de l'ONF de Jacques Leduc," undated [September1990], 2 pp. Unpublished. Collection

Denys Arcand. • Speech for Arcand's nomination to the Great Montrealers, 8 November 1990, 1 p. Collection Denys Arcand. • "Présentation de *Vue d'ailleurs,*" 1991. • "Commentvous avez imaginé votre dernier ou votre prochain film ?" *Lumières*, n₀ 27, Summer 1991, p. 39. File on the Quebec imagination. • Letter to Gilles Jacob on the Cannes festival, 15 August 1991. Collection Denys Arcand. • Letter to Marc Gariépy, 15 September1991. Collection Denys Arcand. • "If You Were Given an Unlimited Budget, and Were Under No Obligation to Distribute it, What Film Would You Make ?" *Projections. A Forum for Film Makers*, n₀ 1, 1992, Faber and Faber, London, p. 124. • "Montréal," in Véronneau, Pierre, *Montréal, ville de cinéma*, Montréal, Cinémathèque québécoise/Musée du cinéma, 1992, p. 64. • Letter to Marie Laberge, 22 February 1992, 1 p. Collection Denys Arcand. • Acceptance speech for the Molson Award from the Canada Council for the Arts, 3 March 1992, p. 1 Collection Denys Arcand. • Letter about the "Canada 125" scandal, 24 September 1992. *Le Devoir, Le Journalde Montréal, La Presse, 24 images* and *Lumières*. • "Deux souvenirs d'Hollywood," *Lumières*, n₀ 29, Winter 1992, p. 12. • "What Kind of Movies Do You Imagine Might Emerge in the Next Millennium?" *Projections. A Forum for Film Makers*, n₀ 2, 1993, Faber and Faber, London, pp. 43–44. • "Éloge funèbre de Mankiewicz," undated [August 1993], 2 pp. Unpublished. Collection Denys Arcand. • Letter to Stephen Grenier Stini, 24 October 1993, 1 p. Collection Denys Arcand. • Letter to Christopher Young, 28 October 1993, p. 2 Collection Denys Arcand. • "La maison est ouverte . . . ," *Les 12ₑₛ Rendez-vous ducinéma québécois*, February 1994, p. 4. • "Denys Arcand, pourquoi faites-vous ducinéma?" undated [1995?]. Unpublished. Collection Denys Arcand. • Communication for a literature conference in Bologna, 1995. • "Préface," for Machiavelli, Nicolas, *Le Prince*, Montréal, Boréal, 1995, pp. 7–8. • "Protestation des professeurs dephilosophie," 1995, p. 1 Arcand comments on the abolition of philosophy teaching in Cégeps. Collection Denys Arcand. • "Célébrons le centenaire (pendant qu'il est temps)," *Les 13ₑₛ Rendez-vous du cinéma québécois*, February 1995, p. 4. • Honorary doctorate from the Université de Montréal. Speech, 6 April 1995, 2 pp. Collection Denys Arcand. • "La rigueur du sport. Troisième version," October 1995, p. 6. This text, rewritten for the radio, is slightly different from the versions published in *La Gazette de Lausanne, Format cinéma* and *Liberté*. Version read by Arcand in the documentary *Denys Arcand. Un portrait pour la radio*, by Jean-Sébastien Durocher, February 2004. Collection Denys Arcand. • "Introduction," November 1995, in Girard, François and Don McKellar, *Thirty-two Short Films About Glenn Gould*, Toronto, Coach House Press, 1995, pp. 7–8. Translation by the author, December 2002. • "Présentation de *Joyeux calvaire,*" undated [1996], 3 pp. Collection Denys Arcand. • "Questions d'Adriana Schettini," undated [August 1996], 5 pp. • "*Stardom*. Director's Statement," undated [2000], 1 p. Translation by the author, 2003. • "Festival du film de Québec 2000," 2000, 3 pp. Collection Denys Arcand. • "Mot de Denys Arcand, Président d'honneur," *Festival Images du nouveau monde*, March 2001, p. 3. • "Mondialisation: L'état du cinéma vu par 50 cinéastes de la planète," *Cahiers du cinéma*, n₀ 557, May 2001, pp. 52–53. • "Préface," for the published version of *Les invasions barbares*, Montréal, Boréal, 2003, p. 7.

2. THEATRE

Un peu plus qu'un peu moins, December 1979, 32 pp. "Le titre définitif sera probablement *La fin du voyage.*" Collection Denys Arcand. Excerpts in *Copie zéro*, n₀ 34–35, December 1987–March 1988, pp. 20–21. • Dompierre, François, *Fin de siècle. Opéra en trois actes*, 18 pp. Opera based on an idea by Denys Arcand, François Dompierre et Jean-Jacques Stréliski; dramatic concept: Denys Arcand. Collection Denys Arcand. Excerpts in *Copie zéro*, n₀ 34–35, December 1987–March 1988, pp. 18–19. • *Mousse. Petite variation sur un thème de Claire Bretécher*, July 1980, 9 pp. Collection Denys Arcand. •*Les Lettres de la religieuse portugaise*, June 1990, Théâtre de Quat'sous, 46 pp. Collection Denys Arcand. Besides the play there is a presentation of the original work and a description of musical passages. Collection Denys Arcand.

3. FILM PROJECTS AND SCRIPTS

Champlain. 1) *Samuel de Champlain, une réévaluation*, script, August 1962, 24 pp. Collection Cinémathèque québécoise; 2) script, 14 January 1963, 17 pp.; 3) scénario, 1964, 29 pp. Collection ONF. • *Les Découvreurs [La Route de l'Ouest]*. 1) synopsis, August 1963, 5 pp. Collection ONF; 2) script, August 1963, 28 pp. Collection ONF; 3) script, 10 September 1963, 19 pp. Collection Cinémathèque québécoise; 4) commentary, 13 April 1964, 11 pp. Collection Cinémathèque québécoise; 5) commentary, August 1964, 18 pp. Collection Cinémathèque québécoise.• *Entre la mer et l'eau douce*. 1) synopsis, undated [1964], 1 p. Collection NFB; 2) script, undated [1964], 54 pp. Collection Cinémathèque québécoise; 3) synopsis written in collaboration with Michel Brault, September 1964, 19 pp. Collection ONF; 4) script, 30 December 1964, 54 pp. Collection ONF. • *Parallèles et grand soleil*, commentary written in collaboration with Jean Lemoyne, Office national du film du Canada, 1964, 6 pp. Collection ONF. Commentary on a 40-minute film directed by Jean Dansereau. Another film of 10 minutes, *Appuis et suspensions*, was made from the footage shot for *Parallèles et grand soleil*. The commentary is attributed to Arcand, LeMoyne and Roch Carrier. • *Volleyball*, script, October 4, 1965, 6 pp. Collection ONF. • "Notes du scripteur sur le développement de l'émission *Minute Papillon*," 16 January 1967, 3 pp. Collections of Radio-Canada and the Cinémathèque québécoise. • *Les Parcs Atlantiques*, film project and research report, undated, 11 pp. Collection of the Cinémathèque québécoise. This document resembles a somewhat free-form synopsis and notes for the mise-en-scene. • *Les Informateurs [On est au coton]*. 1) research report, 17 March 1968, 24 pp. Collection of the Cinémathèque québécoise; 2) film project, 21 June 1968, 7 pp. Collection Cinémathèque québécoise; 3) film project, 18 October 1968, 9 pp. Collection Cinémathèque québécoise. • *Duplessis est encore envie [Québec: Duplessis et après . . .]*, film project, 15 March 1970, 12 pp. Collection Cinémathèque québécoise. • *Les Terroristes*, film project, June 1970, 5 pp. Collection Cinémathèque québécoise. • *La Chine des poètes*, film project, Office national du film, 1971, 5 pp. Collection Office national du film. • *Réjeanne Padovani*, script written in collaboration with Jacques Benoit, 1972, 90 pp. Collection Cinémathèque québécoise. • *Réjeanne Padovani; dossier établi par Robert Lévesque sur un film de Denys Arcand*, Montréal, L'Aurore, 1976, 111 pp. Scene breakdown of finished film along with a file of articles. • *Gina*. 1) *Les Jarrets noirs/Gina*, film project, April 1972, 6 pp. Collection Cinémathèque québécoise; 2) synopsis, undated [1972], 2 pp. Collection Cinémathèque québécoise; 3) script, November 1973, 59 pp. Collection Cinémathèque québécoise; 4) script, February 1974, 135 pp. Collection Cinémathèque québécoise. • *Gina; dossier établi par Pierre Latour sur un film de Denys Arcand*, Montréal, L'Aurore, 1976, 126 pp. Scene breakdown of finished film, along with a file of articles. • *Nesbitt's Trip*, script written in collaboration with Jacques Méthé, August 1976, 160 pp. Collection Denys Arcand. • *Mémo*, September 1976, 3 pp. Project for a film on tourism. Collection ONF. • *Québec et après . . . [Le confort et l'indifférence]*, film project, 16 June 1977, 10 pp. Collection Cinémathèque québécoise. • *Duplessis*, Montréal, VLB, 1978, 489 pp. • *Empire Inc. 1944. 4 ͤépisode: "Les gens adorent les guerres,"* February 1980, 76 pp. Collection Cinémathèque québécoise. • *Maria Chapdelaine*, in collaboration with André Ricard. 1) script in 6 episodes, March 1979, 111 pp. Collection Cinémathèque québécoise; 2) script, December 1980, 182 pp. Collection Cinémathèque québécoise; 3) script, February 1981, 118 pp. Collection Cinémathèque québécoise. • *La fin duvoyage*, project for a film based on the play *Un peu plus qu'un peu moins*, 2 August 1982, 5 pp. Collection Cinémathèque québécoise. • *En mai, nos amour s . . .* 1) *1960 (En mai, nos amours)*, script, 11 October 1982, 46 pp. Collection Denys Arcand; 2) *En mai, nos amours . . . Cinquième épisode de "La Maison du Carré Saint-Louis,"* script written in collaboration with Louise and Andrée Pelletier, 11 August 1986, 55 pp. Collection Denys Arcand. • *Le crime d'Ovide Plouffe*. The first stages of writing for *Le Crime d'OvidePlouffe* were done by Lemelin alone over 1981 and 1982. At that point, the project was called *Les Plouffe (II)* and *Ovide Plouffe 1949*. When he started to collaborate on the project, Denys Arcand says he wrote the feature screenplay with Lemelin, in the first stages. Episodes 5 and 6 of the television series were then scripted from the initial screenplay for film. 1) episodes 5 and 6, synopsis, undated [1982], 18 pp. The authors are not specified. Collection Cinémathèque québécoise; 2) episodes 5 and 6, film version, script written in collaboration with Roger Lemelin, undated [1983], 95 pp. Collection Cinémathèque québécoise; 3) script written in collaboration with Roger Lemelin, 1 June 1983, 123 pp. Collection Cinémathèque québécoise; 4) script written in collaboration with Roger Lemelin, 12 July 1983, 121 pp. Collection Cinémathèque québécoise. • *Émile Nelligan*. 1) film treatment, undated [1983], 2 pp. This text precedes a 41-page synopsis written by Aude Nantais. Collection Cinémathèque québécoise; 2) script written in collaboration with Aude Nantais and Jean-Joseph Tremblay, first version, undated [1984], 240 pp. Collection Cinémathèque québécoise. • *Le déclin de l'empire américain*. 1) *Conversations scabreuses*, project, 14 August 1984, 4 pp. Document related to a project called *Groupe de travail cinématographique,* which brings together five projects, synopses or scripts for feature films, dated 6 September 1984. Collection Cinémathèque québécoise; 2) *Le déclin et la chute de l'empire américain*, script, first draft, November 1984–February 1985, 244 pp. Collection Cinémathèque québécoise; 3) script, second draft, May–June

1985, 241 pp. Collection Cinémathèque québécoise; 4) script, third draft, July–August 1985, 192 pp. Collection Cinémathèque québécoise. • *Le déclin de l'empire américain* (published version of script), Montréal, Boréal, 1986, 173 pp. • *Jésus de Montréal.* 1) draft for a pre-synopsis, December 1985, 1 p. Document included in the project called *Demande de scénarisation conjoint (package),* presented by Les Productions Oz and dated 11 April 1986. This dossier also includes the synopsis and development budgets for three feature films, as well as related documents. Collection Cinémathèque québécoise; 2) script, second draft, April 1988, 224 pp. Collection Cinémathèque québécoise; 3) script, fourth draft, July 1988, 216 pp. Collection Denys Arcand. • *Jésus de Montréal*, Montréal, Boréal, 1989, 188 pp. • *Vue d'ailleurs*, script written in collaboration with Paule Baillargeon, 16 April 1990, 12 pp. This script is part of a document composed of all screenplays for the "omnibus" film *Montréal vu par . . . Six variations sur un thème.* Collection Cinémathèque québécoise. • *La femme idéale*, 10 April 1991, 173 pp. Collection Denys Arcand. • *Dernier Amour*, second version, October 1991, 174 pp. Collection Denys Arcand. • *La Vie éternelle*, script, 1991. Script not found. • *C'est la vie*, fourth version of *La femme idéale*, *La Vie éternelle*, *Dernier Amour*, 1993–1994, 99 pp. Incomplete. Collection Denys Arcand. • *Stardom.* 1) *Beautiful*, script, 24 October 1995, 191 pp. Collection Denys Arcand; 2) *15 Moments*, script written in collaboration with Jacob Potashnik, 25 January 1998, 143 pp. Collection Cinémathèque québécoise; 3) *15 Moments*, script written in collaboration with Jacob Potashnik, June 1998, 133 pp. Collection Denys Arcand. • *Les invasions barbares.* 1) first draft, April 2002, 117 pp. Collection Denys Arcand; 2) second draft, June 2002, 115 pp. Collection Denys Arcand; 3) final draft, August 2002, 128 pp. Collection Denys Arcand. • *Les invasions barbares*, (published version of the screenplay) Montréal, Boréal, 2003, 216 pp.

4. PUBLISHED INTERVIEWS

1958   Lafontaine, Raymond, "Arcand s'envole de nuit," *Le Sainte-Marie*, 29 November 1958, p. 8.

1962   Grenier, Serge, "La première en avril. *Seul ou avec d'autres . . . ,*" *Le Quartier latin*, 8 avril 1962, pp. 4–5.

1971   Houle, Michel, Jacques Leduc and Lucien Hamelin, in "Entretien," *Cinéastes du Québec 8, Denys Arcand*, Montréal, Conseil québécois pour la diffusion du ciné-ma, 1971, pp. 12–31. • Perreault, Luc, "La violence d'un cinéma (jusqu'ici) doux," *LaPresse*, 29 May 1971. • "La genèse du film. Une entrevue avec Denys Arcand," *Cinéma Québec*, vol. 1, no 2, June–July 1971, p. 32. • Arcand, Denys and Gérald Godin, "Un film didactique," *Cinéma Québec*, vol. 1, no 2, June–July 1971, p. 33.

1972   Tadros, Jean-Pierre, "*La Maudite galette,*" *Cinéma Québec*, vol. 1, no 9, May–June 1972, pp. 26–29. • Salducci, Christiane, "*La Maudite galette*: les gangsters québécois, vus par Denys Arcand, réalisateur licencié en histoire et ex-conseiller pédagogique" *Nice-matin*, 8 May 1972. • Arcand, Denys and Gérald Godin. "A Didactic Film," *Transformation*, vol. 1, no 2, été 1972, pp. 41, 43. • Scully, Robert Guy and Laurent Laplante, "L'espoir du film documentaire. . . Le désespoir d'être constant," *Le Devoir*, 23 June 1972. • Perreault, Luc, "Duplessis n'est pas encore mort," *La Presse*, 24 June 1972. • Lévesque, Robert, *"Duplessis et après . . .* de Denys Arcand. Tout ce qui grouille, grenouille et scribouille dans la politique," *Québec-Presse*, 25 June 1972. • Thibault, Louis Claude, "Le réalisateur de *La Maudite galette* encore fasciné par la pègre," *Le Grand Journal illustré*, 14 August 1972. • Lanken, Dane, "Denys Arcand — a Director on the Move," *The Gazette*, 26 August 1972. • Tadros, Jean-Pierre, "Disséquer l'homme politique québécois," *Cinéma Québec*, vol. 2, no 1, September 1972, pp. 18–22. • "Denys Arcand: une 'maudite galette' au poker du cinéma!" *Dimanche-vedettes*, 3 September 1972. • Lévesque, Robert, *"La Maudite galette.* Une vraie vue pour le monde ordinaire," *Québec-Presse*, 3 September 1972. • Scully, Robert Guy, "Denys Arcand 'au milieu de labébelle,'" *Le Devoir*, 9 September 1972. • Hennebelle, Guy, "Brève rencontre . . . avec Denys Arcand," *Écran 72*, no 9, November 1972, pp. 26–28. • Lévesque, Robert, *"Réjeanne Padovani.* Une soirée avec 'le beau monde' du dernier film de Denys Arcand," *Québec-Presse*, 26 November 1972. • Johnson, William, "Nothing's Changed since Duplessis, Maker of Banned Film Says," *The Globe and Mail*, 27 December 1972.

1973   Péclet, Manon, "Denys Arcand joue aussi avec 'les bons et les méchants,'" *Dimanche matin*, 1973. • Marcorelles, Louis, "Entretien avec Denys Arcand," *Image et son*, no 270, March 1973, pp. 81-94 • Tadros, Jean-Pierre, *"Réjeanne Padovani.* Un film dramatiquepour provoquer une série de sentiments," *Cinéma Québec*, vol. 3, no 1, September1973, pp. 17–23. • "Nouveaux cinéastes québécois. Denys Arcand," *Téléciné*, no 181, September 1973, p. 21. • Amiel, Mireille, "Denys Arcand," *Cinéma*, no 180, September–October1973, pp. 102–5. • Lionet, G. et N. Ghali, "Denys Arcand: le chemin d'uncinéaste québécois," *Jeune cinéma*, no 73, September–October 1973, pp. 22–26. • DesRosiers, Hélène, "Denys Arcand s'explique sur . . . *Réjeanne Padovani,*" *Le Journal de Montréal*, 26 September 1973. • Malina, Martin, "Quebec's First in New York," *The Montreal Star*, 29 September 1973. • Perreault, Luc, "Arcand: créer une sorte d'inquiétude," *La Presse*, 29 September 1973. • Perreault, Luc, "Un cinéaste qui prenddes risques," *La Presse*, 29 September 1973. • *"Réjeanne Padovani*: de Montréal à NewYork via Paris," *Montréal-matin*, 30 September 1973. • Lévesque, Robert, *"Réjeanne Padovani.* Un film pour la campagne électorale," *Québec-Presse*, 30 September 1973. • Bonneville, Léo, "Entretien avec Denys Arcand," *Séquences*, no 174, October 1973, pp. 4–11. • Lanken, Dane, "A Hard Look at Quebec Politics," *The Gazette*, October 1973. • Scully, Robert Guy, "Denys Arcand réalisateur: de la justesse au cinéma audésespoir en politique," *Le Devoir*, 6 October 1973. • Daigneault, Claude, *"Padovani, Duplessis et après . . .* Denys Arcand?"

Le Soleil, 27 October 1973. • Hennebelle, Guy, "Entretien avec Denys Arcand," *Écran 73*, n₀ 19, November 1973, pp. 61–63. • Fleouter, Claude, *Le Monde*, 8 December 1973. • "Denys Arcand: la conscience politique des Québécois," *Perspectives*, 22 December 1973.

1974   Bastien, Jean-Pierre et Pierre Véronneau, "L'équipe," *Cinéastes du Québec 12. JacquesLeduc/essai de travail d'équipe*, Montréal, dans Conseil québécois pour la diffusion du cinéma, 1974, pp. 10–16. The interview with Jacques Leduc contains several comments made by colleagues, including Denys Arcand. Some of the quotes from Arcand are taken from *Cinéastes du Québec 8. Denys Arcand*, 1971. • Bechstein, Joseph, "The Wit and the Widsom of the Canadian Film Industry," *Take One*, vol. 4, n₀ 4, 1974, pp. 22–23. • Perreault, Luc, "*Gina*: la recette d'un bon scénario, le laisser mûrir," *La Presse*, 16 March 1974. • Ibranyi-Kiss, A., "How to Have Your Cake and Eat it Too . . . à a Denys Arcand," *Cinema Canada*, vol. 2, n₀ 13, May 1974, pp. 56–58. • McLarty, James, "Canadian Film. Denys Arcand," *Motion*, May–June 1974, p. 12. • Wright, Judy and Debbie Magidson, "'Making Films for Your Own People': An Interview with Denys Arcand," *This Magazine*, vol. 8, n₀ 4, November–December 1974.

1975   "Entretien avec Denys Arcand," in *Cinépix présente "Gina": le nouveau film de DenysArcand*, Cinépix, 1975. • Hofsess, John, "Denys Arcand," in *Inner Views: Ten Canadian Film Makers*, McGraw-Hill, 1975, pp. 145–57. • Maulucci, Anthony M., "Comment on Cannes. Three French-Canadian Film Directors Talk about Cannes," *Motion*, vol.4, n₀ 2, 1975, pp. 36–38. • Malina, Martin, "Reality as Fiction," *The Montreal Star*, 25 January 1975. • Perreault, Luc, "Denys Arcand veut pêcher son marsouin," *La Presse*, 25 January 1975. • Tadros, Jean-Pierre, "Le textile et le viol de la strip-teaseuse," *Le Jour*, 25 January 1975.

1976   "Une réflexion sur l'état actuel de la civilisation," in *Réjeanne Padovani, dossier établi par Robert Lévesque*, Montréal, L'Aurore, 1976. • Bouthillier-Levesque, Jeannine, "Entrevue avec Denys Arcand," *Positif*, n₀ 187, November 1976, pp. 20–22.

1977   "'Quand il parlait des gens d'ici, tu sens dans sa voix qu'il était ému' – le réalisateur de *Duplessis . . . et après,*" *La Presse*, 10 September 1977.

1978   Mercier, Johanne, "*Duplessis*. La mini-série de l'année," *TV-Hebdo*, 4 February 1978. • Tadros, Jean-Pierre, "Si Duplessis m'était conté . . . ," *Le Devoir*, 11 February 1978. • "*Duplessis*: la télé ne nous avait pas tout dit," *La Presse*, 22 November 1978.

1979   "Documentary on Referendum Planned. Filmmaker Handles Hot Potato," *The Gazette*, 29 May 1979. • Winters, Robert, "Denys Arcand va tourner pour l'ONF un film sur le référendum québécois," *La Presse*, 30 May 1979.

1980 "Arcand: Duplessis et après !," *La 8ème Semaine du cinéma québécois*, 3 to 12 October 1980, p. 4.

1982 Bégin, Jean-Yves, "Le confort et l'indifférence. Entrevue avec Denys Arcand," Office national du film, undated [1982], 4 pp. • Lemieux, Louis-Guy, "Misères et grandeurs d'un film sur le référendum," *Ariae Soleil*, 6 February 1982. • Perreault, Luc, "Machiavel au secours d'Arcand," *La Presse*, 6 February 1982. • Royer, Jean, "Denys Arcand. À quoi rêvent les Québécois ?" *Le Devoir*, 6 February 1982. • Corbeil, Carole, "Little Comfort, No Indifference in Arcand's View of Referendum," *The Globe and Mail*, 10 February 1982. • Corbeil, Carole, "*Empire* Built on Two Solitudes," *The Globe and Mail*, 13 February 1982. • Petrowski, Nathalie, "*Empire Inc.* Scènes de nuit en Amérique," *Le Devoir*, 20 February 1982. • Gay, Richard, "La part des scénaristes," *Le Devoir*, 6 March 1982. • Cusson, Normand, "Denys Arcand, cinéaste québécois," *TV-Hebdo*, 17 April 1982, pp. 19, 21–22. • Gural, Anna et Benoît Patar, "Denys Arcand: silence, on tourne," *24 images*, no 13-14, July–August 1982, pp. 47–56.

1983 Petrowski, Nathalie, "Denys Arcand remporte le Prix de la critique," *Le Devoir*, 30 March 1983. • Bazzo, Marie-France and Bernard Boulad, "Les maîtres de la saga québécoise," *Temps fou*, no 31, September 1983, pp. 46–49.

1984 Petrowski, Nathalie, "Silence! On tourne! Les frères Arcand occupent le plateau chacun à sa manière," *En route*, August 1984, pp. 42–47. • Lamon, Georges, "Arcand prévoit un destin populaire pour *Le crime d'Ovide Plouffe*," *La Presse*, 28 August 1984. • Patar, Benoît, "Denys Arcand. Le refus de la ligne juste," *24 images*, no 22-23, Autumn 1984–Winter 1985, pp. 35–40.

1985 "*Le crime d'Ovide Plouffe*," *Les 3 e Rendez-vous du cinéma québécois*, January–February 1985, p. 9. • Leroux, Pierre, "Jamais le cinéma québécois ne pourra faire ses frais!" *Le Journal de Montréal*, 2 February 1985.

1986 "Entrevue/Interview," *Cahier de presse du "Déclin de l'empire américain*," 1986. • Sklar, Robert, "*Decline of the American Empire*. An Interview with Denys Arcand," *Cineaste*, vol. XV, no 2, 1986, pp. 48–50. • Wera, Françoise, "Entretien avec Denys Arcand. 'Je voulais que la caméra trahisse les personnages . . . ,'" *Ciné-bulles*, vol. 5, no 3. 1986, pp. 28–30. • Dussault, Serge, "Cannes ovationne Arcand," *La Presse*, 10 May 1986. • Guez, Gilbert, "Denys Arcand libère le Québec," *Le Figaro*, 13 May 1986. • Scott, Jay, "*American Empire* Conquers Cannes," *The Globe and Mail*, 13 May 1986. • Pinard, Guy, "La personnalité de la semaine. Denys Arcand. Son dernier film est porté aux nues par la critique," *La Presse*, 25 May 1986. • Petrowski, Nathalie, "Denys Arcand. La renaissance de l'empire québécois," *Le Devoir*, 31 May 1986. • Perreault, Luc, "Denys Arcand. 'C'est moi, schizophrène,'" *La Presse*, 14 June 1986. • Lemieux, Louis-Guy,

"Arcand parle d'amour mais surtout pas d'eau fraîche," *Le Soleil*, 21 June 1986. • Ducasse, Christiane, "L'ascension de l'empire Arcand," *Qui fait quoi*, no 28, 15 July 1986, pp. 9–10. • Archambault, Claude, "Denys Arcand, la gloire lui est venue de Cannes," *Allure*, August 1986, pp. 28–29. • Bazzo, Marie-France, "Denys Arcand. Le syndrome de la table de cuisine," *Québec Rock*, August 1986, pp. 74–75. • Bacon, Suzanne, "Avec *Gina*, j'étais sûr de faire un hit," *Le Fil*, autumn 1986, pp. 12–13. • Racine, Claude, "Denys Arcand. Le confort après l'indifférence," *24 images*, no 28–30, Autumn 1986, pp. 28–32. • Demers, Pierre, "Denys Arcand cinéaste," *Mouvement*, vol. 4, no 1, September–October 1986. • Kirkland, Bruce, "Fest Opens with a Verbal Bang," *The Toronto Sun*, 3 September 1986. • Lefebvre, Martin et Suzan Ayscough, "'This Is How We Live and Love,'" *Daily Festival*, 5 September 1986. • La Roche, Paule, "Denys Arcand et *Le déclin de l'empire américain*. D'abord un film sur les passions," *Le Droit*, 6 September 1986. • Taylor, Noel, "*Decline of the American Empire*," *The Citizen*, 6 September 1986. • Harkness, John, "Arcand's Hilarious Sex Romp Fetches Critical Acclaim," *Now*, vol. 6, no 2, 11 September 1986, p. 13. • Base, Ron, "Talking Frankly of Sex — and Empires in the '80s," *The Toronto Star*, 12 September 1986. • "Film Marked by Cold Desperation," *The Calgary Herald*, 13 September 1986. • Dussault, Serge, "Denys Arcand au festival de New York. 'La vraie bataille reste à venir. . . ,'" *La Presse*, 29 September 1986. • Dorland, Michael, "Renaissance Man," *Cinema Canada*, no 134, October 1986, pp. 15–19, 21. • Rudel-Tessier, Danièle, "Quand Carle et Arcand 'placotent,'" *L'Actualité*, October 1986, pp. 168–69. • Kleinman, Dena, "A Reporter's Notebook: Hollywood on the Hudson," *The New York Times*, 1 October 1986. • Schneider, Pierre, "Un film à réflexions qui ... passe par le sexe! *Le déclin de l'empire américain*," *La Semaine*, 4 October 1986. • Dodd, John, "Ex-Girlfriends Provided Film Fodder," *The Edmonton Journal*, 11 October 1986. • Insdorf, Annette, "Director Surveys *American Empire*," *L.A. Times*, 25 December 1986. • Perreault, Luc, "Heureusement qu'il reste la gloire!" *La Presse*, 27 December 1986. • Stoler, Peter, "Sex and Success in Montreal," *Time*, 29 December 1986, p. 61. 1987 Corbeil, Normand, "'Ma solitude diminue' (Entretien avec Denys Arcand)," *Philosopher*, no 3, 1987, pp. 7–17. • "Denys Arcand: le sexe? Parlons-en . . . ," *Elle*, January 1987, pp. 64–65. • Riou, Alain, "Le premier film qui ne parle que de sexe," *Le Nouvel Observateur*, no 1160, 30 January 1987, pp. 66–67. • Alion, Yves, "Entretien avec Denys Arcand," *Image et son*, no 424, February 1987, pp. 16–17. • Ciment, Michel, "Entretien avec Denys Arcand sur *Le déclin de l'empire américain*," *Positif*, no 312, February 1987, pp. 16–20. Reproduit dans *Petite planète cinématographique*, Stock, 2003. • Parent, Denis, "Denys Arcand. Le nouveau désordre amoureux," *Première*, no 119, February 1987, p. 24. • Frois, Emmanuelle, "*Le déclin de l'empire américain*. Peut-on être plus heureux ?" *Le Figaro*, 4 February 1987. • Rouchy, Marie-Elisabeth et Raphael Sorin, "La chaire est triste, hélas, en Occident," *Le Matin*, 4 February 1987. • Andreu, Anne, "Denys: 'Les Québécois sont des parasites logés sur le dos de la baleine américaine,'" *L'Événement du jeudi*, 5 February 1987. • Pantel, Monique, "*Le déclin de l'empire américain* de Denys Arcand. Le film où on ne pense et on ne parle que de "ça"»*, France soir*, 5 February 1987. • Robitaille, Louis-Bernard, "Des critiques élogieuses pour *Le déclin* à Paris," *La Presse*, 5 February 1987. • Robitaille, Louis-Bernard, "Un Oscar à portée de la main. Denys Arcand ne se laisse pas monter la tête," *La Presse*, 14 February 1987. • Grousset, Véronique and Alix de Saint-André, "Sexe-solitude: l'étonnant film qui sonne l'alarme," *Le Figaro*, 14 February 1987, pp. 68–69. • Nuovo, Franco, "Denys Arcand un an après *Le déclin* . . . ," *Hommes*, no 5, printemps 1987, pp. 50–51. • Alaton, Salem, "Hollywood Can't Keep Arcand from Party," *The Globe and Mail*, 13 March 1987. • Brownstein, Bill, "The Rise of Denys Arcand," *The Gazette*, 21 March 1987. • Taylor, Noel. "Denys Arcand – Skeptical About his Oscar Chances," *The Ottawa Citizen*, 21 March 1987. • Perreault, Luc, "*Le déclin*: pas d'Oscar," *La Presse*, 31 March 1987. • Nuovo, Franco, "Les Oscars 87. Arcand pas trop déçu," *Le Journal de Montréal*, 1 April 1987. • Pinard, Guy, "La personnalité de la semaine," *La Presse*, 3 May 1987. • Hébert, Isabelle, "Un pas vers des ententes et un avenir meilleurs. Contrat-type prêt à être négocié," *Lumières*, vol. 2, no 9, September–October 1987, pp. 4–5. • Côté, Roch, "Personnalité de l'année de *La Presse*, Denys Arcand ne risque plus de tomber dans l'oubli," *La Presse*, 13 October 1987. • "Film Directors Hate Commercials," *The Chronicle-Herald*, 16 October 1987. • Dussault, Serge, "Téléfilm Canada: un trou de $48 millions. L'excellence au travail," *La Presse*, 27 October 1987. • Jutras, Pierre, Réal La Rochelle and Pierre Véronneau, "Conversation autour d'un plaisir solitaire," *Copie zéro*, no 34–35, December 1987–March 1988, pp. 4–12. • Roy, Mario, "La pub comme un des beaux arts," *La Presse*, 12 December 1987.

1988   "Le cinéma et l'argent," *Lumières*, no 12, March–April 1988, pp. 8–9. • "Le succès a-t-il changé Denys Arcand ?" *L'Actualité*, vol. 13, no 4, April 1988, pp. 176–79. • Perreault, Luc, "*Jésus de Montréal*. Denys Arcand soulève le premier voile," *La Presse*, 30 August 1988. • Peary, Gérald, "From *American Empire* to *Jesus of Montreal*," *The Toronto Star*, 3 September 1988. • "Le réalisateur d'un film est-il un auteur ?" *Lumières*, no 16, November–December 1988, pp. 5–7.

1989   "What Has Winning a Genie Meant to You?" *Cinema Canada*, no 160, February–March 1989, p. 35. • Élia, Maurice, "Denys Arcand. Interview/entrevue," *Cahier de presse de "Jésus de Montréal*," March 1989. • Tadros, Jean-Pierre, "The Second Coming of Denys Arcand?" *Cinema Canada*, no 162, April–May 1989, pp. 11–12. • "Pour Denys Arcand, un risque sans peur," *Le Journal de Montréal*, 22 April 1989. • Brownstein, Bill, "Rollercoaster Starting Again for Arcand," *The Telegraph Journal*, 29 April 1989. • Haas, Christine, "Cannes 89. En compétition. *Jésus de Montréal*," *Première*, no 146, May 1989, pp. 142–45. • Gaudreault, Léonce, "La crise des valeurs selon Arcand," *Le Soleil*, 6 May 1989. • Josselin, Jean-François, "Jésus sans tentation," *Le Nouvel Observateur*, 11 May

1989. • Goddard, Peter, "Canada Could Do it With Arcand," *The Toronto Star*, 15 May 1989. • Tranchant, Marie-Noëlle, "Denys Arcand: le charme d'un tyran," *Le Figaro*, 15 May 1989. • Scott, Jay, "Critical Hosannas Greet Arcand's *Jesus*," *The Globe and Mail*, 16 May 1989. • Boujut, Michel, "Le Christ recrucifié, version québécoise," *L'Événement du jeudi*, 18 May 1989. • De Maulde, Françoise, "*Jésus* sur la Croisette," *V.S.D.*, 18 May 1989. • Perrin, Gilbert, "L'Évangile selon Denys Arcand," *La Vie*, 18 May 1989, pp. 61–63. • Macia, Jean-Luc, "Entretien avec le réalisateur de *Jésus de Montréal*. "Retrouver l'authenticité du message du Christ," *La Croix*, 20 May 1989. • Rechtshaffen, Michael, "Arcand Moves Out of *Decline* with *Jesus*," *The Hollywood Reporter*, 22 May 1989. • "À propos de *Jésus de Montréal*. Propos de Denys Arcand," *OCCF*, 25 May 1989, p. 5. • Johnson, Brian D. et Nathalie Petrowski, "Jésus of Cannes," *Maclean's*, 29 May 1989, pp. 54–55. • "La face cachée de *Jésus*. Le cinéma et l'argent 5," *Lumières*, no 19, Summer 1989, pp. 44–48. • Marsolais, Gilles et Claude Racine, "Entretien avec Denys Arcand à propos de *Jésus de Montréal*. Le jeu, la vie, l'histoire, le cinéma," *24 images*, no 43, Summer 1989, pp. 4–9. • Bonneville, Léo, "Denys Arcand," *Séquences*, no 140, June 1989, pp. 12–19. • Garel, Sylvain, "*Jésus de Montréal*. Le déclin de l'empire catholique," *Cinéma 89*, no 458, June 1989, pp. 7–8. • Ramasse, François, " tre tendre malgré tout. Entretien avec Denys Arcand," *Positif*, no 340, June 1989, pp. 12–17. • Rousseau, Yves, "Entretien avec Denys Arcand. '*Jésus de Montréal*, c'est aussi l'histoire de ma vie,'" *Ciné-bulles*, vol. 8, no 4, June–août 1989, pp. 4–7. • Lachance, Micheline, "Saint Denys Arcand," *Châtelaine*, August 1989, pp. 29–30, 32, 34. • Jean, Marcel, "Entretien avec Denys Arcand. Je me souviens," *24 images*. no 44–45, autumn 1989, pp. 46–53. • Fortin, Marie-Claude, "Denys Arcand. Chasseur d'images," *Vous*, September 1989. • Kirkland, Bruce, "A Question of Faith," *The Toronto Sun*, 6 September 1989. • Roy, Pierrette, "Denys Arcand. Un réalisateur aux portes grandes ouvertes," *La Tribune*, 9 September 1989. • Taylor, Noel, "With *Jesus of Montreal*, Arcand's Hotter than Ever," *The Ottawa Citizen*, 16 September 1989. • Haeseker, Fred, "Arcand Surprised by Church Reaction," *The Calgary Herald*, 1 October 1989. • Roberge, Huguette, "Denys Arcand/Prix Albert-Tessier. Le confort et la fin de l'indifférence," *La Presse*, 11 November 1989.

1990   Abel, Marie-Christine, "Denys Arcand. Réalisateur/scénariste/acteur/monteur," in Marie-Christine Abel, André Giguère and Luc Perreault, *Le Cinéma québécois à l'heure internationale*, Montréal, Stanké, 1990, pp. 109–14. • Sklar, Robert, "Of Warm and Sunny Tragedies. An Interview with Denys Arcand," *Cineaste*, vol. 18, no 1, 1990. • Barker, Adam, "Actors, Magicians & the Little Apocalypse," *Monthly Film Bulletin*, vol. 57, no 672, January 1990, p. 4. • Andrew, Geoff, "Messiah's Handle," *Time Out*, 3 January 1990, pp. 22–23. • Chabot, Jean et Paul Tana, "Cheminements d'une écriture»," *Lumières*, no 22, printemps 1990, pp. 17–21. • De Billy, Hélène, "The Triumph of Denys Arcand. *Jésus* et après," *En route*, March 1990, pp. 64–77. • Garel, Sylvain, "Denys Arcand: prophète en son pays," *Cinéma 90*, no 465, March 1990, pp. 11–12. • Curtin, John, "Denys Arcand Offers a *Jesus* for the 1990's," *The New York Times*, 20 May 1990. • Toumarkine, Doris, "Post-*Decline* Satire and Drama in Arcand's *Jesus of Montreal*," *The Film Journal*, vol. 93, no 5, June 1990, pp. 14, 28. • Burnett, Ron, "Denys Arcand – *Jesus of Montreal*: A Discussion," *Critical Approaches to Culture, Communications and Hypermedia*, 29 June 1990 (www.eciad.bc.ca). • Fortin, Marie-Claude. "Denys Arcand. L'évolution tranquille," *Voir*, 25 October 1990. • Dupont, Sylvie, "Denys Arcand," *Elle Québec*, November 1990. • "Denys Arcand Takes the Stage," *The Globe and Mail*, 13 November 1999. • Charlebois, Gaetan, "Capitalism and Christ," *Mirror*, 22 November 1990.

1991   *"Vue d'ailleurs*. Entretien," *Fiche du film "Vue d'ailleurs,"* undated [1991]. • Vigeant, Louise, "Adaptation des lettres écrites, jouées, filmées. Entretien avec Denys Arcand," *Cahiers de théâtre Jeu*, no 60, 1991, pp. 93–99. • Lacroix, Laurier, "Entrevue avec Denys Arcand," *Continuité*, no 50, Summer 1991. • Bergeron, Johanne, "Denys Arcand scénariste," *Séquences*, no 153–54, September 1991, pp. 80–83. • Harris, Christopher, "'Success Is the Strangest Thing to Explain,'" *The Globe and Mail*, 4 November 1991. • Mietkiewicz, Henry, "Denys Arcand's Horizons Extend Beyond Quebec," *The Toronto Star*, 9 November 1991. • Dansereau, Suzanne, "Une occasion unique d'explorer l'œuvre complète du cinéaste," *L'Express de Toronto,* 12 November 1991.

1992   Perreault, Luc, "Arcand va tourner en anglais *Unidentified Human Remains*," *La Presse*, 10 January 1992 • Conlogue, Ray, "Arcand to Film Fraser's Hit Play," *The Globe and Mail*, 11 January 1992. • Léger, Marie-France, "Denys Arcand se plaint à son tour d'avoir servi, à son insu, de propagandiste de l'unité nationale," *La Presse,* 27 September 1992.

1993   "Production Notes," *Cahier de presse de "Love and Human Remains,"* 1993 • "Written interview with Denys Arcand," *Cahier de presse de "Love and Human Remains."* 1993, 2 pp. • Coulombe, Michel, *Denys Arcand: La vraie nature du cinéaste*, Montréal, Boréal, 1993, pp. 12–124. • Roberge, Huguette, "Arcand et le choix de Toronto: pas un pied de nez au Québec," *La Presse*, 13 September 1993. • Gagnon, Véronique, "Rencontre avec l'archange Arcand," *Clin d'œil*, November 1993. • Perreault, Luc, "Denys Arcand – Roger Frappier: toujours le beau fixe," *La Presse*, 7 December 1993.

1994   Fourlanty, Éric, "Sexe, mensonge & vidéo," *Voir*, 1994. • Privet, Georges, "Garde à vues," *Voir*, 3 February 1994. • Charbonneau, Alain, "Entretien avec Denys Arcand," *24 images*, no 72, Spring 1994, pp. 6–11. • Hays, Matthew, "The Cultural Abduction of Denys Arcand," *Mirror*, 10 March 1994. • "Du *Déclin* à *De l'amour*," *Le Journal de Québec*, 12 March 1994. • Blanchard, Louise, "Denys Arcand mise gros!" *Le Journal de Québec*, 12 March 1994. • Delagrave,

Marie, "Le désarroi des jeunes adultes a touché Denys Arcand," *Le Soleil*, 12 March 1994. • Delagrave, Marie, "Haro sur le nationalisme protectionniste à outrance," *Le Soleil*, 12 March 1994. • Roberge, Huguette, "'Ce que je voudrais faire, à chaque fois, c'est un chef-d'œuvre absolu ... ,'" Denys Arcand," *La Presse*, 12 March 1994. • Tremblay, Odile, "Un film est un film est un film," *Le Devoir*, 12 March 1994. • Brownstein, Bill, "Arcand: Hoping for the Best," *The Gazette*, 18 March 1994. • Knelman, Martin, "Denys Arcand Turns his Camera on Generation X," *The Financial Post*, 19 March 1994. • Castiel, Élie, "Denys Arcand. Le confort sans l'indifférence," *Séquences*, no 171, April 1994, pp. 14–16. • "Notes de production," *Le Magazine de cinéma Cinéréseau*, no 4, 1 April 1994. • Conlogue, Ray, "Arcand's Not So Excellent Adventure," *The Globe and Mail*, 4 April 1994. • Johnson, Brian D., "Remains of the Night," *Maclean's*, 4 April 1994, p. 58. • Brownstein, Bill, "Arcand Makes a Rough Sortie into English Movies," *The Ottawa Citizen*, 8 April 1994. • Chartrand, Luc et Louise Gendron, "La jeunesse sur un plateau d'Arcand," *L'Actualité*, 1 May 1994, pp. 10–12. • Privet, Georges, "Arcand, le coton et l'indifférence," *Voir*, 6 June 1994.

1995 Capatorto, Carl, "An Interview with Denys Arcand," *Urban Desires*, 1995 (www.desires.com). • La Rochelle, Réal, "Sound Design and Music as *tragédie en musique*: the Documentary Practice of Denys Arcand," In *Auteur/Provocateur. The Films of Denys Arcand*, Wiltshire, Flicks Books, 1995, pp. 32–51. • Loiselle, André, ""I Only Know Where I Come From, Not Where I Am Going": A Conversation With Denys Arcand," in *Auteur/Provocateur. The Films of Denys Arcand*, Wiltshire, Flicks Books, 1995, pp. 136–61. • Joanisse, Marc André, "Même Arcand doit attendre," *Le Droit*, 11 November 1995.

1996 Brioni, Bruno, "À la découverte des arcanes de Denys Arcand," *6 Bears*, undated [1996] (www.6bears.com). • Meunier, Robert, *Présentation de presse de "Joyeux calvaire*,*"* undated [1996], 3 pp. • Kelly, Brendan, "*Joyeux calvaire* Takes Arcand Back to French Roots," *The Gazette*, 24 October 1996. • Langlois, Claude, "*Joyeux calvaire*, le nouveau Arcand, parle des sans-abri," *Le Journal de Montréal*, 24 October 1996. • Privet, Georges, "Denys Arcand. Retour aux sources," *Voir*, 21 November 1996. • "The Low Life and the High Road," *Hour*, 28 November 1996. • Barrière, Caroline, "Un *road movie* à pied. *Joyeux calvaire*,*"* *Le Droit*, 30 November 1996. • Perreault, Luc, "Denys Arcand: un auteur en quête d'inspiration," *La Presse*, 30 November 1996.

1997 Lamarche, Claude, "Denys Arcand," *Les Diplômés*, printemps 1997, pp. 32–33. • Brioni, Bruno, "Annexe 1: Interview avec Denys Arcand réalisée à Montréal le 25 février 1997," dans *Évolution de la société québécoise depuis 1970 à travers le cinéma de Denys Arcand*, mémoire de maîtrise, Université libre de Bruxelles, Faculté de Philosophie et Lettres, 1997–1998, pp. 120–34.

1998   Holste, Jens W., "Appendiks A: Interview med Denys Arcand" and "Appendiks B: Interview avec Denys Arcand," in *Variationer I Forestillingen Om Lykke. Québec og Arcand: film og deres billede af samfundet*, M.A. thesis, Institut for Romansk, Odense Universitet, 12 June 1998, pp. 76–91. Interviews in French attached to a thesis written in Danish.

2000   "L'entrevue avec Denys Arcand," *Showbizz.net*, undated [2000](www.showbiz.net). • Beaudin, Monique, "Denys Arcand Tackles *Stardom*," *Canadian Screenwriter Magazine*, undated [2000] (www.writersguild-ofcanada.com). • Schwartzberg, Shlomo, "Cannes 2000: Out of Competition, *Stardom*," *FilmFestivals.com*, 2000 (http://www.filmfestivals.com/cannes). • Cassivi, Marc, "*Stardom* en clôture: Arcand est heureux," *La Presse*, 19 April 2000. • Rioux, Daniel, "Le dernier film de Denys Arcand clôturera le Festival de Cannes," *Le Journal de Montréal*, 19 April 2000. • Tremblay, Odile, "Denys Arcand clôture le bal avec *Stardom*," *Le Devoir*, 19 April 2000. • Rioux, Daniel, "Avec son film *Stardom*. Denys Arcand entre dans l'histoire . . . en anglais," *Le Journal de Montréal*, 21 May 2000. • Cassivi, Marc, "La célébrité fast-food, selon Denys Arcand," *La Presse*, 23 May 2000. • Tremblay, Odile, "Les mirages de la célébrité," *Le Devoir*, 23 May 2000. • Peranson, Mark, "Arcand Ponders Beauty's Trap," *Eye*, 31 August 2000 (www.eye.net). • Alioff, Maurie, "Denys Arcand's *Stardom*. Media Mania and the Beauty of Beauty," *Take One*, vol. 9, no 29, Autumn 2000, pp. 8–12. • Coulombe, Michel, "Entretien avec Denys Arcand," *Ciné-bulles*, vol. 19, no 1, Autumn 2000, pp. 4–9. • Letarte, Valérie, "Denys de Montréal," *Clin d'œil*, September 2000. • Bilodeau, Martin, "Arcand et la fascination de la célébrité," *Le Devoir*, 8 September 2000. • Griffin, John, "Beauty Has a Hold on Denys Arcand," *The Gazette*, 8 September 2000. • Brazeau, Renée-Claude, "Rencontre avec Denys Arcand," *En Primeur*, October 2000 (www.enprimeur.ca). • Anderson, Jason, "Shooting Stars: *Stardom*," *Eye*, 26 October 2000 (www.eye.net). • Harkness, John, "Fashion Victim," *Now*, 26 October 2000 (www.nowtoronto.com). • Koepke, Melora, "Fame Is Funny That Way," *Hour*, 26 October 2000. • Latimer, Joanne, "Shooting *Stardom*: Denys Arcand on Fleeting Fame, Mid-life Crisis and Jessica Paré," *Hour*, 26 October 2000. • Ruer, Juliette, "*Stardom*: La guerre des étoiles," *Voir*, 26 October 2000. • Villeneuve, Paul, "Denys Arcand parle de la "célébrité pour rien"», *Le Journal de Montréal*, 28 October 2000. • Perreault, Mathieu, "Denys Arcand. L'esclave de la beauté," *Séquences*, no 210, November-December 2000, pp. 52–54.

2001   Gagné, Jean-Simon, "L'indifférence tranquille," *Le Soleil*, 16 March 2001.

2002   Brunet, Mathias, "Denys Arcand," in *Paroles d'hommes*, Montréal, Québec/Amérique, 2002, pp. 17–75. • "The Directors," *Sight and Sound*, vol. 12, no 9, September 2002, p. 40.

2003 Marcotte, Pascale, "La croisée des chemins," *Famous Québec*, vol. 2, n₀ 2, April–May 2003, pp. 30, 32–33. • Petrowski, Minou, "Entretien avec Denys Arcand," *Cahier de presse "Les invasions barbares,"* May 2003. • De Billy, Hélène, "Le monde selon Arcand," *L'Actualité*, vol. 28, n₀ 7, 1 May 2003, pp. 52–56. • Frois, Emmanuèle, "Denys Arcand: Le déclin, la mort, le rire," *Le Figaro*, 21 May 2003. • Ferenczi, Aurélien, "Denys Arcand, réalisateur des *Invasions barbares,*" *Télérama.fr*, 22 May 2003. (www.cannes.telerama.fr). • Pliskin, Fabrice, "Rencontre avec Denys Arcand. *Le déclin* 'reloaded,'" *Le Nouvel Observateur*, 22 May 2003. • Ruer, Juliette, "Entrevue avec Denys Arcand. Penseur d'Amérique," *Voir*, 29 May 2003. • Dumas, Hugo, "Cannes, ça ne change pas le monde, mais ça aide un film,'" *La Presse*, 30 May 2003. • Blanchard, Louise, "Le livre lu par ... Denys Arcand. 'En vieillissant, j'ai tandance à relire les classiques,'" *Le Journal de Montréal*, 13 September 2003. • Libiot, Éric, "Du *Déclin* aux *Invasions*. Rencontre avec Denys Arcand, réalisateur des *Invasions barbares,*" *L'Express*, 18 septembre 2003, p. 62. • Guilloux, Michel, "Rencontre avec un Québécois qui ne chante pas. Denys Arcand," *L'Humanité*, 24 September 2003. • Mury, Cécile, "*Le déclin de l'empire américain*, suite ... et fin? L'empire, de pire en pire," *Télérama*, 24 September 2003. • Davtyan, Masha, "Sex Is Talk: Denys Arcand: 'All My Heroes are Dead,'" *Moskovsky Komsomolets*, Moscou, 25 September 2003. • Dolin, Anton, "To Smoke a Pot of Marijuana Facing Death," *Gazeta*, Moscou, 25 September 2003. • Ciment, Michel et Philippe Rouyer, "Denys Arcand. Comme le sourire d'une nuit d'été," *Positif*, n₀ 512, October 2003, pp. 8–12. • Coudé-Lord, Michelle, "Denys Arcand. L'homme de l'année," *Le Journal de Montréal*, 27 December 2003.

5. AUDIO-VISUAL MEDIA INTERVIEWS

Échange avec Denys Arcand, Premier festival du cinéma québécois de Blois. Archives Pierre Gaffié. • *Parler pour parler*, Radio-Québec, September 1986, 52 minutes. Round table about *Le Déclin de l'empire américain*, in which Arcand participates. The main theme of discussion is relationships between men and women. • *Le Point*, Radio-Canada television, January 1987, 31 minutes. Round table about *Le Déclin de l'empire américain*, in which Arcand participates along with four actors from the film (Louise Portal, Gabriel Arcand, Geneviève Rioux et Pierre Curzi) and Nathalie Petrowski. Is presented as "a discussion of the serious questions brought up by *Le déclin de l'empire américain.*" • *The Magical Eye*, a film by Terrence McCartney Filgate, 1989. • *Le Mouton noir*, film by Jacques Godbout, Office national du film, 1992, 2 episodes of 119 and 114 minutes • *Contact*, Radio-Québec, 1993, 49 minutes. Interview with Stéphan Bureau. Arcand talks, among other things, about his childhood, his parents, his arrival in Montreal and his discovery of culture. • *Tête à tête*, Productions Points de mire, 1993, 48 minutes. Interview with Lise Payette. • *Une leçon de cinéma*, Festival de Namur, 1994. • *La Conquête du grand écran*, film by André Gladu, 1996, 108 minutes. • *Gros Plan sur Denys Arcand*, Image Diffusion

International/Musiqueplus, 1996, 23 minutes. Interview with Anne-Marie Losique. • Interview with Michel-M. Campbell and Denys Arcand, 1998, Direction des infrastructures technologiques d'enseignement et de recherche, Université de Montréal. • *À l'ombre d'Hollywood*, film by Sylvie Groulx, Office national du film, 2000, 112 minutes. • *De l'art et la manière chez Denys Arcand*, film by Georges Dufaux, 2000, 60 minutes. • *Entrée des artistes*, Le Réseau de l'information, 2000, 22 minutes. Interview with Marie-Claude Lavallée. • Interview with Patrick Damien Roy and Denys Arcand, Festival du cinéma panaméricain, Autumn 2000. Not broadcast. • *Les Francs-tireurs*, Télé-Québec, 2000, 10 minutes. Interview with Richard Martineau. • *Luce Guilbeault, explorActrice*, film by Marcel Jean, Office national du film, 2000, 45 minutes. • *Le Septième*, Télé-Québec, 2001, 25 minutes. Commemoration of fifteen years of distribution of *Le Déclin de l'empire américain*. • Interview, David Cantin with Denys Arcand, Vancouver Festival, Summer 2001. • *Paroles de stars*, Radio-Canada radio, July 2001, three 24-minute broadcasts. Minou Petrowski interviewed Arcand in Vancouver on his promotional tour for *Stardom*. • *Voir Gilles Groulx*, film by Denis Chouinard, Office national du film, 2002, two episodes of 38 and 47 minutes. • *Arcand*, TVA, 2003, 21 minutes. Interview with Denys Arcand and Rémy Girard on Paul Arcand's program. • Interview, Première Chaîne, Radio-Canada, with Nathalie Petrowski, 2003. • *Les Héritiers du Mouton noir*, film by Jacques Godbout, Office national du film, 2003, 80 minutes. • *Le Point*, May 2003, 13 minutes. Interview with Stéphan Bureau after the presentation of *Les Invasions barbares* at Cannes. • *Viens voir les comédiens*, programmes 38 and 39, Zone 3, October 2003, two 51-minute programs. • *Denys Arcand en personne*, 40th anniversary of the Cinémathèque québécoise, November 2003. Archives Cinémathèque québécoise. • *Denys Arcand. Un portrait pour la radio*. Five 52-minute broadcasts. *Réalisation*: Jean-Sébastien Durocher. *Scripts and interviews*: Réal La Rochelle. *Commentarie*: Gisèle Trépanier, Geneviève St Louis. February 2004. Broadcast of Radio-Canada's cultural network. • Entretien avec Charlie Rose, PBS, February 2004.

II. SELECTIVE BIBILIOGRAPHY

1. GENERAL WORKS

Cahiers de l'AGEUM (founded and directed by André Brochu), Université de Montréal, Association AGEUM, 1962–1963. • *Maurice Séguin, historien du pays québécois vu par ses contemporains suivi de "Les Normes" de Maurice Séguin*, Montréal, VLB, 1987, 308 pp. • *"Parti pris et après," La Barre du jour*, n₀ 31–32, Winter 1972. • Brault, Jacques, *Agonie*, Montréal, Boréal, 1993, 78 pp. • Brault, Jacques, *Poèmes choisis 1965–1990*, Saint-Hippolyte, Éditions du Noroît, 1996, 136 pp. • Brochu, André, *La Croix du Nord*, Montréal, XYZ, 1991, 114 pp. • Brochu, André, *L'Instance critique*, Montréal, Leméac, 1974, 376 pp. • Brochu, André, *Le Maître rêveur*, Montréal et Echternach, XYZ/Phi, 222 pp. • Brochu, André, *La Vie aux trousses*, Montréal, XYZ, 254 pp. • Gagnon, François,

Données sur l'économie du scénario au Québec pour le long métrage de fiction. Répertoire 1968–2000, Montréal, Centre de recherche cinéma réception/Cinémathèque québécoise, 2002, 458 pp. • Guilleragues, *Lettres portugaises suivies de Guilleragues par lui-même*, Paris, Gallimard-Folio classique, 220 pp. • Klibansky, Raymond, Erwin Panofsky and Fritz Saxl, *Saturne et la mélancolie*, Gallimard, 1989, 738 pp. • Lever, Yves, *Le cinéma de la Révolution tranquille, de* Panoramique *à* Valérie, Y. Lever éditeur, 1991, 732 pp. • Loiselle, André, *Stage-Bound. Feature Film Adaptations of Canadian and Québécois Drama*, McGill-Queen's University Press, Montreal and Kingston, 2003, 260 pp. Includes an analysis of the film adaptation of *Love and Human Remains*. • Ricard, François, *La Génération lyrique*, Montréal, Boréal, 1994, 282 pp. • Sebald, W.G., *Les Anneaux de Saturne*, Arles, Actes Sud, 1999, 352 pp.• Sebald, W.G., *Austerlitz*, Arles, Actes Sud, 2002, 350 pp. • Sebald, W.G., *Les Émigrants*, Arles, Babel/Actes Sud, 1999, 276 pp.• Sebald, W.G., *Vertiges*, Arles, Actes Sud, 2001, 240 pp. • Sebald, W.G., *De la destruction comme élément de l'histoire naturelle*, Actes Sud, 2004. • Tolstoï, Léon, *La Mort d'Ivan Ilitch. Nouvelles et récits (1851–1885)*, Paris, GF-Flammarion, 1993, 416 pp. • Tolstoï, Léon, *Résurrection*, Paris, Gallimard-Folio classique, 1996, 646 pp. • Tremblay, Michel, *Les Vues animées suivi de Les Loups se mangent entre eux*, Montréal, Leméac, 1990, 190 pp.

2. GENERAL ARTICLES

"L'année cinéma," *L'Actualité*, vol. 29, no 1, January 2004. • "Son histoire est une épopée. L'Université de Montréal fête ses 125 ans," *Les Diplômés*, no 450, Autumn 2003, 60 pp. • "Une pétition contre le *Dossier Nelligan*. Le ministère des Affaires culturelles étudie la possibilité de le retirer," *Le Devoir*, 16 May 1969. • "Université de Montréal 125 ans," *Le Devoir*, 10 January 2004. • Arcand, Suzanne, "De la bureaucratisation policière," dans *ACSALF: Colloque 1980. Travailler au Québec*, Éditions coopératives Albert Saint-Martin, pp. 323–34. • Castiel, Élie, "Denise Robert. Le charme discret de la Séduction," *Séquences*, no 225, May-June 2003, pp. 34–35. • Cornellier, Louis, "Les désenchantés de la Révolution tranquille," *Le Devoir*, 6 July 2003. • Descôteaux, Bernard, "Bourgault l'indépendantiste," *Le Devoir*, 17 June 2003. • Des Roberts, Gilles, "L'invasion Robert," *Commerce*, December 2003, pp. 10–12, 14, 16, 18. • Devarrieux, Claire, "W.G. Sebald (1944–2001). Le devoir de mémoire inachevé. L'écrivain allemand meurt dans un accident," *Le Devoir*, 18 December 2001. • Dubé, Frédéric, "Des images de l'Elysée à SoftImage," *Le Devoir*, 17 May 1995. • Fortier, Monique, "Le pré-vu et l'imprévu ou les charmes discrets du montage," *Copie zéro*, no 34–35, December 1987–March 1988, p. 47. • L'Hérault, Pierre, "L'intervention italo-québécoise dans la reconfiguration de l'espace identitaire québécoise," in Fratta, Carla et Élisabeth Nardout-Lafarge (sous la direction de), *Italies imaginaires du Québec*, Montréal, Fides, 2003, pp. 179–202. • La Rochelle, Réal "L'économie du scénario au Québec," paper delivered at the 16th Congrès mondial du Conseil international d'études francophones, Abidjan, May 2002. Unpublished. • Lapierre, Michel, "Rhinocéros des neiges," *Voir*, 27 February 2003. • Leclerc, Jean-Claude, "Est-ce la fin de la machine à distribuer faveurs et subventions?" *Le Devoir*, 22 March 2004. • McIntosh, Andrew, "I Want to Suck Your Funds: The Cultural-industrial Split and the Survival of English Canada's Means of Cultural Expression," *POV*, no 51, Autumn 2003, pp. 20–23. • Paquet, Diane T., "C'était hier," *L'Hebdo de Portneuf*, 29 September 1975 [interview with Colette Bouillé and Horace Arcand in Deschambault]. • Poitras, Huguette, "Un scénariste. Jacques Benoît," *Séquences*, no 100, April 1980, pp. 30–39. • Prévost, Jean-Guy, "Compte rendu de Crapez, Marc, *La Gauche réactionnaire*," *Revue canadienne de science politique*, vol. XXX, no 3, 1997, pp. 583–85. • Rérolle, Raphaëlle, "À la recherche du "sentiment de l'éternité"», *Le Monde*, 8 November 2002. • Tassinari, Lamberto, "Au-delà de la "culture"», *Le Devoir*, 31 December 2002; *Montréal Cultures*, no 2, 28 February 2003. • Tremblay, Odile, "Cinéma québécois: grande cuvée 2003," *Le Devoir*, 3 January 2004. • Venne, Michel, "Successeurs de Bourgault," *Le Devoir, 18 June 2003*.

3. MONOGRAPHS ON DENYS ARCAND

Cinéastes du Québec 8. Denys Arcand, Montréal, Conseil québécois pour la diffusion du cinéma, 1971, 51 pp. Presented by Réal La Rochelle. With the collaboration of Denys Arcand, Alain Dostie, Gérald Godin, Lucien Hamelin, Michel Houle, Jacques Leduc and Bertrand St-Onge. • Brioni, Bruno, *Évolution de la société québécoise depuis 1970 à travers le cinéma de Denys Arcand*, M.A. thesis, Université libre de Bruxelles, Faculté de Philosophie et Lettres, 1998, 108 pp. • Chevrier, Henri-Paul, *La Distanciation au cinéma: application dans les films de fiction de Denys Arcand*, M.A. thesis, Montréal, Université de Montréal, 1982, 201 pp. • Coulombe, Michel, *Denys Arcand. La Vraie nature du cinéaste*, Montréal, Boréal, 1993, 134 pp. • Jutras, Pierre, Pierre Véronneau et Réal La Rochelle (direction), "Denys Arcand. Entretien, points de vue et filmographie," *Copie zéro*, no 34–35, December 1987–March 1988, Montréal, Cinémathèque québécoise/Musée du cinéma, 76 pp. Texts by Denys Arcand, Denis Bellemare, Roger Bourdeau, Fulvio Caccia, Henri-Paul Chevrier, Véronique Dassas, Marc DeGryse, Claire Dion, Michael Dorland, Monique Fortier, Gérald Godin, Luce Guilbeault, Marcel Jean, Pierre Jutras, Marguerite Lemay, André Pâquet, Denise Pérusse, Réal La Rochelle, Michel Larouche and Pierre Véronneau. With the collaboration of Nicole Laurin and Carmen Palardy. • Latour, Pierre, *Gina, dossier établi par Pierre Latour sur un film de Denys Arcand*, Montréal, L'Aurore, 1976, 126 pp. Presented by Pierre Latour. Includes reprintings of texts by Denys Arcand, Serge Dussault, Gilles Marsolais, Luc Perreault and Denis Tremblay. • Latour, Pierre, *La Maudite galette, dossier établi par Pierre Latour sur un film de Denys Arcand*, Montréal, Le Cinématographe et VLB, 1979, 105 pp. Presented by Pierre Latour. Includes reprintings of texts by Denys Arcand, Robert Lévesque, Louis Marcorelles, Gilles Marsolais, Claude Mauriac, Hubert Niogret, Luc Perreault and Robert Guy Scully. • Lévesque, Robert, *Réjeanne Padovani, dossier établi par Robert Lévesque sur un film de Denys Arcand*, Montréal, L'Aurore, 1976, 111 pp. Presented by Robert Lévesque. Includes reprintings of articles by Denys Arcand, Jean-Louis Bory, Claude Daigneault, Claude Fleouter, Yves Lever,

Robert Lévesque, Luc Perreault and Pierre Vallières. • Loiselle, André and Brian McIlroy (Edited by), *Auteur/Provocateur. The Films of Denys Arcand*, Wiltshire, Flicks Books, 1995, 195 pp. Texts by André Loiselle, Brian McIlroy, Réal La Rochelle, Denise Pérusse, Bart Testa, Pierre Véronneau, Gene Walz and Peter Wilkins.

4. ARTICLES ABOUT DENYS ARCAND

"L'Amérique a du cul," *Libération*, 12 May 1987. • "Le cinéma d'auteur est menacé," *Le Devoir*, 16 December 2003. • "Denys Arcand a renoué avec l'espoir," *Canoë*, 22 May 2003. Interview with Denise Robert (www.infinit.com). • "Denys Arcand, Denise Robert *Playback*'s Person(s) of the Year," *Playback*, 24 November 2003. • "Document. Table ronde sur le cahier "Arcand"», *Champ libre*, no 3, November 1972, pp. 68–76. • "Études de mœurs franco-québécoises," *Le Monde*, 20 November 1975. • "Forum. Après *Les Invasions*: le débat," *La Presse*, 21 May 2003. • "Off-screen: Arcand 'fan of euthanasia,'" *The Globe and Mail*, 6 September 2003. • "*Réjeanne Padovani*," *The Independent Film Journal*, vol. 73, no 1, 10 December 1973. • Allard, Gérald, "Variations sur des thèmes évasifs," *Argument*, vol. 6, no 1, Autumn 2003–Winter 2004, pp. 47–56. • Atkinson, Michael, "The Parent Traps," *The Village Voice*, 19 November 2003. • Azoury, Philippe, "Des "barbares"bien bavards," *Libération*, 22 May 2003. • Bachand, Denis, "Denys Arcand, réalisateur et scénariste. Les voies du documentaire et de la fiction," 2003. Unpublished. • Barbe, Jean, "L'air du temps," *Voir*, 18 et 25 May 1989. • Baril, André. "Voir *Les invasions barbares* avec Sollers," *Le Devoir*, 17 March 2004. • Baril, André, "Voir *Stardom* avec Freud," *Le Devoir*, 19 March 2001. • Barrette, Pierre, "La fin des bacchanales," *24 images*, no 115, été 2003, pp. 4–5. • Beaucage, Paul, "Une réalisation impersonnelle," *Ciné-bulles*, vol. 15, no 4, hiver 1997, p. 42. • Beaulieu, Carole, "*Le déclin* entre à Paris avec fracas," *Le Devoir*, 3 February 1987. • Beaulieu, Étienne, "Le cinéma québécois et l'écran de la communauté," *Le Devoir*, 20 June 2003. • Beaulieu, Étienne, "La rédemption de la fiction: Denys Arcand et la crise de l'image-mouvement," dans *Sang et lumière. Du sacré et du saint dans le cinéma québécois*, M.A. thesis, Université de Montréal, 2003. • Beaulieu, Janick, "*Gina*," *Séquences*, no 80, April 1975, pp. 21–22. • Beaulieu, Victor-Lévy, "Le cul du Québec," *Le Couac*, vol. 3, no 10, July 2000, p. 10. • Benoit, Jacques, "Mon travail de scénariste pour Denys Arcand," *La Presse*, 26 May 2003. • Bersianik, Louky, "L'empire du statu quo," *Le Devoir*, 9 August 1986. • Bilodeau, Martin, "La traversée des images," *Le Devoir*, 28 October 2000. • Bissonnette, Lise, "La vengeance et le mépris," *Le Devoir*, 30 January 1982. • Blumenfeld, Samuel, "La caricature complaisante d'une génération," *Le Monde*, 24 September 2003. • Bonitzer, Pascal, "L'espace politique," *Cahiers du cinéma*, no 249, February-March 1974, pp. 39–42. • Borde, Dominique. "Hymne à la vie," *Le Figaro*, 24 September 2003. • Bourdeau, Roger, "Au-delà des *Invasions barbares*. Le cinéma québécois caméra au poing," *Le Monde diplomatique*, October 2003. • Bourgault, Raymond, "Jésus, Denys Arcand et nous," *Le Devoir*,

12 August 1989. • Bouzet, Ange-Dominique, "Canada dry. *Les invasions barbares*, sympa sans plus," *Libération*, 24 September 2003. • Brunn, Julien, "Les désespérés du Québec," *Libération*, 21 June 1976. • Burdeau, Emmanuel, "*Stardom,*" *Cahiers du cinéma*, no 551, November 2000, p. 98. • Charbonneau, Hubert, "Les "barbares"excès de la fiction," *Le Devoir*, 30 May 2003. • Charron, Claude G., "Arcand, le Big Business et George W," *Le Couac*, vol. 7, no 6, March 2004, p. 5. • Charron, Claude G., "Les Ti-Counes de Denys Arcand," *Le Couac*, vol. 6, no 10, July 2003, p. 4 • Chauvet, Louis, "Nos cousins du Saint-Laurent," *Le Figaro*, 21 June 1976. • Chazal, Robert, *France soir*, 19 novembre 1975. • Cherneaud, Bill, "La semaine cinéma," *Libération*, 4 February 1987. • Conlogue, Ray, "Arcand's Paradise Lost," *The Globe and Mail*, 4 February 1997. • Côté, Audrey, "*Les invasions barbares* vues par ... nos camelots!" *L'Itinéraire*, no 106, June 2003, pp. 12, 33. • Courville, Léon, "La vraie nature des *Invasions,*" *Le Devoir*, 4 March 2004. • Couture, Daniel, "L'historien qui ne comprend rien à l'histoire," *Le Devoir*, 27 May 2003. • Del Pozo, José, "*Les invasions barbares* et l'histoire," *Le Devoir*, 27 May 2003. • Delahaye, Michel, "Montréal: trois festivals en un," *Cahiers du cinéma*, no 190, May 1967, pp. 8–11. A brief appreciation of *Les Montréalistes* on page 10. • Demers, Pierre, "Le Montréal itinérant (et le cinéma d'ici) revu par Denys Arcand. *Joyeux calvaire,*" *Factuel*, vol. 9, no 2, March 1997, p. 18. • Denby, David, "Close to the End," *The New Yorker*, 24 November 2003, pp. 113–15. • Douhaire, Samuel, "*Le déclin de l'empire américain,*" *Libération*, 9 October 2003. • Dufresne, Jacques, "La claque constitutionnelle," *Le Devoir*, 24 April 1982. • Durbin, Karen, "Decades Later, a Cast of Players Faces the Biggest Chill," *The New York Times*, 16 November 2003. • Dussault, Serge, "La personnalité de la semaine," *La Presse*, 25 March 1990. • Falardeau, Pierre, "La soupane et la marchette," *Lumières*, no 31, Summer 1992, pp. 58–61, 63–64. Text reprinted in *La Liberté n'est pas une marque de yogourt*, Montréal, Stanké, 1995, pp. 18–24. • Ferenczi, Aurélien, "*Les invasions barbares,*" *Télérama.fr*, 22 May 2003 (www.cannes.telerama.fr). • Fournier, François, Jean-François Thuot and Daniel Villeneuve, "Déclin d'un empire ou échec d'une génération ?" *Le Devoir*, 25 August 1986. • Fraser, Matthew, "Riding the TV Bandwagon," *The Globe and Mail*, 10 November 1984. • Gill, Alexandra, "Arcand's Film Opens Festival," *The Globe and Mail*, 5 September 2003. • Gravel, Jean-Philippe, "Denrée périssable," *Ici*, 26 October 2000. • Gravel, Jean-Philippe, "*Les invasions barbares*. Denys Arcand, d'un *Déclin* à l'autre," *Ciné-bulles*, vol. 21, no 3, Summer 2003, pp. 22–29. • Gravel, Jean-Philippe, "Sauve qui peut (la mort)," *Ici*, 8 May 2003. • Griffin, John, "Arcand's Brilliant Reunion," *The Gazette*, 9 May 2003. • Griffin, John, "Is That All There Is? Arcand's *Stardom* Is a Shallow Look at Shallow People," *The Gazette*, 27 October 2000. • Gusse, Isabelle, "Les évasions barbares," *Recto verso*, July-August 2003, p. 32. • Habib, André, "*Les invasions barbares* ou le triomphe d'un malentendu. Et in arcandia ego," *Hors Champ*, March 2004 (www.horschamp.qc.ca). • Harcourt, Peter, "Wotcha Lookin' at, Anyway?" *Cineaction*, no 61, 2003, pp. 2–9. • Hardy, Dominic, "Denys Arcand a longtemps cru pouvoir mener sa carrière de Deschambault," *Le Soleil*, 30 December 1989. • Haskell, Molly, "Bedding Down With Power," *The Village Voice*, 18 October 1973. • Hays, Matthew, "Close-up on Denys Arcand," *Montage*, autumn 2003, pp. 20–26. • Hays, Matthew, "Epidemic Amnesia," *Mirror*, 31 July 2003. • Hétu, Richard, "Le Québec de

Denys Arcand," *La Presse*, 23 November 2003. • Honorez, Luc, "Mourir de rire pour vivre," *Le Soir*, 23 May 2003. • Howell, Peter, "A Director in His Prime: Denys Arcand's *Les invasions barbares*," *Take One*, no 43, September–December 2003, pp. 28–31. • Jasmin, Claude, "Arcand est un moraliste moderne," *La Presse*, 18 May 2003. • Jasmin, David-Barrière, "D'intenses questionnements," *La Presse*, 18 May 2003. • Jean, Marcel, "L'histoire chez Denys Arcand: la marque du présent sur les temps passés," dans *Cinéma et histoire. Bilan des études en cinéma dans les universités québécoises*, colloque de l'Association québécoise des études cinématographiques, 15 November 1986, p. 49-53. • Jean, Marcel, "Le théâtre de la mort," *24 images*, no 115, Summer 2003, pp. 6–7. • Jeancolas, Jean-Pierre, *"Gina,"* *Positif*, no 171–72, July–August 1975, pp. 64–65. • Kapica, Jack, *"Gina*, Vision of Quebec Psyche," *The Gazette*, 25 January 1975. • Katadotis, Dimitri, "Last Defence." *Hour*, 8 May 2003. • Kelly, Brendan, "Arcand Stumbles in Film about Homeless," *The Gazette*, 29 November 1996. • La Rochelle, Réal, "Denys Arcand. Une carrière en dents de scie," in *9 e Festival international du film francophone*, Namur, 1994, pp. 120–21. • La Rochelle, Réal, "Descente aux enfers," *Ciné-bulles*, vol. 14, no 1, Winter–Spring 1995, pp. 19–21. • La Rochelle, Réal, "Le remake d'*Aurore* ne se fera pas," "Revoir *Gina*," dans *Cinéma en rouge et noir*, Montréal, Triptyque, 1994, pp. 111–16. • La Rochelle, Réal, *"Réjeanne Padovani*. Petite chronique d'un choc culturel," *24 images*, no 100, Winter 2000, p. 27. • La Rochelle, Réal, *"Stardom. La Traviata* selon Arcand," *24 images*, no 109, Winter 2002, pp. 36–37. • Larose, Jean, "Savoir et sexe dans *Le déclin de l'empire américain*," *La Petite Noirceur*, Montréal, Boréal, 1987, pp. 9–17. • Lavoie, André, "Entre Buffalo et Beyrouth," *Ciné-bulles*, vol. 15, no 4, Winter 1997, p. 43. • Lavoie, André, "Retour sur *Le déclin de l'empire américain*. Sous les pavés du bavardage, une plage de non-dit," *Ciné-bulles*, vol. 21, no 3, Summer 2003, pp. 18–21. • Le Chroniqueur masqué, "Madame la productrice," *Ici*, 4 March 2004. • Le Course, Rudy, *"Le déclin* a déjà récolté $13 millions. Qui va empocher, mis à part le nettoyeur de la salle de cinéma? ..." *La Presse*, 4 April 1987. • Leduc, Jacques, "Culde- sac," *Objectif*, no 62, July1962, pp. 26–30. • Lefort, Gérard, "Triste est ressuscité!" *Libération*, 16 May 1989. • Légaré, Anne, "À propos de quel déclin ?" *Le Devoir*, 23 August 1986. • Legault, Josée, "Le confort et l'indifférence, prise deux," *Le Devoir*, 2 June 2003. • Léonardini, Jean-Pierre, "Une agonie humaine bien orchestrée," *L'Humanité*, 22 May 2003. • Levant, Victor, "Sainte Louky, pensez pour nous !," *Le Devoir*, 30 August 1986. • Lévesque, Robert, "La mort à l'aise," *Ici*, 22 May 2003. • Lévesque, Robert, "Le sexe et rien d'autre," *Ici*, 7 March 2003. • Lord, René, *"Gina* soulève des problèmes qui concernent notre région," *Le Nouvelliste*, 29 January 1975. • Luissier, David, "L'héroïne pour soulager la douleur," *Le Devoir*, 5 June 2003. • Lussier, Marc-André, *"Les invasions barbares* remporte l'Oscar du meilleur film étranger. La consécration d'Arcand," *La Presse*, 1 March 2004. • Lussier, Marc-André, *"Joyeux calvaire*. Le dernier film de Denys Arcand," *La Presse*, 30 November 1996. • Magny, Joël, *"Jésus de Montréal,"* *Cahiers du cinéma*, no 421, June 1989, p. 52. • Major, Robert, "La critique d'art. 1 – Denys Arcand," *Parti pris: idéologies et littérature*, Montréal, Cahiers du Québec/Hurtubise HMH, 1979, pp. 176–79. • Malina, Martin, "Mind, Blood and Flesh," *The Montreal Star*, 25 January 1975. • Mandelblatt, Bertie, "Carry on Declining," *Mirror*, 8 May 2003. • Mandolini, Carlo, "Papier glacé, média froid et cinéma muet," *Séquences*, n₀ 210, November-December 2000, pp. 50–52. • Marsolais, Gilles, "Denys Arcand. Un pessimisme justifié?" *Vie des arts*, n₀ 80, Autumn 1975, pp. 64–65. • Marsolais, Gilles, "Un cinéma au temps présent," *24 images*, n₀ 91, Spring 1998, pp. 6–7. • Martin, Robert, "Arcand's Bitterness Ultimately Buries *Gina*'s Fine Points," *The Globe and Mail*, 23 June 1976. • Martineau, Richard, "*Le déclin de l'empire américain*. Ils ne militent plus, ils baisent," *Allure*, August 1986, p. 15. • Martineau, Richard, "Lettre à Denys Arcand," *Voir*, 15 May 2003 • Masson, Alain, "*Les invasions barbares*. Dans les catacombes," *Positif*, n₀ 512, October 2003, pp. 6–7. • McSorley, Tom, "Between Desire and Design. The Passionate, Sceptical Cinema of Denys Arcand," *Take One*, n₀ 4, Winter 1994, pp. 6–13. • Mérigeau, Pascal, "Le film qui a fait pleurer la Croisette," *Le Nouvel Observateur*, 18 September 2003. • Morgenstein, Joe, "*The Barbarian Invasions*," *The Wall Street Journal*, 21 November 2003. • Mosk., "*Réjeanne Padovani*," *Variety*, 13 June 1973. • Murat, Pierre, "*Les invasions barbares*," *Télérama*, 24 September 2003. • Nestruck, J. Kelly, "Arcand Leading Canadian Contigent," *National Post*, 28 January 2004. • Perreault, Luc, "L'Arcand nouveau," *La Presse*, 10 May 2003. • Perreault, Luc, "Heureusement qu'il reste la gloire !," *La Presse*, 27 December 1986. • Perreault, Luc, "Intellos psychorigides, Arcand réac," *La Presse*, 24 May 2003. • Perreault, Luc, "Plus avec moins," *La Presse*, 30 November 1996. • Perron, Éric, "Le cinéma québécois va-t-il vraiment bien ?" *Ciné-bulles*, vol. 21, n₀ 3, Summer 2003, pp. 2–3. • Petrowski, Nathalie, "Serge Toubiana: savoir attendre un film," *Le Devoir*, 27 October 1986. • Pevere, Geoff, "The *Decline* Continues. *Les invasions barbares*." *Cinémascope*, n₀ 15, Summer 2003, p. 40. • Piégay, Baptiste, "*De l'amour et des restes humains*," *Cahiers du cinéma*, n₀ 542, January 2000, pp. 67–68. • Pomerleau, Joël, "Denys Arcand à l'émission *Tête-à-tête*. Drame télévisuel. Denys Arcand ou les angoisses du cinéma petit-bourgeois," *Hors Champ*, 29 August 1997 (www.horschamp.qc.ca). • Privet, Georges, "*Joyeux calvaire*. Macadam cowboy," *Voir*, 28 November 1996. • Provencher, Normand, "Les seigneurs de Montréal," *Le Soleil*, 6 December 1996. • Ranger, Pierre, "*Les invasions barbares*. Pour la suite du monde," *Séquences*, n₀ 225, May-June 2003, pp. 32–33. • Renaud, Nicolas, "Le secret honteux du *Déclin de l'empire américain*. Histoire d'un malentendu," *Hors Champ* (www.horschamp.qc.ca). • Riou, Alain, "De l'émotion ... Un film qui parle de nous," *Le Nouvel Observateur*, 18 September 2003. • Rioux, Christian, "Un hôpital ou un pays?" *Le Devoir*, 20 June 2003. • Rioux, Michel, "La crotte de nez sur une nappe," *Le Couac*, vol. 6, n₀ 10, July 2003, p. 4. Reprinted in *Le Devoir*, 12 March 2004. • Robitaille, Antoine, "Le boomer et la mort," *Le Devoir*, 26 May 2003. • Robitaille, Louis-Bernard, "*Les invasions barbares* créent la polémique en France," *La Presse*, 24 September 2003. • Robitaille, Louis-Bernard, "Ovation présidentielle pour les *Invasions*," *La Presse*, 10 September 2003. • Rousseau, Yves, "Le confort et l'indifférence de Monsieur Canada 125," *24 images*, n₀ 62–63, September–October 1992, pp. 22–23. • Rousseau, Yves, "La maudite galère," *24 images*, n₀ 86, Spring 1997, p. 42. • Roy, André, "*Stardom* de Denys Arcand. Le déclin de Denys Arcand," *24 images*, n₀ 103–104, Autumn 2000, p. 87. • Roy, Jean, "Le bon bec du Québec," *L'Humanité*, 24 September 2003. • Royer, Philippe, "*Les invasions barbares* de Denys Arcand," *La Croix*, 24 September 2003. • Ruer, Juliette, "Nous nous sommes tant aimés," *Voir*, 8 May 2003. • Sabouraud, Frédéric, "Le téléphone rose," *Cahiers du cinéma*, n₀ 393, March 1987, pp. 48–49. • Sansfaçon, Jean-Robert, "Mature, mais fragile," *Le Devoir*, 2 March 2004 • Sauvé, Mathieu-Robert, "De nouveaux pères qui n'en sont pas. Les personnages masculins qui ont une image de losers même dans *Les invasions barbares*, *La Grande Séduction* et *Gaz Bar Blues*," *Le Devoir*, 11 March 2004. • Smith-Debanné, Cheryl, "*Joyeux calvaire* Was Fine Portrayal of Street Life," *The Gazette*, 7 December 1996. • Sotinel, Thomas, "Sitcom amère sur l'échec d'une génération," *Le Monde*, 23 May 2003. • Sotinel, Thomas, "*Les invasions barbares*, de Denys Arcand. Finalement l'âge rattrapa les babyboomers," *Le Monde*, 24 September 2003. • St-Onge, Josée, "*Joyeux calvaire*. Bénévoles et intervenants de l'Accueil Bonneau ont apprécié," *L'Itinéraire*, February 1997, p. 31. • Stursberg, Richard, "L'avenir du cinéma québécois passe aussi par la diversité des entreprises partenaires des créateurs," *Le Devoir*, 22 December 2003. • Tessé, Jean-Philippe, "*Les invasions barbares*," *Cahiers du cinéma*, n₀ 582, September 2003, p. 36. • Teisseire, Guy, "Un cinéma canadien très "dry"au Festival international de Paris," *L'Aurore*, 19 November 1975. • Testa, Bart, "Before the Barbarians. The Films of Denys Arcand," *Cinematheque Ontario*, vol. 14, n₀ 1, Autumn 2003, p. 46 • Thivierge, Renée, "De la symbiose à la solitude," *Le Devoir*, 30 August 1986. • Tison, Jean-Marie, Cylvie Gingras, Nathalie Labonté et Serge Lareault, "*Joyeux calvaire* de Denys Arcand. Des malades 'manteaux' sans-abri," *L'Itinéraire*, January 1997, pp. 26–27. • Tremblay, Odile, "Déception," *Le Devoir*, 23 May 2003. • Tremblay, Odile, "Denys Arcand au pays des barbares," *Le Devoir*, 16 April 2003. • Tremblay, Odile, "Du cynisme à l'émotion," *Le Devoir*, 9 May 2003. • Tremblay, Odile, "Orage dans le ciel serein de notre cinéma," *Le Devoir*, 20 December 2003. • Tremblay, Odile, "Pas d'Alliance pour Arcand (et vice-versa)," *Le Devoir*, 6 November 1996. • Tremblay, Odile, "Le piège du réel," *Le Devoir*, 7 December 1997. • Tremblay, Odile, "Le regard des sans-abri," *Le Devoir*, 4 December 1996. • Tremblay, Odile, "Une première pour les sans-abri," *Le Devoir*, 24 October 1996. • Trudel, Clément, "*Le confort et l'indifférence*. Une leçon de politique," *Le Devoir*, 29 January 1982. • Vandelac, Louise, "Le déclin. . . enfin . . . ," *Tribune juive*, January 1987, pp. 46–47. • Véronneau, Pierre, "*Champlain* de Denys Arcand (1964)," in *La Production canadienne-française à l'Office national du film du Canada de 1939 à 1964*, a doctoral thesis presented at UQAM, December 1968, pp. 424–431. • Weiler, A.H., "*Réjeanne Padovani*," *The New York Times*, 2 October 1973. • Yakabuski, Konrad, "Vive la différence!" *The Globe and Mail*, 7 August 2003.

UNPUBLISHED INTERVIEWS AND ARCHIVES

INTERVIEWS

The transcriptions for the following conversations were all revised by their authors. André Brochu supplied notes and written replies, as did Monique Fortier.

- Denys Arcand. 30 November and 14 December 2002; 31 January, 22 Marchand 13 June 2003; 7 January 2004; 14 May 2004. • Jacques Poulin. 13 August and 14 September 2002. • Suzanne Arcand. 14 April 2002; 31 July 2003. • André Brochu. 26 May, 25 September and 2 October 2002. • Denise Robert. 17 February 2003. • Monique Fortier. 26 February 2003. • Yvon Rivard. 15 May 2003. • Johanne Prégent. 13 February 2003. • Marc Laurendeau. 23 July 2003. • Clémence DesRochers. 20 November 2003. • Jacques Benoit. 7 May 2003. • Jacques Brault. 29 January 2003. • François Ricard. 10 April 2003. • Édith de Villers. 27 November 2002; 20 January 2003. • Gilles Messier. 3 June 2003. • Jacques Wilbrod Benoit. 27 November 2002. • Isabelle Dedieu. 16 January 2004.

I also had a number of informal conversations with filmmakers Jacques Leduc, Marcel Carrière, Catherine Martin, Colin Low, as well as the producers, technicians, actors and sound mixers for *The Barbarian Invasions*.

ARCHIVES

- National Film Board of Canada, La Cinémathèque québécoise, UQAM (Université du Québec à Montréal. Service des archives et de gestion des documents. Archives, Collège Sainte-Marie, 6 pp.), La Bibliothèque nationale du Québec, Radio-Canada, Les Moulins de La Chevrotière in Deschambault, the private collection of Suzanne Arcand.
- The NFB Archives also exhumed the script for *Nominingue* by Jacques Leduc, as well as *Histoire de l'anarchie* and *Descendre dans la rue*, by Hubert Aquin and Jacques Godbout, and *Violence* by Louis Portugais.

- Luc Desjardins, *Notes de séminaire sur le cinéma québécois à travers l'œuvre de Denys Arcand*, directed by Pierre Véronneau, Université Concordia, 1995. Includes a comparative analysis of the versions for Brad Fraser's script for *Love and Human Remains*, as well as the summary of an exchange with the director, 4 April 1995.

- François Gagnon, *Découpage après montage de la version originale d'*On est au coton, *(1970)*, 2002. [scene breakdown of original version of *On est au coton*]

- François Gagnon, *Analyse comparative des scénarios et des montages de films: Entre la mer et l'eau douce, La Maudite galette, Réjeanne Padovani, Gina,* la télésérie *Duplessis, Le déclin de l'empire américain, Jesus of Montreal, Stardom*, 2003. [comparison between the screenplays and edited film versions of the abovementioned works]

- Secretariat of Rideau Hall, *Press kit for the launching of "The Barbarian Invasions"in Moscow and Saint Petersburg*, 2003.

CLOSING TITLES

This book owes a great deal to researcher and film studies graduate François Gagnon. His perseverance and discipline, not to speak of his great interest in the subject, nurtured the biography, down to its minute details. Gagnon sifted through and examined the archives of Collège Sainte-Marie at UQAM, those of the Association des étudiants de l'Université de Montréal, the Cinémathèque québécoise, the NFB, and numerous Internet sites. He compiled all Arcand's interviews since 1958, analyzed his screenplays and montages, and put together complex files such as the one on the original version of *On est au coton* (1970). Gagnon was also responsible for assembling the data for the biblio-filmography.

I also wish to acknowledge the indomitable and cheerful sleuthing mind of Bernard Lutz, in charge of the NFB archives, who managed to unearth documents one might have thought were lost or nonexistent. Also, I thank the indefatigable teamsmanship of the staff at the Cinémathèque's Médiathèque Guy-L.-Côté—the guardians of its film vaults, the projection booth, and the friendly assistance of all the employees of this institution. Moreover, René Beauclair, the Médiathèque's director, agreed to make a place for all the documents used to create this book and put them at the disposal of the public. So now it is possible to examine in detail all the files on Arcand that have been filling up since 2002: screenplays, projects, interviews, correspondence, unpublished writings. Anyone who wishes is now welcome to peruse them!

Denys Arcand himself contributed a colossal effort to this archival task. He emptied his filing cabinets and boxes, opened up his photo albums, handed over a copy of his baptism certificate. Others assisted him in this quest. Suzanne Arcand, who remembers all the stories from Deschambault and the Arcand/Bouillé families, also talked about her work as criminology consultant for her older brother's first fiction films. Édith de Villers made several interesting contributions about the filmmaker's youth at the NFB.

Thanks also go out to those who kindly agreed to share their memories and impressions of the director's personality and his works: Jacques Poulin, Denise Robert, Yvon Rivard, Monique Fortier, Johanne Prégent, Jacques Benoit, Jacques Brault, François Ricard, Gilles Messier, Jacques Wilbrod Benoit, Isabelle Dedieu, as well as filmmakers Catherine Martin, Marcel Carrière, Jacques Leduc and Colin Low. André

Brochu, in particular, wrote several pages on the young Arcand at Sainte-Marie, the Université de Montréal and *Parti pris*. Also thanks to the entire shooting and post-production crew for *The Barbarian Invasions*, who honoured this "barbarian"with their warm welcome.

Very special thanks to Clémence DesRochers and Marc Laurendeau, who livened up this book with their original monologues. Many thanks to Jean-Sébastien Durocher, who lent his ear and recorded long hours of interviews and readings by Denys Arcand without baulking, and who, with this material, composed the five-hour radio broadcast *Denys Arcand: Un portrait pour la radio*, whose title is a tribute to Glenn Gould's sound work for CBC radio, Toronto. Hats off to Pierre Jutras for having first suggested the idea for this radio series and to Andrée Girard for welcoming it on Radio-Canada's cultural channel.

And finally, many thanks to all the others who accompanied the writing of this essay: Fabien Philippe, Claude R. Blouin, Jean-Pierre Bibeau, Fernand Aubert, Luc Desjardins, Denis Bachand, Patrick Damien Roy, David Cantin, Pierre Gaffié, Minou Petrowski, Michel Martin, Luc Trépanier, Robert Daudelin. A research grant from the Conseil des arts et des lettres du Québec (CALQ) helped make this book possible.